PRAIRIE BLITZ:

High School Football on America's 50 Yard Line

by

David Almany

*Dedicated to Mom and Dad; and to all those
Boys of Fall - past present and future - to the young
who dream of what will be and to the old who
remember what was.*

*Oh, the days of the Kerry dancing,
Oh, the ring of the piperís tune,
Oh, for one of those hours of gladness,
Gone, alas, like our youth, too soonÖ*

Acknowledgements

Special thanks to three of the best head coaches to be found anywhere in high school football: Dan Imdieke, Jeff Gross and Chris Koetting. Their trust in allowing my unlimited access to their programs was instrumental in the successful completion of this project.

Others whose contributions should be noted and appreciated, in no particular order or significance: Tim Dockter, Paul Keeney, Wade Huber, Al Bjornson, John Gumb, Chad Lyons, Scott Mollring, Russ Schlager, Jeremy Yilk, Bill Ramsey, Jeff Ellis, Tim Garcia, Clint Coleman, Nick Umscheid, Berry Schaeffer, Tom Lentz, Eric Ramsey, Taylor Liess, Craig Campbell, Hayden Merket, Tim Fletcher, Jeff Isom, Kolt Littley, Johnny Hudson, Ronel Saenz, Grant Norgaard, Jerry Smith, Rick Haney, Darin Nichols, Dennis Berry, Tim Almany, Caitlin Almany, Andrew Almany, Kyle Lynch, Rick Berry, Allan Burke, Mark Webber, Laurie Ezzell Brown, Andrew George, Shari Skiles, Lisa Almany, Mark McCombs, Bob Elder, Micah Lewis, Jackie Wald and Sam Potter.

Special thanks to these talented photographers whose work appear in the color insert found in this book: Steve Kodad, Alan Hale, Steve Towery, Mark Weber, Jim Baker and Colyn Suda. Also, special thanks to Kevin Kraus for his editing work.

Table of Contents

A Message from Hall of Fame Coach
Tom Osborne

A native of Hastings, NE, Tom Osborne's coaching career at the University of Nebraska was nothing short of remarkable. From 1972 to 1998, Osborne's NU teams compiled a 255-49-3 record for a winning percentage of .836.

Osborne's coaching career came to a climactic end in the 1998 Orange Bowl. In his final game, the Huskers defeated No. 3 Tennessee, 42-17, giving him a share of a third national title in his final four seasons. Nebraska in Osborne's last five seasons strung together the best five-year run in collegiate football history with an amazing 60-3 record, including five consecutive 11-win seasons.

Under Osborne, University Nebraska football became famous with its renowned walk on program, most of whose ranks were filled by small town farm kids from the vast Nebraska Plains. Since 2007, Osborne has served as the university's Athletic Director, overseeing a growing University of Nebraska athletic program.

I grew up in Hastings, NB playing all sports at the local high school. I made the decision to stay home and attend Hastings College without a scholarship because I wanted to play both basketball and football. The coaches in both of those sports at Nebraska offered me scholarships, but both said I had to choose between the two sports and could not do both. I worked construction during the summers to pay my tuition at Hastings College so I could play both sports. I guess in a lot of ways, I was a four year walk-on in two sports myself.

High School football is very important to the people of Nebraska. The citizens of Nebraska come from tough stock. People here had to be tough to survive the harsh climate and still prosper as farmers on the open plains. It just follows that tough people would look upon a tough sport like football with favor.

While coaching at Nebraska, we were well known for taking players from small towns as walk-ons. In the mid 1970's, the NCAA dramatically reduced the number of scholarships that Division I schools could award. It went from 45 initial football grants each year with no total limit to a total limit of 105. In 1978 the limit was lowered to 95 and in the early 1990's to 85.

That became the basis for starting our walk on program at Nebraska. We needed more players than we had scholarships for. There were years, especially when we still had freshman programs, that we might have 100 walk-ons. With numbers like that, you will always be able to find a few players, at least, who have Division I ability, but for some reason were overlooked out of high school.

We treated the walk-ons the same as we did scholarship players. The person who earned the spot in practice is who would play on Saturday. We would normally try and keep five to seven scholarships open each year to award to players who had come to us as a walk-on. We did a study over a five year period and it averaged that of our 60 players on our travel squad each year, 24 had come into the program without a scholarship.

Football is a developmental game. So much more than say basketball where most kids out of high school are ready to play on the college level. A small town Nebraska kid might not be physically ready to play at age 18, but give him a couple of years and get him into our strength program and he goes from 6'4 and 220 pounds to 6'4 and 290 pounds. Now he can physically compete. Our strength and conditioning program in the 1970's and 1980's was well ahead of most others. That really helped a lot of our small town Nebraska kids who came to us as walk-on lineman. We found a lot of good players that way. High school coaches around the state knew their kids would get a fair chance with us and would encourage their players to come here. Anytime you can play a lot of in-state young men; that will create interest and loyalty in that boy's home town and that loyalty will build over the years.

I always felt we had the hardest working teams in the nation. Year in and year out, we would win because our kids just worked harder than they did at other schools. I attribute that to the tone set by the walk-ons. Just by the nature of a young man who is willing to turn down a scholarship at other schools, and many did, to come and walk-on here, with no promise of a scholarship, then that is a player who is confident in their own abilities and is going to overachieve. They are going to be hard workers. Remember, we had so many of them, often times 40% of our roster. If you are a scholarship player and you see a guy without a scholarship who plays your position who is working twice as hard as you are, then that is going to get your attention. You can either buy-in, picking up your effort level, or you will not be around here very long.

Tom Osborne
Lincoln, NE
Transcribed October, 2011

Chapter 1

A Glory Field

Dark and silent late last night
I think I might have heard the highway calling
Geese in flight and dogs that bite.
James Taylor, *Carolina on My Mind*

I went to the woods because I wished to live deliberately, to front
only the essential facts of life, and see if I could not learn what
it had to teach, and not, when I came to die, discover that I had
not lived.
Henry David Thoreau, *Walden*

In little towns like mine, that's all they've got
Newspaper clippings fill the coffee shops
The old men will always think they know it all
Young girls will dream about the boys of fall
Kenny Chesney, *Boys of Fall*

It was the most poignant moment in an adventure full of poignant moments. On a fall evening, close to dusk, following on the heels of an Indian summer perfect weather day, I stopped at a small cross roads town in South Dakota. It could have been in Texas, Oklahoma, Kansas, Nebraska or North Dakota; didn't really matter; as I found many such towns in those states as well, but, for the record it was South Dakota. It was a depressed looking little hamlet, holding on by an economical thread; similar to hundreds of other dying little towns on the High Plains I had driven through.

It was the middle of October, 2011 and I was two months into a three month journey. I called my adventure the "ultimate road trip for a high school football junkie." I spent the fall roaming up and down US Highway 83, from Westhope, North Dakota to Laredo, TX – the Canadian border to the Mexican border – documenting the unique role high school football plays in small town America. As a part of my project, I was photographing every high school football field along Route 83; the last non-interstate highway to run unimpeded from the USA southern to northern border. My timing, as I almost always inexplicitly found it to be on this trip, was perfect.

The man approached me as I stood in the west end zone of the poorly cared for field, trying to get just the right camera angle with the setting sun at my back. He looked no more prosperous than the town we were in. After his inquire as to my task, I gave him the standard rendition of my project goals. As always, it was a great ice breaker and he, as most all males did on this trip, willingly told me his story from his gridiron glory days of long ago.

"Right where you are standing, right here, well it was over 40 years ago, but I scored a touchdown," he drug out the last syllable of "touch-doooowwwnnnn," for dramatic effect. "How about you," he asked me, "did you ever score a touchdown?" A couple, I said. "You know," he continued, "my life ain't been much, married and divorced three times. I can hold a job; always work around here to be had, but none (that) ever pays much. Even the Army wouldn't take me after high school, and back then, they took everyone," he showed a small grin, missing several key teeth, and shook his head in tired resignation of his failed life.

"Lived here all my life and will probably die here, but one night, much like this night, right here on this spot, I scored a touchdown and the whole town stood and cheered for me. Never scored another, I wasn't very good. Matter of fact, the pass I caught for my touchdown wasn't even thrown to me, it bounced off a couple of other people's hands and landed in mine, and I was standing right here. TOUCHDOWN. One of the few lucky breaks I ever have had." I smiled, for as I could see in his eyes, it was 40 years ago again, and my new friend was suspended Peter Pan like, celebrating in the end zone of eternal youth. If only the real world was so clear cut.

"A lot of people make more out of themselves than I have, but you know, they ain't in the club, like you and me. The banker here, over the years, has taken back a couple of my cars, my house and once even my john boat. I know he looks down on me and I got no one to blame for my failures but myself; and I am sure you can see, I am not much to look at. Still, I grew up with that banker and every time I see him on the street, I think, I scored a touchdown and you never did."

The wind had started to pick up, as it often did at dusk on the arid high prairie. I needed to get back to my picture taking task.

"You know where you are standing," he asked me, waving his arms spread wide?

I looked around and took it all in: goal posts that were badly leaning; trash – probably from the last game- blowing around a dirt track long ago abandoned from any serious attempt at running; weeds everywhere, choking out what little turf fescue this badly worn field once held; drooping and unsteady wooden bleachers on each sideline, peeling what little paint was left on their surface; and a scoreboard, I would bet, that was old enough to have witnessed my new friend's touchdown of over 40 years ago.

"No," I answered, "where am I standing?"

"This" he said, in a voice suddenly swollen with pride, "is a Glory Field."

Chris Koetting jumped into his pickup truck, threw the transmission into reverse and began to wheel his age-worn white Chevy from his reserved parking spot behind the high school gymnasium. Koetting is the head football coach of one of the most decorated small school programs in the football crazed state of Texas. His Canadian High School Wildcats, would in less than seven hours, open their 2011 season ranked as the number one Class 1 team in the whole state of Texas. This will be Koetting's second year as head coach.

Koetting's parking spot is still marked with the name of the man he succeeded, Kyle Lynch. "We need to get that changed, or maybe I am still an interim coach" chuckled Koetting. Kyle Lynch had a hugely successful run as head football coach of the Panhandle school. Lynch is considered a hero by many in the community, including Koetting, for resurrecting what had been a long suffering program. Lynch's Wildcat teams won state titles in 2007 and 2008, narrowly missing a third consecutive championship by dropping the title game in 2009, by a mere five points.

After the 2009 season, Lynch made the move up into the district's vacant Superintendent position. One of his first moves from his new office was to promote Koetting, his long-time offensive coordinator, to the head football coaching slot.

Going back to the tardiness in having the name in the parking lot changed, Koetting, who is known for his self-deprecating -aw shucks- sense of humor and dry as West Texas wit, suggested, "Maybe they are waiting to see how I do this year." Not likely. Koetting has not only adequately filled Lynch's parking spot, but also his huge coaching shoes. Last fall, Koetting's initial Wildcat team finished the season with a 13-1 mark, falling in the state semifinals, in a game he says eight months later, "we should have won." Koetting, by his first year performance, had shown the people of Canadian that they still have the right man for the job of leading their number 1 community treasure, their Wildcat football team.

At noon on the day of the season opener, Koetting was on his way to a Lions Club luncheon/meeting, where he along with his three senior captains would address the local civic club. The low key head coach is right at home and comfortable in his element as he shared with the audience a pre-game reality check: "You know, with the first game (which was seven hours away) you just never know what is going to happen. Last year we also opened against River Road. We take the kickoff, get too cute with it, fumble the darn ball backwards and fall on it at about our own 6 inch line. I mean that sucker was about as close to the goal line as you can get. Then we jump offside on the first play from scrimmage and we get a half the distance to the goal penalty, about 3 inches. That may be the shortest penalty in the history of football. I remember thinking, 'this is not the way I planned on starting my head coaching career'," he related, while laughing along with his audience. It is doubtful anyone has ever accused Koetting of taking himself too serious.

If Chris Koetting is nervous with the opening game looming, he does not show it. Dressed in blue jeans and a polo shirt with the Canadian Wildcat emblem embroidered on to his left pocket, the 44 year old non-descript pickup driving Koetting could have easily been mistaken for just another sun drenched rancher in town for lunch. Instead, he shoulders an enormous burden; he is the man responsible for the collective dreams of a small town.

It is game day in Canadian, Texas. You can smell it and you can feel it. From the appearance of the crown jammed into the high school gymnasium on this Friday, for a 3:00 pep rally, the whole town of 2,000 is here. The community of Canadian, with an itchy trigger finger, is cocked and loaded, ready for some high school football. All that is needed now is an opponent to play the role of sacrificial lamb. In a few hours, the River Road Wildcats would arrive from Amarillo in two purple and white painted Blue Bird school busses, and nicely fill the bill.

You know you are coaching football at small high school if you measure the quality of your victories against fast food franchises. Dan Imdieke, long-time coach of the Linton, North Dakota Lions has compiled a 35 year head coaching record of 288-67. Last fall (2010), Linton traveled south to play the squad representing the much larger town of Mobridge, SD. Overcoming a two touchdown deficit in the 4th quarter, the Lions rallied for a 34-28 win. One excited Lion player informed the coach after the game that "they (Mobridge) have a McDonald's AND a Pizza Hut. We have beaten a lot of Dairy Queen towns, but never a McDonald's or a Pizza Hut, and they have both!!"

Jeff Gross squinted and looked directly into the western sky. Fighting the setting August sun, the coach surveyed the distant horizon, searching for any sign of a surge of late afternoon bad weather that was forecast for the High Plains. In his 14 years as head football coach of the McCook, Nebraska Bison, Gross had learned to respect what nature could dial up on short notice on a hot summer evening for this sparsely populated land. Now into the second week of preparing the 2011 edition of McCook's hometown warriors for the upcoming season, and with the season opening game less than two weeks away, Gross knew that time was of the essence. He did not want to have to move another practice inside to the school gymnasium basketball court, as had been the case the previous week, when an evening hail storm pounded the west side of McCook. As the 16 to 18 year old players began to file from the locker room to the adjacent practice field to begin their work, one of Gross' assistant coaches said in a kidding manner, "come on Coach, let's just take the night off. It is only football." With a reserved grin, Gross responded, "tell that to them," motioning with his right hand to a parking lot past a far sideline, where a group of local supporters had gathered to watch the evening practice.

Later Gross would lament philosophically while discussing his life's calling, the head coach of a small town football team with a tradition so rich that winning was not only expected by the locals, but demanded. "There is no other job on earth quite like this one," stated Gross, who has won two state championships in his career at McCook. "Yeah, but the last one was eight years ago," pointed out the coach. "That is too long for these people. But you know what; it is also too long for me. We have the talent this year. We have the speed we have not had in the past. I owe it to my boys, to their parents and to this community to set the bar high, to demand that we always stride to accomplish the difficult. We set our goals high here. Football is a big part of this community, but in a positive way. That is what makes this such a special place. It is hard to put into words, but look at my actions, and that tells you what I am having a hard time expressing. I came to McCook 14 years ago for my first head coaching job, thinking this would be a stop along the way, a launching pad to a bigger and better job. Now after 14 years I can tell you, for Jeff Gross and his family, there is no better job. There is no better place to coach, no better place to teach, no better place to raise a family than McCook, NE."

I started this adventure with a bushel basket full of tough questions jotted in my leather cased notebook that I go nowhere without: Does small town America, so immortalized in Norman Rockwell paintings and Jimmy Stewart movies, still exist? Is small town America, a century after the population shift from the farm to the city and then to the suburbs, still the bastion of character, honor and truth we so long for in moments dominated by the stress of our 21st century urban existence? Or is it all a myth, a figment of a nostalgic imagination holding no validity in the 21st century?

Has the internet world of instant communication and overwhelming information available at the click of a mouse, forever bridged the gap between rural and urban? Does a teenager raised in a rural middle of America small town setting have a better chance of a childhood devoid of the temptations so prevalent in urban and suburban schools; drugs, alcohol and risky sexual behavior? Or is it all a social collective wish, a nirvana that exists only in our minds; a therapeutically, but momentary mental vacation of longing for a time when we as a nation were less rushed, less driven and less harried?

Has this slice of Americana on the High Plains, from North Dakota to Texas, been swallowed up by a world economy that demands global solutions? At a time when thousands of American jobs, many formerly in rural communities, are disappearing overseas, can rural America ever swing back the pendulum of population shifts that has seen most small towns on the High Plains lose half of their population in the last 20 years? Has the monster that began as just another five and dime store on the town square of a small Arkansas burg in the 1950's, forever doomed the commercial survival of the independent   rural merchant? Does the construction of a new Supercenter hasten the boarding of store fronts in countless small towns, not long ago vibrant with the life of Main Street America, but now mere ghost towns, as dead as the summer weeds that spring from every crack of their neglected pavement? To put it in simple terms, can rural communities on the High Plains survive in today's global economy?

A lot of tough questions, for sure. I took to Highway 83 in the fall of 2011 looking for answers.

What started for me as a quest to chronicle the unique dynamic of high school football in small town America, soon became much more. I set forth on this discursive journey seeking to understand the almost fanatic love some small towns in America have for their successful high school football teams. I was startled by what I found. In time, I began to see an affiliation between three small "football towns," each a thriving oasis of survival and growth in a desert full   of its failing neighbors;   a conjunction of sorts between a healthy community and a strong school system, with football the magnetic lure that pulled the entire dynamic together.

Do not underestimate the extraordinary effect that a winning high school football team has on the very survival of a small town, isolated on the vast open prairie of our nation, fighting an uphill battle for survival. Sociologist and economists tell us these towns are dying. Some even go as far as suggesting that the government buy back much of the Great Plains and turn the land into a refuge for the American Bison; that the land is unfit to support the human population currently calling the area home.

But I know of at least three small towns that are not dying. I spent the fall of 2011 as a witness to their successes.

I witnessed three communities on these same High Plains- or Buffalo Commons, as two East Coast Professors would rename the area- who are thumbing their noses at the big city academic naysayers making these doomsday predictions, daring non-believers to come see for themselves how their communities are not only surviving, but thriving. The common denominator for the three towns I visited? Simple: outstanding high school football programs that are the pride of the community. I am convinced that if high school football were for some reason suddenly abolished in these three towns, we would see an immediate and marked downturn in their civic fortunes, especially in three areas that dictate their very survival: community pride, community activism and community cohesion. I saw repeated examples that validate in mind the paramount necessity of a strong school/town bond in rural communities, if small town American life is to survive in the 21st century. I found that nothing solidifies that community bond like long term success under the "Friday Night Lights."

But what is the order of development; a strong football program creating a vibrant community or a vibrant community giving life to a strong football program? Or could they both flourish and prosper in collusion, feeding off of each other? I have tried to sort this out in my own viewings of what I witnessed this past fall in Linton, ND, McCook, NE and Canadian, TX, connecting the resulting dots, my journalistic challenge.

The level of fanaticism shown by many hard core high school sports fans can best be explained away with one word: loyalty. "Those are our boys. We birthed em, we raised em, we passed a bond issue to build that new weight room for them; and by god, we are better than those bastards down the road, (insert rivals name here)."

I write these thoughts at a time when it seems big time college athletics are ready to implode. This past twelve months, we have witnessed a sorry parade of one collegiate athletic scandal after another. The allegations of rampant sexual abuse at Penn State has ensnared the man who before was considered untouchable by mere human accountability, Joe Paterno, and cost him his job of nearly 50 years.

Schools threatening to jump conferences, players taking illegal payments, sexual abuse scandals, coaches lying to investigators; it has been a long year for college athletics.

The system of big money college athletics, as it now stands, cannot survive. In time, it will crumble under its own hypocritical polices. There is too much money, in the billions of dollars, being made off the backs of amateur "student athletes."

A billion is 100 million $100 dollar bills. Think about that. If money corrupts, then why are we crying out in self-righteous pain for what is happening right now to the NCAA? We should have seen it coming.

Jim Tressell, the Ohio State head football coach, resigns because he lies about his players trading awards for tattoos. When you have coaches making four million a year, like Tressell was making; and the true valuable commodity, the players, get nothing but a scholarship – and a few free tattoos -

then it will be just a matter of time until the structure crashes from within, which is precisely what I see happening now.

In the NBA this past season, if you remove former Los Angeles Lakers Head Coach Phil Jackson from the equation, then added together the salary of every other head coach in the league, it would not equal what LeBron James made alone for this past season. This is proof beyond a doubt that on an open market, free from the artificial financial restraints that colleges place upon their athletes, it is proven that the players are the valued commodity, not the coaches.

The NCAA men's basketball tournament is big business- and it has nothing to do with education. If you think it does, you are a fool. The TV contract alone that CBS recently signed with the NCAA is worth over $10,000,000,000. That is a lot of 00s. And that is only the tournament. What would happen if on the Saturday morning of the final four, all 40 players for the four final teams came together and declared, "We are all sticking together on this, we each want $20,000, or we are not playing." What would those in charge do? They would pay up, and don't doubt it for a minute. What is the alternative? Watch John Calapari and Clark Kellogg play one on one? Think CBS paid 10 billion for that?

College athletics are much too mercenary for my tastes. But high school athletics, especially small town high school athletics, is different. Those grid iron heroes are our kids, because we raised them right here where I was raised. The star quarterback, the town's shining knight in armor, who miraculously pulled out a victory in the game Friday night, is the same pimple faced kid who will be bagging your groceries at the local IGA on Saturday morning. The star running back, who the paper says might just break the school rushing record this year; why, you babysat for him when his mom went back to work ten years ago; and you smile as you remember how you had to wipe his snot nose. That strapping and snorting linebacker, striking terror in the hearts of opponents every Friday night from August to November, he may look mean now, but you remember not all that many years ago when he lived next door and cried every day the first two weeks he got on the bus to go to Kindergarten.

That is why high school football in towns like Canadian, TX, McCook, NE and Linton, ND will never die. It is too pure. As the locals will tell you, "they are our kids."

As the calendar turned the page to the month of July in the year 2011, reality hit me like a ton of bricks: In less than two months school would open and for the first time since I was five years old, it will open without me. No new teacher to get to know; no new season to prepare for, no new students to acquaint with, no new challenges.

For the first time since I had started Kindergarten, almost a half century ago, my fall calendar was wide open. After a 31 year career in public education that had run the gamut of positions in the field: classroom teacher, high school coach, high school building principal and collegiate coach, all following 18 years of unbroken attendance as a student and an athlete through the completion of my college years, I was now off the sidelines, relegated to the bleachers, a mere spectator.

Two years previous I had completed item number 4 on my bucket list: to successfully write and publish a book. My efforts produced _Riding the Storm Out: A Year of Inner City High School Football_. I had spent a calendar year following the 2008-09 Roosevelt High School Roughriders football team. The St. Louis, MO school was only a few years before considered the worst high school in perhaps the worst school district in the nation. The ghetto school had recently undergone a much needed infusion of new leadership, in both the offices of principal and head football coach. I greatly admired the work of these two men on the grass roots level as they were in constant torment due to the actions of the men and women in the upper level administrative positions of the St. Louis Public School District. The way the system ran was outrageous. The needs of the students under the care of those at the top of the district command were seldom considered and received little more than lip service from the downtown gang, as I came to call the incompetents who ran the city schools. The story of the Roosevelt High School football team was both inspiring and enraging, and I portrayed it as such.

The book, for a first time author's effort, has done well. It was picked up in 2010 by a national distributor and can now be bought nation-wide.

My publisher, in the summer of 2010, suggested a trilogy of works, the second to focus on small town high school football and its effects on the local communities. She suggested that I do my research thoroughly, taking the necessary time to find just the right school to follow, and plan on the 2011 season to chronicle that very journey.

I liked this idea and in the spring of 2011, after I had resigned my college coaching job, began looking for the right school to cover. In 2008, Roosevelt's locale, since I live in St. Louis, had allowed me to report their story and still hold down my college coaching job. Now with no team to coach, I was free of the constraints of a limited area to search for a suitable school, and having always loved to travel, I began a nation-wide search.

I wanted to find a team with a long standing reputation for excellence, one that embodied the spirit of the entire community. I spoke to several schools, even visiting a couple in the winter/spring of 2011, but I just did not get a good feeling for the cooperation and administrative support for the necessity of full access I would need. In many ways, as a retired school administrator, I understand the reluctance of school leaders to throw open fully the doors of access. We live in a lawsuit happy society and schools are the new targets of many "ambulance chasing" law firms. It is a nation-wide problem and has hurt public education by shackling any new and innovative ideas, hamstringing innovative thinkers in the educational field.

As spring turned to summer in 2011, I still needed to find a suitable school. One evening, as July 1 approached, and as I scoured the national atlas, my gaze fixed upon US Route 83. It appeared to be, for the most part, a two lane road, the kind that would run through the type of "off the beaten path" small towns I was looking for. As I researched the route, I learned that US Route 83 is the last road in our national system that is not a free-way (limited access) road that runs from the Mexican border in the south to the Canadian border in the north.

The romantic and exotic appeal of "get your kicks on Route 66" is nothing but a memory for most Americans. If you travel cross country today, you do it on a ribbon of unbroken concrete that by-passes the small towns for the sake of speed and efficiency. A cross country journey by car today is about getting from one place to another as quickly and safely as possible. Hard to argue that logic, but it has destroyed the slower pace of yester-year when a cross country traveler would actually encounter stop lights in small towns. The exception is US Route 83; and that perked my Americana seeking radar. Why not travel the route from north to south during high school football season and tell the stories of multiple teams representing the towns on this route, as opposed to just one team, I wondered? After several frustrating months of agonizing over my failure to find a suitable school, the light of inspiration had clicked on, my excitement becoming invigorating.

This would be the dream road trip for someone like myself; a high school football junkie.

I spent a solid two weeks researching, looking for just the right schools. I settled on three. I wanted my teams spread out from one end of Highway 83 to the other. I used the internet and publications such as _Texas Football Yearly,_ and narrowed my search down to six, all sharing a common Main Street; Route 83. My finalists all had outstanding football resumes and high expectations of competing for a state title in the upcoming season. I decided three would be the maximum I could cover and give justice to their season, so I designated a "first team" of three and a "second team" of three. On August 2, 2011, I sent my first choices the following information:

I explained that I was a writer who had a contract to publish a trilogy of books about high school football. My purpose for contacting the school was that my second book would focus on small town high school football and the role it plays within a community. After some research, I had decided that instead of focusing on only one school, I was going to use US Highway 83 as my anchor and visit schools that lie on this route, from North Dakota to Texas.

Along the way I expected to find a "true America" that gets little play from the national media. I explained that I wanted to report on three high school programs that lie along the route, encompassing the states of North Dakota, South Dakota, Nebraska, Kansas, Oklahoma and Texas. I wanted the story to be steeped in small town life - not just football - but also focusing on the societal role high school football plays in small town culture.

I informed my prospective schools that I was a retired coach, classroom teacher and building administrator. I attached my resume. I told each school leader that I could understand their initial reluctance at this out of the blue request and could anticipate, and appreciate, the questions they had in regard to it. I informed each that I expected to find a positive story in each respective community and that I had no interest in writing a negative story for the simple reason that it would not sell.

I explained in detail how I would conduct my research when in their community and that it was vital that I be given access to the everyday operation of not only the football program, but the school and community as well.

I attempted to pacify any resistance that might have been created by my open ended request by stating that while doing my research, I was very impressed with not only the success of each school's athletic program, but also the high academic achievements. I emphasized how as an experienced public school educator, I believed with all of my professional soul that the two went hand in hand. The qualities that allowed for a school to achieve athletically also drove the same students of those schools to academic success. That, I stated was the story I wanted to tell.

I knew that my request would be met with raised eyebrows; but I once again reiterated my desire to write a positive story. If for some reason, after visiting a school I did not feel I could honestly portray their football program, school and community in a positive light, then I gave my professional promise that I would inform them as such and that I would not write the story.

My strategy must have worked, as within 48 hours I had received positive acceptance calls from all three of my "A" team. I never had to go to the bullpen for my second team choices.

The itchy feet of the wandering vagabond have never been fully appreciated in modern American society. To the contrary, often the wander is regarded with distain, a loafer failing to be slotted to fit within the 9 to 5 work day of normal Americans. Webster defines a vagabond as "One who wanders from place to place, having no fixed dwelling, or not abiding in it, and usually without the means of honest livelihood; a vagrant; a tramp; hence, a worthless person; a rascal."

Despite society's condemnation, I have always longed for the freedom of the open road. A train-whistle will grab my attention - and my imagination - the sound of an 18 wheeler rolling down a nearby interstate will be cause for a brief pause from everyday life and the contemplation of how near freedom is. It is a romantic way to daydream. If I want to get my blood rushing, even today, all I need is a full tank of gas, a bag of sunflower seeds and an open road.

As a teenager, I devoured Jack Keourec's classic 1950's bohemian howto handbook on vagabonding; <u>On the Road</u>. I considered the rumpled and down home news correspondent Charles Kuralt to be the luckiest man in America, the holder of my ideal dream job. For 20 years, Kuralt wandered the back roads of America looking for human interest stories. He specialized in recording inspiring and light hearted three minute news segments that would typically play several nights a week at the end of the CBS Evening

News with Walter Cronkite. In those pre-cable 24 hour TV news day, Uncle Walter, as Cronkite was known, was the most trusted man in America. Kuralt's light hearted stories, celebrating the strength that the original thinkers of this nation brought to our national mental well-being, was the perfect balance for the often much too sobering and disturbing stories that Cronkite reported. And Charles Kuralt held an oft stated hatred of interstate highways. He said, "Interstate highways allow you to drive coast to coast, without seeing anything." How could a closet hobo like me not love the guy?

Over the years, I continued to dream of the open road. A periodic vacation, travel in relation to work; even the moderately out of the norm decision to take the back roads as opposed to the more efficient and faster interstate while traveling, were always anticipated by myself with eagerness, a harmless expression of my desire to break free and hit the open road. I considered my silent daydreams to be a mild form of defiance on my part to the responsibilities I knew I must fulfill as father and spouse. But still, I could dream of someday, some far off day, when those responsibilities would not shackle me to such a grounded life.

In 1970, I was a very impressionable junior high student. That year, NBC-TV came out with a short lived one hour dramatic series named "Then Came Bronson." The series plot dealt with a young man, Jim Bronson, who had become disillusioned with the American rat race, a common theme in many media productions of the time. To drop out of a society he found to be lacking in values and substance, Bronson took to the open road on his Harley Davidson Sportster motorcycle for an extended look at America.

The series featured, in the leading role of Bronson, Michael Parks. He portrays a young newspaperman who becomes despondent after the suicide of his best friend. A subsequent argument with his editor-boss over the type of stories that Jim should cover and write pushes Bronson over the edge. He jumps on his bike and takes to the nation's highways, a modern day cowboy, sans a horse, but nicely substituted for with his classic Harley.

Vagabonding across the nation, Bronson enjoys a freedom very alluring to a young man, such as me, trapped in the mundane life of a Junior High student. The show became for me a weekly diversion from the tedious boredom of my everyday colorless routine. "*Then Came Bronson*" became a way to divorce myself from reality and join Bronson, if only for an hour, basking in the freedom of the open road.

Each week, for the introduction to the show, Jim pulls up on his motorcycle to a stop light and finds himself waiting alongside a middle aged man in a station wagon. Dressed in a suit and tie - we assume the nameless man is on his way to a well-paying, but boring office job- a true victim of the suburban middle class, the very lifestyle Bronson himself so detests and is himself fleeing. In a scene played out each week, the man in the station wagon asks, "Where are you headed?" Bronson responds, "Oh, I don't know, man, where ever I end up I guess." The man at the wheel looks tired and disillusioned. "Man, I wish I were you," he sighs. "Well, hang in there, you'll make it," Bronson states in a non-believing tone, as he guns the engine of his Harley, headed down the highway, off on another weekly adventure.

After all these years, at age 54, I had a strong sense that it was now time for me to stop "wishing I were you," and head out to live a life with little restraints, one I had dreamed of for years - to set my destination for "where ever I end up, I guess." At my age, I questioned as to how many more years I would have the stamina to handle the miles of travel I was now proposing on this extended football road trip. If I wanted to experience the open road, then I needed to do it now, before the aching joints of an aging body made the comforts of home- a warm fire and soft bed- too inviting to leave for the lonely back roads of the wanderer.

I realized, I had better find where I want to go and get there while I still could.

After much research, I felt I had made three great choices for the schools on Route 83 to chronicle: **Linton, ND, McCook, NE and Canadian, TX**. All three schools have long traditions of success in football, but even more importantly, have great reputations for academic excellence. As I traveled up and down Highway 83, I found many inspiring American success stories beyond football – more than I could ever have hoped to record in the limited pages of this book. I found many whose very style of living validates the belief that there is still a core of values found in the heart land of this great nation that is above reproach, not for sale. And, boy, did I ever meet some characters.

We realize, but often do not appreciate just how vast and empty many areas of the American West are. Viewed from a jet plane window at 30,000 feet, the landscape is impressive; but from ground level, it is daunting.

Having traveled the 1,000 miles along Highway 83 - from Westhope, ND to Laredo, TX - several times, I have a firsthand appreciation of how open this marvelous land is. Close to 1/3 of the trip's route lies in what I have come to call the state of NPR. You are traveling through the state of NPR when you push the scan button on your car radio and it spins like a Las Vegas roulette wheel, stopping only once each cycle, at the precise same spot, 88.9, home on the dial of National Public Radio.

On my first visit to Canadian, TX, a hot, late August night, the eve before the local Wildcats would open their 2011 football season, I walked across Route 83 from my motel room at the Canadian Courts to a convenience store to buy a 99 cent fountain Pepsi. For a short interlude, US highway 83 was absent of the large 18 wheelers that seemed to constantly be engaged in hauling oversized oil field equipment and supplies from Pampa and Amarillo to the nearby booming oil and natural gas fields.

The lull in the volume of this busy road gave me a moment to stop in the center of the two lane ribbon of concrete. Standing square in the middle of the Canadian, Texas Main Street, I could gaze to my left and marvel at the thought that I was standing on the same road that would wind its way through the Texas and Oklahoma Panhandles, navigate the entire length of the state of Kansas and finally to the Sand Hills of southern Nebraska until highway 83 turned into the Main Street of McCook, Nebraska, a distance of 500 miles. If I was to continue my northward trek another 500 miles, I would find myself on Main Street, Linton, ND. The Lions, the Bison in McCook, NE and the Wildcats of Canadian, TX, were all diligently preparing for their respective season opening games, all the next evening. I thought of how this over patched and worn pavement linked together these three diverse towns, and how in each of these high plains hamlets, young men were retiring for an evening of restless sleep, dreaming the dreams of small town football heroes, hoping and praying that this would be the year they were to lead their teams and communities to the promised land of a state high school football championship.

I needed no GPS to find my way on this trip. I was truly blessed for three months to traverse, back and forth, this road. Along its' route I found the "true" America- one of real people whose solid but common everyday lives never make the national news. I intended to record the human drama that is so unique, and so American, to small town high school athletics. This goal I have accomplished.

I found a 180 degree difference in environment along rural Highway 83 from what I found at inner-city Roosevelt High School in St. Louis, MO, the team whose season I chronicled in 2008, (www.stlhsfb.com). What proved to be no different in Linton, ND, McCook, NB and Canadian, TX, from what I found in St. Louis, MO, was the passion of teenagers to succeed, and the unqualified support of their family and community in that noble quest.

As I lean against my economy sized rental car in a McDonald's parking lot in Pierre, SD, a middle aged man, coffee in one hand, brief case in the other, rushes to his car, parked in the slot next to mine. He glances my way and nods, as well-mannered strangers will. I reach out and he accepts my non-verbal invitation to hold his coffee and brief case as he fumbles in his dress slacks' pockets for his keys. It is five minutes to 8 am. I assume, from his hurried manner, he is due in some nearby office by 8 am. "Thanks," he said, as he eases himself into the driver's seat, retrieving from me his coffee and brief case. "Where you headed," he asks, out of politeness, I assume, as he had not the time to listen to the whole description of my adventure. For a reason I know not why, I said, "Oh, I don't know, man. Where ever I end up, I guess." He turned the key, revved the engine, and just before putting the Mazda into gear, looked me square in the eye and said through the open window, I swear to God, "Man, I wish I were you." It is a moment worth the 40 year wait.

David Almany
December, 2011

Chapter 2

The Generals

The very essence of leadership is that you have to have vision. You can't blow an uncertain trumpet.
Theodore M. Hesburgh

The secret to winning is constant, consistent management.
Tom Landry

In a crisis, don't hide behind anything or anybody. They are going to find you anyway.
Bear Bryant

Football may be the best-taught subject in American high schools because it may be the only subject that we haven't tried to make easy.
Dorothy Farnan, Former English Department Chairman, Erasmus Hall High School Brooklyn, New York

Jeff Gross, McCook, NE

If there has ever been a high school football coach waiting for the proverbial other shoe to fall, it is Jeff Gross, head football coach of the McCook, NE Bison. The mentor has known nothing but success, almost from the beginning of his tenure at the school on the High Plains in the Nebraska Panhandle, and all from a head coach who himself questioned his readiness when the McCook Public School Board of Education in the Spring of 1998, tabbed Gross as the man to lead their beloved red jersey clad Bison.

As an untried rookie head coach, Gross' first two first teams in a town known for winning football, were at best mediocre, finishing 4-6 and 4-5. Since then, over the last 10 years, his Bison have compiled a gaudy record of 119 wins and 13 losses. Along the way they have won two state titles (2003 and 2004), just missing a third consecutive title in 2005, when they, in heartbreaking fashion lost the title game on a last second play. A third straight state championship would have been a Nebraska state record, a huge accomplishment in a state that ranks success on the gridiron right behind God and family. The Bison also claim, over the last decade, two state second place finishes and an incredible 72 game regular season winning streak.

Gross spent the first eight years of his coaching career at his home town Hays, KS High School, a two hour drive across the state line from McCook. "I got into coaching very early," said Gross. "My dad passed away young, at 45 years of age. I was in college at the time and needed to take on the responsibility of running the family farm. I also started coaching at Hays High School while I still had two years left in college. I was an assistant at Hays for 8 years (1990-1997). I never did teach at the school, I just coached. Along with farming, I also got into private business in the Agriculture field. At one time, I had wanted to teach Agriculture, and that is what my degree is in, but I never put it to use in Hays."

A down swing in the farming economy in the late 1990's, and the responsibility of a recent marriage and a future child made Gross reexamine his family's needs and his personal finances. "I just couldn't make it anymore without a teaching job. I needed to be on staff, but that just wasn't going to happen at Hays, at least I couldn't get a promise (that there would be a teaching job) for me. If something would have opened on the faculty at Hays, I am confident they would have taken me, but it was anyone's guess as to when or how something would open. So I started looking for a job outside of Hays, but in the area."

Gross' eventual landing in McCook, was like many of life's fortunate bounces, a product of several lucky happenings. "Bob Fuller was the Coach here at McCook at the time. He was also the high school principal. He had taken the Hays job for the next year and wanted to promote me to his offensive coordinator job," says Gross.

In late spring, Fuller called with the news that the search to replace him as Head Coach at McCook had stalled. "They offered the job (at McCook) to two different individuals and each turned it down," remembers Gross. Why the difficulty in filling a position that would seem on the surface, due to past tradition, a very choice gig for any ambitious football coach? According to Gross, the attachment that came with the job description gave many a willing suitor cold feet. "The district was starting an alternative school," explained Gross, "and the new head football coach was going to have to start the school and then run it. And it was going to be a one man show."

Almost immediately, Gross became McCook's new number one candidate. "It was getting late, the coach recalled, "school was almost out and they needed someone in place before the summer started. I was most definitely in the right place at the right time. Thankfully, for my future, the other candidates did not want to mess around with the alternative school."

McCook put the offer on the table for Gross; Head Football Coach and head of the new alternative school.

With the promise of a career move upwards in coaching at Hays, but no guarantee of a teaching job, opposed to a full time coaching and teaching position in McCook, Gross now had to make a tough decision. "I am a Kansas guy, knew nothing about Nebraska and was willing to push my luck, hold on to the hope that a faculty position would open for me and go to work for Bob in Hays, a guy I still consider a mentor." After much contemplation, Gross decided that the offer forthcoming from McCook was too good to pass on.

Gross took McCook up on their offer.

"I knew going in the job had been offered twice to coaches who turned it down, before I ever interviewed for it," recalls Gross. "That didn't bother me at all, I was just glad to have a full time job."

An alternative school is an innovative way for public schools to deal with troubled students. For many reasons, behavior based mainly, students sent to an alternative school are ones who have not functioned well in the regular school setting. Once placed in the alternative school, students are allowed to work at their own pace, primarily through computer generated programs, to complete the needed class work to graduate. Students will typically attend classes for four hours a day and are then expected to hold down a steady job in the community. For many, it is their last chance at a high school diploma and avoiding the life time stigma of being labeled a high school dropout.

More often than not, a troubled student who graduates from an alternative school will be met with skepticism. "We do hear some that our program is watered down," says Gross. "Sometimes a student can come in here and get as much as three semesters credit in one. The work is not watered down. We have the documentation to show that. What happens, is the work is structured, and for many of these kids, that structure is what they were missing in the regular classroom. Our kids earn their credits."

Landing in McCook on the run in the summer of 1998, Gross got right to work. "A first time head coach and the duties of creating an alternative school from scratch was a full plate, no question," he recalls. "The district was reasonable, they said they wanted the alternative school up and going by the start of second semester and we actually opened the doors by November 1," Gross states proudly. He retains the title of principal of the alternative school today, but has added a full time teacher and two full time aides to help with his duties. "Last year, we started taking middle school kids, with the hope of returning them to the regular classroom after some modifications to behavior and some remedial work to get them caught up academically. The program has never stopped growing."

A program he started from scratch, a responsibility several contemporaries wanted nothing to do with, is now one Gross has watched over the years grow and produce tangible, life changing results. He sounds much like a proud parent. "We definitely have filled a need. A lot of kids who were not going to make it through the regular school setting have come to us, gotten their diploma and moved on to live productive adult lives," Gross states.

As for the football side of his assignment, Gross knew expectations would be high. Small towns on the High Plains, he knew, developed and measured their self-esteem based on the success of the local football team. The late 20th century farm economy in the Panhandle of Nebraska was, to say the least, grim. Yes, the economy has gone bad; farmers were being foreclosed on in record pace, multi-generational farm families found themselves homeless, banished from not only their property, but their heritage. But come Friday night in the fall, all that becomes null and void. Our best is going to strap it on against the best the rival town has to offer, and for an all too short interlude, the real world will take a back seat to high school football. "This town needs football," Gross succinctly summed up the community pressure put upon him, an outsider, to give the town hope at a time when hope was all many had.

Current McCook High School Principal Jerry Smith came into the district that same summer that Gross began his tour of duty. "We got ripped by many in the public," recalls Smith. "People said 'the guy has no experience.' Jeff had a lot of doubters to overcome." But the McCook populace turned into a fair one, willing to give the new coach time. It didn't take long for

McCook to become enamored and charmed by the outgoing new head coach. "Jeff cares, and that comes across immediately and sincerely," said Principal Smith. "It is just not in football, but overall. He takes a sincere interest in the kids and he has been like that since he arrived here. He attends games he doesn't have to: girls' basketball for example; he goes to school plays, music concerts; he wants to show his support. He doesn't do it in a 'showy way,' but the community knows he cares about the kids in this town, not just the star football players."

Athletic Director Darin Nichols is entering his fourth year of directing the MHS athletic program. Nichols admits that football is a major player on the athletic landscape at MHS, a sort of "flagship" status in comparison to the other program's offerings. "No doubt, football is going to generate most of the attention in McCook," Nichols admitted. "But we do have balance. Look at our numbers in other sports. (55% of McCook High School's student body was listed on a fall sports roster in 2011, a very high percentage.) "Our other sports might not get the notoriety that football does, but we support them just the same. Sure, we get the complaints from some members of the community that football gets too much, but also, don't forget that football gets the scrutiny that others don't. Coach (Gross) and his players are under the microscope 24/7. Other coaches and athletes don't have to deal with that. And Jeff addresses it (responsibility) constantly with his team."

Carrying the pride and hopes of the community into battle each Friday night in the fall is a responsibility that Gross takes serious and his administrative bosses' appreciate it. "Our kids represent us well," says Principal Smith. "It is something Jeff stresses. It is a great 'life lesson' for our kids. Very seldom does one of our athletes screw up to the point that we have to step in."

When Gross arrived in 1998, he knew that a quick turnaround with the fortunes of Bison football would not happen, but there was hope not far down the line. "We went 4-6 the first year and 4-5 the second (1999). But we had a great group of 8th graders when I got here and we knew they were going to be good. They were the core of our first state championship team in 2002."

Success breeds success, and the first sweet taste of a state title propelled the Bison into what would become a state dynasty in the first decade of the new millennium. "The next few classes didn't have the talent that the 2002 group did," recalls Gross. "And were not as successful on the Junior High level as the 02 group, but we had a move in at QB from Pratt, KS that really helped in 2003 and 2004 and the winning just dominoes. It became a case of attitude. Each senior class would say 'we will not be the group that doesn't win.'"

The Bison dominated Western Nebraska as they won a second state Class B title in 2003 and finished runner-up in 2004, 2005 and 2007.

Every young coach needs someone to give them a break, a friendly nod from the god's of fate. "Everyone wants experience (when hiring a new coach). But how do you get experience if no one will give you that first job," Gross asked rhetorically?

Gross was thankful that community expectations were not real high the first couple of falls. The administration allowed him to grow into the job, but a defining moment came during his first season. "Lexington was our big rival at the time. We had not beaten them in several years. They killed us during the regular season, but we sneaked into the playoffs as the number 16 (and last) seed with a 4-5 record. We drew the #1 seed, Lexington, in the first round at their place and somehow we upset them in overtime. That really solidified what we were doing, and gave me confidence as a young head coach that I could succeed. Looking back now, I don't know if we would have ever reached the heights we have for this long of a run without that win. It gave me standing in the community and bought me time." said Gross.

Max Broderson came to McCook in 1970 to run the defense for the now defunct football program at McCook Community College. He also served as the college's Athletic Director. Broderson's coaching career was short lived as the college board of trustees voted to drop the program after his first season. Despite his short tenure, he and his wife had grown comfortable in the community and made the decision to remain and raise their family. Broderson left coaching and entered the area banking market, but still got his football fix by getting behind the local high school program.

"I came here for a salary of $4,325 in 1970. I guess it was enough, cause I am still here," the man whose is identified by a local leader as "a good guy, a little colorful, very outspoken, but as big a supporter of Bison football as you will find."

Broderson claims that Gross needs to know how much the community is behind him. "My boys played for three coaches and each had their strengths," said Broderson. "But Jeff is the first coach who has come in here and stayed. He has the community behind him in a way you just don't see in this day and time. Small towns are hard to coach in. We had some good coaches before (Gross), guys who won at schools before they came here and won at schools after they left here, but Jeff is the first who stayed, made a long term commitment to the kids of McCook and made this program flourish."

Broderson says that although a good tactician of the game, Gross' strength in grounded in his ability to understand people. "Jeff's strength is he knows how to place kids. He does a great job of evaluating his talent and then figuring out a way to get the most out of that player at that particular position. He knows people, how to motivate kids, how to make them feel they are important to the success of the team. Not only the stars, but also the kid on the end of the bench."

Gross admits that he suffered early self-doubts about his own abilities as a young coach. He gives a great deal of credit to the long standing and experienced coaching staff he has. "I came in here the first year and we ran a kind of Mouse Davis Run and Shoot offense. It didn't work," Gross admits now with a shake of his head and a grin when remembering how badly he misjudged the needs of his first team.

"It was a disaster," Gross remembers. "I had to humble myself and say to our coaching staff, 'listen, I need your expertise. I need your help.' We developed a variation of the veer that we run from an I-Back formation and it has been our bread and butter, year in and year out. This is Nebraska. We run the football. We play hardnosed football. Ideally, we are going to throw the ball five times a game because we are going to whip you at the line and don't need to pass. Don't matter how big you are, we will beat you with our technique. I bought into that with help from our assistants. Our kids also bought into it. Our kids now run the I-formation from the time they start in 5th grade."

Dennis Barry carries the double hat duties as both the Mayor of McCook and the Junior High School Principal. He came to McCook in 1984 and has since coached almost every sport the district offers. "Jeff is the key to why this program is what it is," says Berry. "He is fair with kids and that has earned him a lot of support. Is it because he wins? Sure, that always helps. But when parents comment on Jeff they always commend him for the interest he takes in each kid. He gets people involved. It is not just Gross' team; it is the community's team. We have all shared in the many successes of our teams, but we also together shoulder the few disappointments we have had. Jeff does a great job of teaching our young people about life. And often you learn more about life in times of disappointment and loss than you do when you win."

One particular monster loss brought the Bison nation to its knees, cutting much deeper than any disappointment on the scoreboard: the death of long time and popular assistant coach Ron Coleman. "Ron was my right hand man. He was here when I got here and was deeply rooted in the community. Everyone liked Ron and everyone respected him. He was just so special to so many people. He taught me so much," says Gross. "He and I ran the offense together, but I learned so much form him, about both football and people."

On November 29, 2004, shortly after a heart breaking last second loss in the state finals, a setback that denied the Bison a third straight state title, tragedy struck suddenly. "I was going over to pick up Ron at his house," recalls Gross, still obviously emotional seven years later when recalling the event. "He was going to ride with me to Lincoln to an awards ceremony. It was on a Sunday. I couldn't get anyone to answer the door, so I walked around back and that is when I found him."

Coleman had climbed onto the roof of his house to dislodge some ice that had formed overnight. Somehow, he had slipped and fallen, resulting in serious head injuries. "Ron was still alive when I found him," says Gross about his 52 year old colleague. "We got him to the hospital, and they airlifted him to Omaha, but by the next day, he was gone."

The news of Coleman' death spread quickly and was a punch in the collective gut of the town of McCook. The community went into shock. "I still remember it taking several days for the fact he was gone to settle in. It was like a bad dream," says Gross.

"We are as close as a town could be and this was just so tragic and so unexpected," recalls Max Broderson. "RC taught elementary PE and the kids loved him. He was a big man (6'5", 240 pounds), but he was just a big old teddy bear to those kids." As those elementary kids have grown and moved up to the high school, Coleman's name has not been forgotten, says Broderson.

At a mid-season practice in 2011, John Gumb, the veteran of the McCook staff, with almost 40 years of service to the Bison program, recalled his longtime friend and colleague, "If RC were here right now, and he would be almost 60 years old, he would be right over there with the punters, his right shoe and sock off, out kicking everyone. That is just how he was; a big old kid that never stopped being a kid. He was one of those people that everyone loved just being around him."

As Broderson noted, many of the current Bison came under Coleman's influence when they were elementary students. Even today his legacy and influence, seven years after his death, lives on. "I know there have been times coaches have referred to Ron's memory when challenging our players to meet a problem head on. He had that kind of influence on people," says Gross.

The Gross family consists of four, and leading the household is wife Diana. "I get the kids where they need to be. I am the facilitator," she says with a laugh. The wife of a coach is never an easy life. When compounded by the drama that comes with the closeness of a small town, especially when your spouse is arguably the most recognized person in the community, the role can be full of pit falls. The Gross', who are raising two children, 12 year old Lexi and 10 year old DJ, have learned to negotiate that landscape well.

"I enjoy my role as the coach's wife," says the 46 year old Diana, three years the senior of her husband. "Football has always been a part of our lives. In fact I met Jeff when he hired me for a job when he was in private business and we were located in Great Bend, KS. I was raised just across the border from here (McCook) in Phillipsburg, KS and I had just recently moved back from Kansas City when Jeff hired me. I had season tickets to the Chiefs games and I kept them when I moved back. When Jeff found out I had the tickets, I sure saw a lot more of him," she says with a laugh.

"The time demand for not only football, but all the other things Jeff is involved in is tough," the coach's wife admits, "but Jeff does a great job of keeping family involved. My son is very involved in helping his dad with coaching duties and we never fail to make Thursday night family night. And another big help has been the advances in technology."

To illustrate her point, Diana tells a story from her early days as a coach's wife. "When Jeff was an assistant at Hays, he was always at school. All the film work, all the scouting; anything to do with technology in those days, had to be done at the school. The wives never knew when their husbands would be home. One night, one of the other assistant's wives finally had enough. Her husband had said he would be home at 7:30. When he was not home by 9:00 pm, she took matters into her own hands. She drove to the school, broke into the coaches meeting and announced she had had enough. We laugh about it now, but there were times when I never saw Jeff except for a few passing moments in the morning. Now, he can do all of his preparation at home and so can the other coaches. They spend Saturday getting the films broke down, uploaded into the computer and then Sunday evening they are over here in our family room getting ready for the next Friday's game. But at least it does keep them around the house on the weekends."

Having learned early in his head coaching career not to micro manage his staff has been, according to the head coach, a major factor in the long running success of his program. "I was the head coach of the staff, but I was also the pup," says Gross, reflecting back to that first season in 1998. "What a great staff I have been blessed with."

Gross' ability to prepare a team for any opponent is legendary amongst his peers. Steve Kodad is the Sports Editor of the daily McCook newspaper. A news room veteran of many years in western Nebraska and Wyoming, Kodad enters his third year of covering the local sports scene. Ironically, Kodad came to town the week after the Bison's 72 game regular season winning streak had been stopped with a loss to Aurora.

"I get to work on Monday morning," recalls Kodad, "and on my desk is Jeff's scouting report for the upcoming game. I have never seen anything like it. Plays, tendencies, defensive schemes; it was all there. I knew right then two things about the man; he didn't spend a whole lot of time feeling sorry for himself about a loss; and if his team was going to be beat, it was not going to be because they were not prepared. My initial assumptions, I have found from now having been around Jeff for a couple of years, were right on the mark."

The Coaching staff returns the complements when praising the head coach's leadership style. "The man has been great to work with," says longtime assistant John Gumb. The veteran coach has been in the McCook system for near 40 years and is the elder statesman on Gross' 14 man coaching staff. "I enjoy it so much, that I now volunteer my time," Gumb admits. "I don't get paid. I am here because the man listens. He lets us coach. I feel involved, I feel respected and I feel needed. And that all goes back to Jeff's leadership style. I am too old to be out there at practice every day, standing in the heat and cold, if I am not contributing."

Watching Gross at one of his Sunday evening coaches meetings in early August, drove home the skill he possesses in walking the fine line between leader and dictator.

As he works the white board he has installed in his family room/coaches meeting room, he constantly seeks input and validation from his staff. "We got to get Cherry off some of these special teams," Gross states as the staff works on early season depth charts. "Get him off the kickoff team is my thought," the head coach throws out to his staff. "If we are kicking off, we just scored, give him a break, get a drink and then get him back on the field." What do ya think," Gross polls the staff as he erases Cherry's name from the white board. "Bad idea," one assistant offers. "I agree we need to get him off, but not the kickoff team. We need him as a gunner. We score and the worst thing that can happen is they run it back up our ass on the kickoff for a TD. Game changer. We need guys who can tackle and he is one of the best. How about getting him off the punt return team," offers the assistant, one of the younger staff members. "Okay," says Gross, "Cherry stays on the kickoff team," as he rewrites the young man's name on the board listing the specialty teams, "and he comes off the punt return team. Everybody agree." The group nods in unison.

Gross was both lucky and smart at the same time when he arrived in McCook in 1998. Lucky in that he already had a talented staff of assistants in place, smart in that he (in time) recognized the talents of his staff and developed a managerial style that allowed for the utilization of those talents.

"I have been very blessed," states Gross. "The last fourteen years have been more than I could have ever dreamed of when I took this job. We have a home in McCook; we have a community here that supports us. Now, we need to go and get another state title."

Dan Imdieke, Linton, ND

Dan Imdieke is a big man. Even at 57 years of age, preparing to enter his 36th year of coaching the football Lions' of Linton, North Dakota – 35 as head coach- it is not hard to imagine his as the collegiate wrestling and football star he was as an undergraduate at nearby Jamestown (ND) University. "I came here out of college," says Imdieke, "not knowing how long I would stay. I was lucky, met a great woman and have raised a great family (three grown children) right here in this town. Linton has given me everything I could have ever wanted. I have had a great life here. No complaints."

Imdieke is a man who has known nothing but coaching success after spending his first year in Linton as an assistant football coach and head wrestling coach. He remains today as the head mentor of the Lions' grappling program, but it is ön the gridiron that he has made his mark, compiling a resume that almost guarantees a future hall of fame induction. With a record of 288-67, highlighted by four state championships and five state second place finishes, Imdieke has left his mark on this small farming community that lies in the center of the state, 20 miles north of the South Dakota boarder.

The veteran coach knows how to keep his success in perspective. "The kids, man we have had some kids who could play, no doubt," says Imdieke. Still, few Division I coaches have made their way to Linton to show interest in the Lions' school boy stars. "Our kids know if they are going to play beyond high school, it will most likely be at a small school."

North Dakota high school football, even its most vocal supporters will admit, is a barren hunting ground when it comes to latching on to Division 1 recruits. In the history of the NFL draft, 26 North Dakota natives have heard their name called by a NFL suitor. There are high schools in Texas that alone have had more NFL alumni. The list starts in 1939 with Charlie Gainor of Milnor who went in the 18th round to the Philadelphia Eagles; and ends, for now, with Greg Eslinger of Bismarck, who attended the University of Minnesota and was a 6th round pick of the Denver Broncos in 2006. Grand Forks native Brooks Bollinger had an outstanding collegiate career quarterbacking some great University of Wisconsin teams. He was a 6th round draft pick of the New York Jets in 2002. A decade later, he is back home in Grand Forks, far removed from the bright lights of the NFL. He served as the head linesman for Linton's season opener against Mobridge, SD.

The Northern Plains coaches at smaller Division II and III programs, plus many of the area NAIA schools, know Imdieke's program well. "If our better kids want to play in college, we have found them a place," says Imdieke. "I played at a small school and it was a great experience. I had a great deal of respect for my college coach, Rollie Greeno. He coached for years and he influenced a lot of young men like me. He kept things fun. We worked hard but it wasn't drudgery. I have tried to always make playing football here fun."

Imdieke has a low key personality that belies his physical presence. He looks like a football coach. Even at 57 years of age, he still maintains a muscular build. However, after only a short time watching Imdieke apply his coaching skills, he immediately impresses with his patience with his players. Mistakes are corrected, but seldom does the coach raise his voice or let his frustration with a player's mistake show.

According to former players, Imdieke has followed his college mentor's example well; he has made football at Linton High School fun. Mark Weber is the Sports Editor of the weekly Linton newspaper. He played for several of Imdieke's early teams, graduating in 1981. When the Coach is asked in the presence of Weber to elaborate on the writer's skills as a player, both laugh and give no further insight. Regardless of his on field success - or perhaps lack of- Weber has fond memories of his days as a Lion. "Coach always made it fun," remembers the reporter. "Some of my favorite memories of high school are riding the bus over to practice each day and listening to Coach talk. He was really funny. Once we got to the field, it was time to get serious, but when it was time to have fun, we had fun. That is really the genius of Coach, he brings great balance to everything he does," says Weber.

"It has to be fun," states Coach Imdieke. "Many of our kids over the years have been farm kids. They work hard and it hasn't always been the best of economic times for farmers and ranchers here on the High Plains. You have to take that all in to account, look at the whole picture in these kids' lives. Football for most is a fun diversion. We expect to win, but when we don't, we don't blame the kids. When you win as much as we have over the years, the pressure mounts each succeeding year, to continue to win. I try to take that pressure off the kid's shoulders and place it on mine."

To prove his point, when Imdieke is asked about the only team in his long head coaching career that did not finish the season on the winning side of the ledger, recording a 4-5 record, he will not discuss the season, will not even name the year. "You can look it up if you want to. Those kids worked just as hard as some of our state championships teams. It just didn't come together that year like it has in others, but it wasn't because they didn't try."

Superintendent Al Bjornson remembers how impressed he was when he took over the helm of the Linton Public Schools several years back. "I walked into the gym and immediately saw all the banners on the wall for football," he recalls. The tributes to the many state qualifying teams coached by Imdieke cover a large portion of the south wall of the gym. "But once I was here, I was even more impressed with Dan's program from the aspect of how he treats his players. He is a leader and a teacher. He has to a lot of grown men in this community, been a role model and a mentor. His impact cannot be measured. It is too great."

"Every coach loves to win," states Imdieke. "Getting your butt kicked is no fun. But we never want our program to be measured strictly against a win and loss record." His boss agrees with that standard. "It took us a while to lose, after I first came here," remembers the Superintendent. "When it did happen, the behavior of our team and our coaches was very impressive. They lined up and shook hands and moved on. No excuses. No pouting. Just an attitude of 'let's get ready for the next game.' That is leadership and that is why Coach is so well respected here and why he is so important to this community."

Even in a state that distrusts big government and questions, almost across the board, any hint of a tax increase, the tax payers of Linton should feel they are getting their money's worth when Imdieke cashes his monthly pay check. At 7:30 am on a September Wednesday morning, he is already on duty. As the coach walks the hallways of the high school he is greeted warmly, "What's up, Mr. I?" one senior girl inquires.

The early arriving students are headed to the cafeteria to take advantage of the school's breakfast program. "Big game tonight," the coach says to a group of senior volleyball players. "Better be ready," he encourages. The Lions volleyball squad will have a home game this evening, starting with a freshman game at 5 pm; followed by junior varsity and varsity contests. Athletic Director Imdieke will be late arriving, as he will not drive the bus containing his football team back from practice at Seeman Park until about 6:15. This will follow a day that sees him teach four physical education classes and supervise a study hall. He has two hours during the day to fulfill his Athletic Director duties. Back at school for the evening's volleyball match, he will supervise the concession stand - he uses the profits for the benefit of the athletic program- and make sure that the gate money is secured and counted. He will also watch as much of the volleyball match as possible, after which he will pay the two volleyball officials he hired to work the evening's match. He will make sure the lights are turned out in the gym before, at 9:45 pm, he heads home. Imdieke also drives the team bus to all away football games.

Weber can remember when the Lion football program was not the power house it has been for the last 35 years. "I started going to games when I was 10 years old, several years before Coach came. It was win some, lose some. Not a real big deal. The parents went to the games and some of the students to the home games, but nothing like what you see today. Don't let anyone tell you otherwise, Coach Imdieke made this program what it is today. Coach is football in Linton."

Claiming to have never entertained any serious thoughts of leaving Linton, despite the obvious offers from rival schools seeking to employ such an ultra-successful coach, Imdieke considers himself a perfect fit for the remote school. "I met a great woman here and raised three great kids. I love to hunt and fish and it doesn't get any better for those than right here. All three of my children got a great education here and had great childhoods. My daughter (28 year old Vanessa) and my two sons (26 year old Ben and 24 year old Dan) are all successful adults. Two (Vanessa and Dan) are in the National Guard and have served tours in Iraq. Ben is a successful young coach." Ben was recently engaged and Vanessa will be expecting the coach's first grandchild later in the fall. All three children reside in Fargo, a 3-1/2 hour drive from Linton.

"I was able to coach my sons in both football and wrestling. It was over-all a good experience," Imdieke said. "It is always hard to coach you own kids, but probably harder on them to be coached by their dad. But we all handled it well. The two boys won nine (Dan won a state high school title as an 8th grader) state wrestling championships between them," the proud father states.

The relationship with the "great woman" Imdieke met and married in Linton got off to what, at best, would be described as a rocky start. "He stood me up on our first date," says Cathy Imdieke. "My brother was on the school board at the time and he kept trying to arrange a first date, and then I got stood up," laughs the almost 30 year wife of the coach. "I grew up here, one of ten kids," she states. "When I first started dating Dan, I was in between changing jobs from Aberdeen (SD) to Bismarck, but I always knew I wanted to move back home."

Educated as a dietician, an emerging field in the mid 1970's when Cathy earned her Bachelor's Degree; she readily admits she has had to make sac-rifices to remain in both her chosen profession and her home town. "I trav-el a lot on my job. I mostly work in Bismarck now, but I also do a lot of train-ing of staff in other parts of the state. As far as I know, I am still the only dietician in the three county area."

With a husband who has as demanding a job as hers', adaptions had to be made to fill the role of full time professional, full time mother and full time wife of the coach. "I came in with my eyes open to this marriage," she recalls. "It was clear right away that Dan is a coach. It is what he was meant to be and he is very good at it. Never would I ask him to give that up. It is too much of who he is. Fortunately, all three of our children were very athletic, so it (school and athletics) just became our lives. We were always on the go, to a game, to a match, to a practice. It just flew by. But the results were well worth all the schedule juggling. Our kids had a great upbringing in Linton. This is my home. This house we sit in was my mother and father's house. Most of my nine brothers and sisters live here. What more could we want? Dan always said that as long as we both had jobs, Linton is where we would stay. I don't see us ever leaving here. It is home for us both and it has been a very good home."

Imdieke has immersed himself in bettering his home town. So committed is the coach that recently he has taken to wearing another hat, as a civic leader. "I am on the city council," he relates. Those who know him could never have seen him in his younger years taking on the role of a politician. "I know it seems out of character for me, but I have enjoyed it. We are very proactive in promoting Linton. We need jobs to survive. Many good communities up here, a lot similar to Linton, have dried up and blown away because of the loss of jobs. I don't want to see that happen here and I want to do my part to see that it doesn't."

Much like a team that loves to run the ball- as Imdieke's teams' do- a football team must still possess, to keep the defense honest, at least a threat of a passing game. Using that analogy, the coach explains why he does not want to see his town become too one dimensional. "We will always be a farming/ranching community. No one disputes that. But we need other industries to fall back on. We have a good hard working and stable work force here. I am interested in promoting the area to potential businesses that might move in."

Steadily over the years, the Lions have grudgingly earned the respect of area schools. It has become accepted, that if you have the Lions down in a game, you had better bury them.

"We don't quit, ever," says Weber. "We have had some great comebacks over the years. Now other teams expect it. It is like we are in their heads and they expect to lose a close game to us."

Imdieke shows his "old school" side when disclosing the secret to his team's fourth quarter heroics. "It's The Hill," he simply states.

"Oh my, The Hill," laments former player Weber. According to both, The Hill, a steep incline of about 50 yards, located just to the south of the team's practice field, has become a rite of passage amongst the young men who have passed through the Lion's program over the last 35 years. "It is not that bad," says Imdieke, with a sheepish grin. "Oh my God," disagrees Weber. "A lot of us still have nightmares of The Hill, and it's been over 25 years!"

"The Hill" is located at Seeman Park, 1-$^1/_2$ miles east of town, where the Lions have practiced for as long as anyone can remember. Seeman Park is an idyllic spot to spend an Indian summer early fall day. A creek runs through the middle of the well cared for park grounds. The team practices on a softball field that is unlined for the use of a football team, the outfield fence surrounding the field, in many places, falling down.

When conditioning on The Hill, players sprint up one side and back down the other, in a circular movement. Sometimes it is a lonely chore, with a solo player singled out by Imdieke for a set number of reps up the incline. "Jayden, give me two," the coach yells out at one practice, not happy with a player whom he catches walking between drills. For 35 years, every Lion player knows what "give me two" means. No discussion - practice continues without interruption, minus one team member for a few minutes.

On Monday, Tuesday and Wednesday, work days for the team, the players can expect to finish practice with a conditioning session on The Hill. Imdieke is careful to make sure it is not viewed as punishment. He will stand at the bottom of The Hill and place a senior leader at the top. Both become cheerleaders, as the rest of the team runs up and down for a predetermined number of repetitions.

The record for reps on The Hill is legendary amongst current and former Lions. "About 15 years ago," Imdieke recalls, "I had a boy who lived out on a ranch. One morning, he didn't come to 7 am practice during the summer. He called me and said, 'Coach, I was just too tired. I will take my punishment tomorrow.' That was the kind of kid he was. He could have lied to me, but he didn't. The next day, I asked him, like I often do, 'how many do you think you should do to make it right.' He said, 'what is the record." I said, '15'. He said, 'then I think I should do 16.' Just to make sure, he did 17, and that was at the end of a four hour summer practice. Nobody has been crazy enough since to offer to break 17."

Running the incline has been a great conditioner for the Lions over the years. The Head Coach claims that the effect is more mental than physical. "Four (repetitions) is about the most we will ever run," says Imdieke. "But it is a challenge and you have to gut it out to finish after a hard practice. Then when the fourth quarter comes around and the game is on the line, our players remember The Hill and we really believe it gives us an advantage. When you sell out and really pay the price to achieve something you feel is important, then that makes it harder to give it up without giving all that you have, and people will tell you, the Linton Lions give all they have."

Chris Koetting, Canadian, TX

Chris Koetting, head football coach of the Canadian, TX Wildcats, could not have jumped into a hotter fire for his first head coaching assignment. After spending seven years as the offensive coordinator for Canadian Head Coach Kyle Lynch, Koetting was promoted to the head coaching position after the 2009 season when Lynch decided to accept the district's offer to become Superintendent of Schools. Lynch, with Koetting as his main assistant, had built a dynasty on the isolated plains of the north Texas panhandle. His Wildcats won two state championships, in 2007 and 2008, just missing a third title with a runner-up finish in 2009.

A state championship in Texas is never earned without many trials and much tribulation. While many states have added layer upon layer of classifications to their systems, diluting and cheapening what a state title once stood for, in football crazed Texas, a team must first qualify through district play and then, in Class 1A where Canadian resides, win six consecutive games to claim a state title, a momentous challenge, to stay the least. One bad game, one ill-timed injury and you pack up the equipment for the year, the dream dead.

Lynch says he can give the exact date and person responsible for initiating the movement that has turned this small cross roads town into the football envied program in the Panhandle. "Paul Wilson is the man who got it all started here in football. We had limited success before Paul, but since he came in 1990, things have taken off. We had never even won a playoff game in the history of the school until 1992. Paul was an innovator. I learned so much from him. On offense, he was running empty backfield sets while everyone else was in the full house or wishbone. He was just ahead of his time." When Wilson left in 2000 to return to his roots in Fort Gibson, OK, his trusted assistant, Lynch, was ready to step in and the program didn't miss a beat, climaxing with the two state titles late in Lynch's coaching career.

"I will miss it," Lynch said in response to hanging up his whistle. "But the timing was right. The Superintendent here decided to retire and if I turned the job down, who knew how long it would be before it opens again? And Chris was sitting there ready to go. He needed to be a head coach and I knew I was leaving the program in good hands. Everything just came together to show me it was the right move at the right time. But yeah, there are times I miss the coaching."

Lynch stepping down left big shoes to fill. The position of head coach was never opened up for outside application; the Wildcats had their man in-house. Despite a resume that was void of any head coaching experience, the nearly 20 year assistant coach knew he was ready. Koetting didn't blink and neither did the district. "We knew all along that Chris was our man," said newly seated Superintendent and recent Head Coach Lynch. "I wanted someone to keep the tradition alive. I felt very comfortable recommending Chris to our Board (of Education) and he has done nothing to make me, even for one second, question my choice."

Accepting a new job position required many changes in Koetting's life, not only professional but also his family life. He and his wife Rosemary are raising three children; 13 year old daughter Lauren and 10 year old twin sons Bill and Jack. The couple were high school sweethearts, but as Mrs. Koetting points out, "we did go to different colleges. If it was not meant to be, we figured the college separation would let us know." They were married when both completed college. Rosemary is a nurse in an area clinic.

"I was athletic when I was younger," she states. Still an active runner, Rosemary carries an athletic build, and like her husband is high energy. "I knew what I was getting into as a coaches' wife," she says, "but to be honest; I love it. It is such a part of our lives. Sometimes I wish football season lasted year round. I miss the excitement in the off season," she says with a laugh.

As most coach's wives must, Mrs. Koetting has learned to shoulder a disproportionate load of parenting duties. "Chris is so busy; it does fall on me quite a bit. Good thing all the kids are athletically inclined. We are just starting to get into the age of the traveling teams with the boys. And that, I am told by many, will really take over our lives. We did the basketball with the boys last year, but we made them wait until, in the 5th grade, to let them do football." What, the football coach's sons in a football town had to wait an extra year to start? "I know," says Rosemary with a laugh. "According to the boys, we were the worst parents ever!"

As with most football staffs, the wives on the Canadian football coaches have become socially dependent upon each other. "Especially in season," Rosemary says, "we try to help out. We work together and fix lunch for the coaches on Saturday and we always try to ride to the away games together. Chris has a great coaching staff, and they all have great wives. We have had the same group for a long time and we are very supportive of each other, and our roles as wives and mothers."

When stepping up to the head coach's position, changes were inevitable, Rosemary says she knew, but for the most part she sees little difference in her husband. "Chris is really good about keeping an even keel. He doesn't bring the job home with him often. Sometimes I wish he would talk more about his day, especially if it is a bad day. But Chris is not really a talker."

With the tragic death this past summer of the mother of a JV football player, Mrs. Koetting has seen, up close, how the town pulls together. "People here are very supportive. I know everyone in town has let that young man know that whatever he needs, the town is here to see he gets it. There is a strong sense of community here."

Due to her nursing job, Rosemary is aware that there are pockets of poverty in the community. She is an active member of a loose knit group known as Helping Angels. "By design, we are pretty low key," she states. "But we have resources that if it is brought to our attention – often by teachers – that if a student in town needs some basics, we see that they get what they need."

We love it here," Mrs. Koetting states. "Now that Chris has the opportunity to be a head coach, I don't see us leaving here. He really enjoys the job and I like the role I play as his wife. We are very comfortable professionally, and as a family, in Canadian. I am afraid the town is stuck with us," she says with a laugh.

Chris is aware also, of the role his new job plays in the dynamics on the home front. "I do put in more time than I did as an assistant," he says. "Maybe not so much in season, but more so in the off-season. In the spring, as Athletic Director, there are a lot of events I attend, when in the past I would have been home."

As a first year head coach last fall (2010), all Koetting did was take the Wildcats to within one heart breaking loss of a fourth straight state title game. Canadian finished the season with only that one semifinal blemish on its record, giving the rookie head coach a season mark of 13-1.

"That loss still gnaws at me," said Koetting after the conclusion of a hot practice and 48 hours before he would lead his second addition of Wildcats on to the artificial turf of Canadian Stadium for the season opener. "We lost some very good kids, but we have some good ones back. I think we are going to be pretty good again this year (2011)."

An offensive coordinator or a defense coordinator on a football coaching staff is a unique assignment in the world of coaching. While technically still an assistant, the coordinator is given virtual carte blanche control of his side of the line of scrimmage. They develop the game plan and then take the hands on operation of play calling and in-game management. In no other sport is this true. Even with a pitching coach in baseball, the manager will make out the rotation schedule; decide when to lift a pitcher and choose the reliever inserted into the lineup. But in football, if you are the offensive coordinator, then you are responsible for the offense. Totally.

Because of this level of responsibility, the coordinator has become a very glorified position. Many excellent coaches have been content to stay in this type position their entire career, satisfied with their autonomy and power bestowed a coordinator, never seeking a head coaching job.

Koetting never saw himself as a lifetime coordinator. "I knew somewhere down the line, I would become a head coach. I am just thankful it came when it did here in Canadian. My game responsibilities have not changed that much. I still run the offense and cheer for the defense. The difference is all the organizational duties I have now as a head coach. It is year round, something not so much true for the coordinator. I am also responsible for a lot of public relations that I wasn't as an assistant. I am more the face of the program now as opposed to the more anonymous role of an assistant."

Koetting, who also serves as the district's Athletic Director, readily accepted the challenge of leading a team that the community has come to expect to win. "I want high expectations," he stated. "I expect us to compete every year for a state title. Some years that may not be as realistic of a goal as some others, but I always want that to be what we play for. I will not have it any other way. This town wants a winner. I would not be here if they didn't. We use that type of pressure to motivate myself, our staff and our players. It is my job to guard against complacency. Our kids do not want to be the group to let the tradition fall and let the town down. We use pressure to make us better. We don't run from high expectations," said the Head Coach.

Koetting then reverts back to "coach talk," lamenting for sympathy for his (he would like you to believe) overmatched team. "Can you believe those suckers picked us number 1 in the state," he pity mouths to an assistant. "Hey, we lost two DI linemen, and you don't replace those that easily in our size school," Koetting said in response to a just released state wide pre-season poll picking the Canadian Wildcats to wear the crown of state champions come December.

The 103 degree August temperature drove home Koetting's final words of wisdom. "It is a long time until December." At least he managed to avoid the over used cliché of every sandbagging coach sitting with a stacked hand, "we play em one game at a time."

Canadian High School principal Rick Berry use the same word as the coach when describing what allows Koetting to maintain such a high level of success: priorities. "Chris is a good educator," says the 59 year old Berry, starting his 11th year as high school principal at his alma mater. "He helps keep balance and priorities in check, which is not always that easy to do when you are running such a high profile program as Canadian." Berry points to the two recent Division I signees, Class of 2011, as proof that the substance of the Canadian High School Football program goes way beyond the mere final score on Friday night. Taylor Chappell, on full football scholarship at Big 12 power the University of Missouri, was a state academic champion in science, Berry points out. He adds, "Ryan Alexander, who is at West Point, was the state debate champion. We are very proud of both of them because they are good kids who worked hard and deserved the (awards) they received. But even more, it is says a lot about our school that two such highly rated football players also had the balance, and most importantly, the adult guidance to achieve academically."

After having spent several years in bigger towns than Canadian, along the way of his coaching journey, in 2002 Koetting and his wife Rosemary made the decision to return to the panhandle to raise their family of three children. The twin boys are constants at practices and games, filling roles as water boys, which on this particular 103 degree August day, is arguably the most important job on staff.

Koetting describes his staff's approach to coaching. "We are not yellers and screamers. As coaches, we get excited and we try to convey that to our players. We want enthusiasm on the field. We go hard all the time that is our motto and what are known for. We are not going to wait for you. We play FAST. If we want to play up tempo, we have to practice up tempo. But we want kids to also have fun. My gosh, what a great time in their lives. They are local heroes. But we got to; as I said earlier, get them to outwork the other team. We have to guard against complacency."

One could take the route, it is pointed out to Koetting, a program such as he inherited at Canadian has Sir Isaac Newton to deal with, in other words, there is nowhere to go but down. "You could lose a lot of sleep thinking like that," the coach said with a chuckle. "But we tell our coaches and players to worry about what we can control and not the things we can't. If we work hard, the winning will take care of itself. And along the journey, let's not forget to have fun."

Superintendent Lynch applauds the way his former assistant runs the program. "We do things with class, and Chris demands that from his players."

Koetting deflects praise for the conduct of his athletes to Lynch. "Kyle demanded as head coach that we win with class, we lose with class. I learned that from him and have carried on with it. We respect every opponent we play. If you trash talk you don't play for Canadian, that simple. You don't win games with your mouth; you win by outworking and out performing your opponent. We hate to lose, but we don't act like fools when we do. That is why we get the support in the community that we do. Our kids represent Canadian in a way that our community can be proud of. We can never make exceptions for poor behavior on the football field. If your jersey on the front says, 'Canadian', then you better conduct yourself the Canadian way."

Watching the season opening game against River Road High School of Amarillo, and witnessing Koetting's defensive players fly around the field fearlessly making crisp, hard and legal tackles, one cannot help but to ponder his edict to his team: "You trash talk, you don't play." This, a true fan of the game thinks, is how the game should be played. We are bombarded each Sunday afternoon with overpaid, over-muscled buffoons who seem to think the simplest tackle requires a self-congratulatory celebration befitting of the curing of cancer. Watching to the point of nausea, a true fan has to better like the modus operandi of Koetting's Canadian High School team. It seems to go something like this: Step 1: Knock him on his ass. Step 2: Pick him up. Step 3: Pat him on the back. Step 4: Repeat steps 1 through 3.

"I have a great staff here," Koetting concluded. "What a great place to work and live. I have no thoughts of looking for any other job. As long as they want me, I will be here."

A first year season with a 13-1 mark it is a pretty sure fire way to see that the welcome mat stays out.

83

Junction, TX

"If you quit here, you will quit on the goal line." *Paul "Bear" Bryant, Junction, TX, August 1954*

It is striking how barren this place is, even by West Texas standards. I have driven 350 miles south on US Highway 83 from Canadian, TX, burning a tank full of $3.57 a gallon gas in the process, just to reach this particular patch of arid Texas rangeland.

I am here to pay homage.

I am in the small town of Junction, TX, standing on ground that, 57 years ago, was witness to perhaps footballs' most legendary ever two weeks of summer practice. Coach Paul "Bear" Bryant brought his 1954 Texas A&M team, his first at the College Station school, to this 400 acre "campus" to conduct for his Aggies a pre-season training camp. The Bear intended to find out quickly who of the 114 prospects he brought west to Junction wanted to play football, and who didn't.

The facilities for the camp, as Bryant had demanded, were Spartan. In 1954, this area of West Texas was in the midst of the worst draught anyone could remember, in a summer that had seen the thermometer climb over 100 every day for six straight weeks. In 2002, when the movie The Junction Boys was made, to reconstruct the environment of the camp, the filming was done in the Australian Outback.

Bryant's methods were brutal, maybe even inhumane. By today's standards, they would be considered criminal.

Practices started before dawn and, with only a few breaks throughout the day in barracks lacking air conditioning, lasted until dark. Water breaks were not allowed during practice and it was not unusual, due to the sweltering heat and humidity, for a player to lose 10% of his body weight in one day. Bryant's methods were not for the meek. According to sportsjones.com, during the camp, Bryant head-butted tackle Henry Clark after a blown assignment, leaving the player on the ground, dazed and holding a broken nose.

Dr. Arnold LeUnes is today an A&M professor of sports psychology. He was an A&M undergrad during the years the Bear ran the Aggies football program and has studied Bryant's methods. According to LeUnes, Bryant's word was the law in a time, especially at a military school like A&M, that authority was not questioned by subordinates. "He was strict, enforcing iron discipline," LeUnes said. "At the time, a coach could get away with pretty much anything. You wouldn't find something like that today."

LeUnes is correct. The sport will never again see the days of the Bear Bryants. The lawyers will see to that. Legend has it that of the 114 players who went to Junction in August of 1954, by the end of the two week camp, the roster had melted away in the West Texas desert sun to only 27. The hand full of survivors became the legendary "Junction Boys."

Four busses took the squad to Junction. Only one was needed to transport those left, back to College Station. Those who did persevere through the two weeks of pure torture at Junction, two years later, formed the core of A&M's only national championship football team.

The 1950's was a time when the legendary football coach, especially in the South, was a symbol of unquestioning and unbending discipline. He was often larger than life. His word was the law. This strong jawed, no nonsense coach was often viewed as unapproachable by parents, players, boosters, and in extreme cases, even the college president. The 1950's were the peak decade for the limitless power of coaches like the Bear. As the nation rode the wave of the radical 60's into the "me generation" of the 70's and 80's, the likes of these giants disappeared like dinosaurs from the college and high school football landscape, many, like Bryant, riding off into legendary status.

It is surprising that Junction's local chamber of commerce has not attempted to cash in on the famous events of over 50 years ago that occurred in their back yard. The civic boosters of Junction are not exactly working with the Garden of Eden when attempting to convince outsiders to spend their tourists' dollars in this barren land. Yet the county tourism web site does not even mention the Junction Boys. It does promote the area's hunting, fishing, canoeing and other outdoor activities; and plugs the area museums that depict early life in the west Texas desert; but not a hint of the Bear and his legendary two weeks spent in Junction. There is not even a small marker at the site to recognize what took place here.

In 1979, the survivors of this football style death camp held a 25 year reunion. Bryant was invited back as a special guest of honor. Some of these men - his boys- Bryant had not seen since his coaching days at A&M. He was not sure as to what kind of reception he would receive. He need not have worried. The reaction of the players to their demanding old coach was one of, if not love, then of genuine respect. A commemorative ring had been minted for each of the players and Bryant. It was a memento that linked these men and their coach together in a special bond. As a group, they had endured a living hell that would forever bind them as one. No matter what else these, just over two dozen men had accomplished in life, they would forever be known as "The Junction Boys."

Bryant went on to win three national championships. Yet when he died in 1983, his wishes were that the only piece of jewelry commemorating his great career that he would wear into the here-after would be his Junction Boys ring.

After asking directions, I locate, what I am confident, is the site of the camp. A few out buildings still stand, a former mess hut and several barracks are upright, but crumbling. The open area is over grown with weeds and littered with trash. It takes some liberal use of my imagination to picture in my mind how this neglected piece of desert could possibly have been the setting for the legendary events of the summer of 1954.

As a nation that loves our heritage, it is startling that this important part of football lore has been left with no care taker. Along Highway 83 alone, for commercial purposes, we have immortalized the world's biggest prairie dog, largest buffalo, largest ball of string and Lawrence Welk's birth place; but we have forgotten the Junction Boys.

It is not near as hot today as it was that drought summer of 1954. The four hour drive down required the use of the rental car air conditioner, but right now, it is comfortable outside. The sun is setting, the dry desert wind from the south beginning to pick up. If I close my eyes and use my imagination, I can hear the shrill whistle from almost 60 years ago, blown by a no nonsense and focused coach determined to build champions under a relentless West Texas desert sun, no matter what the cost; calling a dwindling group of exhausted but determined non-quitters to the next descending level of hell.

Chapter 3

Out of the Gate: August
Weeks 1 and 2

The harder you work, the harder it is to surrender.
Vince Lombardi

On this team, we are all united in a common goal; to keep my job. *Lou Holtz*

Truth is tough. It will not break, like a bubble, at a touch; nay, you may kick it about all day, like a football, and it will be round and full at evening. *Mark Twain*

Sectional football games have the glory and the despair of war, and when a Texas team takes the field against a forcign state, it is an army with banners. *John Steinbeck*

Week I – Game on
August 26

Canadian will open their season hosting the Amarillo River Road Wildcats.

A class 2 school with twice the enrollment of Canadian, River Road would appear on paper to be outclassed, if not outnumbered. Only two starters on each side of the ball return from last year's 4-6 squad. River Road Coach Jayme Carr does have some tools to work with, primarily running back Trey Evans. Fast and tough, his rushing prowess will be much needed to compensate for a very inexperienced front on both sides of the line of scrimmage. Carr will be coaching his first game as head coach at River Road.

"You never know about a first game," said Canadian Head Coach Jeff Koetting. "We have some questions to answer on the line. We have some very good talent returning at the skilled positions, so we should be pretty set there. We lost two Division I (to the University of Missouri and the US Military Academy) level linemen and in a school our size, that is not easily replaced. We should be able to put points on the board and our defense pursues to the ball well. We will hit people. We have to stop Evans and force them to go to more inexperienced people. If we contain him, we should do all right. I am confident we can score points."

The McCook Bison will open on the road at Scottsbluff. The season opener will be a big test for the Bison. Although McCook has not dropped a game to Scottsbluff in five years, the last few have not been easy wins. Last year, at home, the Bison had to erase a 7-0 half time deficit. In 2009, the trip to the panhandle saw McCook need a last second field goal to win, 10-7.

"This is the year they have been pointing to," said Bison head coach Jeff Gross on the opening week's opposition. "They have a very athletic junior class and a three year senior starting quarterback. They might be the only team we play all year that is faster than we are. We have our work cut out for us. They made the playoffs last year and I know they want to build on that." The 260 mile bus ride to get to Scottsbluff also has Gross concerned. "I think it is worth a touchdown to the home team," Gross said expressing his concerns on how the long trip to the far western panhandle of Nebraska would affect his team's focus.

"We better get used to it (the travel)," the coach said. "We got two more trips out there in weeks 3 and 4. Our schedule is frontloaded as tough as any I have had here in 14 years. After week four, if we are still standing, we are going to have a pretty good team." Gross also noted the first home game, in week 2, was also a stiff assignment. "Next week we get Aurora. We have not beaten them in five years. We could start the year 0-4 and still have a good team by the end of the season. These first four weeks will tell a lot."

Although both teams are Class B schools, Scottsbluff is one of the larger in the state, with double the enrollment of McCook. Gross notes that the Bison newcomers to the starting lineup will need to grow up fast, with a baptism under fire.

Dan Imdieke will launch his 35th Linton Lions team with a home game against Mobridge, SD. The Mobridge game has, in recent years, become a hotly contested rivalry, with the Lions winning last year in heart stopping fashion. "We went down there last year and overcame a 21-6 deficit in the final quarter," remembers Imdieke. The veteran coach sports a remarkable winning percentage of over 81% (288-67). Mobridge defeated the Lions in 2009 in Overtime and Linton eked out a 6 point win in 2008.

The contest will be the only non-regional game on the Lions schedule, and Imdieke expects a hard fought game. "We need to replace almost all of our skilled players from last season," he said. "I am sure the butterflies will be there for our young kids. Mobridge should have a very strong passing game this year, so our defense will be tested right away. Our skilled position players are all new, including our QB, but I am convinced this (offense) is going to be a strength of our team by the end of the year. You never know," said the future Hall of Fame Coach, "but I think we are going to have a strong team this year. The good thing about playing a strong team like Mobridge early is that we will know where we stand, what we do well and what we need to improve on right away. That should help us as we head into the rest of our schedule. MoBridge might be the best team we see all year."

"Hurry. Hurry. Hurry," encouraged Canadian Head Coach Chris Koetting. He was putting his Wildcats through a short practice the night before their season opener. The temperature on the digital sign in front of the Happy State Bank in downtown Canadian at 2 pm that afternoon read 103 degrees, five degrees cooler, pointed out Koetting to his team before the practice began, than the reading at the same time the day before. A thermometer laid on the artificial grass of Wildcat Stadium registered a blistering 140 degrees. Koetting and the Wildcats, for several seasons, have adopted a motto of "212 degrees", the point in temperature that water boils. "If you give just that little bit more, take the temperature from 211 degrees to 212, look what happens," explained the coach. "That is what we want to get across to our kids. Just that little bet extra, just one more little degree of effort, and then look what happens, water boils. We always want to keep pushing, not only ourselves, but our opponents." To help themselves remember, and as a subtle reminder to visiting teams, the numbers 212 had been spelled out in block letters by the formation of large rocks that were hauled in and anchored on a hillside behind the south end zone.

Koetting uses the word "hurry" repeatedly throughout the course of a practice. The Canadian team employees a potent spread offense. He and his staff want their players to be in constant attack mode. "We sprint to the line of scrimmage, we don't wait for anyone. We want to get inside the defense's head. Give them no time to rest. It helps, in that it limits the opportunity that the defense has to use situational substitutions (send players best suited for particular down and distance situations. For example, a heavier player sent in on the defensive line on a short down situation, such as 3rd down and 1 yard). The main reason we use the hurry up offense is that we want the defense to know we are always coming after them. With the skilled players we have, we want to run 80 to 100 plays a game. If we can do that, we are going to score a lot of points. We play pretty good defense as well. I like that combination," Koetting stated.

The coaches on the Canadian staff are not "screamers," so common in earlier eras of high school football. "We encourage, and when we are critical, we always want to stay constructive," says Koetting. "We want our kids to stay focused and they know how important that is. Our kids want to win. That is the way it is in Canadian. We don't have to instill a will to win in these kids. It is already there. The tradition here for winning is strong and expected. We don't have to scream at them to get them ready to play. When it ever becomes to the point that we do, then we are in trouble."

Quarterback Braden Hudson is the poster boy of this year's team. As a junior the previous season, he threw for a head spinning 46 touchdowns and over 3,600 yards. Hudson had received the lion's share of the pre-season publicity amongst the Wildcat players. His 5'10" stature has scared off some Division I coaches, but Hudson insists he is not concerned about stats or his height. "I have confidence in my ability. I am not worried about college. I just want to win, one game at a time, but eventually a state championship. I will not allow our team to settle for less. We want it all and we want it badly."

Any team with a 17 year old leader receiving as much "ink" as Hudson is a prime candidate for bad locker room karma. Hudson acknowledged how he carried himself - how he managed all the attention he received - was critical to ward off any jealousy and make sure his teammates did not feel like Paul Revere's horse, in other words: "we do all the work and he gets all of the credit."

"I always make sure my teammates, especially my line, know how important they are and that I know I could never complete even one pass without them. We are a cohesive group. We want to win, and that comes from the coaches. They will not let us get big headed." Hudson, whose father is the Canadian High School boys' basketball coach, plays his role as team leader well.

Coach Koetting often compliments Hudson's poise. "He is a coach's son," says Koetting. "That shows in how Braden conducts himself. He is humble. He has been raised around sports and knows a team must play together. He handles the notoriety well and that is a real strength in making him a team leader. I sense no jealousy toward him from anyone in our program and I give Braden the credit for that."

Hudson and his favorite target, senior Isaac Lewis, both realize they are leaders of not only their teammates, but also role models for the next generation of Wildcats. Tradition is not a word thrown around lightly in Canadian. The varsity players know they have a huge legacy to live up to. They are also the role models for the next generation.

The team's female cheerleading squad is in charge of a program called "Walkout Buddies." Each Friday afternoon during the season, the varsity football players and the varsity cheerleaders go into the elementary school classrooms to visit with the younger students. "We love doing it," says Lewis. "It is the coolest thing to hang out with those little guys," affirms Hudson. "I remember when I was that age and looking up to the players on my dad's teams. Now the little guys are looking up to us. One week last year we had to cancel and I remember that we were more disappointed than I think the little guys were."

The quarterback admitted that he would have a few butterflies, despite his success and experience, before the next night's 7:30 kickoff, but said he would be concerned it he didn't. "I can handle the nerves. I have learned over the years to even make them work for me. After that first good hit I take on the field, I will be ready. The worst part will be how long tomorrow drags on until we do get on the field." Lewis agreed with his pitch and catch buddy. "Yes sir," the senior answered when asked if he was ready to finally play a real game, the first in 9-1/2 months. "Yes sir," he repeated. "The whole town will be here and we will not let them down. This is Canadian football. Are we ready to play? Oh yeah, can't wait."

After the short practice, Koetting reminded his troops to stay hydrated. The record heat was just a touching finish to the warmest and maybe driest summer on record. An arid region to start, the Panhandle averages about 23 inches of rain a year. So far, in the first 8 months of 2011, a scant 3 inches had fallen. But, as Koetting reminded his assembled team, the opposition would also have to play in the heat.

The team huddled at midfield and broke off the last practice of the pre-season to a unison chant of "FAST."

GAME TIME!

Sixty young men, in grades 9 through 12, filled out the roster of this year's Canadian High School's team. Since there were only 96 boys enrolled in the high school, and of those 96, six were ESL (English as a Second Language) students, none who participate in football, the turnout for the team was exceptional, but expected. "Our numbers, compared to most class A teams are always pretty good," said Koetting. "But still, even we get hurt in a numbers crunch sometime."

The Thursday practice saw a sparse group of 29 on the field ready to participate. Those same 29 would compose the varsity roster for the next evening. On Thursday, Canadian had sent 31 junior varsity players to Amarillo for a game, giving the practice field a more barren look than normal. Those making the 100 mile trip on the school's two black and gold painted buses would not be able to play the next night. The UIL (the Texas Governing Association for high school athletics) rule of only one game a week conflicted with what most other states allow. Other than Texas, the limit is either two games or 6 quarters a week. This more liberal approach allowed kids who played on JV squads to also serve as fill-ins on the varsity, especially helping fill out special teams. "We are used to it," said Koetting, "It forces a lot of our varsity kids to play both ways, but all Class1A schools have this numbers problem. We think the JV experience is very important to the continuity of our program. Last year's JV went 10-0, and we should have another good one this year." The younger Cats would make short work of their River Road counterparts, winning the Thursday night game in a walk-over fashion, 47-6.

The Canadian Wildcats lived up to the pre-season hype as the #1 ranked Class 1A, Division 1 team in the state of Texas, racing to a first quarter 35-0

lead and cruising to victory by the final score of 48-13. River Road's pair of scores came late in the game against the Canadian second team.

The tone of the game was set on the opening kickoff, when reserve junior linebacker Tyler Lynch threw all 170 lbs. of his lanky body at full speed into the sternum of the River Road return man. The opponent out weighted Lynch by 30 lbs. Didn't matter. POW! The force of Lynch's blow stood the white clad return man for the visitors straight up and then slammed straight backwards into the steaming artificial surface. Lynch's first hit signaled "game on" for the Wildcats. The season was finally here and Koetting's crew sent a clear message they were going to make short work of RR. Before 1 minute had run off the clock, Canadian had forced a punt, subsequently scoring on its second offensive play of the game.

At times during practice in the week leading into the opener, the Wildcats had seemed lethargic. Very catchable balls in practice were dropped. Several times each day assignments were missed, forcing coaches to shout our repeatedly, "No no, do it again." But when the clock struck 7:30 p.m. on Friday night, it was game time and Canadian played flawlessly. "We are not a super practice team," head Coach Chris Koetting said of his Wildcats after Thursday's practice. "But when it comes game time, we strap it on." To show how dominant and efficient Canadian was in the first half of the opener, in racing to a 48-0 lead, the ball touched the ground only one time, due to an incomplete pass. No fumbles. "You won't lose often like that," said the Coach.

Koetting proved to be a wise prophet in more ways than one. He "scripts" his first ten offensive plays for each game, meaning that the plays are pre-set and his offense ran through the sequence each day in practice. The play calling will not be audibled or changed, regardless of down and distance, or defensive alignment. The theory behind "scripting" is that you get good reads of the defensive reaction to each play. The coaches in the booth can identify and dissect both defensive line play, and pass coverages used by the opponent. Koetting will then take what he learns from the defense's reactions to the first 10 plays to develop "counters" to that reaction, thus setting up successful plays later in the game.

This is a method developed by the legendary coaching innovator, the late Bill Walsh. He won three Super Bowls with the San Francisco 49'ers in the 1980's. Walsh is considered the father of the West Coast Offense, the prelude to the spread, the short and precise passing game that evolves from the shotgun alignment, a formation that is so popular today at all levels of football. Walsh and a little heralded bench warming quarterback, and late round draft choice from Notre Dame, named Joe Montana, both used the West Coast passing game for a ride all the way to the Pro Football Hall of Fame.

The 10th and final play of Koetting's pre game list was a 10 yard touchdown pass from QB Braden Hudson to do it all wide out Isaac Lewis. The TD and subsequent PAT made the score 29-0 in favor of Canadian. There were still three minutes remaining in the first quarter. Koetting was reminded after the game to save this particular script. It had worked pretty well, he was told.

The Cats scored again, to up the first quarter lead to 35-0. Koetting gathered his troops during the intermission between the first and second quarters. "Don't let up," he encouraged. "We need to stay focused and we need to work on our conditioning. Now is a great time to do that. We are starting to drag. Get hydrated and let's keep this pace going," he implored his team.

The only part of the first half that threw a pall over the halftime locker room, with the Cats now staked to a 48-0 lead, was the injury to senior linebacker Colton Cates. The injury occurred on the first play from scrimmage when Canadian forced a River Road fumble. Cates took a direct helmet blow to the inside of his right knee. He made it off the sideline on his own but was in obvious pain. "Felt like it broke loose and is just hanging," he told the team doctor on the sideline. After performing several field tests, the Doc told Cates, and his mother-who had come down from the stands to the sideline- "It's not an ACL (anterior cruciate ligament), which is good. But being on the inside, I think you have strained your MCL (medial collateral ligament)." Both are major ligaments, one of four in the knee. The good news was that the MCL, the Doc felt, would heal on its own without surgery. With intense therapy Cates could be back on the field in four weeks. "If it was an ACL," Brian Mullins, the team trainer explained, "You would probably be out for the year."

"That is the one position (linebacker) we have a little room to move people around," reasoned defensive coordinator Craig Campbell, as the coaches gathered in their office at half time. "But darn, you feel for the kid. He has worked really hard to get where he is and his attitude has been such an improvement, and then he gets hurt on the first play." Campbell let his last words drag on as he shook his head side to side in quiet dismay. Cates had been picked by Texas Football Magazine as the pre-season defensive player of the year for District 1. He would not be easy to replace.

There is no medical redshirt in high school, as there is in college. This would be Cates' last season as a high school football player, injured or not.

It was a sad sight watching the young man pace the locker room at half time with his pads off and adorned only in his game pants. His frustration, cast amongst his teammate's giddiness over an almost perfect first half of play, was a striking contrast. Cates seemed to at one minute be ready to cry, the next to punch something, or someone. He watched the second half from the bench in his street clothes. "We won't know for sure until we see the scan on Monday," the Doctor told Koetting after the game. "But right now, plan on four weeks."

The first team players of Canadian were limited in the second half to the role of cheerleaders. When River Roads pulled off several long runs against the second team defense, one assistant asked the head coach about subbing back in at least a couple of first teamers. "NO," was the one word, emphatic answer from Koetting.

River Roads and its new coaching staff were able to score 13 unanswered points in the second half to make the final score a more respectable 48-13. After the game the rookie head coach for the Amarillo school, Jayme Carr, sought out Coach Koetting in the middle of the field and thanked the older coach for calling off the dogs. "You could have buried us; you and I both know it." Koetting offered a few words of encouragement to Carr - and one piece of advice - no short cuts.

After the game, back in their office, the coaches anxiously searched the internet for scores that were coming in from other games around the area and the state. Former head coach and current superintendent Kyle Lynch dropped in to congratulate the staff. He made a point of kidding Koetting in front of the rest of the staff, "He didn't take the starters out for the second half to be a nice guy, but to make sure no one on his side got hurt."

The combination of Hudson to Lewis, so publicized in the off season, lived up to its' billing. Hudson was the consummate team leader. He had the swagger, but not the cockiness. He was a "yes sir" kid who knew he had a special opportunity in front of him and he was not going to let it slip away. "So smart," said Koetting in describing his QB as the final seconds ran off the game clock. "He threw a couple of lasers and didn't have one bad read the whole night. In our offense, that is saying something."

Lewis had practically buried the visitors single handedly in the first two minutes of the game. So quick were Canadian's first two touchdowns, some of the late arriving home crowd had not yet settled into their seats in the sun soaked east bleachers. Lewis caught a touchdown pass of 11 yards on Canadian's first play from scrimmage and then after a three and out by River Road, returned the subsequent punt 68 yards to the end zone. Later in the first quarter Lewis found pay dirt again with a 48 yard run. Three touchdowns in the first quarter, one on a pass, one on a return and one on a run; was not a bad start to his senior year.

Lewis had his heart set on attending Texas Tech and playing Division I football. First appearances are deceiving in regard to the well-mannered young man, whose father served as the Wildcat Booster Club President. He was fast, a sub 4.5 40 yard dash time, run at several of the numerous camps he had attended on college campuses the proceeding summer; and strong with a 300 pound plus bench press on his resume. But he stood only 5'8, and small stature would scare off many of the potential college football suitors. "I said before the season that we got to get him 15 touches a game," said Koetting. "Tonight he only got nine, be he just played a half. But I will tell you one thing, and I know I am not very smart, but if I was Meade (the Kansas school who would be next week's opponent), on the top of my scouting report, in big old black letters, it would say: 'don't kick it to 5.'"

The staff now knew that they had on their hands a group of athletes with the talent to be a special team, and that this fall had the potential to turn into a special season. But there was a lot of work to do. "Enjoy it tonight," Koetting told his players as they huddled in the south end zone after the game, "But be here at 10 tomorrow morning for film. We've got to go to Meade next week, and we know how bad they want a piece of us."

One game down, Fourteen to go.

The McCook Bison got their season off to a positive start with a solid 28-6 win on the road against a very good Scottsbluff team. Coach Gross felt, prior to his team taking the field in their visiting white jerseys, that his team would get a very good test against Bluff. After the game, on the long bus ride back from the Panhandle through a very dark western Nebraska night, he gave his team high marks for the opening effort.

"Jumping on them quick was the key," Gross said. "Returning the opening kick to the seven got us off and running and had them back on their heels. We fumbled it right back to them, but then I was really proud of how we stuck the next two drives in the end zone. We could have let the fumble stop our momentum, but we didn't. I like the mental toughness of this group. They are going to need it to get through the first half of our schedule."

The first quarter scores came on a 37 yard run by Senior quarterback Matt Chitwood and a 30 yard run by fullback Justin Terry. Junior tailback Jake Schlager scored on a 6 yard run two minutes before the half giving the Bison a 21-0 half time lead. For all purposes in terms of a solid challenge, the game was over. "Tough to come back from three scores down in one half against a good team," said Gross. "Two, maybe. That is why that score by Jake right before the half was big. It gave us some breathing room."

Schlager scored again in the fourth quarter. Chitwood converted on all four extra-point kicks.

Gross had taken some good natured ribbing from his coaching staff over the summer when he would announce that "we will throw it 20 times this year, we got the quarterback." True to his linemen's roots, Gross always coached a conservative run first offense, built on solid blocking. Control the line, and control the game, is the motto of every line coach. His coaching staff, as they did every year, took an "I will believe it when I see it," approach to Gross' new proclaimed love for the forward pass.

In Scottsbluff, quarterback Chitwood completed 2 of 6 passes for 23 yards. He ran the ball for 89 yards. "Didn't need it tonight," was Gross' face saving response, when kidded about the puny air performance.

What the coach did like was his defense. "I thought we played lights out on defense. That is what you like to see on the road. We really rose up. We really met the challenge. We showed our toughness early, and I really liked that."

"Next week is big for us,' Said Gross. "We want to take what we can from this week. We will break down the film and see what we liked and what we didn't like. This was a good first step, but I am sure we are going to see some things we can do better."

Jake Schlager, junior running back and linebacker, was held under wraps, the coach felt. Many thought the talented Schlager was a Division I recruit. He had spent the summer traveling from college camp to college camp, and the exposure paid off, as he was now on the radar screen of multiple Division I programs.

As high tech and competitive as college scouting has become, an athlete needs to be labeled a prospect by their junior year to get him an invite and a good look at the "combines" that would take place the summer before his senior year. "He has the speed and you can't teach or coach that," said his head coach. "Jake is a legit 4.4 guy, and we haven't had that around here for a while," commented Gross. "That type of speed makes him quite attractive."

The Linton ND Lions did not fare as well as they dropped their season opener 26-12 to a very good team from Mobridge, SD. The game became a showcase between two quarterbacks. Linton senior QB Tanner Purintun made his quarterbacking debut a memorable one, as he set a school passing yardage record, completing 17-27 passes for 209 yards. The previous season, Purintun had played tight end for the Bison. His efforts though, were not enough as the South Dakota school countered with a solid duo of their own, quarterback Bailey Friesz and his twin brother, and favorite receiver, Payton Friesz. The brothers connected on three passes for 91 yards.

"They are both real good athletes," observed Imdieke. "The quarterback really hurt us more running than he did passing, but he did make a couple of really nice long throws to his brother." The signal caller ran for a whopping 183 yards from his quarterback position.

A 13-6 half time deficit was not a big concern for Imdieke. He told his players during the intermission break that they were still in the game. Later he said, "We needed that one big play to jump start us in the third quarter, and we didn't get it." Instead, the visitors tacked two more touchdowns- 13 points- on to their side of the ledger during the critical third stanza.

Dan Imdieke has lost very few games in his 36 years at the North Dakota school, but on the rare occasions his Lions have come up on the short end of the scoring stick, he knows there are lessons to learn from losing. Always in control of his emotions, by the 4th quarter having accepted this game's outcome, Imdieke didn't want to risk a serious injury to a key player that could have put the rest of the season in peril. He huddled his dispirited team late in the fourth quarter and went into teaching mode. He asked his team to look at the big picture. "We need to act like men now," he instructed. "We have a lot of season left to play. We need no injuries the last few minutes of this game. You played hard and we did some good things. Now we regroup and get ready for the regionals. Show some class, because they played a great game, and tonight were the better team."

At Linton, ND, you don't shoot the survivors because you lost the battle. You regroup and get ready for the next battle and hope, in the end, that you win the war. That is the way Imdieke has done it for 35 years and he had no intention of changing now.

Week 2 – The Aurora hex
September 2

Two years ago, on the hallowed ground of McCook's own stadium, Aurora broke McCook's 72 game regular season winning streak. However, according to Coach Jeff Gross of the Bison, revenge is not a factor. He simply wants his team to continue to get better.

Aurora is a game that has become very meaningful to the Bison faithful, as well as the coaches and players. The Huskies have won five games in a row against McCook, including two playoff wins. The number represents almost half of McCook's losses in the past decade. No other program has dominated Gross' Bison in such fashion. He is tired of hearing in the community that Aurora has his number. "We need to get a streak going the other way," he stated at his Sunday night coaches meeting.

McCook has not defeated Aurora since the third week of the 2008 season. That win was a resounding 42-7 thrashing. However, in the playoffs, Aurora regrouped and defeated the Bison in the state semifinals in a thriller, 37-33. The next week, Aurora claimed the Class B state title. In last year's regular season game at Aurora, Gross' outmanned crew put a heavy scare into the Huskies, before allowing two long punt returns to stem the tide and push momentum back in Aurora's favor on the way to a final score of 43-28. The Huskies then ended McCook's season in last fall's playoffs, leaving no doubt this time who was the better team, with a convincing 27-0 shutout. "It will not take much to get our kids motivated for this one," Gross told his staff Sunday night.

Although Gross will not mention it to his players, Aurora was given a much tougher than expected tussle last Friday night in their opener against Seward. The rumor all summer was that this could be a transition year for the Huskies, having graduated a number of players from last year's team that lost in the state finals to Crete. Coach Gross will tell you it doesn't matter, you have to win on the field before you declare yourself better, and that is something McCook, in regard to Aurora, has not done for the past several years. The players are tired of hearing it, but Gross said it at least three times at the Tuesday practice, "They are the favorites, until we beat them, they are the favorites." Maybe, but two of the three state wide polls have the

Bison ranked second behind defending champion Crete. Aurora was ranked 5th in one poll, 6th in the other.

Gross, like most coaches, is always worried about a letdown after a big win to open the season, such as his Bison gave him in week 1 at Scottsbluff. He intended for his squad to spend the week of the Aurora game working on a few kinks in the offense, especially offensive line blocking assignments.

Gross and his large and able staff worked hard at Tuesday's practice to reinforce the importance of consistent line blocking. Gross was, as always, high energy, despite the heat of the afternoon and the length of the workout. The instruction from the coaching staff was constructive and non-stop. "Son, I would love to play you," Gross says in an almost pleading shout to one large lineman, near the end of the workout. "But you got to hit people. All you do is lean. You weigh 280 pounds. You could dominate, but you don't, you just want to leeeeean," as Gross stretches out his last word for emphasis. The coach is now almost nose to nose to his target, as the offense huddles nearby. He finishes his short tutelage on the need of aggression in football on a positive note. "You are going to do it, and I mean on this play, right now, you are going to do it." The effort from the young man on the next play satisfies the veteran coach. "Better, much better. Son, you could make us so much better with your size, so much better," Gross praises in a softer voice, but then immediately turns the volume back up to as high as his raspy and hoarse voice would allow, "But you got to want to." A work in progress, Gross seems to be saying.

If you like good coaching (teaching), McCook is a great team to watch practice. Players and coaches interact with each other on the practice field in an efficient manner. There is no wasted time or effort. The instruction from the coaches is non-stop. After almost each play, three of four mini lessons, between player and position coach, will break out simultaneously all over the practice field, yet this teaching does not slow down the practice pace. Point is made, reinforcement is given, and on to the next play. Gross seems to be unconcerned on most plays as to what his coaches are instructing to the players assigned to them. He says he trusts his staff to that degree. His attention is with his area of responsibility, the offensive line. But every so often, maybe just to keep everyone on their toes, he will take time between scrimmage snaps to address something he does not like outside the world of the offensive line. On Tuesday, he took the time between scrimmage snaps to correct one of his quarterbacks when he did not like a particular read on an incomplete pass the young man had just thrown. "Why do you throw into double coverage when the flat is wide open? Read your progressions."

A Bison workout will exhibit all the strategies of a good classroom presentation in the world of academics: an excellent practice (lesson) plan, implemented with solid coaching (teaching) and reinforced with consistent repetition (homework); all tied together with enthusiastic, constructive and immediate feedback, with Friday night's scoreboard serving as a report card. It is a formula that can produce a student scholar in the class room, or a championship football team on the gridiron; or both, if a school is fortunate enough to have this type of teaching/coaching talent. If one subscribes to the theory that excellent coaches make excellent teachers, and vice versa, then witnessing a McCook Bison football practice will validate your beliefs.

By midweek, Gross was in overdrive. He was even more demonstrative than usual at practice. His assistants, who know his moods well, felt the head coach was feeling confident. Practices, as always, were long. Gross' well-earned reputation as a fanatic for detail and preparation would allow for no less against a team that had defeated his squad five straight times. "Their size worries me," Gross repeated several times to his staff during the week. The Huskies would start a front three on defense that went 270 lbs., 280 lbs. and 270 lbs. Garrett Johns, center and defensive tackle for Aurora was cast as a sure bet Division I signee come next January. Gross called him the best Class B football player in the state.

"When these two teams play, throw out the records and just tee it up. It will be a war in McCook on Friday night," he predicted. Still, Gross' sense of confidence, to players and coaches both, was a good sign. It was not in anything he said; it was in how he said it. "When he is chewing on us, you got to figure out is he mad or is he excited," said Quarterback Matt Chitwood. "This week, I think he is excited. I am tired of losing to these guys, so I know he is too."

As Gross had pointed out to his team, especially his 12 seniors as they began the week of preparation Monday afternoon, "Guys, you might not get another shot at these guys. With the new playoff format, it is highly likely we would not see them again until the championship game. You better take advantage of this chance, 'cause there might not be another."

What Gross would not mention was his own personal stake. He had lost to Aurora five straight times. It was eating at him, gnawing at his confidence. On the surface, he knew his record and resume left him respected around the state, especially amongst the coaching fraternity. Still, five straight losses for a man who won over 4 of every 5 times he sent his team onto the field, was unacceptable on the most personal of levels. He really believed that this year he had the better team. Another loss, under those circumstances, was a constant nudge of motivation to make sure this week's preparation was flawless. "For me," he confided on Friday afternoon, "this is a must win game."

It might always be a stretch to call the second game of the season a must win situation, but Linton really needed to come out with a "W" on Friday night as they entertained Oaks High School.

Last week's Linton loss to Mobridge, SD, 26-12, will have no bearing on the post season hopes of the Lions. It was a non-regional game. All games the first week of the season for North Dakota schools are non-regional encounters. The next seven would all be regional games and count toward the end of the regular season standings, when determining who makes the playoffs and where teams are seeded on the bracket. To better understand the North Dakota system, think in terms of a one game exhibition season and a 7 game championship schedule. From here on in, as head coach Dan Imdieke stressed to his Lions, they are all for keeps. Adding significance to the game with Oaks is that it is a Lion home game and Oaks is picked in the local media polls to finish third in the region behind Linton and Milnor.

Imdieke, low key as always, plays down the significance of the regional opener. Claiming to have no sense of panic, but maybe just a little sense of urgency, he told his players after the Mobridge game that with a good week's practice, the Lions would be a better team for the Oaks game than they were for the Mobridge game. "We will get there," said Imdieke. "We had a new man at quarterback and I was real proud of him. Tanner played a very good game. We are still adjusting to new positions, new roles, and we got beat by a very good team. We will still have a lot of football to play after Friday, regardless of if we are 1-0 in the regional standings, or 0-1, but obviously, I would rather be 1-0."

When you have won 82 percent of your games over a 35 year career, all at the same school, you have earned the right to be philosophical about winning and losing. Still Imdieke knew his current crew was untested and an 0-2 start might permanently reduce their roar. The Lions, for many reasons, needed a win on Friday. Imdieke knew it would not be easy.

Canadian will travel out of state to Meade, KS for a matchup with numerous interesting subplots. Canadian is the state of Texas' number one ranked small school, quite an honor to claim in a state with so many great small school programs. Meade returns a majority of its team that won the Kansas Class 1 state title. Their only loss during the year was to Canadian.

The mighty Wildcats should beware the Jayhawkers. Here is why:

Subplot 1: The Wildcats of Coach Chris Koetting looked unstoppable in Week 1 in their first quarter 35-0 blitzkrieg of River Road. The squad from Amarillo and their new coaching staff were in shock at the instant and intense onslaught that Canadian hit them with. Could a letdown be in the cards?

Subplot 2: Meade was manhandled by Canadian at the Texans' field last fall. As with this year, it was the Kansan's first game of the season. Meade marched through the rest of their schedule and state playoffs to win the Kansas state title for small schools. Could revenge be a factor, especially with the game at Meade and the Kansans hearing all off-season that they cannot compete with a Texas school? If Meade won a state title last year, even if it was in a basketball state, they must have talent. (I will be hearing from my Jayhawk friends on this one. But hey, how many Texans are on K-State or KU rosters? How many Kansans are on the Longhorn's roster? Point proved).

Subplot 3: Meade runs a single wing offense, and I do not mean a hybrid of the spread or the wildcat. I mean the traditional single wing with all backs often lined up inside two tight ends. It is a hard-nosed offense and harkens back to the days of Red Grange, Bronko Nagurski, and leather helmets. The Canadian crew has shown that with their speed and fearless play on defense, a spread offense will have problems against them. The Wildcats pursue to the ball too fast and hit too hard. But what about some smash mouth football, from a team, like Meade, who feels they have something to prove?

Subplot 4: The state of Kansas follows the National Federation of High Schools standard rules. The state of Texas does not, choosing instead to subscribe to the rule book of the NCAA, with a few notable exceptions. Since the game is in Kansas, the contest will fall under the jurisdiction of NF rules. The hash marks are farther apart, blocking below the knees is not allowed, the defense violating the neutral zone before the snap of the ball is not a penalty, and several other subtle differences that could affect the game's outcome.

The steady and mature hand that Coach Koetting provides for his program is paramount in the Canadian success story. This team looked like a nearly completed Van Gogh last Friday, a work of art. However, there are a lot of red flags blowing as the Wildcats prepare to travel north up Highway 83 to the Jayhawk state. On the other hand, Canadian is not ranked #1 for no reason, so why worry, think many of the Wildcat faithful.

A tradition in McCook, NE: the day before the first home game of the season, the senior captains paint the large block letter "M" in the center of the field at Bison Stadium.

Football is a game of tradition and small town high schools are steeped in just such community rites of passage. In McCook, NE the painting of the "M" signifies "game on."

Another tradition involves a local motorcycle gang who call themselves the Bison Fury. Although not school sanctioned ("don't know those guys," one administrator told me, with a laugh), for the last six years the McCook Bison football team has had a motorcycle escort for their team bus as they travel from the school to the stadium on game night.

Members of the escort are all decked out in typical "biker" attire – lots of leather and chains. A bigger guy – they were all big – who seemed to be the leader would not disclose to me his name - something to do with warrants or statute of limitations – something about the legal system, he said. The number of bikes for the escort is between 6 and 10, "depending who is in jail already by 6 on Friday," said the leader. "We never know till we get here."

The Fury, so they claim, are in charge of security for the game's officials - in a way. "If we win we protect them to get them out of town. If we lose, we are the ones who chase them out of town," another member told me.

I am sure he was just kidding. They claim to be nice boys just supporting their team. But then who in McCook does not support the Bison?

Senior Captains Clint Beguin, Austin Sis, Matt Chitwood and Justin Terry took a "break" from their painting chores to sit in the shade of the empty bleachers of Bison Field. In a little more than 24 hours, a seat in the same bleachers will be a hot commodity. "Just wait until tomorrow night,"

said Quarterback Chitwood. "This place will be packed." Added Terry, "They will be standing all around the field. There will be no seats."

Terry remembers attending games here as an elementary student. "I always knew I would play here someday," he says. "But now that I am a senior, I realize I don't have many games left. It makes each game even more important." Does that significance add extra pressure? "Not really," says Terry. "It is just I want to win here. I know the guys that played before still talk about games when they played on this field. Some of them are old men, but they still remember. I want my memories to be good ones."

As for the Captains' future memories, none would be better than to knock off the visitors from Aurora tomorrow evening. "Oh yeah, real sweet," says Andrew Sis. The fourth senior captain had moved to McCook from nearby Concordia before his freshman year. Both towns are a lot alike, Sis agreed. "Very similar, yes, McCook is not a whole lot different than Concordia," he says. "Except for only one area, that is, and that area is football. Worlds of difference between here and there in football," he concurs. "McCook is so much better of a program. I am lucky my dad got a job here. I have loved the experience and would have never gotten this in Concordia."

Lineman Beguin knows that the Bison faithful are counting on the line, that he anchors, to handle the larger Husky interior line. "We know they are big and we know the line is their strength. If we get it (the football) into the hands of our speed people, we got 'em. They lost a lot from last year with their skilled positions. We don't have to whip their line, just hold them to a draw. If we play them even, then we are going to win, and I don't want to go my whole career saying I never beat those guys."

The searing Nebraska Panhandle sun was relentless, the heat overbearing. It had been this way all up and down the high plains, starting in late spring, carrying through the whole summer, and now with fall knocking on the door, no letup was in sight. It was not only hot, 103 degrees, at the beginning of McCook's Thursday "short" practice, but also a record drought had added torment to much of the region.

On Thursday, for the second straight day, McCook High School students were, to compensate for the parts of the campus that were not air conditioned, dismissed at 1:30 in the afternoon. Football practice began at 2:30.

One elderly farmer at the local Casey's General Store on Thursday morning said that in 70 years of living in the Panhandle, he had never seen a heat wave that had lasted this long, and this far into September. "It was so hot yesterday," he told the young clerk ringing up his soft drink purchase, "that I looked out in my back yard and saw a squirrel pouring Gatorade over his nuts." Even by the hearty standards set forth by the off- spring of fearless pioneers who now inhabit this area; that is hot.

On Thursday afternoon, Coach Gross wants to hear nothing of the heat, or the supposed demise of Aurora. "If you think they are not coming in here intending to rip us apart, then you don't have a clue. Did they lose some good players from last year's team? Yes. Probably the best Class B quarterback I have seen. But good programs graduate kids. They also replace them, and that is what they have done. They also have, don't forget, the best Class B football player in the state," Gross warned his staff.

Penalties had been a problem at the Scottsbluff opener. The Bison had two touchdowns called back and several good drives stalled by major holding penalties. Defensive coordinator Russ Schlager, at Sunday's coaches meeting commented, "We could have easily won the game 56-7, if we hadn't hurt ourselves." Gross, during the week, several times mentioned penalties to his team, but he did not harp on them. After one practice he told his coaches, "All of the penalties (at Scottsbluff) are correctable and several were just because we were giving an extra effort. I like that." Once again, outside of Gross' ear shot, several assistants commented on how relaxed and confident the head coach seemed considering the Aurora game was on the near horizon. All knew that Gross' sunny disposition could change at any time. All it would take on the practice field tomorrow was one player not being on the right special team, and the old fire breathing Gross would be back.

Aurora's three year starter at offensive center, Garret Johns, concerned Gross. He had earlier called him the best Class B player in the state and a sure Division I signee. Gross shows the ultimate sign of respect for Johns, by changing his defensive alignment for this game. The Bison will go to a four man defensive front, removing their nose guard and leaving the center uncovered at the line of scrimmage. By making this adjustment, Johns will have to move up field and block a linebacker. "He is that good," praised Gross. "He can disrupt our whole defense in he can block someone at the line. This way he has to move. His feet are not bad, but I would much rather have that big old boy stumbling around five to ten yards down field trying to block one of our quick linebackers, as opposed to locking up our rush at the line. I think we can neutralize him, and if we can, our chances go way up."

Gross assembled his team at the end of Thursday's practice to again test their collective understanding of the next night's strategies. Always the master planner and ready for any new wrinkle the opposition may throw his way, Gross systematically ran through every scenario his squad might face the next evening. He told his team, in a very confident tone, that they were ready to play and defeat a very good opponent. "Trust in yourself, but also trust in your teammates. Do your job and have confidence they will do their job. That is what makes a good football team. Don't beat yourselves. Matt do you trust in Javier? Javier, do you trust in Matt? They run a pattern you read as a hitch Matt, do you have the confidence to know that Javier has you covered if you misread? Or do you have to worry about him biting on the swing pattern when that is not his man? You have to have faith in each other. Do your job, and we will be fine. Now the tunnel..."

Gross took the time to instruct his team on the details the pre-game procedure. "We line up on the hash mark, helmets on. When I say 'helmets,' right before the national anthem, take your helmet off, place it under your right arm and turn and face the flag. Don't do anything that will bring dishonor to us. You are standing quietly and showing respect for our country. No talking. No laughing. No scratching your stuff. The anthem is over, then we kick ass, but we show respect during the song."

Detail conscious as ever, Gross gave his team ten minutes of instructions on how the starting lineup would be introduced and the role of those not being introduced. The starters, when their name was called, were to run through a tunnel of two long lines formed by their teammates. The instructions came with a warning.

"This should be a highlight for the starters," Gross said. "They have earned this. Let me tell you a story. About seven years ago we had a kid who moved in from Minnesota. Not a bad player, but not real smart, and he loved to take cheap shots in practice. So he is not too popular. First game of the year the starters run through the tunnel, and as everyone pats them on the shoulder pad as they go buy, this guy throws a full forearm shiver into one of our seniors and knocks him down in front of 3,000 people. Well for the next two weeks, before every practice, he got his ass whipped, until he finally moved back to Minnesota. Just tap 'em on the shoulder pad, understand?"

The Bison coaching staff gathered in the coaches' locker room at 4:30 on Friday, thirty minutes before they will meet with their team. The coaches' locker room is sufficiently large enough to accommodate the staff of 14. Gross has the biggest desk, square against a far wall. Four other desks are spread about the room, shared by the assistants. There are no outside windows and only two entry doors, one to an adjacent hallway and the other to the team locker room. The windows are covered with shades that are constantly pulled down. The atmosphere is one of a subterranean cave.

The mood of the staff is light, not what one would expect 2-$^1/2$ hours before a big game. The fact that the Aurora Huskies, who have defeated McCook five consecutive times, almost one half of all the losses Gross' teams have suffered the last 10 years, are barreling west in two chartered buses and will arrive at Bison field within an hour, has not dampened the social mood in the coaches' office. The tone is sophomoric and fraternal, but light and welcoming.

One assistant coach is bragging about the weight he has lost. "Down to 275, baby!" he crows. "Dropped 25 pounds in two weeks, just like that," has says as he snaps his fingers. "Can you see "it" yet when you pee?" asks another assistant, bringing a howl of laughter from the other coaches. "Haven't seen it for years, have you?" a second assistant kids. The talk turns to story time, with many of the long time assistants chiming in with fraternity style tales of long ago coaches' clinics, epic victories and humorous side bars in praise of past Bison heroes.

Coach Gross pulls out his cell phone, "Hey, look who had a baby," he states as he passes around the phone displaying the picture of a newborn that had been texted to Gross that afternoon. The new father had been an outstanding player a few years back, but from the comments made by coaches, not always in lock step with the mainstream. "At the banquet that year," an assistant reminisces through a stifled laugh, "I will never forget when he got up and said, 'they should have given me the ball on every play.'" This brings a new round of laughter from the coaches. "Maybe we should have," says Gross, "At least maybe a couple of games. But the best was when he went down with a bad leg and RC (late assistant coach Ron Coleman) runs out on to the field, bends over and says, 'you all right?' He looks up at RC and says, as serious as could be, 'Yeah coach, don't worry,

I'm going to make it, but how are my fans taking it?' I thought RC was going to kill him."

Gross stops talking and looks at his watch. 5:00. "Let's go win a football game," he says, heading out the door to meet with 60 nervous young men waiting down a hallway in the band room.

The Bison Stadium, a football only complex, is located on the campus of McCook Community College and was originally built to host both the college's football team and the high school Bison. At the time of the stadium's construction, in the 1930's, the "junior college"- as it was known in those days - and the high school were both controlled by the same elected school board. The college was the first junior college in the state, and was part of the McCook School District.

Bison Stadium is unique in that the spectator stands are almost on top of the sidelines. There is no eight lane running track, as at most stadiums, to provide a buffer zone. The whole place has a Wrigley Field cozy feel about it. There is barely enough room in the corners of the end zones to fit a legal playing field. Bleachers and press boxes line both the east and west sidelines, and a woods covered hillside rises just behind the west end zone goal posts. The east end zone is over looked by the college's student union. On evenings of Bison home games, parking is a major issue as the college campus lies in a residential area. The stadium sits down in a natural bowl with spectators entering from above through ticket gates at ground level. The playing field is below ground. The whole set up ekes of tradition, as it should, for it has witnessed over the past seven decades the many heroic feats of McCook Bison gridiron stars.

After the 1970 season, the newly formed college board of trustees, no longer affiliated with the high school, voted to drop the college's successful football program. The move was a surprise and blindsided many college supporters. Over 40 years later, the hard feelings persist. "Was no need for dropping football," says Max Broderson, who at the time was athletic director at the college. "There was one woman behind all of that, and everybody in town still knows who it is." His use of the present tense demonstrates that the hard feelings still exist. The axed gridiron program has several times been rumored for resurrection, but no serious steps have ever been taken to restore it.

I get to the stadium early –"If you aren't an hour early, you will have no place to park;" I was told numerous times. I arrive at 5:45 for a 7:00 kickoff. I only have to walk a few blocks from my car to the stadium gates, but I don't make it as far as the gates. A Booster Club member, manning the truck entrance gate, recognizes me. "You are the writer guy," she says. "I saw your picture in the paper today." As she waives me in, she must also be reading my mind, "Here get in line, I bet you haven't ate yet." For $4.75 I am treated to a Bison Dog, a cup of baked beans. two (gloved) hands full of chips and an ice cold Pepsi in a plastic bottle.

I take my supper on a nearby park bench behind the west end zone. The weather has taken an unexpected turn for improvement. The showers have stopped, the sky has cleared and the temperature has dropped over 25 degrees in the last 24 hours to a now very comfortable 81. The football gods are once again smiling on Bison football.

As I eat my dinner, which is made to order perfect, for this made to order perfect moment –the only improvement might have been a glass bottle for my Pepsi, like when I was a kid – I stop for a moment to take it all in. The weather, the cozy and rapidly filling stadium, the coaches of both staffs milling together on the grass eye blinding green field, renewing old friend-ships – these are two stable and long-time staffs who truly respect each other - the Bison band marching into the stadium to take their seats in the south bleachers, the players, out of sight in their respective locker rooms, dressed in battle gear, adorned in the colors of their home town; nervously awaiting the agonizingly slow count-down to kick off.

The bench where I sit will accommodate three. A well-dressed couple whom I judge to be in their 70's appears. The gentleman asked in a polite voice if the two seats next to me are taken. I wave for them to join me. It is nice to have company at such a time, someone to share in this pristine, mid-dle of America special moment.

I ask where they are from and the man informs me "Aurora." He appears to be someone who at one time worked a white collar job. He does not have a farmer's hands and his complexion is fair, hints of a man who spent his working years inside an office. He speaks quietly, but his diction is clear. I imagine this man a success in whatever he did. He has that air of quiet con-fidence that successful people exude, and the ability to make a stranger feel comfortable upon a first meeting.

The couple has a grandson playing for Aurora, I am told. "We never miss a game. We will also be in Lincoln for the game tomorrow. We do like football," he says. The University of Nebraska Cornhuskers open their season tomorrow at home. The University of Nebraska football team is a state wide treasure, even in the western portions of the state, four hours from Lincoln. The stadium, in Lincoln, which holds just less than 90,000, has been sold out for every home game since the 1960's, making Memorial Stadium, on game days, the third largest city in Nebraska. "But," my new friend informs me, "I like the high school games better. If I had to choose between one and the other, I would be here." I nod in agreement

After several minutes of idle chatter about the merits of the university's recent move from the Big 12 Conference to the Big 10, I ask how far Aurora from McCook is. "About 90 minutes," he says. Before I can respond, the nicely dressed wife seated to her husband's left, who has not yet spoken and who reminds me somewhat in her neat dress and stately manner given off by her lady like and feminine body language, of my own sainted mother, finally joins the conversation, "But not too far to come to kick McCook ass," she says. The man laughs nervously, the wife says no more.

The Aurora vs. McCook game lived up to its pre-game billing, and then some. If ever a football game can take the wind out of spectators, as well as the players, this was the one. When the game finally ended, after nearly three hours of constant drama, it was an exhausted and breathless crowd that exited the site.

If someone in Hollywood would ever decide to make a movie about the life of former New England Patriot and Notre Dame Football Coach Charlie Weis, Jeff Gross would make a perfect double for the role of Weis. Gross, despite the high expectations and scrutiny the community places upon his work, is adamant about making the sport fun for his players, his coaching staff, and himself. For example, the ritual of the spy plane. It is tradition that when the team is on the practice field, if a low flying dust cropper comes overhead, as they often do in the summer in western Nebraska, regardless of the importance of what is transpiring at that moment in practice, Gross will yell, "hit it," and the whole team, along with coaches, drop to the ground and cover their heads. Gross will then shake an angry fist towards the heavens and the trespassing pilot shouting, as he did the week of the Aurora game; "It's those damn Aurora spies again!" He is in many ways a recreation of everyone's favorite uncle- a huggable personality that makes the day better and lightens the mood for all around.

It is a different Jeff Gross who now stands at the portable blackboard in his team's makeshift locker room under the north bleachers at Bison Stadium. In twenty minutes, his team will receive the kickoff from his personal nemesis and tormenter, the Aurora Huskies. The Bison have gathered amongst lawn mowers, hoses and other such maintenance gadgets in the room they share with grounds keepers to hear their coach's final pre-game words.

Although not near worthy of a Bobby Knight blast, Gross for the first time I have witnessed, peppers his talk with a few profanities; referring several times to "kicking ass." On three separate occasions during the five minute pep talk, the coach will challenge his troops to "do your job." He mentions trust and team work and the ability to rise to a challenge. He in particular points to the David vs. Goliath battle looming in the trenches. Aurora's inside three players, on offense and defense, weigh between 260 and 280 pounds, at least a 25 pound per man advantage when compared to their Bison counterparts across the line of scrimmage. "Technique, sure, but give me guts and heart even more than technique, and you can handle them. Hit them every play. Keep wearing on them. Who they have out there are very good. But they have no depth at those positions. Trust me on this one. We keep pounding on them, every play, never take one off; and by the 4th quarter they are worn out," Gross pauses for effect, "and then we got their asses."

The tone for the game was set early. McCook fumbled the second play from scrimmage and Aurora recovered on the McCook 20 yard line. One running play, behind the big three in the center of the offensive line that so consumed concern of McCook's coaching staff, pushed the ball to inside the Bison 10 yard line. First and goal to go from the five yard line. One the next play, another full back dive, the white jersey Aurora runner appeared headed to the end zone, when a Bison arm came in from the side and punched the football loose, just before the Husky runner crossed the goal line. McCook recovered in their own end zone for a touch back. A near disastrous start had been averted.

Gross had warned before the game that this could well be a low scoring contest, and the outcome predicated on field position. He noted that his team had the better kicker and the better punter and that could spell the difference. Junior punter Matt Collicott had boomed spiral after spiral in practice and Gross was convinced that when adding Chitwood's skills as a placekicker to the formula, he would have, at his disposal, the best one-two kicking punch in the state. He took the kicking game serious and spent hours perfecting it. His senior center, Austen Sis was being shown Division I recruiting interest due to his specialty skill of long snapping for punts and field goals. The Bison holder for place kicks, junior Austin Cherry was sure handed in performing this often overlooked but critical part of the kicking game. Ironically, Cherry's older brother Josh had just completed a stellar career as the place kicker for the Kansas State Wildcats. Josh Cherry filled the kicking shoes of Trent Lyons, who as a Bison, kicked a state record 30 field goals between 2000 and 2003 seasons. Trent is the son of Bison assistant coach Chad Lyons and went on to an outstanding career at the University of Nebraska-Omaha.

All the success that Gross' teams have had over the years with punters and place kickers is not a happenstance of luck, but due to the cause and effect of planning. "I used to use Ray Pleffley kicking camp and have them come in to do a one day clinic," Gross said. "Now I use the former kicking coach at Kansas State. We have one day summer training with a professional. I will have 15 junior high kids who want to kick. By the time they get to be freshman in high school, they have whittled themselves down to 5 or 6. By the time they are varsity level we will have three. We kick as a group every Sunday night in the summer; kickers, punters, long snapper and holders. We think it is very important."

Collicott had a tough night during the season home opener. He shanked his first punt badly to the left, for a net of less than 10 yards, giving Aurora the field position they would need to produce their only touchdown of regulation. His third punt of the first half was a wobbler that preceded a rare bad snap from Sis. But it was his second punt that had Gross half way on the field, livid as he met Collicott. With the ball resting on the Aurora 35 yard line, Gross wanted to play field position and wanted his punter to pooch kick the ball high and short and let the coverage team down the ball deep in Aurora territory. Instead, Collicott kicked the ball long and high in the air, and it flung into the end zone. The subsequent touch back brought the ball back to the 20 yard line, a net of only 15 yards on the punt. "Do your job," Gross screamed as he stood face to face with the junior. "You made no effort to place the kick; you just kicked the hell out of it. You worried about your average? Do your job or I will find someone who will."

Gross was already steamed about the two plays before Collicott's punt, but had not had the chance yet to vent face to face on the perpetrators, quarterback Chitwood and running back Cherry, as neither had yet come off the field since the plays that raised Gross ire. That did not, however, hinder Gross from expressing his displeasure to the two from the sideline. On the third down play before the wayward punt, Chitwood, facing a 3rd and 8 from the 15 yard line, had been sacked for a 20 yard loss, effectively taking the Bison out of field goal range. Ignoring several opportunities, as his protection broke down, to simply throw the ball away and kick the field goal on 4th down, Chitwood had continued to reverse his field as he scrambled backwards, hoping to make a dramatic big play, before finally being sandwiched by two Aurora linemen for the big loss. The play before, on 2nd and 2 from the 9 yard line, Cherry had been given the ball on a sweep to the left. Gross felt he had not run hard to get to the corner, instead reversing his field and being dropped for a six yard loss by a pursuing defensive end. The combination of the three plays, Gross would say later, was a microcosm of the dumb decisions his playmakers had made in the first half.

Perhaps the most crucial time of the game came at the end of the first half with the Bison down 7-0. Aurora had controlled the line of scrimmage on both sides of the ball, dominating the line play. In the trenches, always a macho point of emphasis by Gross, his team had gotten, as he accurately and succinctly said at half time, "our asses whipped." Still, it was only a one score deficit, but Aurora was moving the ball, ripping runs of 10 to 15 yards on three straight plays. With the ball resting on the Bison 7 yard line, Aurora was only yards away, perhaps requiring only one more push behind their dominant interior offensive line, from taking a 14-0 lead into halftime. Such a score would perhaps seal the fate of a dispirited McCook team. However, Aurora had used all of its available timeouts and, facing a third down, decided to pass. The Aurora staff knew that if they were stopped short of the goal line, tackled inbounds and with no time outs, the half would end before they could get off a 4th down play.

The attempted pass into the Bison end zone was intercepted by Jake Schlager and the half ended with a badly outplayed McCook team down only 7-0.

After the game, Gross gave the Aurora staff the benefit of the doubt. "I am sure they were aware of the time out situation and were afraid they might not get another play off if they ran it and we stopped them short." But Gross also admitted his defense had been rocked back to its knees and it would have been highly doubtful they could have withstood two more rushing attempts by a team that needed only seven yards to score.

"You are very lucky it is not 28-0 right now," said Gross in his halftime address to his team." He then lit into Chitwood, Cherry and Collicott.

"Chitwood, Cherry, you can't score a touchdown every time. We talked about field position, and then you just killed us on those back to back plays. Matt, if it is not there, throw it away. Austin, you got to run hard to where the play is supposed to go. You can't tiptoe and then just go and do your own thing. Your letting your teammates down, Matt (Collicott), do your job. Pay attention to your drop (of the ball when punting). You took your eyes off of the first one, but no excuse for just blasting that one through the end zone when we needed the pooch kick. That is just you saying I only care about me." He then shifted his attention to the whole team. "We are down 7-0 and look at you guys. You are whipped. You are beat. Is anyone out here having fun? Justin, how about you," he asks senior linebacker Justin Terry, who had made several hard hitting tackles to drop Aurora ball careers for loses? "Yes sir," was the enthusiastic response. For the soft spoken Terry, a two word answer was a speech. "You know why he is having fun," pleaded the coach, to the rest of his team. "Because he is not scared. He is doing his job and he is kicking some ass because he is taking it to them, not sitting back and waiting for them to come hit him, like the rest of you are."

Gross let his words linger and set in. The head coach is a gifted orator, one of the few who can raise and lower the spirits of his audience as he sees fit. Gross takes the last few minutes, as an assistant holds up four fingers to show the head coach how much time is left in the intermission, to put some air back in his deflated team.

"Listen," he says now in his normal calm voice. "We are one play away from tying this sucker up. We are in this game. Matt (Chitwood), this is your chance. Jake (Schlager), this is your chance. You skill people, we been blowing you up all summer in the media. And this is why, right here, right now. You are going to shine this second half. They are big, and right now we don't have an answer for that. But listen, they are playing those big guys every snap. No rest. They will wear down. Just start taking it to them."

Gross would turn out to be dead on bull's eye accurate with his prediction.

Jake Schlager is the Bison getting the most attention from the Division I scouts. He has burning speed that sets him above the field. A 23 foot long jumper in track, he also posted a FAT (fully automated time) of 10.8 in the

100 meter dash last spring. On the Bison's first possession of the second half, he took a quick pitch for a sweep to the left side, the short side of the field. In terms of blocking schemes, it might be the simplest play in the vast McCook playbook. The purpose is simple, get the ball to the guy with speed and let him make something happen. The simplicity worked to a tee. With the snap coming from the Bison twenty yard line, Schlager was being checked at the line of scrimmage simultaneously by the two Huskies assigned to guard the perimeter on the short side. They were a fraction of a second slow. The two defenders collided head on into each other, grasping for the red jersey that had passed between them only a fraction of a second earlier. The strong side safety attempted to give pursuit, but by the fifty yard line, encouraged on by a suddenly energized home cheering section, it was obvious no one was going to catch the track star in the open field. Chitwood's PAT tied the game. As Gross had predicted at half time, one big play, and it's a whole new ball game.

Before addressing his team during the half time intermission, Gross gathered his assistant coaches to get group agreement on what for him was a tough decision. "We got to go to the one back set and we got to go to the shotgun formation," he said with displeasure to his assembled staff. They all agreed. Despite his protests to the contrary, Gross is a meat and potatoes coach. Control the line, win the game, it is that simple. True to Nebraska roots, the community shares his conservative approach. It fits well in rural Nebraska, an area inhabited by simple people who do not like gadgets or short cuts. Outwork your opponent, and in the end, you will come out on top. But the first half proved that if this game, on this warm September night, were to be decided in the trenches- between the tackles - then it was a game the Bison could not win. Slugging it out in the first half had result-ed in a seven point deficit, that all agreed could have easily been 28 points. McCook had been outplayed that badly.

Gross admitted after the game that it was one of only a handful of times in his coaching career that he had to concede that his team could not win the battle in the trenches heads up. It went against all the offensive principles he had built the Bison attack on over the years, but Gross was a coach who desperately wanted to break a five game losing streak to Aurora. He had no other choice than to concede defeat on one front, gather his troops, and attack on a new one.

After the game, Gross admitted it was a tough call, but the right one. For the second half, the Bison all but abandoned their traditional two back set with the QB under center, and went to a one back, or in some cases, a no back set, with Chitwood in the shot gun formation. It worked. The game moved from the trenches to the perimeter, where the Bison would win any game against the bigger Aurora squad that was decided strictly on speed. More important, it made the Aurora interior linemen pursue hard and up field on each play. As Gross had accurately predicted at half time: take it to them on every play and they will by dragging in the dirt by the 4th quarter.

As the second half progressed into a fourth quarter 7-7 deadlock, it was obvious the tide was turning the home team's way. The vicious Huskies pass rush of the first half, that had Chitwood scrambling for his life, was now nonexistent. On nearly every pass play, operating five yards behind the center in the shot gun formation, Chitwood had ample opportunity to run or throw. His decision making, as Gross would inform the QB after the game, was much wiser in the second half than in the first.

Yet, the score remained tied as the regulation clock ticked to zeros. Like two heavyweights staggering into the 15th round of a title fight, the two premier Class B programs in Nebraska over the last decade, fought to a regulation deadlock, neither able to deliver a decisive knockout punch.

It was fitting that in the end Chitwood would fill the role of hero. Typical of a good athlete on a small school team, he seldom leaves the field. During the overtime session, the senior went from hero to goat and then back to hero, all in a span of about five minutes of time. In the first overtime, he found pay dirt on an open field run, improvising on a broken pass play, to score from eight yards out on 3rd down, giving the Bison a 13-7 lead. Inexplicably, Chitwood, the kicker Gross calls the best in the state, hooked the extra point kick wide to the right.

On their overtime possession, Aurora used a shovel pass to walk, unmolested, into the Bison end zone on the first play of the series. It was way too easy and appeared to be a play that would give the Huskies their sixth straight win over McCook. Needing only an extra point kick to seal the big road win, and with the large McCook crowd deathly quiet, almost in acceptance of their fate and the Aurora jinx, the Aurora's kicker also hooked his extra point kick attempt, this time wide left. Still deadlocked at13-13, the game now went into overtime number two.

In the second overtime, Aurora had the ball first. After a penalty, an incomplete pass and a loss of five yards on a roll out by the quarterback; Aurora had been pushed out of the range of its kicker and faced a 4th and hopelessly long 22 yards to the end zone. Gross, speaking over his headset to his assistants up in the press box, informed them, "If they don't score, we are kicking it on first down."

Chitwood, now at defensive back, broke up the subsequent 4th down pass, heaved into the end zone, to deny Aurora any points on their offensive possession. Coach Gross did not hesitate. He immediately sent Chitwood back onto the field, but this time with his kicking tee. The senior nailed the 27 yard kick dead center and, as the standing room only home crowd rushed the field, a huge burden was lifted from the backs of Coach Gross and his team. The Aurora hex had finally been broken.

In a game that saw more twists and turns than an Ozark Mountain logging road, Chitwood's field goal exorcised some long standing Bison demons. His kick broke three years of futility that McCook had endured at the hands of the Huskies.

Any coach as successful as Jeff Gross, despite his refusal to verbalize it, is eaten up inside with losses to a competitor who seems to have his number. It is no longer us or team or program; it is me. It eats away at the insides of the hyper competitive coach. No matter if the opposing victorious coach is a good friend – it is obvious that the McCook and Aurora staffs have great and genuine respect for each other – it stills eats away at a proud coach.

Gross' coaching psyche, with a long awaited win over the Huskies, was finally freed of an aggravating itch three years in the scratching. "It goes back to 08," he said, after the game and while slumping down in his office chair with a loud exhale. "We were the best team in the state. We beat Aurora 42-7 in the regular season game and then get beat by them in the playoffs. I can't explain it. Now that we have finally broken the streak, I will admit it did bother me. Made me in some ways question what we are doing. In the end, I would always come back to the conclusion that we are doing what we need to do; that we have a solid philosophy and we are not going to go for radical changes because we have a bad run against one team. Still, this one means a lot, probably more to me personally that anyone else in this office or in this locker room."

Aurora headed home bemoaning lost opportunities. In the first half the Huskies drove inside the McCook ten yard line four times and did not score. A blocked field goal, two fumble recoveries, plus an interception; all at the hands of an opportunistic McCook defense that bent most of the night, but refused to break. The home standing Bison, incredibly, only snapped the ball on their own side of the 50 yard line once in the first three quarters, and did not force a Husky punt until the 4th quarter; and yet a Jake Schlager touchdown scamper of 80 yards in the 3rd stanza had the game tied 7-7. It was the one big play Gross had begged for from his team at halftime.

Come Sunday evening, Coach Gross and his staff will gather in his family room, as they do each Sunday in the fall, to begin preparing for next week's game. They will, as coaches do, concern themselves with fumbles, botched special teams play, missed assignments and other such deficient parts of the game as the omnipresent game film will show them. Doesn't matter, for tonight all things in this small town on the high plains of Nebraska are good. Aurora has been beaten. The world is once again, until at least next Friday night, spinning in greased grooves.

Linton won a nail biter over regional foe Oaks, final score 12-7. The Lions scored the winning touchdown with 5:30 left in the 4th quarter, then held on for dear life as a last second Oaks pass fell incomplete in the end zone, but not before being tipped and hanging in the air for what seemed to Linton fans to be an eternity, until it final hit the turf just ahead of a diving Oaks receiver.

The first half was a defensive battle, as neither team amassed over one hundred yards of total offense. The Lions took the initial lead of the evening, in a contest played before another large crowd at their field, when Jayden Gross made a diving catch in the corner of the end zone on a 4th down and 11 pass with under a minute left in the first half. Linton Head Coach Dan Imdieke says that Gross is having a solid season. "He has turned into a real solid player for us. He made a real nice catch for our first score." The point after kick failed.

The Lions, however, would have to stop one last drive of the half from Oaks. A 45 yard kickoff return to the Lions 34 yard line put the visitors in a scoring position. Oaks took advantage of the good return, moving the ball to the eight yard line with six seconds left in the half when Lion Defensive Back Dillon Doolittle came up huge, picking off a pass in the end zone, preserving Linton's half time lead. "Looking back," says Imdieke, "that might have been the play of the game. Going in at the half with a lead was a big lift for us."

The Lions attempted to start the second half with a bit of trickery, a rarity in the Imdieke years. An onside kick did not fool the visitors who recovered, then took advantage of the short field handed them by marching six plays to their first points of the game. The extra point kick gave Oaks the lead, 7-6. "We were concerned about kicking it deep," said Imdieke, "Because they had run the one before the half back so deep. But (the onside kick) didn't work and really pushed the momentum their way."

The Oaks one point lead lasted until the 4th quarter when the Lions' do it all quarterback Purintun hit Gross with a 3rd down two yard touchdown pass. On the second and goal play prior to the score, Purintun had to leave the field with an injury. On third down, he returned to launch the decisive throw to Gross, the second aerial hook up for pay dirt for the senior pair in the game.

With a 12-7 lead, the Lions needed to run 5:33 off the clock to wrap up a big regional win. It turned out to be a long 5:33 for Lions fans.

After forcing an Oaks punt, Imdieke had his team milk the clock by keeping the ball on the ground and forcing Oaks to exhaust its three second half time outs. It proved to be a smart move. With 1:58 left in the game, the Lions lined up to punt the ball back to Oaks. However, Coach Imdieke had one more trick up his sleeve; he had his team execute a fake punt. "We were on their 36. If we punt it into their end zone, it is only worth 16 yards net. Plus, we were concerned about a bad snap of a blocked kicked. And our kick coverage is something we got to get better on. I thought it was worth the risk," the veteran coach explained about the unorthodox strategy.

The fake punt fooled no on, gaining only one yard and Oaks took possession of the ball needing to cover 65 yards in less than two minutes to pull out the big road victory. They came much too close for the comfort of the huge Lions home town crowd.

Before sending his defense out, Imdieke told them, "This might be our whole season right here. We got to tighten up, and we need one more stop."

After three first downs, while conserving as much time as possible with no timeouts, Oaks found itself, with only seconds left on the game clock, 4th and goal from the Linton 19. They took one last shot at a touchdown with a desperate hurl to the end zone. "They had to throw it up and we needed to bat it down. Unfortunately, we batted it up instead of down and it seemed like the ball hung in the air forever," said Imdieke. The ball finally fell harmlessly to the turf, between two Oaks would be heroes, desperately diving for the ball.

Linton had escaped with a much need win, 12-7.

Imdieke, after catching his breath, praised his team. "We had some great individual efforts tonight, kids who rose up and made critical plays. That shows a lot of heart and (that is) one of the reasons I am high on this team.

We have had teams in the past with better players that is for sure. This is not one of our most talented groups, but they are showing me they will not back down, and we can build on that as the season goes along."

"The O line continues to be a concern. We are just not as big as we have been. Where our tackles a lot of years would go 240, this year we are 210. We do pick up a young man this week that is just now getting eligible and has played on the line for us in past years. He is a good kid; just got a little behind in his grades, but he is going to be a good addition to have at practice this week."

For a team with as many question marks as the Lions brought into the season, to have your toughest games front loaded on your schedule, Imdieke had fretted all summer that this year could easily start his 35th season as Linton head coach at an unprecedented record of 0-3. "We could be 1-2 after next week, and still have a good team. We have had teams lose two games early in the season before and go on to become state champions. We are not out of the woods yet."

The Lions have a well-earned reputation as a fourth quarter team. Much of it has to do with the way Imdieke trains his athletes. Other schools in the area try and defuse the reputation the Lions have for strong finishes. "Our kids all know about the Linton tradition," said one area coach. "The Hill, and the belief they are a fourth quarter team with some kind of magic for last second wins. We talk to our kids about it, but it gets in your head and sometimes I think we are better off to not even mention it to our players."

Maybe it is the placebo effect, or maybe Imdieke, with all of his years of experience, really has developed a training regime that allows for the fourth quarter heroics his teams have become known state wide for. But something is there. As the old saying goes, "champions win the fourth quarter."

2010 was an unusual year for the Lions, in that they went through the regular season and first round of the playoffs undefeated, including a win over rival Milnor, only to fall 17-14 in the second round of state play to the same Milnor team. "It still stings us," said Imdieke.

The Lion's week 3 opponent will be the hated Milnor, and Imdieke has a score to settle.

The Wildcats of Canadian traveled north on Highway 83 to Meade to take on the defending champions of the small school division in Kansas.

The outcome was not to the Texans liking, as they dropped a close 24-18 decision.

Canadian knew going in that the trip would be one ripe with pitfalls. The start of the game was ominous, to say the least. Meade's Jett Little returned the game's opening kickoff 90 yards for a touchdown. "That set the tone," said Head Coach Jeff Koetting after the game. "We knew coming in that we would be faced with adversity. We saw none in our opener (a romp over River Road). I was anxious to see how we would respond."

"We turned it over way too many times," said Koetting. "It seemed we were in the red zone all night but couldn't score. I don't know how we still had a chance to win at the end, after playing so poorly against such a good team. Maybe that is a positive," the coach said, searching for a silver lining somewhere in the Kansas night.

Koetting applauded his team's defensive effort. "I thought, defensively, we played good enough to win," Koetting said. "Our number one concern going in was stopping that single wing and we gave up two long runs, but that was about it for the whole night."

The bad news for Canadian only grew as the first quarter unwound. Sophomore Bo Daniels went down first, with a leg injury. Later it was determined that the sophomore had torn his ACL and was done for the season. Within a few minutes, senior defensive back and tight end Chance Walker was helped off the field. Both injuries were untimely for the Wildcats. Koetting did some quick assessing with his assistants about the best way to compensate for the two losses. All suggestions had drawbacks. "We are so light in the line to begin with," Koetting would say at halftime. "Right now we don't have a good option. Let's just get through tonight the best we can," he instructs his staff, before returning to his team's locker room, where he and his assistants would frantically work to construct their now make shift offensive line.

Canadian had 413 total yards (262 passing, 151 rushing), but Koetting said his team was not efficient in taking advantage of scoring opportunities. "We reached the red zone four times and didn't score a point. You can't do that and expect to win," Koetting repeated.

The Wildcats held Meade to 271 total yards and recovered a fumble. "Our defense played well enough to win," Koetting said." The loss breaks a Wildcat sixteen game regular season winning streak. "We just made too many mistakes and had too many turnovers," Koetting said.

Canadian was preparing to score in the final seconds of the game to come within an extra point of a win, but the offense was derailed by the fifth intercepted pass thrown for the evening. After the game, Quarterback Braden Hudson was noticeably down, as he slumped in the losers' locker room. The poster boy for Class 1 Texas football had thrown only 9 interceptions in 14 games in 2010. Throwing five picks in one game was hard for him to take. It was obvious he was personally shouldering the bulk of responsibility for the loss.

Koetting tried to lessen the load for his despondent QB. "I put you in some bad spots," Koetting said, in trying to soothe the pain. "That first one was on the O line; you got hit just as you threw. The last one doesn't count. It was a 'Hail Mary.' We had no choice but to throw it up for grabs. The others, we all take a role in. The routes we gave you tonight were not the best. It was just one of those nights. You are still the best around."

Hudson's head stayed down, but his shoulders began to rise. He was listening. Maybe tomorrow, the coaches soothing critique would make the young man feel better. But when you are the senior all-state quarterback of the Canadian Wildcats, you are expected to throw touchdowns in the closing minutes of close games, not interceptions. Right now, in the visitors' locker room in Meade, KS, Hudson felt his whole world was falling apart.

Koetting was still calm the next day, as his players came in for the Saturday film session. He told his quiet team, "No excuses from us. They are a very good team and they really hit us hard. We are banged up right now, and that worries me more than anything. We will learn from this. We coaches will be good teachers next week. We had our chances, but just didn't get it done. We will be all right."

The road for Canadian will continue to be a tough one. Koetting knows that his schedule is front loaded with bigger schools and is always concerned as to what the constant pounding will do to his team. "Depth is always a concern, but we will play with what we have. We have some talented kids on the JV and if need be, we will fill holes from there. Chance Walker was hurt early, and that limited us," Koetting noted the importance of losing the services of the senior defensive back and receiver. "We think he will be okay. We lost another lineman to what we think is an ACL. That (the offensive line) is getting to be an area we are thin in."

The loss was the first regular season defeat for the second year head coach, but Koetting was gracious after the game. "They are a class outfit," he stated in regard to the Meade team. "They wanted this game badly, they hit us very hard. It was a big win for them. You could tell last year's game (a 36-6 Canadian walkover) had them motivated. It was a harsh environment for us to walk into. Bottom line, they beat us."

Being a small school powerhouse, filling Canadian's six game non-district schedule is always going to be a challenge. Add to the mix Canadian's remote location, and the problem multiplies. Most small schools do not want to tangle, year in and year out, with Canadian. But, it is also hard to convince bigger schools to add the Wildcats to their dance card. Everything to lose and nothing to gain in playing a smaller school that, year in and year out, is capable of administrating an embarrassing loss on larger schools. Thus the explanation of why Koetting has schools from New Mexico and Kansas on his non-district slate.

With the River Road and Meade, KS games already completed, the other non-district games are filled with long time local rivals, all but one, with much larger enrollments that Canadian. None will be walkovers for the Wildcats. All four will be against bigger schools; including the above mentioned visit by Clayton, NM High School. Week 3 will see the Wildcats travel to Perryton, a Class 3 team. Also on tap will be a trip to Sanford-Fritch, a playoff team from Class 2 that returns enough firepower that they are picked to win their district. Week 6 will be a home game with Panhandle, a long-time rival in Class 1A, who competes in District 2.

The loss will mean that Koetting's team will now drop in the rankings, vacating the #1 state wide ranking, which is ok with him. "The only ranking we are concerned with is at the end of the season. The (pre-season) ranking, and the publicity it brings our kids is nice, but the game is played on the field," the coach said.

Does playing such a killer schedule toughen the Wildcats for a deep post season run? Texas Preview, a widely read publication, had the Wildcats ranked as #1 pre-season in the state for Class 1A- D1. Greg Tepper is an associate editor at the magazine. He explained to the Canadian Record why he placed Canadian at the head of the class. Besides leadership, solid coaching and two very talented skill position players, Tepper pointed to the challenging schedule of the Wildcats. "This is a team that knows how to win the big game," the reporter stated. He emphasizes his belief that when a team like Canadian, who chooses to play a challenging non-conference schedule, as opposed to loading up on cupcake teams, will be battle tested come play-off time. "They are well coached and they are experienced in knowing how to win the big playoff game," explained Tepper, in defense of his choice to hoist the state trophy in December.

Koetting is astute enough to know that football is, in many cases, a game of attrition; you have to be healthy come playoff time. Of course, a star play-er can be injured just as easily in a blow-out win against an overmatched opponent, as in a street fight with a capable nemesis, such as what his Wildcats ran into on their foray into Kansas. "What we saw in Kansas was adversity," said Koetting. "That it what toughens you for the post- season run. We can preach and preach about being prepared, attention to detail, and all the little things we harp on in practice. But do they really listen? If we go into Meade and pull that game out, do our kids listen as well this week as they will after a loss? You allow the opening kickoff to be run back for a touchdown; then don't tell me you are ready to play. We will get that point through to them this week, that's for sure. You can sit around and pout about it or you can move on," Koetting said on Monday. "We watch film Saturday morning and then we're done with it. (We want to) move on, get better."

Canadian is not a team or a community that has seen many setbacks on the gridiron in recent years. "We don't like to lose. When we do, we will do so with class, and we did that Friday night. No excuses. Congratulate the winners. But still, this stinks, and we hate it. We are ready to get things righted. But boy, it don't get any easier," said Koetting.

"I hate to say it, but sometimes (losses) they're a good thing," Koetting said. "If you go about it the right way, you can improve after a loss."

Always teaching, Koetting knows he has a long season yet to go; and sometimes a loss early is just what a state contender needs. But he also knows his team right now is beat up, both physically and mentally, and next week's encounter promises to be a tough assignment for a wounded former state #1 ranked team. Little did Koetting know, the week he was now preparing for would be a nightmare no coach could ever see coming, nor be prepared for.

Chapter 4

Last Town Standing

Everybody wants you to do good things, but in a small town you pretty much graduate and get married. Mostly you marry, have children and go to their football games. *Faith Hill*

I am a big rock star, I got a beautiful girl, and they still call me a fag. It's like high school never ends. The jocks are always on top. *Jonathan Davis*

I firmly believe that in any man's finest hour, the greatest fulfillment of all that holds dear is the moment when he has worked his heart out in a good cause and lies exhausted on the field of battle, victorious. *Unknown*

Leadership rests not only upon ability, and not only upon capacity; having the capacity to lead is not enough. The leader must be willing to use it. His leadership is then based on truth and character. There must be truth in the purpose and willpower in the character. *Vince Lombardi*

All three of the Highway 83 towns have similar beginnings. The railroad's arrival in each was a life line of survival. As the railroad moved west, it would need a refueling point every 8 to 10 miles to restock its engine with coal and water. Many little whistle-stop towns around Linton, McCook and Canadian did not survive; most are now only a side note in local histories. For various reasons, Linton, Canadian and McCook took root and grew.

All three towns are also county seats. The jobs generated by the government services provided by a county seat are imperative to the healthy economies of all three. All three are the main office locations of Cooperative electric services. Multi- county areas are supplied power through these energy cooperatives. The resulting production, maintenance and office jobs generated are instrumental to the economic health of all three towns.

For school districts to remain strong and vibrant, they need students. It is that simple. School budgets are enrollment driven and Linton is fighting an uphill battle in terms of enrollment. McCook and Canadian are growing. For school enrollments to grow, jobs for constituents within the district boundaries must be ready and available. All three communities are engaged in proactive plans to lure top paying industries to their respective communities. The Linton population decline is met with little reservation by those running the schools. Most feel that in time there will need to be a county wide consolidation of the three school districts in Emmons County and that Linton, with its central location and largest campus, will be the site chosen for a county wide school. Most predict this will take place within a decade.

The world is shrinking due to the world-wide web. Small rural towns who hope to survive must learn to harness the potential of the internet to help stimulate their local economies. All three Highway 83 towns have invested heavily in their technological infrastructures. Wireless internet connections are readily available throughout all three downtown commercial areas. All three school districts offer distance learning opportunities, such as an online German class for McCook High School students. These long distance opportunities were not available a decade ago.

New industries have expanded and relocated in all three towns. These new employers provide well-paying jobs for an already in place workforce. New industry will also attract skilled workers who are college educated graduates. Many are enticed to move to isolated areas for the quality educational systems found in towns like Linton, ND, McCook, NE and Canadian, TX. Any small town would welcome this type of professional skilled worker. The opportunity to raise a family in a small caring community with a sound school system is the best sales pitch any chamber of commerce type can ever hope for. Many relocating white collar move-ins are individuals whose job, by utilizing the internet, will allow them to work from home.

However, Linton, McCook and Canadian are the exception to be found along Highway 83. As I travel up and down "America's 50 yard line," it is much more common to view great vast open terrain, broken every 20 to 30 miles by communities in the obvious throes of economic depression.

As the national press has drilled into our consciousness, challenges for 21st century small towns on the High Plains are numerous and enormous. Many of these hamlets along Highway 83 could be labeled as still functional, but barely. A faint pulse is still present, pumping a minimum amount of oxygen into the few operating businesses that are still open. But it is obvious that a slow and irreversible death is occurring. Government social service programs on the High Plains can at times appear to be nothing more than a hospice for dying communities, making those left behind as comfortable as possible, as they wait for the inevitable end.

When I take the time, as I sometimes do, to stop and talk to the few old timers still hanging out in these depressed towns, my simple inquiry as to local history will almost always unleash a stream of community pride, based on "how things used to be." Tales of famous sons who moved away and made good or the undefeated 1948 high school football team- "line outweighed Kansas State's line that year" – or the town doctor who worked until the day he died at 93 years of age, or how many troop trains use to pass through and stop each day during the war; all told with a pride that defies the downtrodden current state of a once thriving community.

Many other small towns along Highway 83 are even worse off, having not survived, falling into the state of a ghost town. Despite that most are no longer even listed on a map, I still, on my travels, must pass through their decayed remains, municipal road kill, and a rotting carcass on the side of the road. The crumbling buildings tell the story of a community that, for whatever reason, did not adjust its' sails to the changing economical winds. Now mere memories -deserted and forgotten - boarded up buildings that once housed a living community. It is sad even to a stranger like me, passing through at 65 miles per hour. The demise of each town and the broken dreams that accompany any failed community, I am sure, would make a good book in itself. However, is anyone left to tell the tale?

In almost every one of these deserted burgs I encounter, I can identify the building that once was the community school. I speculate that the section of the "school house" that is two stories tall was the gymnasium. I imagine years of basketball games played on frigid January Friday nights when two small prairie towns packed it to the rafters, necessitating the opening of the windows, just to cool the crowd down. From the banker to the town drunk, everyone was here to witness the drama and the heroics of the local team, a respite for one night a week to the drudgery of life in a lonely prairie town. And I wonder what happened to the trophies, earned by sweat and blood, and once displayed with such pride, won on those long ago cold winter nights?

In many ways, 2011 is the worst of times for rural areas historically dependent upon agriculture. It is a two sided sword. The farming economy on the Great Plains, I was told over and over this fall, is at an all-time high. In the north, a combination of good rainfall and a weak American dollar have created bumper harvests – wheat at $8 a bushel - and high demand in European markets for American grains. Still population shifts away from the rural northern plains continue unimpeded.

Since the end of WWII, population shifts have been constant. Young people have moved from the High Plains to the cities in search of steady and well-paying jobs. With them they take their school aged children. Without a solid population base, over the last three generations, rural schools have seen an inexorable decline in their enrollment. Small towns have lost not only their schools, but their community identity. For most isolated small towns, the school is the social anchor that gives the community life. When the school dies, soon so does the town. It is a dynamic that has sadly been played out across the High Plains now for the last fifty years.

The major contributing factor to the decreasing farming area population is the technology boom that has revolutionized modern farming. To afford the high dollar machines that now drive the huge production increases seen in the last fifty years, production per acre for each operation must increase accordingly. For those farm operations able to grow large enough to afford the new and much improved equipment, the profits in this period of boom have been huge. However, the small family farm is disappearing, swallowed up by growing neighbors who, for many reasons, have conquered the complexities of the modern farming economy. Economical Darwinism has taken root on the high prairie; the strong get bigger, the weak move to Bismarck.

In simple terms, increased volume plus decreased man hours per unit of production equals a high profit, but fewer family farms.

Many multi-generational farms on the High Plains have been sold in the last decade, the retirees moving to town, their children off to the cities in search of a new life. The aging population left behind drains social services, in particular medical needs, while producing no tangible economic benefits for the local economy. While these retirees have, through a lifetime of toil on family farms, earned these retirement benefits, for the first time there is no one taking their place in the farming production line. The next generation, for lack of jobs and opportunities, have cut family farm ties and moved to the cities.

So how have my three Highway 83 towns –Linton, ND, McCook, NE and Canadian, TX – held up so well against these grim rural economic trends? Surprisingly, they are all doing quite well. All three have low unemployment. All three have adequate medical facilities with well-staffed hospitals. All three are area commercial hubs with vibrant and growing downtown business sections. All three have strong school systems. The pride of the community in their schools is obvious in the sense of ownership seen in the economic support the community provides for each, is impressive. And all three - not to lose track of the original purpose of my travels - have outstanding high school football programs.

Is town pride why these three are thriving while their neighbors are dying? I asked this question repeatedly over the three months I spent on Highway 83. The answer, I found, is complex and did not come to me through a lightning bolt of enlightenment from above, but instead with a slow realization that formulated in time as I learned to separate expert perception from everyday reality. But let's start with the experts.

As I traveled Highway 83, I found no more despised term than "Buffalo Commons." The simple verbalization of the words would raise the ire of even the most laid back good ole boy I would meet. At best, my inquiry would elicit responses from locals like "arrogant" or "egg head liberals;" at worse, a tongue in cheek (I think) suggestion of old time frontier justice for any easterner proponent of this fool hearty plan with the stupidity to have stepped foot on the High Plains.

In 1987, two eastern college professors developed a proposal to return the High Plains area of the north central United States to its primitive state, a nature reserve that would drastically decrease the current population and reintroduce the Bison to the area. The area would be renamed the Buffalo Commons.

Frank and Deborah Popper, husband and wife and Professors at New Jersey's Rutgers University, developed and conducted the controversial study and were meet with the expected distain from locals when they visited the High Plains to promote their proposal.

The Poppers suggested that the large area of the American heartland known as the Great Plains be turned over to ranching and that farming be slowly, but totally, eliminated as a use of the land. The result would be a decrease in human population, as a ranching economy needs fewer workers and thus less social support systems than a farming economy requires. They projected up to twenty million acres should be returned to natural grass lands, devoid of cultivation and fertilizer. The Department of Wildlife should then reintroduce large Buffalo herds to the restocked grazing lands, the Federal Government overseeing its future day to day operation.

The professors argued that history and science was on their side and such events as the Dust Bowl of the 1930's proved that the area was not meant to be farmed. The duo also pointed out that over the last eighty years the area had continuously seen its population decline, a phenomena seen nowhere else in the nation. Population in the region had fallen by one third to one half since 1920. They argued that this constant decrease in human population validated their theory and that their proposal was already in motion, stimulated by nature and the rules of supply and demand economics. It was now, they reasoned, up to the Federal Government to close the deal.

The Poppers suggested that one way to successfully return the land to its native state was for the federal government to pay farmers for a fifteen year period what they would have earned each year, if they harvested a cultivated crop. During this time of government support, farmers would plant native grasses and help the Prairie re-establish its natural state (pre-white man) of vegetation. At the end of fifteen years, the government would buy at fair market value from the farmers what their land was worth. The two professors argued that in fifteen years the natural cycle of continued farm failures in the region would have reduced the human population anyway. They argued that their plan was a fairer one to farmers than foreclosures, and it gave people who called the "Buffalo Commons" home (some families for over five generations) time to adjust and move to more human suitable areas of the country.

Needless to say, those living in the Buffalo Commons, especially farmers, did not take kindly to being called intruders and prime candidates for a conservation based eviction. The Poppers academically based study met with all the favor of a rattlesnake at a Sunday social to the longtime residents of communities like McCook, NE, Linton, ND and Canadian, TX. The locals decided to figuratively waive their middle finger at the eastern elite. The Poppers' found that in McCook, NE, they were about as popular as a hard working meter maid.

In 1995 the McCook community staged the first "Buffalo Commons Storytelling Festival."

The challenge presented to local folk tale enthusiasts was to try and come up with a bigger fairy tale than the Poppers had devised with their proposal to all but eliminate the thriving community of McCook, NE. The first year of humorist "whoopers" was a huge success. The sarcasm directed at a far off and often unseen enemy in the East, was therapeutic to the town; as the taller the tale spun, the more laughter would be directed at these educated fools and outsiders. The event went over so well, that it remains today an annual late summer staple on the area's community calendar.

With the demise of the Poppers' plan, to the point that today it is considered a dead idea and recorded in McCook town lore as a win for the little guy, the Festival has taken on more of a light hearted approach. And the Buffalo Commons Plan, although still in the name of the festival, is most years not even mentioned. Still, town leaders have not let their guard down, always leery of the next liberal crack pot idea to come from an Eastern intruder.

Tom Bredvick, Vice President of the McCook National Bank gave me his view of the Buffalo Commons issue; "Many here in McCook were insulted by the whole idea. The High Plains were settled by people with character. Many families have made a living from this land for five generations. They survived Indian attacks, droughts, prairie fires, horrific winters and countless other challenges. Some of those same challenges we still face today."

My conclusion on the Buffalo Commons: It took tough people of hearty stock to settle and build a community like McCook. It is going to take more than a couple of eastern college professors with what the locals call "screw ball" ideas to run these multi-generational families off of what they now consider their ancestral homeland.

Editor of the McCook Daily Gazette, Shary Skiles, cuts the Buffalo Commons folks a little wider path of leeway. She hits home with a good counter point when she says: "Some of what they proposed was taken out of context. Their point was that there are areas up here so sparsely populated that we cannot afford to provide them governmental support and infrastructure that are needed for populations this spread out. We have a county west of here that is down to 800 residents. How do you provide them the government services they expect?"

There is no grander sight in the world of sports than a perfectly punted football. When hit just right, the ball flies effortlessly off the foot in a tight spiral, ascending into the sky, the nose of the sphere bent ever so slightly up. The ball reaches its upward apex and levels off, traveling however far the laws of physics will allow, until the nose of the ball, still in a tight spin, turns downward, beginning the descending process. Gravity finally returns the football to the ground and depending on the skill of the kicker, anywhere up to 70 yards from where it was launched.

Punting a football is turning into a lost art. Coaches have discovered that the prettiest and longest of kicks are not the best in terms of net yardage gain. Top flight punters are now told to not kick the ball too long, or they will out kick their coverage, allowing for a long return. The rugby style punt has become very popular, at all levels of today's football. The ball is punch kicked on the run with a sideways swing of the kicking leg. The low, line drive end over end kick, almost impossible to block, will normally hit the ground before a return man can catch it in the air, often then rolling in the direction of the receiving team's goal line. The roll on many kicks is longer than the distance the ball was in the air. Because the ball is bouncing, the timing of the return team is thrown off and blockers have a hard time setting up in an organized manner for the return.

The rugby style kick is very productive. It is also ugly as hell.

It is July, 1970 and the location is Hattiesburg, MS, on the campus of the University of Southern Mississippi. The New Orleans Saints are holding their pre-season training camp, utilizing the practice fields at USM. I am 13 years old. In the midst of a family vacation, I find myself, along with a handful of other boys my age, shagging footballs for a group of four would be Saint's place kickers. The Saints are not a very good team, a recent expansion franchise, now entering their fifth year of existence and still over a decade away from their first winning season.

One of the field goal kickers we chased balls for that day, the incumbent, was Tom Dempsey who wore a unique kicking shoe. Dempsey was born without toes on his right foot and no fingers on his right hand. He wore a modified shoe with a flattened and enlarged toe surface. This club like device would help Dempsey in 1970 to set the record for longest field goal ever kicked in an NFL game, a 63 yard game winner. The record distance has since been tied twice, but never broken. The NFL eventually outlawed the type of shoe Dempsey wore for his record kick.

On an adjacent practice field I became fixated on a lone player practicing his punting skills. With four balls at his disposal, he systematically lifts one booming punt after another, all spirals that seem to cover the entire length of the practice field. After four punts, he will jog down to the end of the field, retrieve the balls, turn the other direction and give a repeat performance. I watched in awe for a good 15 minutes. He never mishit a kick. They were all perfect. His form was breathtakingly beautiful. With a whip like motion, his right kicking leg would raise in follow through above his head - as straight as a gymnast - the right kneecap almost making contact with his nose as if he had no hamstrings to limit his flexibility.

For several years I attempted repeatedly to mimic what I had seen that day. It looked so simple, yet I never came close. I finally gave up, accepting that God had only blessed a few with such a gift for punting a football and I was not one.

Later I learned the name of the punter was Ray Guy. He was not even a member of the Saints, but a college player for the Golden Eagles of Southern Miss. He was spending the afternoon working out on his own, preparing for the upcoming college season. Guy would go on to become a six time all pro punter with the Oakland Raiders and the first and only punter to ever be inducted into the Pro Football Hall of Fame.

The image of a young and still unknown Ray Guy, alone on a barren rock hard practice field perfecting his talented gift, is a favorite feel good memory forever etched in the mind of a 13 year old boy; the perfect punt, majestically spinning into the endless Mississippi sunlight.

History

McCook, NB

Census: 7,994 people, 3,371 households, and 2,154 families residing in the city. The population density was 1,485.1 people per square mile (573.7/km²). There were 3,754 housing units at an average density of 697.4 per square mile (269.4/km²). The racial makeup of the city was 97.37% White, 0.18% African American, 0.45% Native American, 0.18% Asian,

0.91% from other races, and 0.91% from two or more races. Hispanic or Latino of any race were 2.53% of the population. The population was 7,410 in 2009.

There were 3,371 households out of which 29.1% had children under the age of 18 living with them, 52.7% were married couples living together, 8.2% had a female householder with no husband present, and 36.1% were non-families. 31.7% of all households were made up of individuals and 15.2% had someone living alone who was 65 years of age or older. The average household size was 2.29 and the average family size was 2.90.

In the city the population was spread out with 24.1% under the age of 18, 9.7% from 18 to 24, 24.2% from 25 to 44, 21.3% from 45 to 64, and 20.7% who were 65 years of age or older. The median age was 40 years. For every 100 females there were 89.2 males. For every 100 females age 18 and over, there were 86.3 males.

The median income for a household in the city was $31,105, and the median income for a family was $40,455. Males had a median income of $28,065 versus $18,516 for females. The per capita income for the city was $16,691. About 7.9% of families and 9.4% of the population were below the poverty line, including 9.7% of those under age 18 and 8.4% of those age 65 or over.

McCook is named in Honor of a Brigadier General, Alexander McDowell McCook, who fought for the Union Army in the War Between the States. The General was well known also for the 43 years he spent on the High Plains fighting hostile Indian tribes. McCook, Nebraska was established as an incorporated city in 1882.

The town, like so many of the plains, owes its beginning to the railroad. In 1882, the Burlington & Quincy Railroad Company and the Lincoln Land Company made a contract between them to build a new rail head near the village of Fairview. It was felt this location, halfway between Denver and Omaha, would make an ideal site for a local rail hub.

In the early years McCook was, as most frontier towns of the time were, rugged. A traditional old west boom town, the area saw its share of lawlessness in the early years. Cattle driven north from Texas, and the cowboys who drove them, became a key component of the early commercial successes found in 19th century McCook.

As a railroad town, McCook quickly became the center of commerce and trade in the Nebraska/Kansas border area. Homesteaders poured in as the railroad now made small farms viable. These small operators were no longer dependent upon self-sufficiency on the lonely prairie. Homesteaders now had the railroad to provide transportation of their produce to big city markets. The railroad also lessened the isolation of the plains. Products from the outside world were now much more available. Trips to visit far off relatives in the east were now possible. The Railroad gave homesteaders the life line they needed to make their small farms both economically profitable and socially tolerable.

The area, in an ironic twist when faced with the 21st century proposal of the Buffalo Commons, played a role in saving the American Bison from extinction. In 1890, the largest herd remaining in the world roamed just outside of McCook. A local rancher, who earned the nickname of Buffalo Jones, laid out several new ranches that specialized in raising the former wandering beast and sold the meat of the animal world-wide.

The Bison herd, once numbered in the millions, had suffered two decades of needless slaughter by white hunters interested in only the hides, leaving the rest of the carcass to rot in the sweltering prairie heat. The species, if not for Jones, in several years would have been extinct. Jones is credited with saving the few survivors and setting up practices where the meat and hides could be harvested, but in a controlled manner that allowed the herd to grow.

Senator George W. Norris was a resident of McCook from 1899 to 1944. Called the father of the Rural Electrification Administration that successfully brought electricity to many rural areas in the USA, he played a major role in opening the prairie to settlement. He strung together an amazing forty years of public service for Nebraskans, all in the US Congress. Norris was elected five times and spent ten years in the House of Representatives. He then moved to the US Senate, winning appointment by the voters five more times, serving 30 years in the US Senate. He was well respected and connected in Washington DC, and was responsible for many federal programs that helped the area weather both the Dust Bowl and the Great Depression of the 1930's.

Norris's house in McCook is now a museum. It is owned and operated by the by the Nebraska State Historical Society. The home is also listed in the National Register of Historic Places. Norris Avenue, the main east/west street through present day McCook is named for the politician.

Always a hotbed of political activity, three governors of Nebraska can call McCook their hometown. The town also had a hand in a fourth, Dave

Heinemann, who spent several years when he was in elementary school living in McCook. He was later elected Governor of Wyoming.

The railroad, though no longer a major employer, does continue to play a role in the area economy. McCook is still a shipping hub. The nation's rail passenger line, Amtrak, makes two daily stops in the town. The only catch is that both east and west bound trains arrive at 3 am.

McCook Air Force base played a major role in the town's development in the war years of the 1940's. The base was one of eleven air bases operated by the military during WWII. Activated in April, 1943, the base operated three full landing strips. Many construction jobs were provided to area residents as eventually 110 buildings were functioning on the 115 acre installation. Many jobs also went to area civilians in the years the base was in operation, making it one of the bigger employers in the area.

According to military records, McCook Air Base, during the WWII years, provided, "final training of heavy bomber crews for the B-17 Flying Fortress, Consolidated B-24 Liberator and Boeing B-29 Super Fortress. Some 15,000 servicemen and 500 civilians were stationed at McCook. Bomber crew members received final proficiency training at the field before deployment in North Africa, Europe, and Pacific Theater of Operations."

The base closed on December 31, 1945, the war having ended that year in August with the surrender of the Japanese. In 1950, the city took over the operation of the airport but the arrangement, due to the distance to town, proved to not be feasible. The state took ownership of the property in 1952 and still, to this day, holds the deed to the property.

McCook today is still an area dependent upon agriculture. However, there has been an organized effort by community leaders to strengthen the local economy by diversification. The town is a shopping hub for a 150 mile radius. Commercial interests are anchored by a large Wal-Mart Supercenter, which economic leaders give credit to for many spinoff businesses that now thrive in McCook. With the railroad still in operation, and cross continent interstate highways not far off, McCook continues to successfully recruit new industries.

Canadian

Census: there were 2,233 people, 869 households, and 625 families residing in the city. The population density was 1,731.0 people per square mile (668.3/km²). There were 1,047 housing units at an average density of 811.6

per square mile (313.4/km²). The racial makeup of the city was 88.94% White, 0.22% African American, 0.76% Native American, 0.13% Asian, 0.04% Pacific Islander, 9.00% from other races, and 0.90% from two or more races. Hispanic or Latino of any race were 18.76% of the population.

There were 869 households out of which 35.0% had children under the age of 18 living with them, 60.9% were married couples living together, 7.6% had a female householder with no husband present, and 28.0% were non-families. 26.1% of all households were made up of individuals and 13.5% had someone living alone who was 65 years of age or older. The average household size was 2.52 and the average family size was 3.04.

In the city the population was spread out with 27.5% under the age of 18, 7.2% from 18 to 24, 26.8% from 25 to 44, 22.9% from 45 to 64, and 15.5% who were 65 years of age or older. The median age was 38 years. For every 100 females there were 91.7 males. For every 100 females age 18 and over, there were 87.0 males.

The median income for a household in the city was $31,929, and the median income for a family was $38,676. Males had a median income of $30,240 versus $17,083 for females. The per capita income for the city was $16,384. About 12.3% of families and 14.1% of the population were below the poverty line, including 19.4% of those under age 18 and 16.4% of those age 65 or over.

The town of Canadian, Texas can trace its roots back as far as 1100 AD when natives inhabited the bluffs along what is today known as the Canadian River. These early native settlers built a long line of "apartments" and home dwellings on the bluffs.

In 1544, the famous Spanish explorer Coronado and his army passed through the region. They carried with them back to Spain stories of a land ripe for development, of "stirrup high grasses and a fierce and dangerous river."

Native Indian tribes, the Apache, then Kiowa and the Comanche, were all war like tribes who for years roamed and fought over the area's vast grass lands. For many years white settlers avoided the area. Rumor and reputation spread of the harsh life of quick-sand filled river banks. Early explorers described the area as one filled with "treacherous quick-sand, scorching summer winds and winter blizzards." These early concerns kept most whites from considering the area for farming and ranching. The fierce reputation of the native tribes mentioned above, who claimed the land as their own, also contributed to the slow rate of white advancement in the area. For centuries, these nomadic tribes had followed the huge buffalo herds through the Texas Panhandle and what are parts of today's states of Oklahoma and Kansas. For centuries, they had warred with each other for the prime camping and hunting grounds found along the Canadian River.

According to local historians, "The first white settlers were only a bit more settled than the Indians themselves." These first ranchers, arriving in the 1860's and 70's, also adopted a mostly nomadic lifestyle, following their own herds of longhorn cattle, moving from one good patch of grass to the next, watering in the three dozen creeks they identified between the two rivers, picking up strays from the old Spanish herds and generally coexisting in peace with the Kiowa and Comanche tribes. That peace was forever shattered when buffalo hunters, buffalo soldiers, the United States Cavalry and the railroad invaded the area in rapid succession.

In the early days of white settlement, the area was a magnet for many colorful characters. Famous heroes, outlaws, Indian chiefs, and Texas Rangers seemed to have all converged on the Canadian River Valley. It would take the area years to live down this seedy reputation.

Hemphill County's first business, Springer Creek Trading Post, was little more than a lean-to that facilitated the needs of the few trackers, hunters and traders who passed through the area. Real commerce and settlement would not come until the land was "tamed." In time, Canadian became the county seat of Hemphill County.

Outlaws and thieves used the area's wilderness as a refuge from the law. When federal authorities could not run out all the outlaws, or even keep a decent watch on their hideouts, the legendary Texas Rangers found their way to the area. For many years, the Rangers were the only source of law in the area. With the area large and the numbers of Rangers nowhere close to adequate for patrol, the land along the Canadian River could for many years be accurately described as "lawless."

The 1880 census "counted 149 people and 9,600 cattle living in the fledgling Hemphill County with Panhandle, 73 miles west, being the closest town."

The laying of the first railroad tracks was the beginning of lawful civilization for the area. In 1887, the railroad created three whistle-stop towns. These stops were built to facilitate the water needed for the steam engines. The three towns were built at eight mile intervals, the distance the train could travel before needing its' next fill up. The three new town sites were mapped out, covering the length of the county. None of the three survive today. They were named Mendota, Glazier and Hogtown.

The name Hogtown, according to local legend, was one of accurate description. History states that the name of the settlement "referred to the hogs who roamed the streets and the general hygiene of the residents and sanitation of the settlement." The town supported at one time "13 saloons, no churches. The residents were almost exclusively railroad workers, gamblers, saloon keepers and ladies of the night."

The name Hogtown was eventually changed to the more social appealing label of Canadian.

In July 1888, Canadian became an incorporated city. That July 4th celebration saw the first recorded organized rodeo in the area. Rodeo competitions remain today a big part of the local heritage.

The celebration that first year was quite a social event. Newspaper detailed "wild rides and roping on the dirt Main Street, gambling, horse races and three days and nights of music and dancing, after which families loaded up on wagons and buggies and returned to the ranches for long days and months of hard work." The 4th of July celebration today, over 120 years after its inception, remains a popular event on the Canadian social calendar.

Local historians state that the early years of Canadian's existence were filled with controversy, questionable justice and many practices that were outside the normal accepted constraints of social behaviors. "Disputed contracts, beginning about 1910, over the building of Hemphill County's courthouse landed the whole thing before the Texas Supreme Court. An infamous railroad robbery and shooting of a popular sheriff, followed by a forged Governor's pardon and jail escape, would result in Canadian's being tagged with a reputation as a place you could get away with murder in Texas. Ironically, when Canadian was born in 1888, it was the site of the first county jail in the Texas Panhandle, holding the worst desperadoes from across the region, or outlaws captured by the Texas Ranger regiment out of Fort Elliott, 30 miles away in Wheeler County. The jail served the Panhandle all the way through prohibition times when it housed the suspected rum runners and owners of stills hidden in the river breaks near Borger and Pampa."

Even the creation of Hemphill County, of which Canadian is the present day county seat, was controversial. Local historians refer to the creation of Hemphill County, which was carved from Wheeler County, this way: "at an election many still claim to have been illegal, as the region's sparse population left the county short of the required number of resident male voters, the head count was rumored to have been increased by registering the horses of at least one ranch's cowboys, 42 "men" voted to have their own County within the State of Texas. Questions notwithstanding, the Texas legislature formed Hemphill County in 1876. However, Hemphill County remained attached to Wheeler County for administrative purposes until 1887."

The Great Depression of the 1930's, as it did all High Plains communities, hit the Canadian economy hard. The drought that caused the Dust Bowl made farming impossible. Some small self-sufficient farmers tried to hang on, but few succeeded. Most farmers gave up on their homesteads, returning the land to the use of grazing for cattle on the few huge ranch operations that remained.

Between 1930 and 1950, the town of Canadian lost almost half of its population, from 5500 down to less than 3000. In 1954, the area's luck finally turned, as oil was discovered just outside the city limits. Hemphill County's first productive well was brought in by Sun Oil Company. In the summer of 1957 the Ray Wilson well # 1-53 was drilled and is still producing today.

In more recent times, natural gas has been a boom to the local economy. The biggest natural gas well ever drilled in the United States, the Gulf-Helton # 1-21, was completed in the Buffalo Wallow field. Today it produces 588,000,000 cubic feet of gas per day.

Growth in the oil industry in the early years of the Canadian fields was, slow due to a world glut, until the next boom hit in the 1970's. This time, due to worldwide shortages, oil prices went through the roof. Population in Canadian again soared to over 5,000.

As the local old timers like to say, "oil can be a harsh mistress." The cycle of boom and bust has become an acceptable burden to locals, an inconvenience to be endured for the pleasure of living in the Panhandle. Improvements in production, due to better technology, have helped temper some of the economic roller coaster ride that oil based economies are known for.

By 1990, the good times were once again over and Canadian, along with most of oil dependent Texas, felt a deep stinging recession. Population in Canadian returned to around the 3,000 mark, where it stands today.

Linton, ND

2000 Census: there were 1,321 people, 613 households, and 386 families residing in the city. The population density was 1,791.4 people per square mile (689.2/km²). There were 701 housing units at an average density of 950.6 per square mile (365.8/km²). The racial makeup of the city was 99.17% White, 0.23% Native American, 0.38% Asian, and 0.23% from two or more races. Hispanic or Latino of any race were 0.68% of the population.

There were 613 households out of which 24.0% had children under the age of 18 living with them, 53.2% were married couples living together, 6.7% had a female householder with no husband present, and 37.0% were non-families. 34.4% of all households were made up of individuals and 22.2% had someone living alone who was 65 years of age or older. The average household size was 2.13 and the average family size was 2.74.

In the city the population was spread out with 22.2% under the age of 18, 4.1% from 18 to 24, 20.1% from 25 to 44, 21.7% from 45 to 64, and 31.9% who were 65 years of age or older. The median age was 48 years. For every 100 females there were 89.8 males. For every 100 females age 18 and over, there were 85.9 males.

The median income for a household in the city was $25,750, and the median income for a family was $33,203. Males had a median income of $26,339 versus $14,355 for females. The per capita income for the city was $14,661. About 10.8% of families and 16.7% of the population were below the poverty line, including 14.1% of those under age 18 and 29.6% of those age 65 or over.

Linton, ND is the county seat and largest city of Emmons County. The town is located 60 miles southeast of Bismarck ND. The commercial hub of Emmons County, Highway 83 runs though the center of Linton, giving the town direct access to nearby Interstate 94. Linton also has direct access to Highway 13, connecting the town to the southeast part of the state. Linton is fifteen miles east of the Missouri River and Lake Oahe and both are critical to the town's development and future growth. Important to the town's appeal to future residents is the full service of medical care available. A hospital, medical clinic, eye clinic, dentist, and chiropractor serve the community.

Two banks serve the economic needs of the community. Two motels, and a bed and breakfast do a good business, due to the many construction projects in the area. The town lodging facilities are also stretched to the limit in the fall, when hunters from all over the nation descend on the area for pheasant season.

Linton has always prided itself on being on the cutting edge. In 1908 The Emmons County Record boasted, "It is doubtful whether there is another town with the population of 500 that has as many cars as Linton, a total of 14." Local historians report that at the time "there were six Buicks, three Fords, one of each, International, Cadillac, St. Lewis, Pontiac, and Rambler. Authorities directed automobile owners to obey driving laws the state legislature had just passed: not to drive faster than eight miles per hour in town, to carry a horn or bell and sound it when coming up to the rear of any animal-drawn vehicle, to use a muffler and carry lights, to stop when so signaled by any other vehicle."

Linton has given birth to several individuals who have provided the town its fifteen minutes of fame. According to local sources, The Linton American Legion Post was named for Dan R. Richardson; the first American casualty of World War I. Linton High School graduate Thomas Barger became chief executive officer of the Arabian American Oil Co. in Saudi Arabia in 1961. Frank B. Irvine was one of the first persons in the state to take an interest in aviation, and was among the first to have a pilot's license. By 1925 Mr. Irvine operated flying schools in Linton and Bismarck. He had owned 17 airplanes before he retired from flying.

The original county seat of Emmons County was Williamsport. The now defunct town was inconveniently located in the northern part of the county. In November of 1896, voters chose a more central location. The new town was given the name Linton in tribute to George W. Lynn, who settled in Emmons County in 1885. Lynn was a practicing lawyer – the county's first district attorney - a successful farmer and for many years, the publisher of the Emmons County Free Press newspaper.

Linton was incorporated as a village in 1906.

Real growth came to the area with the 1902-03 building of a railroad line, connecting the previously remote area with the rest of the rapidly developing nation. Farming now became a much more profitable business. The railroad also lessened the isolation that had made the area unattractive to potential homesteaders.

The area at the turn of the century was seeing a large immigration movement of German/Russians, who were for two decades steadily homesteading the area. Many of the more prominent families in Linton today are direct decedents of this movement.

Seeman Park, where the high school football team has for many years practiced, was donated to the city in 1919 by L. D. Seeman. It became a social hub for the area. Traveling bands of the era were hired to perform at a newly constructed dance pavilion. Roller-skating on the paved paths became popular, as was swimming in the park's pond. To meet the swimmers' needs, a frame bathhouse was constructed. A community baseball diamond and adjacent bleachers were built. The field was well used and the site of many an exciting summer game with neighboring communities.

During the Great Depression of the 1930's, many government programs were tapped into and utilized for Linton's betterment. Using local labor and funded through President Roosevelt's jobs program, known as the New Deal, the Memorial Courthouse was built and dedicated in 1934. It is still in use today.

The town continued to grow during the 1940's. A swimming pool, a 250,000-gallon reservoir, a new mercury vapor street lighting system, and an expanded water and sewer system were all built. A community hospital, drive-in theater, livestock sales pavilion, modern motel, greenhouse, and a parochial school were more projects of growth in the 40's that solidified Linton's infrastructure.

Today, Linton is the byproduct of good foresight used by its early leaders. The town is on solid economic ground and while the farming population of the area is expected to continue declining over the next generation, a diverse economy, today's city leaders believe, will allow Linton to continue to be a thriving community.

Local Press

Canadian Record

In Canadian, TX on Thursdays when you come to town, you look for the flag outside the newspaper office on Main Street. At the Canadian Record, it has been a tradition for over 50 years, back to the days when printers used real ink and editor's slaved away at paste up boards, hell bent on meeting that always imposing deadline. As everyone in Canadian knows, if the flag on Main Street in front of the office is red, then this week's edition of the paper is not ready yet. If a green flag flies, then park that pickup and come on in, your copy of this week's paper awaits. In today's high tech world of communication, the flag system may be closer to smoke signals than cyber space; but it does work.

Laurie Ezzell Brown is the owner and editor of the Canadian Record. The paper, in print continuously since 1893, was bought by her late father, Ben Ezzell, in 1948. The Ezzell family has had the paper rolling off the press every Thursday since. Ben Ezzell was famous, or infamous, depending on one's views, for his outspoken stances on many of the day's critical issues, both local and national. Often, he was a lone liberal voice in a field full of conservatives.

Mr. Ezzell, as both his admirers and critics will both attest to, took his role as the community watchdog seriously. He recognized no sacred cows. From national issues, and his locally unpopular stance against the Vietnam War, to his decade long legal battles with a local county attorney that Ezzell saw as a crook, the slightly built editor never backed down. Threats, both physical and legal, would not deter him from printing what he saw as the truth.

No one, friend or foe, ever accused Ben Ezzell of straddling the fence. In 1986 he even published a quirky little book with the catchy title of *The Editor's Ass*, detailing the many off beat stories he had gathered from fifty years as a small town newspaper man. Ezzell died in 1993, but only after dictating one last editorial from his death bed, his last deadline met.

Shortly into a conversation with the current editor, it was obvious to me that the apple did not fall far from the tree. When Laurie is asked if she has any interest in running for a local political office, her response is direct and tell-tale that she has continued the tradition of the independent voice of the Canadian Record. "My job is to cover the politicians and keep them honest, not join them," she states sternly. "Too much of that goes on in small towns with the politicians and the media. The line between us and the government agencies we watchdog over becomes blurred. That is not healthy for the local citizens. We will always maintain our independence as a paper and we can only do that by maintaining a separation. People need to trust us."

Ms. Ezzell's states, that like her father, she has had to endure her share of an angry town's citizens. The new social media has given critics even more avenues to attack from. The paper now has its own Facebook page. On one day when I visited, a local reader had posted a complaint about several pictures the paper had run on a series of vehicle wrecks on the highway just outside of town. One wreck had resulted in a fatality. The reader commented on Facebook, "Do you really think this is in good taste?" Ezzell was perplexed and surprised by the writer, who left her real name. "She knows me well enough to know what I am doing," the editor stated. "There is nothing gruesome or in bad taste about those photos. I am simply trying to call attention to a problem that has now resulted in a death. It needs to be addressed and that is our job as the community's voice to point this out."

Laurie Ezzell- Brown has occupied a front row seat for the rebirth of Canadian. Literally, she can look out the paper's front office window and see the vibrant commercial activity on Main Street. Only twelve years before, a much grimmer site welcomed the gazer. The town's local business district was in danger of blowing away in the incessant Texas Panhandle winds. "This town was dying and it took a consorted effort by the civic leaders; the county, the city and the school district to turn things around." She described the role her paper has played. "A major problem we face right now is with housing. There is none, either to rent or to buy." With the current national home building industry at a low not seen since the Great Depression, this would seem to be a good problem to have. But as Ezzell points out, the problem is a lack of lots to build on. "It seems crazy, what with all the open space around here, but the ranchers outside of town will not sell, they are sitting of oil and gas reserves; and the few empty lots in town are not for sale."

A quick trip through town validates the editor's point. In a time of home foreclosures, interest rates below three percent, and a glut of houses nationwide on the market; nary a single "for sale" sign can be found in Canadian. "We made the public aware of this problem and we did it graphically," Ezzell says. "The only apartment complex in Canadian was falling down. It was run by out of town people who really only cared about profit. We took pictures of steps that were caved in, walls that were falling down; the place was not fit to live, but it was all we had. That got things started, (got) people talking. The city and the county worked together and now north of town a new moderate income apartment complex is going up. It will really fit a need. We have had people who wanted to move here, good people who would have been an asset to the community, not be able to (relocate) because they couldn't find decent housing. Kyle (Lynch, Superintendent of Schools) lost a teacher last year because of this."

"I don't know what the future holds for me," the Editor states. "I don't know if I will personally be here twenty years from now, but I do know this paper will be. The town needs a strong paper. These are not the best of times to be in journalism. I see a lot of changes coming, and change brings stress.

A lot of changes in the industry have already happened," she says during a Thursday morning interview. "Fifteen years ago we were still doing paste up. I would be up all night Wednesday trying to make deadline, driving the finished copies fifty miles to be printed, all on no sleep. So in some ways the technology has helped. But we have to learn to co-exist with the internet. Those that don't, won't make it. And we have to make it."

A life-long resident of Canadian, the newspaper woman's roots run deep, and she leaves no doubt that her heels are dug deep into the Panhandle soil. "We will survive here. I feel that a good newspaper is critical for the survival of a small town. Right now the natural gas fields are running at maximum and the money is flowing. But I can tell you from a lifetime of living here, oil is a harsh mistress. We have to be prepared to weather the bad times, to diversify and not be totally dependent on natural gas and oil."

Consumer loyalty, she says, is a key. "People need to support the local businesses, not drive over to the Wal-Mart in Pampa when you can buy the same product right here in Canadian. We have to work together. This is a harsh land, it takes all of us working together. It was true in the ranching cowboy days of long ago, and it is still true in the cyber-space age of today."

When Ezzell-Brown's father died, his legacy came home to roost. As his daughter, she came to appreciate even more his unbending journalistic principles. One last story brings that appreciation into sharp focus. "Dad did a lot for this town, and he loved this town," Brown recalls." One of the first calls I got after he passed was from a man he had fought with over town issues for years. He said, 'I didn't always like your dad, but I did respect him.' I hope the citizens of Canadian will someday say the same of me."

McCook Gazette

McCook has been able to maintain its support of a daily paper, hard for a community of 8,000 in this day and age, to do. In accordance with the community's role as a regional commercial hub, the Gazette covers news for a huge three county area, including 23 separate schools. They also provide printing press services for several smaller area community weekly papers.

Shary Skiles is the paper's Publisher. She takes a hardnosed approach as to the role her paper should play as a community watchdog. "We are a small town and that does, in some ways, change the relationship between us and the governmental agencies. We need to look out for the best interest of everyone, but we also want to be civic minded and we do belong to the Chamber of Commerce."

Skiles sees that constant tightrope walk between oversight and support critical for the survival of her paper. "For us to survive, this town has to survive. We need profitable commerce entities here that hire locals and pay them decent wages. Those workers will then buy in our local stores. That keeps our local commerce strong, and that keeps businesses buying ads in our paper, which allows us to pay our employees. I could go on and on, but you get the point. For small towns out here to survive, we all have to work together."

The publisher admits that the current landscape for the print media is at its worst since the invention of the printing press. With a nod of agreement to the reality of tough times, Skiles also sees opportunity, especially for small town papers. "People here still want that personal touch. You will get much better coverage of your hometown football team in the McCook paper than you would if your son played football in the Denver area, for example." That type of recognition would not be possible, she points out, in an urban paper that does not have the space to cover all their area teams to the extent that her paper does.

"I really see the urban papers having to reinvent themselves more than we do." Still, Skiles admits that she is always looking for ways to increase advertising sales. "We are advertising driven," she says. "The advertising drives the circulation numbers, not the other way around. We have to have a strong local commerce to maintain a strong newspaper. There is no way around that."

Skiles admits that it is a challenge to maintain a daily paper in such a rural area. "We are one of the smaller dailies in the nation. It is tough. We are always hustling to produce extra revenue to afford to print daily. Bringing in the printing of many of the area weeklies like we do, has helped. You will see more of collaboration between newspapers today than what you did, say, twenty years ago. It is much like how our ancestors had to help each other to survive as homesteaders in this harsh environment."

The internet age has changed almost every industry, but the newspaper business has been thrown into total upheaval by cyber space. "Once again," Skiles says, "we have to adapt. The internet is not going to go away. How does it affect life in McCook, Nebraska? How is the internet going to affect how we do future business as the McCook Gazette? Those are questions we are constantly asking ourselves as a paper."

The Gazette, as most papers by 2011 have done, offers a subscription rate on-line. Acceptance of the new technology amongst the Gazette readers, according to Skiles, has been slow. "It is going to take some time, but I think there is no doubt that it is the way of the future. Will we ever become a "paperless" society? I don't think so," she says, "But the internet is still such an evolving force, not only in the newspaper business, but in every facet of our lives. We just don't know yet where it will take us. We know, twenty years from now, our industry is going to be much different than it is today, but how different? We just don't know."

Predictions in the 1950's that the new invention of television would doom the major two outlets for entertainment and news in the pre-TV days; the radio and the motion picture shows, proved to be more hype than anything. Skiles sees some parallels. "That didn't happen, but those industries had to adapt. Those that didn't, did not last long. That is the nature of change, but I don't ever see the day that small town newspapers don't exist. We will be here in one form or another."

Skiles addressed the scourge of every small town's commercial survival – Wal-Mart. The giant retailer has been in McCook for over 25 years, and 10 years ago opened one of their signature box stores, a Supercenter. The operation is one of the more lucrative ones Wal-Mart has in the Midwest. A store employee estimated to me that the Supercenter serves the needs of a surrounding area population of about 35,000.

Local Wal-Mart management points out that the store has immersed itself in the local community, a willing partner and donator for many civic causes. Skiles agrees that Wal-Mart has been an overall good addition to the community. But she professes her support with disclosure of a pragmatic view, "we were not going to keep them out."

"Wal-Mart coming in was really not an issue. There were some smaller businesses here that found themselves in direct competition with Wal-Mart. They didn't survive. But there were also new businesses that opened that would not be here if not for the regional trade from people coming from the surrounding areas to shop here. I feel we have co-existed with them well."

Adapting and adjusting to evolving and changing times is a key for small town survival. "Our ancestors that settled this area had to adjust in much more primitive ways, but it was still change or die. We have so much more technology than they did, be we still must maintain that "we can do" attitude they had over 100 years ago. We will make it here. We come from good stock. It is in our genes."

Linton: The Emmons County Record

Canadian is heavily dependent on Oil. McCook is still very much tied to the successes of local farms and ranches. Both towns have made efforts to diversify. Linton, ND is different. Much more than Canadian or McCook, Linton is not trying to economically reinvent itself and diversify from the industry it was founded on, farming.

"People here are schizophrenic when it comes to the government and the role it plays in our lives," says Allen Burke, owner and editor of the Linton weekly paper, The Record. "We have a tea party mentality in that we don't like the government, especially the federal government, and view them as the enemy. That sounds fine, and the rhetoric is at times therapeutic to the frustration we all feel with big government. But the reality is that without the government programs, we would not have near the community here that we do. That is true for the whole Dakota area."

Burke, who also owns a weekly paper in South Dakota, has a deep appreciation for the role a newspaper plays in a small town. "In many ways we are the scrapbook keeper for the community," he states while sitting in his bare bones (concrete floor), but well used office. It is Thursday, and if there can ever be a time that is called a "down day" for a weekly paper, this may be it. The weekly deadlines have been met and this week's addition is in the mail, deposited in the vending machines and posted on the paper's website for its digital subscribers. "We also do a lot of printing locally and that is never slow," the editor corrects an inquiry as to when would be the best time to sit and talk with a visitor.

The 64 year old newsman quickly shifts to a more moderate pace as he is relaxed and gracious in discussing and answering what could be construed as hard ball questions for a small town newspaperman.

The Emmons County Record, Emmons County's oldest business, was established in May 1884 by Darwin R. Streeter, at the now extinct town of Williamsport. It was moved to Linton in February, 1899.

Burke has owned the Record since 1993. "It was in federal government receivership (bankruptcy) when we bought it," he recalls. The paper today is the fifth largest weekly in North Dakota, despite Linton having only the 54th largest population of towns in North Dakota. "We have worked hard to build up our advertising. By having a solid advertising base, we can offer a much larger paper. We have lots of pictures. We cover lots of sporting events, not only Linton, but at the other four schools here in the area. We think that is important because those are always positive stories and they help to bind a community together."

A fine line any small town paper must walk is its obligation as a watchdog for the public and the desire not to alienate local business owners and their advertising dollars. Burke, who spent a long career in public relations work before re-entering the newspaper business in his mid-40's, credits experience gained in PR work with helping him traverse this potential mine field.

"You have to use some common sense," he states. "If the public has a right to know and the story is important to the citizens, then we will print it. It is pretty clear in our country how important freedom of the press is. It is the backbone of our basic freedoms as citizens and newspapers have historically been the leaders in protecting that freedom. Several years ago we had a situation here where we felt the city was violating the law in the way they were collecting deposits for water. We got an opinion from the State Attorney General's Office that confirmed we were right and the city had to refund some money. That made about as many people around here mad at us as those that appreciated what we were doing."

That was a case, Burke states, that his paper initiated the story and was the driving force behind not only reporting the event, but also responsible for its development. Other times, simply covering a news event can cause stress for a small town paper. "We had a situation a few years back involving some illegal sexual activity at the school between employees and students. There were two different cases at the same time, and we reported both stories. We just stated the facts from open court documents. Many people, some at the school, felt we were out of line, airing dirty laundry in public, and should have just ignored the story. I was surprised at the number of people who felt that way. We didn't back down and felt somewhat vindicated when both were convicted," Burke stated.

In an industry undergoing massive upheavals, especially amongst once powerful big city dailies, Burke still claims he sees a bright future for the small down papers, if they are willing to adapt. "We have had to reinvent ourselves the last few years," he says. "It is the digital age and you cannot ignore that. We sell a lot of papers out of the state, mostly to former residents who keep a subscription. The postal service has gotten very expensive and not very dependable (a complaint I heard from all three editors in my Highway 83 towns). Going digital just makes sense. We can send it out in a PDF format and sell you the subscription cheaper. We don't have the paper, ink and mailing expense. You get it right away and in many cases the visual quality is higher than our paper edition. More and more of our out of town subscribers are going to the digital edition."

"Newspapers play a critical role in keeping small towns viable," says Burke, who started in the newspaper business at age 11, throwing papers, before moving into the corporate world of banking and public relations, only to return to his true passion 20 years ago. "We need, like any other business today, to stay ahead of the curve. But we are doing that. It is sometimes a challenge, but we have to. Small town weeklies are too important to let die off."

We Got'em Outnumbered

Paul Wood has been the Willow County, NE Prosecutor for the past twenty years. McCook is the largest city and the county seat for Willow County. Wood is a McCook High School grad, having played football for the Bison in the 1970's. He has also officiated high school football for 25 years. The attorney makes a good point when describing what sets McCook and other rural areas apart from more urban settings when it comes to the good guys and the bad guys; "Here, we still got them outnumbered," Wood says.

The community of McCook had been shocked the previous year when a 14 year old MHS freshman had been murdered. "Nothing like that had ever happened before," stated Wood. He added quickly, "we locked up the guy who we feel did it. He was an outsider." The alleged killer was a 19 year old young man named Stathis Kirkpatrick. He was alleged to have murdered 14 year old Kaliee Clapp, a freshman at McCook High School. The crime was being portrayed as one of passion, as Kirkpatrick had reportedly stalked the girl to the point her family had raised concerns about his behavior to authorities.

"This was a very unusual case," said Wood. "You would have to go all the way back to the 1970's to find another murder here. Justice will be served, but this was an isolated incident, a tragic one, but not reflective of our community or our kids. Remember this kid came up from New Mexico. We knew he was trouble. He came to live with a relative. He tried to get into school here, but McCook High School wouldn't take him."

"We are seeing a lot more transient movement in our population," Wood continued. "Kids move in and move out a lot more than they use to, even in a rural area like Willow County. What I have seen is that when a young person moves in here, and they are maybe sitting on the fence so far as behavior, they could go either way, good or bad - that the good here pulls them in. They get involved in the school activities, sports or other activities and most will then do fine here. I have seen it many times and that is one of the reasons parents want to move here. The school and the whole community take troubled kids in and they straighten up. That is a big key. Kids here have avenues to be a good school student and citizen, if they want to. As long as we have the bad guys outnumbered and the whole community working together to give kids opportunities to do positive things, then this community will continue to be a good place to raise a family."

High school is a tough age for many. Some could argue that all adolescents go through times of anxiety and insecurity. A lack of sense of belonging, experts tell us, is what makes young people, in particular males, in the inner cities so vulnerable to the gang mentality and the legal problems that result from such associations. All young people have a strong sense of wanting to "belong." It is a basic component of the hierarchy of human needs. According to anthropologist Marque Mathias Jensen, gangs flourish when dreams are denied. "Gangs, like bacteria, do not flourish in all environments. Gangs become most attractive to individuals when they are part of a segment of society which is being marginalized and stripped of resources. Then, without positive social support, or basic resources needed to survive, the (gang) community creates alternative social recognition and economies to create their own social system to gain identity and power," writes Jensen. In other words, high school students will find a group, social or anti-social, to fit in with.

Emilyne Nichols is the daughter of McCook Athletic Director Darin Nichols. She has the perspective of what it is like to be uprooted and moved from one small Nebraska school to another at the most inopportune of times; the beginning of her freshman year of high school. "I was scared to death that no one (in McCook) would like me, that no one would want to talk to me, when I first came here," says the MHS Senior. Her fears were misplaced by proof that three years later she is president of her class. "I played basketball with the high school team the summer before I moved, and that helped a bunch. There was a group of senior girls that really went out of their way to make me feel welcome, and that meant so much to me. I try to do that with the younger girls here, now that I am a senior."

Nichols, blond, athletic and intelligent; is an attractive young lady who would seem to have the label of "popular" stamped all over her. Physical appearance, regardless of our unwillingness as a society to admit, still trumps any other factor when popularity and acceptance are measured within a social group, especially with female teenagers. When you are 14 years old and new to a small school, the implications can be clear; and cruel.

What, Emilyne is asked, if she had dropped into the social circle of McCook High School as a new freshman girl with unemployed parents, living in a trailer, 30 pounds overweight with bad skin and no athletic ability? Would her reception, she is asked, have been as warm and as welcoming? "Maybe not with the same group," she admits in an interview a day before the start of her senior year in high school. "But there would have been a group that would have taken me in. I have only seen one instance that I felt was bullying since I have been here and that was really taken care of by students before the teachers even knew it was going on. I feel we are a very accepting school. At the least, you are left alone. Yes, athletics will get you a lot of attention here, but it is not like you are going to be picked on and put down if you are not athletic. The athletes tend to hang around the other athletes. That is true, but that just seems to be natural. We spend so much time together during the season. It is not like we ignore the non-athletes. We just don't have as much in common."

Students who grow up in Canadian, TX know they have a lot to live up to. The school is well known in the area by envious rival schools for not only their success in athletics, but also academics. School leaders are quick to point out the many academic successes of its recent graduates. The class of 2009 sent two students to Harvard University. From a Texas Panhandle school with only 45 graduates in the class, this has to be unprecedented. Last year's graduating class sent members to the US Military Academy, the University of Missouri and Notre Dame. Many other graduates attend more local, but still prestigious, schools.

Seniors Shelby Saul, Carley Knight and Autumn Childester shared with me their experiences of growing up in Canadian. All three students, surprisingly considering the non-transient nature of the area, moved into Canadian from other districts. Carly was in 3th grade, Shelby in 5th grade and Autumn in 9th grade.

"Activities are big here," says Shelby. "I played sports and right away I got onto the traveling teams and made a lot of friends. I have really enjoyed this school. The town is supportive. But you had better behave because everyone will be calling your parents if you are not," she says with a laugh. Carley agreed. "It is not that hard here to stay away from the things that will get you in trouble. If you are into sports, like all of us are, you know you can't be out drinking and stay on the team. If we went to a party, everyone would know right away. There is sooooo much drama here," she says with an exaggeration on the enunciation of the word so.

Carley intends to study business at Texas Tech, Autumn will attend Metro College in Denver, CO on a basketball scholarship, where she will enroll in pre-med classes, and Shelby will study nursing at Wayland Baptist University.

Autumn is ready to navigate bigger waters. "I have enjoyed growing up here. I have gotten a good education here and have been helped by a lot of people. But I want to get into the medical field, and for me to do what I want to do in life, I see myself living in a big city. What has been the hardest here for me, and would be the only negative I can think of, is that this school is so successful in so many areas; it puts a lot of pressure on us. There are not many of us here, so we are expected to be involved in everything. The spring season is really bad. The track coaches want us out there. The basketball coaches want us in off season getting ready for next year and all of the academic state contests are in the spring. Our teachers want us focused on winning there as well. It really gets crazy."

Canadian is the only one of the three Highway 83 schools not to have an overwhelming Caucasian population. The latest figures show the district to closely reflect the census numbers of the city, 60% white, 40% Hispanic. Salvador Escamilla is a senior captain on the football team and seen as a role model for the other Hispanic students. "I moved here half way through my kindergarten year," the 250 pound lineman shares. "When I started school, I spoke no English. Spanish is all that my parents spoke. I was in second grade before I caught up enough to be taken out of the special classes (ESL)."

English as a Second Language (ESL) is a federal program intended for students who come to the public schools with no or limited, ability to converse in English. Most are Hispanic. Special tutors work with these students, with the goal of getting them mainstreamed into the regular classroom as quickly as possible.

Canadian Superintendent of Schools, Kyle Lynch, says that the language barrier students bring with them to the classroom is a major challenge. "If we get them in Pre-School or even 1st or 2nd grade, the transition is much quicker. The environment will teach them as much as the teacher. Playing and talking with friends on the playground, watching TV, working on the computer; just the everyday things in life will improve their English skills. But when they come here at 17 with no ability to speak English, well that is a tough one."

Rick Barry is a native of Canadian and the current high school principal. "We have about 20 ESL students at the High School now," he says. "That is 10% of our enrollment, but they take up much more than 10% of our resources." Berry also confirms that ESL students hurt the district's test scores. "Our Board of Education is very conscious of our test scores. The issue has been raised locally, are we putting too many resources on the kids on the lower end and short changing those at the top? It is a fair question. But often, because of federal mandates, we have no choice. But it is also important to look at our success stories. We have a Hispanic student who came to this country, and our community, as an illegal. He is now attending Harvard University. We are very proud of that. If you were to speak to him, he would tell you that if were not for the people of this community, he would not be where he is today."

One Canadian educator, asking to speak off the record, expounded on a serious problem with educating the Hispanic students in Canadian: many are illegal aliens, in this country without the proper documentation. "We have three girls who are recent graduates," the educator stated. "We worked hard to get them a trade. All three are in school to become beauticians, you know, hair dressers. The problem is that when they graduate, who is going to hire them? They can't get social security cards. The only way to pay them is under the table in cash. I worry about what will happen to them. The lack of proper documentation is a real problem for these kids and seriously limits their future."

Canadian coaches state that the Hispanic members of their team are indispensable. Escamilla sees football as a unifier in the community. In many areas of Texas, especially those along the Mexican border, football has lost ground. The large Hispanic populations that dominate the border areas do not see the sport as part of their heritage. But in Canadian, the success of the team is paramount on getting a large percent of the school's male enrollment out for the sport.

"When you only have 100 boys in the school to start with, we can't eliminate 40% because of their heritage," says Koetting.

"My parents are from Mexico," Salvador states. "Most kids from Mexico, when they move here in high school, they never really get involved because of the language problem. The separation at the (Canadian) high school is not between white and Hispanic, but between those who speak English and those who don't. The Hispanic kids you see here who stay to themselves, because they don't speak English. If you can speak English, then if you are white or Hispanic, you get into activities and your teammates become your friends and that is who you hang with."

Breanna Burgad is President of the 2012 Senior Class of Linton, ND High School. Anna Schmidt is the Student Council President. Robin Weber and Kayln Schnieder are both active student leaders and successful athletes. All four have attended the Linton schools since kindergarten. All are at least fourth generation natives, tracing their heritage, as most here do, to the turn of the 20th century German/Russian immigrants who founded the community.

All four young ladies give testament of the values instilled in them during their Linton upbringing. "You had better behave, or mom will know about it before you get home," offers Kayln. "I just don't see myself moving very far away," said Anna. "I want to be an accountant and the best program in the state is at Dickinson, but that is a long way from home. I think I will spend my first two years at Bismarck, just to stay closer to home."

Robin and Kayln both credit activities and sports for keeping the community spirit alive. "You are pretty much expected to play sports here and to get involved," said Robin. "Our FCCLA (Family Career and Community Leaders of America) is really strong. Everybody knows about how good our sports are, but the FCCLA has been to nationals like forever. People expect us to succeed, even the other towns. They will not admit it, but they are jealous. To beat Linton in anything, for the schools around here, it makes their year."

As noted by Weber, the school's chapter of the FCCLA has been to nationals thirteen years in a row. Chapter sponsor Jackie Wald says that is almost unheard of for a small school. "We stress to our students the importance of not only leadership but also community service. We try to take on projects that benefit the community and then take those projects to the district and then the state competitions with hopes of getting to nationals. Only one team from North Dakota will qualify for nationals from each category, so it is very competitive and takes a big commitment from the kids."

Burgad, along with her duties as class president, is also president of the FCCLA. "I got involved in 8th grade and just loved it," she recalls. "I am very community minded and I like the feeling that comes with knowing you are helping people, making our town a better place to live," she says.

Burgad was a member of a team her sophomore year that qualified for the nationals with a project based on educating the community to the dangers of teen drinking and driving and teen texting and driving. She hopes to again qualify for nationals this year in the senior division. "Mrs. Wald is really good about letting us take control of our projects," Burgad says. "She gives us guidance but she really stresses leadership from us. As a senior and as president of the chapter, I know it is my job to encourage and help the younger members. The seniors when I first started in FCCLA were outstanding and motivated me. I want to be the same type of leader now that I am a senior."

Wald says that Burgad is a talented and capable leader, but also typical of a Linton High School student. "I am fiercely proud of Linton, the school and the community, I make no pretense on that point," she states. "We have great kids. We give them direction and then turn them loose. We expect to win in everything we do and the kids really embrace that type of winning attitude."

Keeping talented young people engaged in productive activities is, according to the veteran educator, the key to the district that has over the years educated herself, her husband and her children. "The school is the community, the community is the school. You can't separate them," Wald declares.

"We have high expectations of our programs. We hear a lot about Lion sports, but Breanna is a good example of a very talented student who is not athletic, but has the same character traits that our athletes have," Wald declares. "She is a leader and a hard worker."

Wald notes the critical importance of the across the board support for kids from the Linton community. The key, she says, is to keep the focus on the kids and their needs. A spirit of cooperation amongst adults is a paramount, as is eliminating adult egos and the jealousy that Balkanizes many small schools. "Not here, we support each other, both faculty and students," said Wald.

A small school, she notes, has to pull together. Wald says there is no jealousy. "Of course not, we are too small for that. I have two sons, a 20 year old graduate and a 16 year old who is now a junior. Both were athletes. The athletes are often also the same kids I take to national conferences. It would be like wishing bad on your own child to hope the teams don't win."

Wald does admit she sees some of the outside world beginning to infringe on the idyllic small town life style Linton enjoys. "The problems are out there. The temptations are out there. No question. But keeping kids involved is important. When you win on top of that, it makes the kids even more dedicated. We start baseball, softball and wrestling in kindergarten; basketball in third grade, for gosh sakes," she laughs. "When does a kid around here have time to get in trouble? But seriously, the problems are out there. As a school, as parents, we have to recognize that and stay vigilant."

"I have never felt that FCCLA was in competition with athletics," says Wald. "I support our athletes 100% and I have always felt the same support from our coaches for my program. Many of my more successful FCCLA members over the years, girls and boys both, have been some of our better athletes. Then there are kids like Breanna who is not in athletics, but who is at every game supporting her athletic classmates from the stands and she knows she has the same support from her classmates for her non-athletic activities."

Leadership through community service is what Wald says she teaches and what pupil Bugard says she will take with her next year when she embarks on her goal of becoming a Pharmacist. "I would love to be able to come back to Linton and not only have a career in pharmacy, but become an adult leader in community service. I want to see Linton continue to be a great place to live."

Kayln seconds her class mate's endorsements of the merits of being a Linton Lion. "I think we are really good here about supporting each other. Most of us have grown up together. We have had a few kids move in, but most don't stay. Of our senior class, most of us have been here since we started school. We support each other. It really is like a family. I know you hear that all the time about everywhere, but in Linton it really is true. We might fight sometime, but we are also going to be there for each other. I think that really makes this school special."

As for career goals for the four- all accomplished students and shining examples that any local school would like to display as a finished product of their school system- all plan to attend college. Career paths vary from

Nurse to dental hygienist to pharmacy; but all agree on one future plan, they all want to live their adult lives and raise their children in Linton. "There is a lot of drama around here," Breanna laughs. "Everybody knows your business and that gets old. But that does keep us out of trouble. There are no secrets in Linton, and that is what I want for my family, just like I have had here."

In Linton the major obstacle for keeping young people out of trouble is boredom. "We are isolated," admits Superintendent of Schools Al Bjornson. "We have problems in rural areas similar to what they have in urban areas." According to the veteran school leader, it takes a community to raise a child. "I know that is a worn out cliché, but it is so true. Around here, families have known each other for generations. Our isolation makes for a stable population base."

Poverty is poverty, Bjornson says, regardless of its locale, urban or rural. "I worked on an Indian reservation down in South Dakota before I took this job and while this is not a rich area, the poverty rates are not near (in Linton) what they were on the reservation. The family ties are stronger here. The abuse of alcohol is not as bad here as there. It makes a difference. Still, we as a school are always striving to lessen the problems we do have. Just because it is not as bad here, does not mean we shouldn't strive to do better. If we have one child with a problem, that is one too many."

Donna Schneider is the secretary at Linton High School. She has raised one LHS grad and has two more now in the high school. Her daughter Kayln is a senior and a star athlete. "There is just not a lot for kids to do around here," she says. "We keep a pretty close eye on our kids here and I don't think the temptations are as great here as in a bigger city, but still, it does get awfully boring for them. School, sports and work can only keep you so busy. And yes, the churches here have a strong influence on our kids, but still, kids are kids and I do worry."

All schools have polices that deal with illegal drug and alcohol use by student athletes. Athletes know if they break the law in regard to substance abuse, there will be consequences that will affect their team membership. In North Dakota, punishments are set by the state association. "Six weeks for the first offense and 18 months for a second violation," says Linton Coach Imdieke. "There is not much ground for negotiating. So our kids know, if you screw up, you don't play. For most of our kids, most of the time, that is enough and they stay pretty straight. They want to play."

Despite the risk, according to the coach, it is hard for his young kids to always stay on the straight path. "That is something that has not changed in all the years I have been here. There is not a whole lot to do. Boredom can get kids in trouble. That is why sports are so important here. It gives kids a safe outlet."

In McCook, the policies are a little more flexible. Athletic Director Darin Nichols is charged with enforcing the district's code of conduct for its athletes. "We try to use some common sense when handing out discipline," says Nichols. "If a kid is in a car that is pulled over and there is beer in the car, but the student/athlete can show they were not drinking, then that might be a one week suspension from activities, if that person had not been in trouble before. If they were drinking, then that would be a harsher punishment, perhaps six weeks."

McCook Head Football Coach Jeff Gross hopes that the policy teaches kids accountability. "Self-reporting is big with us," said Gross. "If you come in and admit that you were at a party where underage drinking took place, turning yourself in, then you are probably looking at a week, if it is the first offense." Gross says the policy has worked well and has served its purpose. "We have had no issues with underage drinking by football players in the last several years. The kids know the rules up front. We talk a lot about being a good teammate and this is another chance for us, as adults, to be teachers. Think before you act. There are consequences for your actions. Is that can of beer really worth letting your family and your teammates down?"

Coach Imdieke agrees. "We had a lot of problems the first few years the state policy was in effect. Kids learned pretty quickly that this was now the state rule and it would be enforced. We lost some kids early, but lately it seems if the kids are still into underage drinking, then they are keeping it real quiet."

Former player turned home town sports editor, Mark Weber, readily admits that he was one of the policy's early victims. "I got caught my senior year between football and basketball seasons and had to sit out the first few games of basketball. I learned from it," he admits 25 years later.

Star Quarterback Braden Hudson of Canadian, TX High School says that for him the deterrence is strong, because he has too much to lose. "This is my senior year and I am not going to risk my whole future by doing something stupid. I will never get this chance again. This is it for my high school career and I have worked too hard to throw it away for a party."

Coach Koetting emphasizes to his athletes at Canadian that they are under the microscope. "24/7, it never stops," says the coach. "Being successful brings with it responsibilities. We preach that to our players. 'Don't embarrass yourself or your families.' It is not worth it. For most of our kids, most of the time, that type of warning is enough."

McCook senior quarterback Matt Chitwood knows that others are watching closely. "When we were in 5th grade, we started in the little league program," Chitwood remembers. "The high school players were our coaches and we just idolized them. Now we are the coaches and I know the little kids look at us the same way. I don't want to let anyone down, and if I did something stupid and got kicked off the team, it would affect not only me; but also my family and all the young kids in town that look up to us the same way we did the varsity players when we were in 5th grade."

The Rebels

They are not hard to find. They form a distinctive part of the student body in schools both big and large. Attend a high school pep assembly and you will have no problem locating them. They sit on the top row, usually isolated, off in one corner. They will not stand for the school song and through their nonchalant and non-attentive behavior, it is clear the distain they feel for their school mates who are the guests of honor at this party, one that requires their mandatory attendance. They dress different and are outspoken when describing their lack of interest in main stream high school social life.

"Football players are pussies," states the young man dressed all in black. He is small in stature and seems to have several nervous habits, such as constantly tapping his foot as he sits and talks. "They run the whole school and think they should get anything they want. Fuck this place. I am sick of everything about this place. Soon as I get out of school I am gone from here. The best thing to happen to this place would be if someone would blow the whole fucking town up."

The makeshift gathering took place down a dead end gravel road, nothing more than an abandoned farm road. "Here is where we come to party," said a young lady, sporting multi colored hair, featuring pink highlights. Her makeup was chalky, her lipstick a deep black. "Everybody knows we come here. So if you are a narc, telling them will do you no good. They know we come out here. I think they leave us alone because it keeps us out of town and out of sight. As you can see, we dress a little different. They all call us 'Goths', and I guess that is cool, that is who we are. We do dress different and we are not hard to pick out."

The group numbered seven. I had asked to be brought along for this after school "social." A marijuana cigarette was soon passed amongst the group. "You sure you are not a narc," a young man confronted me with the same question I had answered in town shortly before we began our caravan out into the country. My interrogator who had multiple facial piercings and was also dressed all in black, was questioning my deferring on the community joint when it reached me. Rest easy, I assured him, the cops don't normally send many 54 year olds to infiltrate high school drug parties. My presence, I told the group, was for educational purposes, only.

"I can't say the jocks bother us," offered another young man. "They just ignore us. That is what most of the town does. The same at school with the teachers, they just ignore us, hoping we will go away. They use to try and make us cut our hair, wear our clothes different. They even took away our chains." He was interrupted by the second young lady of the group who complained, "they threatened to kick me out and take me to court, put me in a home if I didn't stop wearing my dog collar to school. Now what kind of shit is that?"

The group appeared to be intelligent, their ability to discuss issues and argue values impressive. "I don't really care about all the attention this school and town gives the jocks. But it gets old. Sometimes I just want to scream," complained the girl with multi-colored hair. "It is so stupid. Who cares who wins a dumb game?" She admitted that to her knowledge, neither she nor her friends had ever suffered from a major confrontation with the more main stream students of the local school. She even admitted, to at one time, entertaining thoughts of joining the jock culture. "When I was little, I played on the softball teams in the summer. It was fun and I was pretty good. I am still pretty good at the games in PE, when I want to be," she offered. "But as we got older, it got so much more intense. And I didn't have parents who were going to haul me around to all the different towns where the games were to be played. It just was not worth it, so I quit playing. When that happened, it wasn't like the other girls kicked me out of their group; we just didn't have anything in common anymore. It wasn't a big deal. So I started hanging with the other kids who didn't play sports. We just all kind of found each other. I don't dislike the other girls at school, we just don't have anything in common, but it's cool."

A tall young man with a mature build for his age of 16 was the group's vocal leader and the most outspoken. "I could have been pretty good at sports. Up until about the last year, the coaches were always trying to get me to come out, come over to their side. I will admit that I liked the attention and thought about it; maybe going over to the other side. But it just was not going to work for me. I just didn't want to change, you know what I mean? If I wanted to be in football I had to change my hair, my clothes and my friends, so I said 'forget it.' I think they have finally given up on me. I guess I am past saving," he said with a sarcastic giggle. "I live with my mom. She does not care about sports and if your parents don't get interested, it's tough, when you are too young to drive, to start playing."

He took another long drag on the rolled up weed cigarette and passed it to his girlfriend (I assumed), seated on his right. "Hey, after school, we just come out here and get high. How else are we supposed to tolerate this fucking hick town? I just want out. I don't need anyone here saving me. I am just putting in my time, not bothering anyone, until I can get out of here and get someplace where nobody gives a damn who won some silly fucking game."

The weed cigarette exhausted, a cheap bottle of wine was now passed back and forth among the group. The sun was starting to set, the wind picking up and the temperature dropping steadily, as it always did on a late fall afternoon on the idyllic plains of the American heartland. As the bottle reached the tall leader, he tipped his head back to take a long swallow. He then raised the half empty wine bottle in his right hand, a symbolic salute to his friends, and perhaps to his life. He stated loudly, "f#*k football." The group cheered.

Home on the Range

McCook

There is no overland route to McCook, NE that does not include a jaunt through the Sand Hills. The landscape, as far as the eye can see in every direction is stark, open and lonely. It is daunting and humbling when first seen from the air conditioned comforts of a rental car. It must have been knee rattling from a covered horse drawn wagon. I can only imagine how it must have taken the breath away upon first gaze for the many homesteaders who flocked to this area in the last two decades of the 19th century, many coming sight unseen. Some were Pilgrims in the vast wilderness of the American West and would not make it in this harsh land, perishing or retreating back to where they came from.

The local museum in McCook tells the stories of those who did make it. Many of these early homesteaders endured simply because they had no other option. Most had wagered every last dime they had on their success in this new land. Many had been naively mesmerized while back East by slick advertising brochures that encouraged new immigrants from Europe to make their fortunes on the unlimited potential that waited those wise enough to seize a slice, while still available, of the Great American Desert.

This gambling spirit of these early settlers, many who had risked all on the potential of this arid and barren land, can still be found today in their decedents who are the current leaders of McCook. I was told many times by long time McCook locals, always with a voice of confident pride, that they had the same stubborn blood line flowing through their veins as did their distant ancestors who tamed this harsh wilderness.

The people of McCook pride themselves on having fought this arid and unforgiving land for generations, never giving in, no matter the hardships nature threw at them. In due time, as Bank President Brian Esch told me, "We have learned to live with the environment, and not against it." You never win when you fight nature, but if you can reach a truce and learn how to live within nature's parameters, as Esch told me, then the respect you develop for the Sand Hills makes it one of the most beautiful spots on earth.

I would learn, thanks to an education delivered to me by several local experts, that the Sand Hills are surprisingly some of the best grazing land in the world. The top soil is sandy, but is held in place by a hearty and vast root system of native grasses. The loose and coarse top soil helps keep the second level moist, critical in an area that will often receive less than 20 inches of rain annually. It is a fragile ecological balance, but when not tampered with by man, the Sand Hills has proven to be a haven of fine grazing grass for the raising cattle.

The citizens of McCook have learned over the years how to survive the periodic economic roller coaster ride that farming and ranching on the High Plains requires. Due to present world economic conditions, in particular a weak US dollar and high world-wide demand for American grains, in 2011 McCook farmers and ranchers are in a "boom" cycle. Old timers know it will not last. This summer's drought in the southern regions of the High Plains, some are concerned, is a bad sign of things to come.

Respecting the important role that agriculture plays in McCook's past and future is a necessary show of respect, according to today's town leaders. But, these same leaders concur that for McCook to continue to grow, the economy must diversify. Brian Esch is not only the President and CEO of the McCook National Bank, he is also the President of the McCook School Board. "I grew up in a small town just south of here," Esch states. "I went away to school, but I always knew I wanted to come back. This is a great town and we work hard to keep it that way."

Esch is in a unique position to appreciate the close ties between the school and the town. "The strength of McCook," he states, "is the school. We can provide children here with a great education. That draws people to McCook. Keeping a strong school system is the top priority we have as a community. Our future survival is tied to that end, to having a strong school system."

There was a time not long ago, Esch admits, when coming back to McCook after earning a college degree was not a very enticing offer. "I was fortunate that I could come back with a college degree and find a job in my field and still make a good living in McCook. Many of my classmates who went away to college didn't have the same options I did. There were just not the jobs here that fit their skills. We lose a lot when we lose that type of person. We invested in them to educate them and we, as a community, cannot afford to lose that type of talent, that brain power that belongs here. We have to continue to come up with ways to get those types back home. We need their talents."

Tom Bredvick is the Executive Vice President and Chief Financial Officer of the McCook National Bank. He agrees with Esch. "We have to respect the role that agriculture has played in the development of this great town we now live in. But, as Brian was saying, we have got to create jobs that will attract talented individuals to set up shop here, throw down some roots and make a long term commitment to McCook."

Attracting new industry will always be a challenge for small towns. The competition is fierce. What sets McCook apart from others on the High Plains, according to Esch, is the town's workforce. "We have the work ethic in this community that those looking to relocate a business search for. Our people and their belief in an honest day's work is our best selling point to businesses considering McCook as a new home for expansion."

The town's economic development board has in the last few years managed to attract several new businesses. The key, according to Bredvick, is that these new jobs be above the subsistence level. "If the majority of your work force is employed in minimum wage paying jobs, then it is hard for a small town's economy not to stall. We are a regional commercial hub. We need decent wages for local workers and then we need those same workers to re-invest in their own community. That will keep our economy growing. A worker can do that by shopping here and spending locally the money they earned locally. We have everything in McCook a person would need. There is no reason to drive somewhere else to find what you need. We are very dependent in this way upon each other."

A modern 21st century scourge on the modern high plains are the exploitation industries, drawn to the area with intentions of making a quick dollar while leaving more economic misery in their wake than found before their short interlude. Like the carpetbaggers who descended on southern states during the reconstruction years immediately after the Civil War, these opportunists will exploit the high unemployment rates of the High Plains with the promise of jobs in exchange for generous tax concessions and local money to cover their startup costs. The hog processing industry has a reputation for just such immoral and irresponsible corporate behavior.

McCook has two well established industry that contribute to the local economy; Parker Industries and Valmont, Inc. Parker has been operating their plant in McCook since 1971. "The pay here will allow a worker to make a good solid middle class living," says director of Human Resources, Jeff Crick. The company has a generous package of benefits along with a starting wage for skilled workers of $17.83 per hour. Benefits include health insurance, paid holidays and vacation time, profit sharing and a 401k program. "Workers that are willing to take on overtime, and it is readily available here, can earn quite a bit above their base salary," says Crick, a Kearney, NE native who has been at the McCook plant since 1981.

Crick makes no pretense that his company is some kind of a corporate benevolent entity, showering its workers with good salaries and benefits. "We owe it to our shareholders to make a profit, and balancing wages and benefits are always a big expense of operating a plant," he states. "But, our workers are our most important resource. We added 35 positions last year, so it kind of skewed the numbers, but before that our average employee had 25 years with us. Finding, hiring and training new employees are a big expense. And a new employee is not as productive as one who has been here a number of years. When you look at the big picture, if you are smart, then investing in your employees with wages and benefits to create a stable work force is a corporate smart thing to do."

As stated earlier, all three Highway 83 towns are county seats, a boom to the local work force, creating many state and government jobs. All three towns are home for multi county electric coops, responsible for many semi and skilled jobs in the area. All three have strong school districts that hire a large number of certified and non-certified workers.

All good paying jobs, but all are public sectors funded.

Depending upon one's political leanings, public sector job creation projects are a political hot button issue in 2011. Regardless of if you buy the FOX news angle that President Obama has created a runaway and unsustainable tax payer devouring monster with his stimulus works programs, or you lean more to the left and recognize the necessity of the government taking a proactive New Deal and WPA like approach to putting America back to work, simple economic math dictates that private sector jobs should always be at the top of the economic pyramid, supported at the base by a much larger in volume private sector worker pool; and never reversed. Private sector employment, and the taxes generated through it, creates the purchasing power so critical to any growing economy. Public sector jobs are tax based driven and any tax base falls on the backs of the tax paying private sector. Everyone on the political spectrum, from Rush to Jesse should agree with that premise. The argument is how big should the private sector be and who should pay for it.

Brad Trew is an Electrical Mechanical Engineer at Valmont Industries in McCook. The company opened its McCook facility seven years ago. Trew joined the McCook work force five years ago. He is a native of Kearney, NE. "We are tied directly to the farming economy," he says about his company that manufactures irrigation equipment. "Right now the farming economy is in an up cycle and so is our production."

Trew notes that any company that will come into a community like McCook, and make the construction investment that Valmont has to its infrastructure, is there for the long haul. "The quality of the work force in the McCook area is a definite drawing card to corporate America. People here know how to work; an honest day's work for a fair wage." As stated by Crick, Trew recognized the importance of a stable work force. "Most of our jobs here are skill type jobs. We spend a lot of money training individuals and we need to get a return on that from the longevity of those we hire.

It is cost efficient for us to pay a wage that will keep the turnover amongst our work force low."

Both companies are deeply dependent upon a quality local school system. Both can speak from not only a corporate frame of reference, but also from that of invested community members. Both are industries that employee a roughly 80% skilled worker rate. Both still have some production, seasonal jobs, that require little more than an orientation on the location of the rest rooms, before starting work; but those jobs are fewer and fewer with each passing year. Crick notes that in his 30 years the numbers have flip/flopped. "It used to be 20-80, now it is about 80-20," he commented when comparing the breakdown between skilled and unskilled jobs at his plant."

Both companies are heavily involved with the vocational training that takes place at McCook Community College. Trew points out that Valmont has gone as far as to write curriculums, donate training equipment and provide instructors for facilitating some of the Vo Tech courses at MCC. "If they get through that program, then we will hire them and they are ready to go to work. It is another example of how it is smart for the company to work with the community. Those types of relationships are why the community views us as a good partner and we view the community as a good partner. It is win/win for us both, and as long as that continues, then we both thrive and grow."

Bob Elder is a successful businessman, owning several sporting goods stores throughout the Kansas and Nebraska area. He sees the future for McCook as one of optimism. "This town has grown like it has the last few years because we have had good leadership." Elder's McCook store, his main point of operation, is located in a busy downtown area. "Look at Main Street," he says. "The shops are full. We employ people downtown, we serve our shoppers' local needs and we support local efforts to improve the community." Elder is also President of the Bison Athletic Booster Club.

"The school," he states, "holds everything together here. That is why the success of the football team is so important in McCook. It lets the whole state see our pride. People around the state know that when you say McCook football, you are talking about pride, about doing things right, about being a winner. A lot of area towns are envious of us and that is kind of neat, when you stop and think about it."

Elder readily backs up the importance his two banking friends gave to diversifying the local economy. In his retail business he sees trends come and go. To survive in this small market, he must constantly stay tuned into how to increase sales. "If I just sell shoes out of our stores, we limit our market potential," he states. "That is why we have salesmen on the road. That is why we are always knocking on doors. We are not that much different than Jeff and his football team. If we rest on our laurels, we will not be on top long. No matter what you do, you've got to keep working, keep getting better."

All agree that the community has been wise to invest heavily in the infrastructure of the internet. "It brings everything together, reduces what use to be a huge divide between the High Plains and the rest of the world," Bredvick said.

"We are starting to see people who have jobs that allow them to live in McCook," Bredvick continued, "because they can do their job over the internet. I really feel that the internet will be the savior of the small towns. It allows the talented young people who grew up here to have the option to move back here. They can have it all. They can have the slower, more enjoyable pace of small town living, but also the opportunity to advance in their careers. We didn't have that before. I really believe that over the next 20 years we will see the internet responsible for an unprecedented growth in rural areas like McCook. It is exciting to think about."

Canadian

I will admit readily that I was totally wrong on this one. Having never before had the pleasure of visiting a town called Canadian, smack at the very top of the Texas Panhandle, with the next counties to both the east and the north lying in Oklahoma, I expected to find a dusty one stoplight town with memories of "The Last Picture Show" coming to mind. Maybe a convenience store on one end of town, with a couple of checker players loafing away their remaining years in front of the only business left on Main Street, a dilapidated pool hall with a broken screen door flapping due to a wind that in August blew constant and hot. Well, it was hot, but the rest of my assumptions missed their mark badly.

Canadian is alive and vibrant. Despite a drought as bad as any in the last 50 years, the town was ever so green. Everywhere I looked green, very, very green. The proximity of the Canadian River has been a boom to the little town since it was incorporated in 1906. "Never underestimate the importance of a ready water source on the High Plains," I was told by the mayor of McCook, NE. Canadian, an oasis in the middle of a stark desert, is absolute proof of the wisdom of this adage.

Local Canadian leaders like to point out that their local economy has never been as strong, or as diverse as it is in 2011. The local business community proudly touts the present standard of living found in Canadian and swears to maintain a vigilant watch in their continued proactive advancement of the town. A chamber of Commerce document boasts: "The county and City of Canadian have worked hard to reconcile their economic goals, rich history, unique culture and quality of life. Today citizens look forward to a future that preserves a hometown they love and conserves a natural setting they cherish and share with the birds and wildlife that also call it home. They put as much time and thought into questions of developing water and wind energy plans, development and housing challenges, education and work force training as their ancestors did, determined not to be the last generation in the remote, romantic Canadian ."

John Baker is a bank president in Canadian. A Panhandle native, Baker came to Canadian 25 years ago and since has investede much of himself into his adopted home town. He spent 15 years on the city council and for five years sat in chair of the town mayor. In 2010, with his term as mayor expiring, Baker decided against running for re-election, thus stepping away from city office after 20 years of service.

Baker says that the successes in Canadian all come down to community pride. "It is why our downtown is so clean, our store fronts so attractive. It is why our schools can produce so many academic champions, send our graduates to the best schools like Harvard. Pride is why our sports teams at the high school do so well. It is why we have a great and modern hospital to provide health care; why we have one of the best Art Museum's you find in any town, any size. Many area towns are jealous of us, and we like it that way. We are proud of the lifestyle we have built here. It is a great place to live and raise a family."

Baker sees the town's isolated location as both a strength and a concern. "We have to depend on each other, support each other. If we don't, who will? All we have is each other. When I succeed, you succeed. That is the way our ancestors survived in this harsh climate. We haven't always had oil to fall back on. Ranching is what our ancestors built this town on. It is our core. The oil is going to come and go. It took tough hard headed people to survive here. Not only survive, but thrive. Those same blood lines still run through most here. We come from hearty stock."

The isolated locale, Baker says, is not for everybody. "Most of the people here, if they were not born in Canadian, at least grew up in the Panhandle, and they know what the life here is like. For some who move here, the isolation is too much and they don't stay."

Diversity in the local economy, says Baker, is a must for future padding against the inevitable down years in the oil industry. "Oil is a boom and bust proposition," he says. "We all know that. When the bust hits, I mean it hits. You look out one day and all the workers are gone and you say 'what happened?' It happens that fast. That is why we are always looking for other job producing industries to come in and set up shop."

Leaders who have vision, according to Baker, are the key for survival of small towns. "We have had good leadership here, people who were very selfless in how they gave of themselves for the betterment of the community as a whole. We have been lucky to have smart people among us in town that used their skills to get us grants for many of the upgrades we have had the last 20 or so years. What you see around here; the upgrading of Main Street and the downtown area, the hospital, the schools; those type of works took not only vision, but also skills in knowing how to get it done. They saw what was good for the community and they were aggressive in getting the funding we needed to make it happen."

Andrew George is in his second month on the job as Sports Editor of the Canadian Record, the town's weekly paper. The week before the start of the fall football season, George is nervously awaiting the arrival back from the printer in Liberal, Kansas – 80 miles north on Highway 83 - of his first major project, the 2011 Wildcat Pigskin Preview. When the paper is finally delivered, George and his co-workers are pleased. The result of their labors is a slick looking tabloid overloaded with original information on the local team, the players and the coaches. All is tied together with full color photos. The work would have made any big city editor happy. The paper will now be distributed for the enjoyment of a football crazy small town. All in the newsroom congratulate each other on a job well done, each proud of the role they played in the team effort. "It is the most anticipated issue of the year," stated Editor Laurie Ezzell Brown. "Last year it came back and we were not pleased at all with the quality of the color photos. They were fuzzy, not sharp and it was a real downer for all of us. This is much better (this year).

George's route to Canadian is an unlikely one. "I grew up in New Jersey," he states with an eastern accent hard to hide in the Texas Panhandle.

"I just graduated from George Washington University in DC in May. I saw an ad online for this job. I came down to interview and here I am," he states. "This is just such a neat little town. I wanted to write sports and when I found out the relationship between the town and the team, and how they support all sports; I knew this would be a great first job. I can't wait to cover the football games. This is such a unique opportunity. For an outsider like myself, I am just blown away by how much this town loves football, how they support the players."

One area of commerce that is booming in Canadian is the lodging market. "$119 for a motel room?" I asked in disbelief. "In Canadian, Texas! Hell, I got a 4 star hotel room in Philadelphia last month for less than that," I added for emphasis. "Well honey" my middle aged receptionist told me, between drags on her cigarette, "You ain't in Philadelphia anymore, and besides, when was the last time they hit oil in Philadelphia?"

It was a hard lesson in supply and demand economics and the down side of a "boom" economy. My prospective host explained, "The oil was drying up and things here were real slow. Then they hit a natural gas field a couple of years ago and we've been booming since."

I begged shamelessly for some pity and a better rate that would come at least somewhere close to my budget. "Look in the parking lot," she said, motioning with a wave of her right arm to a lot full of pick-up trucks of migrant oil field workers. "We got one oil company that rents out a block of rooms and sometimes they don't use 'em for weeks. They just know they got them if they need them."

So what, I inquired, happens when the new field runs dry in a few years? "Room prices go back to 40 bucks, honey" she said with a provoking laugh made deep by all too many cigarettes over the years.

Due to my charm more than my shameless begging, I am sure, I did get her down to $80 a night, "but no continental breakfast with a rate that low," I was told, "and don't tell anyone." I promised I would not.

Canadian Superintendent of Schools, Kyle Lynch, explains that his future concern for the school district is a unique one for the High Plains. While most of his contemporaries fret over a declining enrollment, his concern is of too rapid of growth. He produces a spread sheet to illustrate his point. "In Pre-K through 2nd grade, our four lowest grades, we have 301 students enrolled. In the high school, our four highest grades, we have 204. That is a big difference. We are making plans to expand at the elementary grades the next few years and carry over long term into the Junior High and the High School."

Lynch explains that with his district so dependent upon the oil industry, the community leaders have learned to not over build in times of boom, knowing that as surely as the summer will be hot and dry in the Panhandle, the oil fortunes will in time down cycle. But this current growth spurt is different. "The city has been very proactive in bringing in industries not tied to oil. The thought is that when oil does a down cycle, we will be better prepared than in the past because we have diversified."

Lynch, a move-in himself, glows when talking about his chosen hometown and the local schools he now oversees. "People know we are a good solid district," Lynch says. "They want their kids to go to school here. This is a great little community and you don't have to be here long to see that. Our biggest problem right now is housing, or maybe I should say, lack of housing. If we get some of the grants the city is pursuing for affordable housing in Canadian, then you are going to see an even bigger upswing in our school enrollment."

Despite its high motel costs, the town is both quaint and charming. A working cinema occupies a spot at the intersection of the two streets that make up the business district. Not a strip mall multi-screen mall type of cinema, but a true old fashion store front, single screen with a working neon marquee sign in the front. Two museums and a huge art museum are impressive points of community pride. A large performing arts center can be found two blocks off Highway 83. The Bellamy Brothers, a 1960's and 70's Country/Rock duo, were a recent act that played to a full house.

There are several mansions, within blocks of the busy downtown district that are absolute marvels. There are also several areas on the west side of Highway 83 that house hovels that will make no chamber of commerce brochure. Much of the housing within the city limits is analogist to the nature of the oil industry Canadian was built on: boom or bust.

Linton

Walking into Linton, ND High School for the first time is like walking into a retro movie scene from the early 1960's. All that is missing are Frankie Avalon and Annette Funicello, the perpetual high school sweethearts, walking the hallways hand in hand.

To be more accurate I should say when I walked into the Linton Public School Building, as all grades, kindergarten through high school, are located under the same roof.

When entering the school building, I was not met at the door with a pat search from a security guard or a required emptying of my pockets of all personal contraband before passing through a sterile contraption known as a metal detector; a common occurrence to gain entry at most of today's American schools.

In Linton, you simply walk in the unlocked and unguarded front door. What I was not prepared for was the first student I encountered, a very cute and persistent young lady who skillfully used her youthful charm to talk me into buying two tickets for the fifty/fifty raffle at that evening's home volleyball game. Both tickets, I found out at that evening's drawing between the junior varsity and varsity matches, were duds.

At 8:30 am, the bell signaling five minutes to the start of the day's first class sounds. Approximately 110 9th to 12th graders begin to shuffle to lockers and on to class. The junior high students, grades 7 and 8, are out of sight. I later learn they have their own space, the junior high hall, down past the common cafeteria that both groups share.

Two benches line the far wall at the end of the main high school hall, occupied by about a dozen boys and girls. I deduce that this must be the territory of the senior class. The occupants of the benches don't seem to be, at the sound of the bell, in quite as big a hurry to get to first hour Anatomy class, where most are assigned. They have obvious status, as evident by their confident swagger and thus through seniority occupy this choicest piece of hallway real estate.

I did find out later that the stage in the darkened Gymnasium is a favorite before school hangout for couples. Hint of a scandal? In straight as an arrow Linton, ND? Relax, I say; even Annette and Frankie had their frisky moments and it didn't keep him out of "State University," nor Annette from her dream of attending cosmetology school, now did it?

One set of actors is missing from this before school ritual, one that is being repeated at thousands of high schools across the nation this very morning. Where are the teachers? Some kind of a meeting in the Library, one student informs me. I later ask a teacher "Isn't it kind of a risk leaving the whole student body unsupervised?" Why, I was told, they know their way to class.

Several minutes after the final tardy bell that signals the start of the first hour of classes' sounds, the library door swings open and the 16 person teaching staff of Linton High School heads out to start the day by greeting their already self-assembled first hour students.

I shake my head and wonder if at 54 years of age it is too late to start my teaching career all over again. I picture in my head my wife's reaction when I ask, "honey, would you want to move to Linton, ND?"

Diana Nagel has taught English at Linton High School for 22 of her 26 years in education. She is a Linton native, as is her husband. They are in the process of getting their youngest two of five children through Linton High School. "We have challenges," the veteran educator shares with me in a conversation in her classroom that takes place during her first hour conference/preparation period. "But this has been a great place to raise our kids. Our kids have all been very involved in the activities here, but most kids are. That is what makes our community so strong. We really need to depend on each other here. When the snows hit in the winter time, the school becomes the social center of the whole area."

Nagel has seen noticeable changes take place over her two plus decades in the Linton system. "Technology has changed everything. We offer a lot more to students now because of technology advancements. Classes on line for college credit are one option our kids can have now that they didn't before."

A lack of student enrollment makes it impossible at many small high schools to offer the higher level math and science classes that are now required by many universities as a condition for acceptance. Nagel, from the view of both a parent and an educator, says that the local district has done a good job of addressing this concern, stepping up to the plate and delivering a home run by making the financial commitment to keep class sizes low.

"We have kept our class numbers small," says Nagel. "My average class size is 15 students. We have two of us teaching high school English, which is not the case in many small schools. I think our kids leave here prepared. Our ACT test scores are pretty good for a rural school. But, and I tell my students this, 'we can prepare you for a certain level of performance on the placement test (ACT), but it is up to you to go above and beyond if you want to be above average.' We have a lot of good programs available on line to help kids prepare. The resources are there, but it comes to a time that it is up to them. We can only take them so far, then they have to go it on their own. But isn't that true in just about anything in life?"

While the local newspaper in Linton serves as the town "scrapbook" for the community, Bob Tschritter might be as close to a local historian as the town has today.

On a brisk September morning, proof positive the waitress at Wobel's Restaurant tells me, that fall is on its way, Tschritter is having his morning coffee at his usual table. Joining him is fellow Linton lifer Melvin Jahner. Both had made a good living in the area as entrepreneurs and are now enjoying well-earned "vacations". Tschritter explains, "we don't ever retire up here. The next step after retirement is the grave."

Both men, now in their 70's, are third generation residents of the county. Both can trace maternal and paternal sides of their family tree back to the German/Russian migration to the area in the late 1800's. For 20 years, Jahner served as the mayor of Linton. Both are deeply vested and proud of their town.

For over 30 years Tschritter and his wife ran a clothing store in Linton. He says they finally closed the store in the late 90's; a victim of the Wal-Mart Supercenter located 60 miles north in Bismarck.

"We did ok until they repealed the blue laws– allowing for store openings on Sunday," says Tschritter. "Before that, a sixty mile trip to Bismarck was too much of an inconvenience. Then, when it became a Sunday option, it just doomed us. Before, after working all day, most did not want to make that long of a drive. But on Sunday, that was another story. People would make the trip on Sunday, make a day of it."

Tschritter places the blame for the decline of the Linton commercial business district squarely on Wal-Mart. "There was a time when we had several clothing stores here in Linton. And shoe stores. But like most small towns, Wal-Mart was too big to fight. We couldn't afford the large volume buying, maintaining the large inventories. Why, they could sell a pair of shoes cheaper than I could buy them wholesale. How are you going to fight that?"

Jahner has followed various career paths. He spent time in the banking business, insurance business and, when the time was right, broke into the landfill industry. He was also involved in the building of power lines throughout the state, an endeavor he still has his hands somewhat in. His sons now run the day to day operation, but he still keeps a watchful eye on the business. "Give us a call and we warm up the truck. Where there is work, we will go. (You) have to be that way to survive. It is a cut-throat world in business right now and you had better be ready to work, ready to go when the phone rings, or you will be sitting back here with the rest of us loafers complaining about the government," he said with a laugh.

The two long-time friends can trace their relationship back over 50 years to battles fought on the gridiron. Jahner grew up in Hazelton, a small town 10 miles north of Linton on Highway 83. Although the school in Hazelton stills operates as an independent entity (have the nicest gym in the area, Jahner claims), they, like many small North Dakota schools, now "coop" their athletic programs by sending their athletes to Linton to participate with the Lions. About 10 Hazelton football players, and their bus driving coach, make the trip south each day for practice at Seeman Field. But back in the day, both friends agree, when enrollments were up and both schools fielded football teams, it was quite a heated rivalry.

"Never lost to them when I played," crows 1955 Linton grad Tischritter. "But after that we had a pretty good run of teams and never lost to Linton," counters transplant Jahner, Hazelton class of 1957.

"I was one of 10 kids," Jahner states. "Don't have big Catholic families like that anymore. It used to be more common than not. The school enroll-ments have really dropped and the coops have been good, but at one time, it was quite a rivalry between the two schools. Back then, it would have been impossible to even have thought of the two towns cooping anything. I guess that is good progress that the kids can now play on the same team."

Tischritter sees a bright future for his beloved hometown. "My wife and I never had kids," he says. A regular and a volunteer at many of the Linton school activates, he explains, "but we have put a lot of time in with the kids that have grown up here. As long as the school is strong, the town will stay strong. This is a great place to live," he emphatically states.

Dan Weber is as qualified as anyone to give insight to the local farm economy and the survival of the Linton Public Schools. For the past 25 years Weber has served as the County Executive for Emmons County. It is a fed-eral job and his office is housed in the biggest office complex on Linton's Highway 83 Main Street. For the past 12 years he has also served on the Linton School Board and is currently the Board's President.

A local by birth (around here there is no other way, he would later tell me), Weber has graduated four sons from the Linton Schools, all, he states proudly, played football and all were members of at least one state championship football team.

"We are a skeptical bunch here," Weber says, seated in a conference room and choosing his words carefully. "I think it is just part of our heritage. To survive in an environment like you find here, you had to have some common sense. If you bit on some half-baked scheme, back in those days, it could be fatal."

"Back in those days," were the final two decades of the 19th century, when Weber, like most long term families in the county, can trace his heritage back to the Russian/German large migration to Emmons County. "We are still an agriculture based economy here, but almost all about farm life here has changed," he says.

Technology has revolutionized the area farms, according to Weber. "You have to be large to afford to buy the expensive combines and other equipment you need to produce at the levels that today's markets require."

With a weak US dollar driving up overseas markets and abundant amounts of rainfall the past several years, the good times are flowing on the high plains of south central North Dakota. "Times are good now, some of the best I can remember," says Weber, pointing to $8 a bushel wheat to prove his point. "But my job is to help farmers level out the highs and the lows. That is why we have federal programs like price supports – although we haven't needed them the last few years, the market has taken care of itself – and crop insurance. It will not always be like this, but by smart planning we can balance out the highs and lows that will always affect farming out here."

Small farms are disappearing from the area. Weber attributes the survival of those who remain to good family planning, in particular a multigenerational plan for land usage. "Really, the large corporate farms owned by people who do not live here is a myth. With one exception, all of our large operations in this county are run by families that have lived here for generations. What we have found is that those who have planned and divided property in order of a timely passing to the next generation have survived. They are also the ones who have bought out their neighbors who for whatever reason are no longer farming. If a farmer has to buy his land from his own family, then he might make it. If it has to be bought again through the family by a third generation, then they don't make it. The debt they have to take on proves to be just too much. That is what I have seen."

Weber is concerned about what happens if services from the Linton local community disappear. "I like to see us be loyal to our neighbors. If I need a part for my combine, I should buy it here. Don't run to Bismarck when you can buy what you need here in Linton. Same thing with a new car. Or with home owners insurance or if I need my fender fixed. We still have all those services available here, but for how long if we don't support them?"

If the area becomes too dependent on jobs from the government, or if private sector jobs disappear, Weber worries that Linton could begin to see the slow commercial drain that has so negatively affected life in many small towns similar to Linton. "We have the county seat here. We have the local electric coop here. We have the regional federal jobs here. And we need every one of them, but we also need to protect our non-government jobs and that will only happen if we are loyal to our local businesses."

Future problems facing the education system in Linton are easy for the Board President to identify. "We are losing too many kids, that simple," he states. "It has been over one generation now since we have seen the end of the 10-12 kid families. Large families use to be the norm up here. It was an economic benefit for a farm family to have as many helping hands as possible. That is not true anymore. Family size in our county is still high when compared to the national average, but not near what it used to be, and each year we (the school) are feeling that more and more."

Population in Linton has fallen every decade since the 1970's. The 80's saw a decrease in Linton's city population of -7.9%, the 90's saw a fall of another -9.7%, 2000's a loss of another -6.3% and the largest drop in 2010, -17.0%. The population high water mark for the Linton was in 1960 with a town population of 1826. The 2010 census showed 1097 residents lived within the city limits.

These numbers, Weber admits are alarming. "And the data, county wide, would show a very similar drop," he admits. "We can't run schools without students."

Young people, who leave the area for an education beyond high school, need a job to return to, points out Weber. "This is a hard life here. Good in many ways, but you are going to have to work to make it. No way around that. Up before dawn for chores, and chores after school when the sun has gone down, is a pretty typical schedule for many of our kids. Some just get tired of it. They can get a city job for more money, less work and more conveniences."

An unscientific yet still striking example of the loss of families with school age children in Linton appeared in the August 14 edition of the local paper. A picture of the reunion of the Linton High School class of 1990 was printed. The article pointed out that the class was holding its 20 year reunion a year late due to "scheduling conflicts" from the year before. Nineteen of the classes 38 graduating members returned for the festivities. The story listed the hometown of each of the 19 in attendance. Only one had a Linton address. Those in the picture would be 38 to 40 year of age, prime candidates to have children 14-18 years of age; students in their high school years.

Further consolidation of shrinking districts is a process many small farm communities will fight until their last breath. For many, when they lose their school, it will be their last breath. "Many small towns around here, the schools are all they have, but you have to have students. When Hazelton up here graduates 12 seniors last May and enrolled two kindergarten students this August, how long can that continue? It can't. I see county wide school consolidation down the road, and not very far down the road," Weber said.

Both Weber and Superintendent of Schools Alan Bjornson point to Linton's stabilizing enrollment as a sign of a healthy local economy and a promising future for the district. We graduated 32 seniors last May," says Bjornson, "and this August we enrolled 32 kindergarten students."

"We use to run about 180 students in the high school grades," says the Superintendent. "We have held steady around 120 for the last few years, and when looking at enrollment numbers in the elementary, we can project we should stay pretty steady at that number for the foreseeable future. I think we are past the crisis point of worrying about enrollment shrinking to the point we are no longer a viable district."

Bjornson does agree with Weber that county wide consolidation is on the near horizon. "We have three schools in the county, which means a lot of duplication of services; three superintendents, three principals, duplicate classes that are very small at each school; or even worse, classes that don't get offered because of not enough students, but put the three together and the class could be available to the students. Often times there are higher level classes that are not being offered, and that is a concern."

Almost all North Dakota High Schools under 150 students coop their sports teams with other small towns with similar enrollments. Linton does with Hazelton, for example. So, if a school can coop for athletics, why not for academics, and for that matter, why not just bite the bullet and start consolidating the small rural district into county wide organizations?

But Bjornson also knows that the closing of a school, to a small town, is a death sentence for that community. Eventually, said Weber, the state will have to step in and force consolidation. "But what politician wants to face the local (constituency) when he or she has voted to close their school." That type of political suicide requires a deep and severe educational financial crisis. North Dakota is not yet to that desperate of a point, "But," points out Bjornson, "we are getting there."

The Less Traveled Road

When an American speaks of driving "cross country," we almost always are indicating an east to west path. From Chicago to Los Angeles or Philadelphia to San Francisco would be common routes driven. Seldom when we talk of a cross county trip, are we discussing a north to south route.

For the first 125 years of its existence, the United States cast its growth gaze to the west. Horace Greeley never suggested "go south young man" when providing advice for the procurement of future riches. The St. Louis Arch does not represent a "gateway to the south."

A trip itinerary that includes a trip across Kansas is universally met with a groan. The reaction is due to past experiences of a torturous and monotonous seven hour trip on Interstate 70 from Lawrence in the east to Goodland in the west. As every Midwest child knows, it is a chore to be endured if you want to see the Rockies.

With Highway 83 being a north/south route, I for the first time experienced the drive across Kansas from a different view. Following a longitudinal line as opposed to a latitudinal one, the perspective is totally different and far less boring.

From Oakley in the north to Liberal in the south, the landscape along Highway 83 is, in reality, more similar, more barren and less populated than the Lawrence to Goodland route. Traveling the I-70 east to west route, the altitude will rise almost 2,000 feet. It is a steady climb, so gradual that you don't notice. The east to west traveler will also cross a time zone, from Central to Mountain Time, picking up an hour in the always futile race with the western setting sun.

The route 83 north/south path will maintain almost the same altitude from Oakley to Liberal. This holds true all the way from the Canadian border to the border with Mexico. The one change I did notice was the length of the hours of sunlight. In North Dakota in the summer, daylight will be about one hour more per day than in South Texas. If I remember my 6th grade geography correctly, this will reverse in the winter time.

I found the drive on Highway 83 through Kansas, for I made it numerous times when traveling between McCook, NE and Canadian, TX, to be therapeutically relaxing with its tediousness. I did some of my best planning for this book while on this route. I learned the landmarks, the towns and when to anticipate the lonely stretches of openness so grand it left me with a calmness that I grew to enjoy. The land is stark but the repetition of the landscape as one traversed it was reassuring. The simplicity of this north to south route required developing a taste for its remoteness, but when acquired, the trip became for me quite scenic.

I was often tempted by curiosity when I passed over a Highway 83 intersecting crossroad, especially if that east/west road was not paved, as to what I would find if I were to journey down it. For example, if I followed the arrow on the sign post and drove the four miles down the dirt road to Akaska, South Dakota, what would I discover? Normally, my schedule would not allow for such dallying, but just so often, to keep the vagabonding karma in balance, I would throw planning to the wind and follow my curiosity to see if there might be an interesting story at the end of the dirt road. Those jaunts down often rut filled unpaved trails are some of my favorite memories of a fall spent on US Highway 83.

Chapter 5
Prospects

It is how you show up at the showdown that counts. *Homer Norton*

Anyone can support a team that is winning- it takes no courage.
But to stand behind a team to defend it when it is down and really
needs you, that takes a lot of courage. *Bart Starr*

Show class, have pride, and display character. If you do, winning
takes care of itself. *Paul "Bear" Bryant*

If a team is to reach its potential, each player must be willing to
subordinate his personal goals to the good of the team.
Bud Wilkinson

Football is an honest game. It's true to life. It's a game about
sharing. Football is a team game. So is life. *Joe Namath*

Playoff Structure

Those is charge of constructing and administrating state high school
football playoffs have always been hamstrung with the burden of
football not being a "tournament" type sport. Because of the physical demands of the game, rest is needed between contests. Most experts
would agree that a seven day interlude between football games is ideal, five
days a minimum, for a player's body to recover. Basketball games can be
played in back to back days, sometimes even multiple games in the same
day, making it an ideal tournament sport. First round games on Thursday,
semifinals on Friday and championship round on Saturday, is a common

format for an 8 team tournament. Baseball, softball, soccer and track; no other sport has the same logistical scheduling problem that football does. An eight team bracket in football should be stretched out a minimum of 2-^{1}/$_2$ weeks.

For these, and other reasons, many states did not offer football state championship playoffs until the 1960's and 70's, a good half century, in many cases later than basketball, baseball and track. Texas was an exception for football (when are they not an exception for football?) with a state play-off series going back to the 1930's. Both Nebraska and North Dakota added football state tournaments to its state activities association offerings in the 1970's.

Before the on-field playoffs, unofficial state wide polls would be held to determine a winner. Some states had multiple polls and thus multiple paper state champs. Sometimes, an entity such as a newspaper, would sponsor a post season game between two selected teams, a sort of bowl game, and declare the winner the unofficial state champ.

Very similar to the BCS system now used in NCAA Division I College football, the process was almost always controversial and most all agree that determining the state champion of the field is a much better option.

Almost all states, over the years have "tweaked" their football brackets in an attempt to bring more stability to their plans. Teams are divided into classes, or divisions, based on school enrollment and geographical locations. Some states, in an attempt to stem the criticism of private schools dominating state play, have added "multipliers" to the enrollment of private schools. The amount of the multiplier varies by state, but a typical example would be 1.5. If a private school had an enrollment of 100 students, then for state playoff classification purposes, the enrollment for that school would be 150. An exception to addressing the issue of alleged private school advantage due to recruitment would be the approach of Texas; they simple do not let private schools in the UIL (the association for the approximate 2000 public high schools in Texas). Private schools in the Lone Star State have two organizations to choose from, the largest being TAPPS, the Texas Association of Private and Parochial Schools. TAPPS will award five state championship trophies in football this year, Classes 1-4 for 11man and a 6 man division.

Currently, there is legislation in the state capital of Austin that would force the UIL to accept private schools. It was recently defeated by a slim margin, but is expected to be shortly reintroduced. Every public school coach I spoke with was against allowing private schools into the UIL play-offs, but most felt it inevitable that the state would force their hand. Member schools of the UIL currently have the option of scheduling private schools during the regular season, and many already do.

In Texas, the number of private schools is large enough that it allows for a viable playoff system, and TAPPS is able to offer a five class playoff system. In Nebraska and North Dakota, due to the very limited number of private schools in the state, less than 10 in both, and the huge differences in enrollment of the few schools, hosting a state football playoff, or even compiling a regular's season schedule with only private schools to pull from, would be near impossible.

A major recent criticism of the system in all three states is that with every added division, the title of state champion is weakened, in essence, its value watered down. In Texas alone, the state associations UIL (public) and TAPPS (private) combined will, in December, award 17 state football championship trophies. Defenders of such a multi layered system point to the fairness issue. Small school would not have a chance, if not for the divisions based on school size. The days of "Hoosiers," the small Indiana school (Milan High School) that defeated all comers in the Indiana "one class fits all" format, to win the 1954 Indiana state basketball crown, lives today only in the movies, supporters of the multiple class systems will say. Even Indiana has gone to multiple classes in basketball. First, in 2001, two classes, and today to four.

Interestingly, all states (with the exception of Kentucky in basketball) have added classes over the years, but there is no documentation of any state ever "contracting" or reducing the number of classes offered for state championship play. The reason for never lowering the number of state championships awarded is a simple one; money.

Yogi Berra, the old time Yankee catcher, famous for his twisting of the English language, was once asked when ordering a 12 inch pizza, did he want the pie cut into four or eight slices, answered; "Better make it four, I am not hungry enough to eat eight." Both Texas and Nebraska state leaders must have been schooled in the logic of Yogi when several years ago they voted to add divisions to their football playoff systems. Texas lists their 11 man teams as divided into classes 1A through 5A. But in each class, there are two Divisions. In December, Class 5A will crown two state champions; a Division I winner and a Division II champ. Divisions are sorted based on school enrollment. 6 men also have two classes. So in reality, there are 12 classes of football public schools in Texas. That sounds pretty watered down. Class 5A Division 1 sounds a lot better than Class 12, regardless of how hungry for pizza one may be.

A further example that an Alice in Wonderland type of logic has taken over at the University Interscholastic League (UIL) is the terminology adopted several years ago when it was voted to add another week to the regular season. Perhaps fearing charges from academic inclined educators around the state of further over-emphasis of football in Texas high schools, a criticism leveled in some form or another for about as long as anyone can remember, to semantically tap dance around the issue, the board labeled the additional week as "Zero Week." Now the fourth game of the season is played in what is listed on schedules as "Week Three."

Canadian, TX will play in Class 1A- Division 1. There will be 5 teams in their district. Three are guaranteed spots in the playoffs. There are 16 districts in Class 1A-D1, some with as few as four teams, others with as many as 6. Eighty two teams are assigned to Class 1-D1. The district race does not begin until the 7th game of the year. The last four games of Canadian's schedule will be district games and the results of those final four games will determine who qualifies for post season play and where they will be placed on the state bracket. A team in Texas can be 6-0 or 0-6 in the first six weeks of the season, it doesn't matter. Come week 7, Canadian and their contemporaries assigned to Class 1A D-1 - Boys Ranch, Stinnett West Texas, Stratford and Sunray – will, for district purposes, all have a clean slate; 0-0 heading into district play.

Nebraska also chooses to carefully label their divisions for state football play, with a nod to the criticism of "watering down" the significance of a state championship. For football, schools are divided into Classes A through D, and 6 Man. Taking a page out of Texas' book, Classes C and D are divided into two Divisions. In reality, including the 6 Man tournaments, Nebraska will crown 7 state football champions for 2011 in five divisions.

The largest 28 schools in Nebraska are placed in Class A. The next 32 fall into Class B. McCook is a solid Class B school, ranking 19th in enrollment among the field of 32. Interestingly, the smallest school in the state to compete in 11 man football is Pleasanton, with an enrollment of 37. Considering that statistically half of that number each year will be girls, the team fills its roster from a field of 18 or 19 boys. The smallest school to compete in 6-man in Nebraska is Sioux County, with an enrollment of 18 students.

Nebraska is the only one of the three states where each game matters. The state has adopted a format that is a compromise in that all game results are factored into the playoff format, but the last three games of the year, Weeks 7-9, are district contests, giving hope to a team who has had a rough first 6 games of the year.

From week 1, in Nebraska, teams are competing for not only the top district slot which automatically qualify a team for post-season play, but also for wild card slots. Points for wins and losses are calculated on a computer system that takes into account strength of schedule, based on an opponent's enrollment and record, ranking each team within its class. These rankings become very important as they will be used to seed the tournament by strength of team, ranking each qualifier from 1 to 16. Unlike Texas and North Dakota, geography plays no role in determining the state bracket in Nebraska. Teams are placed in accordance with the state computer rankings, 1through 16. The # 1ranked team will play # 16, 2 will play 15, 3 will play 14, and so on. The top seed will have the home field for the first game.

Unique also to the Cornhusker state is that the state association establishes each Class A and Class B team's complete schedule. All other states make assignments once district play begins, but allow each school to build their own regular season schedules.

McCook coach Jeff Gross is glad for the scheduling help provided by the state. "Being out here in the west, most area schools are smaller than us and wouldn't want to play us, and we wouldn't want to play them. Get nothing out of it for either team. It would be hard (for McCook) to fill a schedule with teams from the east, as they wouldn't want to travel all the way out here every other year."

Canadian can validate Gross' comments with tales of the difficulty they have in filling the first six games on their non-district dance card. Head coach Chris Koetting knows that his team's reputation scares off most of the Class 1A schools in the area, and even a few of the larger schools. In 2011, the Wildcats will have teams on the schedule from New Mexico and Kansas. "We are isolated out here," Koetting admits. "We have to look far and wide to find teams for the first six games."

North Dakota employees a mixture of the two systems used in Texas and Nebraska. Week one is the only contest on the schedule that does not count towards playoff qualification. It is considered a "non-regional" game, sort of an exhibition game. For 2011, Linton crossed the border the last week in August to play Mobridge, SD. Linton's next seven games will be against regional opponents and count in the standings for qualification for post season play.

North Dakota is also unique in that it does not give small schools the choice of playing the standard 11 man game, or the modified game of either 6-man or 8-man. The 16 teams with the largest enrollments play in AAA. The next 16 teams in are placed in class AA, the next 32 in class A. If a school's enrollment figure is not in the top 64 in the state, then they play in the 9-Man classification. In 2011, 41 schools will play 9 man. Linton is in Class A. Thirty high schools in North Dakota, due mainly to size and budget limitations, will not offer their students football in the fall of 2011.

To earn the title of state champion, Linton will need to win four playoff games, McCook four and Canadian five of six, depending if the Wildcats get a first round state bye. All wins must be consecutive. This is no double elimination format, you win or go home. When it gets to playoff time in all three states, it is survive and advance.

The Linton Lions

Linton, ND High School has won the Region 1 title five of the last six years. There would seem to be no reason to suspect that the juggernaut will be stopped any time soon.

Coach Dan Imdieke, the architect behind this football machine that has won 82 percent of its games since he took the helm 35 years ago, is still a coach, and Coaching 101 demands that you downplay pre-season expectations. "We got a lot of holes to fill, on both sides of the ball. Graduation wiped us out," he cautioned. "We lost Levi Roemmich (OL), Derek Roemmich (LB), Kelsey Larson (QB) and Tobie Wald (WR), "and, he added for closing emphasis, "Levi was the state player of the year."

The Lions have appeared in the state playoffs sixteen straight years. To keep that streak alive, Imdieke says, his 2011 team must have players who grow quickly into key positions. "Everything with us starts on defense," Imdieke said. "We have never lost a game that the other team did not score in," he deadpans.

The veteran coach admits, only several days before the season opener, that he is very concerned about where the offense for his 2011 team will originate from. "Our whole offensive line is going to have to be rebuilt," he stated. As in most small schools, your best athlete becomes your quarterback. Imdieke will move former tight end Tanner Purintun to the signal caller position, in addition to his defensive duties in the secondary. "Tanner can handle it. He has waited his turn to play quarterback. He had an older brother who was a very good QB for us a few years ago. Tanner is cut from the same cloth. He will make plays and that is what our quarterback needs to do."

In a run oriented offense, when you graduate your top three rushers, you have holes to fill. "We have some people who we think can do the job," Imdieke said. "But until we see them under game conditions, we just don't know. Our line is young, but we think they have potential. How long it takes them to jell is the question," Imdieke admitted.

Imdieke's biggest concern entering August pre-season camp is that his young team might not have the time needed to jell. "Our first three games might be our toughest of the year," the veteran coach explains. "I think we are going to be a pretty good team by October. Our line will have had time to adjust, and our quarterback will have his feet wet with varsity experience. But 0-3 would be a tough hurdle to overcome, and that is what we might be after three weeks."

The 2010 offense, by Linton standards was very diverse. "We are known as a running team. Last year we averaged per game 146 yards on the ground and 131 in the air. That is pretty good for us," Imdieke admitted. "This year we may run a little more and throw a little less. We will just have to see what our strengths are."

Imdieke is more confident with how his defense stacks up entering the season. A team that gave up over 200 yards per game in 2010, compensated with 35 turnovers allowing them to hold opponents to an average of under 11 points per game. "We have more experience on the defensive side," the coach stated, "and we should be pretty athletic. We will hit well and that is always a key. This year more than most, we are not very deep. We have got to keep our team healthy. We are hitting less in practice because we know how important staying healthy is. But you got to hit some or you lose that 'edge.' And we have always had that 'edge.'"

Imdieke and his squad will not have to wait long for a first test. "Mobridge (the season opener) might be as good as anyone we see this year," Imdieke confided about the bigger school from South Dakota. "They've got to come here. And then we are right into regional play in Week 2, so we have got to be ready."

Imdieke expects major competition for a Regional 1 crown to come from Oaks, Milnor and Maple Valley. With 35 years under his belt, Imdieke keeps a good perspective. "This time of the year (August), all the teams on our schedule look tough. You had better look at it that way. You have to respect your opponents or they will reach up and bite you. But we have been successful at this for a long time and we expect to continue that way."

Linton's team goals for the season remain the same as Imdieke has set in each of his previous 34 season as the Lions' head coach; a regional title and an appearance in the state playoffs. "We always hope to get past the first round, but you never know," the coach said, obviously remembering last season's unexpected second round loss that spoiled an otherwise perfect 9-1 year. "That loss left an impression on our kids, but this is a whole new season with a whole different group of kids; different leaders, players in different positions. That is what it is all about in small school football, you get good players, you enjoy them, they graduate and you move on to the next year with a whole new group. We will be fine. We have been down this road before."

The McCook Bison

McCook head coach Jeff Gross is unusually optimistic about the potential for his 2011 edition of the Bison. Those that know Gross will tell you this is not his normal "pity" pre-season stance. Football coaches are notorious for down-playing the potential of their teams. Keeping expectations low, for many a small town high school football coach, is an M.O. for survival. Maybe, after 14 years of success at the small school, Gross is feeling a little more secure. Or maybe he really does have a team worthy of his confidence.

What has Gross' optimism at such a high level is that his team will have in abundance this year the one factor normally missing in western Nebraska football; speed. "We finally have some speed at the skill positions," he says before the start of an August practice.

Returning senior quarterback Matt Chitwood and junior running back Jake Schlager are two outstanding athletes. Both were 23 foot long jumpers for the Bison track team last spring. Both are legitimate 4.5 men in the 40 yard dash. Schagler is getting attention from Division 1 suitors, who like his versatility. He is a standout on the defense as a safety/linebacker. Schlager will also be the Bison's main kick return threat. Chitwood will man his quarterback position, as well as contributing as a defensive back. He will be the placekicker for McCook and his coach calls him the best kicker in the state.

Senior Justin Terry is a very capable fullback and gives Gross the third threat in his triple option veer offense. Not possessing the same level of explosiveness that his two teammates have, Terry is a 210 pound wrecking ball that is a force in the center of the line. As fullback, Terry is the first option in the often lauded veer option offense. He is perhaps even more effective on the defensive side or the ball where he holds down one of two inside linebackers slots. "Our defense is predicated on strong play from the linebacker positions," says Gross. "Justin is a very solid tackler. Many of our defensive schemes are designed for the front line to keep blockers off the linebackers. Our linebackers make a majority of our tackles and Justin is one of the best we have had at that position, and we have had some good ones."

The Bison will enter the season with a goal of keeping alive an incredible post- season record of success. The McCook team has qualified for the Class B playoffs each year since 2000. After losing to Hastings in the first round of those 2000 playoffs, the Bison have won at least one playoff game every year since.

The 2002 and 2003 seasons have become mythical in McCook. The Bison posted consecutive 13-0 records those years, both ending with state championship wins. In 2004, the Bison came all so close to a three-peat, winning 12 in a row before falling in the state finals by five points to Pius X High School of Lincoln. In 2005 and 2007, McCook again made it back to the University of Nebraska's Memorial Stadium, site of the Class B title game, where they took second. The years of 2006 and 2008 saw the Bison defeated in the state semi-finals. 2002 to 2008 was a remarkable seven year run for McCook. Two state championships, three state runner up finishes and semifinal teams the other two years; it was a magic time to be a Bison fan. Gross has reminded his team throughout the summer that 2011 is the year to get the Bison program back to the state championship level.

Gross and his staff enter the pre-season camp with a good idea of where this year's edition stands. The majority of McCook players participate in a host of summer camps, and coach Gross said that helps his squad be very prepared for the start of fall camp.

"We have a pretty good idea about a depth chart after we spend all the time in the summer," Gross said. "There's still some competition to be had at certain positions. Hopefully, someone unexpected will catch our eye in two- a- days, which will always help our depth. There should not be a lot of big surprises with personnel when we get to this point. We will now have more time to put the emphasis on X's and O's, or schemes," he said. "We'll try to put as much in as we can, and then really toward the mid part of the first week when we put the pads on, it will be more about honing and refining our technique."

As Gross and his staff prepared at a Sunday evening meeting for the first week of practice, to begin the following morning he commented on the high expectations that will always accompany a program as traditionally strong as the Bison's. "We accept that," said Gross. "As a matter of fact, we embrace it. We use it as motivation for our kids. We tell them all the time that the community is behind them, but they will demand commitment in return for that support. We tell them, 'you can't be out running around partying and doing other such things you shouldn't be. If you do, I will hear about it.' To be a football player here means accountability, not only to me and your teammates, but to the whole town."

The 2011 goals for the Bison are simple, Gross says on the eve of the start of practice. "We want to go deep into the playoffs. We feel, for the first time in several years, that we have the personnel to win the whole thing. But talk is cheap. We need to get it done on the field. We have a lot of work to do, but we also have the tools to get it done."

The Canadian Wildcats

Football hopes fly sky high in Canadian, TX. It is August, 2011 and the Wildcats have nowhere to go but down, as they enter pre-season training camp with a state wide bull's eye attached to their back, they are ranked #1 in Texas Class 1 Division 1. Chris Koetting enters his second year as head coach of the high powered small school program. "There's only one ranking that matters and that's how you rank at the end of the year," Koetting says. "That's the only one that really matters."

"I didn't vote us #1," he says philosophically. "We have some great skill people returning, no question. The unknown quality is our offense line. I like the people we have there, but we are not deep. Any injuries in the line and we will be scrambling to survive."

The Wildcats must replace two linemen lost to graduation who are now members of Division I programs. Most Class 1A schools, such as Canadian, might expect such a single talent to come along once ever decade or so. Having to replace two such talents is, as Koetting knows, a monumental challenge.

2010 team captains Taylor Chappell and Ryan Alexander are now on the rosters of the University of Missouri and West Point, respectively, big steps up from a small Texas Panhandle school. "We can't replace them," Koetting said as the prepared to start pre-season practice for the 2011 season. "But we have younger players who can fill the gaps. Our skilled people will carry us, but you have to look at the whole picture. Everyone has a job to do. Do your job and the rest will take care of itself."

Koetting knows that he and his staff will have to address the high expectations and the pressure that comes with such pre-season accolades. "We have very high expectations of ourselves," said Koetting. "We've had enough success in the past where our ultimate goal of winning a state championship is something we should strive for each year."

Koetting will look to senior linemen Salvador Escamilla and Ty Morrow in his attempt to re-arm his front lines on both sides of the ball. Both players are experienced and both have grown up in the Canadian system. "We know we are losing some size we can't replace, but the technique is there," said Koetting.

Morrow says he is ready for the challenge. He told the Canadian Record, "It's a big spot to fill but I think that me and Salvador, we've been working hard," said Morrow. "We've got a long way to go but I think that if we keep working hard, I don't know if we'll be as good as Ryan and Taylor, but I think that we can do the job."

Escamilla reaffirms that he appreciates the opportunity he has. "We have been working hard. We know everyone is counting on us. We are not going to be as big as last year, but we can get the job done. We are really excited. We think it is going to be a great year."

The senior leader has confidence in their line mates. "I know our other linemen, they'll do their job, and I'm just focusing on mine," said Escamilla. "I'm pretty excited and I think we're going to do some great things. We have a bright future ahead of us."

Koetting knows that his returning skilled players are some of the best in the state, highlighted by the passing duo of quarterback Braden Hudson and his favorite target and classmate, Isaac Lewis. But Koetting knows his talented skilled players will be unable to continue to run up the head spinning stats they compiled last fall, if they do not have the time to run the routes needed in their precise passing game. "We have some young linemen stepping up and trying to help out in those roles and we feel pretty good about it, they've done a great job this off season and we feel like we're going to be fine," said Koetting.

The coach always anticipates that the Canadian game will be circled on the schedule of almost every team they play. "We always get everyone's "A" game," he said. "For many, beating Canadian makes their season. We wouldn't want it any other way."

Koetting and his team start the season with a very challenging non-district schedule. These first six games, under Texas rules, do not factor into post season qualification and seeding. "Factor is a good word," says Koetting. "Don't say the first six don't count. This is Texas. They all count, believe me, they all count."

When Canadian gets to the district play, beginning in week 7, the task will be no easier. "I think most of the teams in our district will be better," said Koetting. "Stratford is always going to be tough, we know that. (West Texas) got into the playoffs last year, so they're kind of on the rise. Sunray has a new coach and I think they're going to be better, Boys Ranch has some really good athletes. I think every team in our district will be better than last year."

Isaac Run

John Updike in 1960 wrote a novel destined to become and American Classic, titled _Rabbit Run_. Updike recorded the unfulfilled life of a 26 year old former high school basketball star turned reluctant salesman, desperately seeking a role in adult life that would recapture the fleeting fame he briefly knew as a 16 year old local athletic hero. _Rabbit Run_ is a dark, brooding and sad story, often boarding on the macabre, but one commonly true in a society that makes a hero of a mere child who can out run, out jump and out throw the best rival towns can offer. It is a sad story played out time and time again in small towns across the land: the fleeting fame of a school boy star that, at 18 years of age, is slapped with the reality that the final whistle has blown and your best days are now behind you. You become yesterday's hero, booted into adulthood and replaced by a new star of the local high school team. You drift to the bleachers, a few rows higher up each year, until you finally stop going at all because it hurts too much.

To provide him the promised anonymity, I will call him Isaac. "Hey man, I got to live here," he told me. In exchange for his candor, I promised to protect his identity. For that reason, we will give the town the fictional name of "Wilson," the school mascot will be the "Panthers."

Short, and of average build, it was hard to see Isaac in the role he had so well played only a few years before; small town football hero. Fulfilling his now adult role as cashier, he gave me my change from a purchase of gas and sunflower seeds I had made at a non- descript convenience store in a sleepy town I was passing through late one fall night. Adulthood had mandated that he trade in his bright red Panther game jersey for a baby blue smock with a button attached to the right breast pocket promising service with a smile. I would never have pegged him as a local legend.

Had business not been slow on that late evening, perhaps neither he nor I would have had the inclination to progress in our conversation past the normal niceties one exchanges with the locals as a faceless stranger in a nameless town. But being as no other customer or employee was in the store as closing time approached, Isaac with no pressing job responsibilities, asked, "where you heading?" Not having any impending place to be that evening myself, I had the time to respond in detail. "Cool," he told me, after I explained my wandering travels of the back roads of the nation's Heartland in search of the social meaning of high school football.

Isaac, I was to learn, was one of only a handful of African Americans in the town of 5,000. "I used to play football," he told me.

Accepting an offer to join me for a beer after work, Isaac readily agreed to fill me in on the local high school football fortunes. "I lock the doors in ten minutes," he said. "Take me ten more minutes to clean up and close out." I waited in the car as he finished his duties.

By ten minutes past 10 pm, we were both seated in a cozy corner booth of an establishment on the town square that served as the local pub, turned sports bar. In a building as old as the town itself, pushing a century of use, the watering hole served as a haven for the loafers and the local sports experts, who were often in this town, Isaac told me, one and the same. It was pure small town America, both inviting and boring, but the hot stove chatter, for a high school sports fan such as myself, was fun to listen to. The pool table was in use, the one TV above the bar broadcast 24 hour sports news and the waitress who took our order had nicotine breath and called me "Hon."

The local team wasn't doing so good, one of the pool playing patrons told me. Even though early in the season, he blamed it on coaching. His 8-ball partner disagreed, diagnosing the problem as one of "a bunch of lazy ass seniors. We need Isaac back out there," he said loudly as he threw his right arm around my new friend. Even as a stranger, in the company of a local legend, I felt at ease.

Our waitress arrived with our first round of beers. She also was pleased to see Isaac, as were the half dozen other locals bellied up to the well-stocked bar, bottles of beer systematically tilted back at least twice a minute. Isaac, I was to learn in the course of the evening's conversation, had carried the local squad to within "one bad half" of post state regional play, hollowed turf never before or since traversed by the local team. The defeat of six years prior was still, I could tell, a bitter pill for the local populous to swallow.

"I came here the in the middle of my Junior year," Isaac said as he began to spin his story of gridiron glory. "I grew up in KC with my mom and step dad. Never played many sports. I quit football my freshman year. Didn't like the coach. The team was terrible. Everything about playing football there was bad. No equipment. Crappy fields. We played our games on Saturday mornings and nobody came to watch us. Coaches didn't care. Half the time the officials wouldn't even show up. It was a waste of time."

Unoccupied time, though, for an unsupervised street kid such as Isaac had become, was a problem. "Too much freedom. I hit the streets and ran with the wrong crowd. I was on my way to the state penitentiary, for sure. We did dumb stuff. Break out car windows and do $600 of damages to steal a pack of cigarettes we could see on the dash." He was caught by the police twice stealing his sophomore year of high school, and twice taken to juvenile court. "I called myself a sophomore because I wasn't old enough yet to drop out, but I had pretty much, by that time, quit going to school. If it was real cold out or I was hungry and wanted a hot breakfast I might go, but I wouldn't stay. No one ever came looking for me. Just one less dead end nigger they didn't have to worry about, I guess."

Isaac's second brush with the juvenile court system landed him a thirty day stay in a county youth lock up facility. "They called it a school, but wasn't nothing more than a jail. Bad, bad, bad. I was in with two fifteen year old dudes that had shot and killed a kid right in the front of my high school in broad daylight. They knew (because of their age) they was only going to be locked up till they turned 21, but man they had the rep now on the street, know what I'm saying? Dudes didn't care. If you weren't strong and wouldn't fight, well come night time, they would make a punk out of you. Wasn't going to happen to me. I'd fight, so most were cool with me."

The month long incarceration was an eye opener for the sixteen year old. "Set me straight and it wasn't anything the system did, either. The school in there was a joke, worse than my public high school. But man, I could see myself as a future con, in and out of the system, if I didn't get it together, know what I mean?"

Upon his release, Isaac had a heart to heart talk with his mother. "She was only fifteen when I was born. She had been in and out of foster care herself. She was more like a big sister to me. I never gave her the respect one should to their mother, know what I am saying? She never talked about my dad much. I never met him. I heard he was a very good athlete himself in the kid programs, but couldn't stay out of trouble when he got to high school, so he never played, just ran the streets and got into the whole gang thing deeper and deeper. The same road I was going down my momma pointed out. I think my dad is in prison now, but I really don't know for sure."

"Hon, you need a refill?" I bought a round for the whole house, including our waitress. Four at the pool table, four at the bar, me and Isaac. Eleven beers, $26.75, total.

"My mom had a cousin who had married a white girl from Wilson and moved here with her. I came to live with them after Christmas my junior year. We thought a small town and a fresh start was what I needed. We never even thought about football. It didn't work out (with his first host family), but by then I was pretty well known in town and one of the teachers let me move in with her and her family for my senior year."

It didn't take long for Isaac to show his new hometown that he possessed the one ingredient that had for years been lacking with the Panthers: speed." I ran track my junior year," said Isaac. "I did it for something to do, to get out of school early and to flirt with the girls, both ours and at the other schools. Only time I really saw many sisters," he said with a laugh.

"It took a while to get me eligible with all the paperwork that had to be done because of my transfer. It was almost the end of the (track) season before I could run in a meet, but I remember I broke the school record in the 200 (meter dash) and that opened some eyes, including mine. To be honest, I don't know how they (local school officials) got me eligible, what with me having basically no grades for about a year and a half, because I was not going to school on a regular basis. But somehow they did and I am glad of it." Glad also would soon be local sports enthusiasts as it took only the first carry of the first football game the following fall for Isaac to find his true athletic calling, running a football.

"I didn't start the first game (of the season)," he recalled. "But I went in the second time we got the ball."

"The plan was for me and another back to share time as the main running back." Isaac said. That plan was soon forgotten as Isaac scored a touchdown the first time he touched the ball. Later, when I talked to the man who was, and still is, the head coach of the Wilson Panthers, he spoke with a sense of awe of how quickly Isaac grabbed the role of savior of the local team. "We threw him a pitch out around the right end," the coach told me. "We (coaches) had questioned some the willingness of Isaac to get hit. He never was much of a practice player, but that first time he touched the ball in a live game, we knew we had something special."

According to the coach, that first carry has become a part of local lore. "We counted on the film; he got hit 14 times and never did go down. He had two on his back he was carrying when he crossed the goal line. We still show that tape several times a month. He went 70 yards for a touchdown, but I swear he ran 150 yards, back and forth across the field, on that one carry. I still get chills thinking of it."

The town had a new hero, and the recipient of the adulation was more than willing to play the part. "I still can't believe how lucky I was," said Isaac. "None of this was planned. I just wanted a new start where I could get my education and stay out of the penitentiary. And then, wow, I am the star. Overnight. Talk about being in the right place at the right time."

Isaac's rookie game showing was no fluke. He went on to break the school rushing record. More accurately, he demolished the school record by over 500 yards, finishing the season as one of a handful of backs in the state to gain over 2,000 yards rushing that season.

Just as quickly as it began, it was over. "We lost a couple of games during the year, but we got into the playoffs and were really on a roll, and all of a sudden, the season was over." One bad half in the third round of the playoffs burst the bubble. "We were up two touchdowns at the half," recalled Isaac, "and then everything went wrong. Fumbles, penalties, you name it, if it was bad it happened to us that night." The locals fell by two touchdowns. "I was just in shock after the game," Isaac reminisced six years afterwards. "I remember after the game, just sitting alone in the locker room not wanting to take off my uniform, not believing it was all over."

For Isaac it was the end of a dream. "I remember how I couldn't wait to go to school each day. Man, would my teachers back in KC been amazed. Me wanting to be in school," he said with a chuckle. "Girls, girls and more girls. I ended up in the back seat of many a white girls' daddy's ride. Know what I am saying? I was in heaven. You know what is funny; I still see a lot of those same girls today, white girls with money. See em when they come home from college. They wave, but don't really have time for me. But I remember, and I know they do too."

His eye popping stats had put Isaac on the recruiting radar screen of many smaller colleges. His high school coach tried to keep his expectations reasonable. "People around here have such tunnel vision. They see a local star and think he is on his way to the NFL. They don't realize how many good players are out there. In some of the better big (high) school programs, Isaac might have never even made the team. Isaac was a very good small (high) school player and I wish we could have had him all four years. But his size and speed said he should be playing at the D II or D III level (smaller school classifications of the NCAA) in college. But Isaac kept waiting for Nebraska, Texas and Oklahoma to come calling, and that just was not going to happen. But you know what, it doesn't matter. What does matter is that for one magical run of a couple of months, Isaac was 'The Man.' He owned this town. How many people can say that?"

As it turned out, the point of what level he could play on was mute. Isaac's lack of academic achievement came back to bite him. He could not muster the tests scores needed to qualify for an athletic grant in aid. Both his ACT national test scores and his local grade point average were insufficient for him to play at an NCAA school. Junior college was an option that was explored by Isaac and his coach, but eventually they settled on an NAIA school whose admission standards were not as stringent as what the NCAA held. It was a bad fit from the start. Isaac remembers, "Coaches there were crazy. I mean it, they were nuts. Some of the stuff they did in practice was just stupid and dangerous."

Isaac's lackadaisical attitude toward practice, coupled with the higher level of competition on the college level, was a combination that doomed the young man who had not been raised in a football culture, not programmed to accept competition as a challenge to improve, to fight through adversity and show the coaches he had the desire to pay the price to play college football.

"I remember my position coach called me in and told me 'when the going gets tough, the tough get going,'" recalled Isaac, "and that is just what I did, got going right back to Wilson," he recalled with a chuckle.

Returning to the only town where he had ever been told he mattered, even if it was just because of football, Isaac was back in Wilson before the end of September. "I found a few odd jobs to keep me going and I loved going up to the school every afternoon to watch practice. And I just couldn't wait until 7 pm each Friday and game time. People (at the game) knew me and spoke to me with respect."

Torn between leaving the only support system he had ever known, but still wanting to follow his college football dream, Isaac once again tore himself away from Wilson and for the second semester of his freshman year, enrolled in an out of state community college. "I liked it all right. Since it was winter, the football was not as intense yet. We lifted and had off season workouts, but it wasn't hard core and I liked my teammates. I was at a school in a small town without many blacks, a lot like I had experienced here and that was cool with me. Tell you the truth, in that environment and being black, I felt kind of special."

The problem with this stop in Isaac's pursuit of a football home was academic. "I just couldn't get the book work done. I tried, I really did, and I didn't do badly, I just didn't do well enough. At the end of the semester, the coach called me in and said that my grades were good enough to stay in school and good enough to be on the team. But since I was from out of state, I had to have a higher grade point average to keep my scholarship, and I didn't have it. If I was to come back to play in the fall, I would have to pay my own way, and I just didn't have the cash to do that."

As a two time loser in the college placement game, Isaac's choices were now limited. He and his high school coach finally found an NCAA Division III school in the north that could parlay a combination of loans, grants and local scholarships to help Isaac generate the $40,000 plus it was going to cost him to attend this private institution with a great academic reputation. "It was the chance of a lifetime, I know that now," he says as he looks back with five years of hindsight. "It was an environment that I had never been in before. Money, money and more money. I think I was the only one who didn't have much. Even the other brothers on the team came from families with money. My (black) roommate's parents were both lawyers. But people were cool with me and I was treated good."

Isaac still has a hard time explaining why he left. "I blew it. I could have stayed. I had a good year, not a star, but a good sophomore year of playing ball. But I just couldn't make myself go back for another year. It just was not the same as in high school. The coaches wanted to win, but not like we wanted to win here. If we lost in college, that year it was no big deal. By the next day we were over it. Academics were more important (than football). You could miss practice with no penalty, if you needed extra time for a class. That would have never happened here (Wilson). And nobody came to our games. People around school didn't treat me special because I had a good game on Saturday. By Monday, I was just another kid in history class. That whole summer leading up to the next year, back in Wilson, I just couldn't get myself motivated to work out. I keep telling myself, 'tomorrow I will get started.' But I never did. By the first of August, I finally was honest with myself and told people I wasn't coming back. I know I let a lot of people down."

Isaac returned to his adopted hometown knowing that, for all practical purposes, his football career was over. "I continued to work out, continued to dream, but deep down inside I knew it was over. And I knew that without football, my life didn't mean much."

Isaac continues to help the local team in a peripheral way. He has considered coaching, but knows that without a college degree and a teaching certificate, all he can do is volunteer work with younger players. "I still go to high school practice a couple of times a week. And I help out with the little league program on weekends, but it just isn't the same. All I want to do is play. You know what is funny about football? When your school career ends, that's it. You are done. With baseball or basketball you can still continue to play; slow pitch softball or city league basketball. The outlet is still there. But with football, it is gone in a flash. I was at the top of my game in that regional, and then bam! We get beat and no more. I know I will never play again. I have accepted that, but it still hurts. What I wouldn't give for just one more week of practice. It doesn't have to be a game. I just want to feel special again. But that ain't going to happen".

"The worst time for me is when that first cool front comes in about the end of September, when you need a jacket at night. It just takes me back, back to that fall. It was magic and I know I will never feel so needed, so purposeful again. On Friday game nights, about 6 pm, the lights go on at the stadium. I can stand outside the store, look across town and see the glow. I close my eyes and remember. It is like I am back there, padded up and ready for war, but in control, because my life has meaning again. Everyone in town is there, young and old, -the whole town - at the game, coming to see me perform. It is my time and my world. It is the best feeling and the worst feeling, all at the same time, all wrapped into one."

Our waitress returned. "It's getting late guys. Ten minutes to closing time. One last round?" she asked as she cleared from the table our night's work of empties.

The pool game concluded and one of its' four players, an overweight middle aged white gentleman with an ample paunch, approached our table. "Let me tell you something," the intoxicated man slurred, as he reached down to hug Isaac. "You should have seen this boy run that football. That is what is a matter with 'em boys up at that school house this year. No speed. What we need is another little monkey like Isaac."

Amongst this backdrop of dead end drunken dreamers, in a small non-descript cross roads middle of America, Highway 83 town, the greatest running back to ever lug the pigskin for the glory of the Wilson Panthers, whose brief career had rocketed him to local star status - a hero and the toast of the town- sadly shook his head side to side in quiet resignation to his fate. After a long swig to empty the final bottle of beer for the evening, the only 2,000 yard rusher in the history of Wilson High stood and headed for the door. It was closing time.

Chapter 6

September: Settling In
Weeks 3 to 5

If you don't make a total commitment to whatever you're doing, then you start looking to bail out the first time the boat starts leaking. It's tough enough getting that boat to shore with everybody rowing, let alone when a guy stands up and starts putting his jacket on. *Lou Holtz*

You have to play this game like somebody just hit your mother with a two-by-four. *Dan Birdwell*

Some people say the real world comes after high school, but high school is as real as it gets. There are many life-defining moments in high school and you have to be around people you don't like, overcome challenges, build friendships, put up with the gossip, the rumors and the drama. *Anonymous*

Week 3- On the road again
September 9

The task gets no easier for Canadian and Coach Chris Koetting. For the first time in his coaching career, Koetting began a game week preparation after a loss. At the Sunday coaches meeting, he was upbeat; reminding his staff they must do the same. "No time for panic," he informed the assistants. "Everybody feels bad enough; we don't need to harp on that with them (players). Perryton will give us enough problems by themselves," he said, stressing once again the importance of avoiding turmoil, especially with a team such as Canadian, which was not well acquainted with losing.

Perryton enters the game with a 0-2 mark, but a dangerous 0-2. "We have to go down there and it is never an easy trip," stated Koetting. Coming off of a 2-7 record in 2010, the Rangers are employing a new coach this fall in David Flowers. Close loses to Dumas and Bushland, have been encouraging to the new staff. The score against Dumas was 21-6. The Rangers fell to Bushland by a count of 28-14, but were in the game for 3-1/2 quarters.

The two head coaches and programs are tightly entwined. Perryton Coach Dave Flowers is a former head coach of the Canadian Wildcats. Chris Koetting's first coaching job was as an assistant at Perryton. "I have good memories of those years," he states. Both coaching staffs are very familiar with each other. "We know each other's schemes well," said Koetting. "I don't think that will have any effect on the game outcome. Coach Flowers is a great guy and both staffs have a lot of respect for each other. He is still very well-liked and thought of here in Canadian. He will get that (Perryton) program turned around, we just want him to wait one more week to get started," Koetting laughed.

"One of the nice things about this profession is that you get to be friends with your fellow coaches. Last week Panhandle played Dumas, and Coach Flowers left there after last season and his dad is now the head coach at Dumas, so we get used to these types of relationships. But for three hours Friday night, that all goes out the window. I will guarantee you he wants a win as badly as we do," Koetting said.

Flowers has brought with him the offense of choice in the world of football, circa 2011: the spread. Perryton is hitching its hopes for success in the spread to a newcomer at quarterback, Cole Underwood. The signal caller has impressive size at 6 foot 3 inches and weighing in at 220 pounds. (One has to wonder what type of Division I interest Canadian quarterback Braden Hudson would be receiving with that type of size. Undoubtedly, an extra box at the Canadian Post Office would be needed for the overflow of recruiting mail Braden would be receiving.) Running Back Kade Keith returns after a junior season that saw him top the 1,500 yard mark in rushing. Possessing 4.7 40 speed, getting Keith to the perimeter and involved in the spread offense, is viewed as a key for Flower's teams success this fall.

Reviews have been mixed as to how the Rangers have taken to the new coaching staff. "I think they looked a lot better in the Bushland game than in the opener (against Dumas)," said Koetting. Perryton is a school with three times the enrollment as Canadian. "They still can only play eleven,"

said Koetting. The coach did admit that the larger enrollment has its benefits, especially in terms of depth. "We were undefeated on the JV level last
year and so far this year," said Koetting. "We have some younger kids who
can play, and if we have to, we can pull them up. We would rather have
them learn and be successful on the lower levels, but we also need to be
ready to play on the varsity level."

With similar offensive schemes, the teams will also mirror each other on
the defensive side of the ball , both using stack three defenses. "They are
bigger than us across the board," said Koetting, pointing out in particular a
6'5" 340 pounder who will anchor the center of the Ranger's defensive line.
"He is a man," said Koetting, "and will be hard to move around."

Fame is fleeting in the coaching business, especially in Texas High School
football, where the message from fans to coaches seems to be, "what have
you done for me lately." Koetting realizes all of this, but says he has things
in perspective, and he believes, so do his players. "Every game is important," the coach says. "But we also know the big prize is down the road. We
want to use the non-district games to prepare, and sometimes experiment,
to find what we do best and what we need to improve on. Last week at
Meade showed us that we have to make better decisions with our passing
game. We can't throw five picks and expect to beat a good team. And it was-
n't all (quarterback) Braden's fault. We put him in some tough situations."

News on the injury front for his Wildcats was good. Senior Colton Cates,
injured on the first play of the season, was recovering nicely. "He could play
this week," said Koetting, "But I think we are going to hold him out for
now." Team trainer Brian Mullins had predicted on the sidelines of the season opener that he felt Cades' injury was an MCL strain and would proba-
ble hold Cates out for four weeks. It now looked more like three weeks. "We
need him back," said Koetting. "He is our best linebacker." Senior Chance
Walker's status was also improving and Koetting was upbeat about the timing of his imminent return. "We were really happy to get the update on
Chance. He could also probably go this week, but we are not going to push
him hard at this point."

Perryton, in many past years, has been the biggest rivalry game on the
Canadian schedule. "It will be the biggest crowd we play before this year,"
Koetting said, a Panhandle native, very respectful of the tradition found in
Perryton. "They are a 3A school. They have lost two tough games. They
have been down for a few years, but it looks like they have things going
back in the right direction."

Would a second consecutive loss find the Canadian mentor in the same positive philosophical state of mind he seems to now be in, after the first regular season loss of his head coaching career? "Let's not find out," he says with a chuckle.

For Week 3, McCook will travel to Alliance in a battle of undefeated 2-0 teams. Alliance has been an early season surprise, starting off the year with a 31-12 win over Gordon-Rushville and holding on last week to defeat Chadron 14-7. The Bulldogs have leaned heavily on a defense that has produced 11 turnovers in the first two games. "The win over Chadron was big for them. They are rivals and over the years Chadron has had the upper hand," said Jeff Gross. "They will come at us with a good quarterback and a very fast tailback. We are back on the road again and need to be ready to play."

Both Koetting and Gross know the importance of timing when it comes to effectively instructing their teams; molding team morale for the long haul -a hopeful deep run into the state playoffs. Lessons learned by September failures, could prove invaluable in November. From the demeanor of the two at the Monday and Tuesday practices, it was impossible, by simply listening to each instruct their respective teams, which coach's squad had, on the previous Friday night suffered a crushing defeat – the first in 16 regular season's games – and which had won an emotional cliff hanger from an arch rival they had not beaten in five tries. Call that good coaching.

Koetting was upbeat, stressing to his team that this season was young and that they had learned much at Meade that would help them as the season progressed- bigger fish to fry, so to speak. Gross was cautious, stressing that weaknesses in the Bison schemes had been exposed by Aurora, on both offense and defense. Now, he told his team at Monday's practice, was the time to correct those.

On Tuesday, to further underline his theme of "time to go to work," the Bison "padded up" in full equipment for a practice session for the first time since summer two- a-days. "We needed to hit some," explained Gross. "We missed too many tackles Friday night." Not wanting to be remiss on a chance to stress fundamentals - and bring his team back to earth after last Friday's classic win – Gross was challenging his team to improve. "After a big win, a football team can get real comfortable. We do that Friday night, and Alliance will hand it to us. We have a responsibility as a staff to see that does not happen," Gross told his assistants at the Sunday night coaches meeting.

Koetting, on the other hand, attempted to sooth psyches and rebuild confidence. It was time to take the foot off the gas, take a deep breath and put everything into perspective. He asked his all-state quarterback Hudson, fresh off a five pick performance, to think back to two years prior. "We had an excellent QB that year and he threw seven picks in one game. That team went on to finish second in the state. Our play calling put Braden in some tough spots. It was far from all on his shoulders. He doesn't see it that way, and that is (a good) quality of a leader, being accountable. But we need to move on and we can't do that with a quarterback dwelling on a past poor performance."

Both coaches showed that they have a firm grasp on understanding adolescent egos. Fragile as they are, an ego after a big win is a buffer to constructive criticism, thus an excellent time for a coach to demand improvement. Conversely, often the best time to back off and rebuild self-esteem is after a tough loss. Both men knew that perspective is important in maintaining a good balance in team morale. Labor Day has just passed. For all high school football teams, state contenders and conference door mats alike, much football remains to be played. The drama is just starting. A football season is a long journey. As both coaches reminded their young men throughout the week, in the end, champions win the last game.

In Week 3, Linton will host Milnor for their homecoming game. The contest will be the third consecutive home game for the Lions to open the season. Last week's 12-7 come from behind win against Oaks was big, as the visitors were picked to finish third behind the Lions in the pre-season regional poll. The task will get no easier this Friday as Milnor was picked 2rd in the same pre-season poll. Minor started their schedule playing up one class and suffered a 28-13 home field loss to Lisbon. Week two saw another home game as the Bulldogs hosted Cass-Northern. They proved to be poor hosts as they destroyed the visitors by a score of 63-0.

Adding to the meaning of Friday's game is a bit of revenge sought by Linton. Milnor knocked the Lions from the undefeated and state wide #1 ranking last fall in the second round of the playoffs, pulling the upset over Linton, 17-14 in overtime. "We beat them in the regular season," remembers

Imdieke. "We have not forgotten. We had a four hour coaches meeting this morning (Labor Day) and we feel we have a good game plan. They have a great quarterback, but our defense is playing well. We got to get it going on offense. It goes against my grain, but the kids are pushing hard to open up the offense, more shot gun and spread. Our skill people have done a great job. We have a tight end, Jayden Gross, who has done a great job catching the ball. I still believe in power football, but if will help us win, I might give in, some. I will have to see how practice goes (this week)."

Linton will spend the week celebrating Homecoming festivities. September 9th seems early for Homecoming. "We only have one more home game on the regular season schedule after this week, and that has to be Senior Night," explained Imdieke. "We didn't have a whole lot of choices, with our schedule starting off with three straight home games. It (Homecoming) can be a distraction if you let it, but our kids will not let that happen. They know this is a big game and they remember what happened last year. We all do."

Life is fragile. In a heartbeat, the whole world can change. This was hammered home in a cruel and resounding manner to the Canadian Wildcats football team on Wednesday. Senior Captain Ty Morrow's father was tragically killed in an automobile accident. At the conclusion of practice, Ty's uncle made an unexpected appearance in the Wildcat locker room. Everyone knew instantly that something serious had transpired. "We need to get to Amarillo as quickly as possible," Ty was told. "Your dad has been in a bad accident. It don't look good, we need to go now."

On a drive that what would seem like an endless journey – a nightmare so surreal that it allowed for a lot of introspection during the drive – it would take the family 90 minutes to get to Amarillo. "I would not let myself think the worst," Ty said later about his thoughts on that frightful trip. "But deep down inside I think I knew. I was just in denial."

When the family arrived, they were rushed into the ICU to see Kirk. "I held my dad's hand," Ty remembered later, "Then he was gone." Kirk Morrow was pronounced dead at 9 pm. "He kept asking the nurses when we would be there, how much longer. I think he was holding on, waiting for us so he could say goodbye. His heart stopped right after we got to the ICU," said Ty.

Kirk Morrow had been in Oklahoma City to watch his older son play for Northwest Oklahoma University in a golf tournament. On his way home, his pickup truck had inexplicably crossed the center line and crashed head on into a tractor trailer truck. The driver of the semi was killed instantly. "My dad had diabetes, and we think he had gone several days without his medicine. He had called his mom on the way back and said he did not feel well. But we don't know, and probably never will know, if that is why he crossed the center line."

In a small town, news, especially bad news, travels quickly. Morrow had been a well-known insurance salesman. For the current group of senior football players, he had been their first football coach, back in the 4th grade little league program. Most of the seniors had remained close to Morrow as they progressed through school and the football program. His house became a familiar hangout for the group. Several players, at the Saturday services, referred to Kirk as a friend, a confidant and a second father figure. Kirk Morrow's loss was a horrible and painful infliction of grief upon the entire team, but especially heartfelt by the seniors.

The entire community went into shock. "It is amazing how fast things can change," said an emotional Chris Koetting on Thursday. "Last Saturday, we are sitting around moping because we lost a football game. This Saturday we will bury a fine man, a man whose two sons need him, but now has been taken. Some of these things make no sense," Koetting said as he slowly shook his head side to side. "Kirk was one of those guys it is just easy to like," said Koetting. "He did a lot of good in the community. This (his death) is just so sudden, so unexpected. It just makes no sense," the coach repeated.

Koetting knew that getting his team ready for a big rivalry game with Perryton that would be played, grief stricken team or not, in the next 36 hours, would not be easy. He spent Thursday morning huddled with players, coaches, teachers, and community members. Everyone, it seemed, wanted to help, but no one knew what to do, or what to say. Funeral arrangements were made, with the wake and burial to take place on Saturday. In consideration of the large expected crowd of mourners, the high school gym, it was decided, was the only venue in town large enough to facilitate the event.

At 3 pm on Thursday the team assembled for afternoon practice, after what had been as solemn a day of school as anyone could remember. Ty Morrow was in his accustomed spot for pre- practice stretching. He was obvious to anyone's eyes, a distressed young man, but also a determined one.

Morrow decided to play the game at Perryton, two days after his father's death and one day before his funeral, because that is, "what dad would have wanted me to do," Ty said. "My dad loved Canadian football," the 6'4", 240 pounder anchor of the line said. "It is something we shared. He was so proud of me and the team. I know he would have demanded I play, 'your teammates need you, now get your butt out there and do your job,' is what he would have said."

To sandwich a game between the death and the funeral of such a well-liked man is a very difficult assignment. "I don't know how we will play," said Koetting on Thursday. "I just don't know and right now I really don't care. It's hard to focus on something that seems so meaningless after what has happened. But we have a job to do and we will do it, but it will not be easy."

On Friday evening, The Wildcats traveled to play their traditional Panhandle rival, Perryton. The Class 3A Rangers entered the evening holding a 37-20-3 advantage in this series that goes all the way back to 1920.

Koetting told his team that he would not cheapen their mournful state of mind by appealing to them to make things all right again by winning a football game. "I don't know what to tell you," the coach admitted in the locker room just before sending his 28 athletes onto the field for the opening kickoff. "I think we all knew it before, but today we really know it; there are a lot more important things in this world than football," said a clearly emotional Koetting. "I am not going to ask you to play this game for Kirk and win for him. What I am going to ask you to do is to play in a way that will honor him."

Canadian scored early, but then fell behind. Perryton was clearly the team with the most depth and the most athletes. Their interior line on offense was controlling the line of scrimmage and opening huge holes for long runs from scrimmage. On defense, the Rangers were having their way as well. Hudson was given little time to throw and was constantly flushed from the pocket.

Koetting knew at halftime, as he gathered his coaching staff around him to discuss adjustments that needed to be made, with his team down by 12 points, that the second half had the potential of an ugly blowout, with Canadian on the wrong end of the final result. Canadian had clearly been knocked back onto their heels by the hard charging Rangers, backed by a large home crowd smelling Canadian Wildcat blood.

"We got to simplify things," he told his staff. "We got to get to the line and we have got to play fast on offense. If this stays a slug out in the trenches, we can't beat them. They are too darn big."

Koetting's talk with his team was short and direct. "We got to play harder," he said. "Right now they are taking it to us. We got to turn that around and we got to do it from the kickoff this half. No need to panic, but we need to bust them in the mouth right away. If not, this will get real ugly. Give me the best quarter of the year, and give it to me right now."

The Wildcats heeded the advice of their mentor, setting the tone by delivering a solid hit on the second half kickoff. They then fulfilled his wish of "your best quarter of the year" by dominating the period. Down by 12 at the half, Canadian scored 20 consecutive points in the third quarter. The good times, though, did not last. The Rangers got themselves up off the canvas, regrouped and responded with the game's last nine points, culminated by a 25 yard field goal with 40 seconds left in the game, pulling out a thrilling 34-33 win.

It was a despondent, confused and emotionally drained group of Wildcats who made the late Friday night 60 mile drive up Highway 83 back to Canadian.

Funeral services for Kirk Morrow were held at the Canadian High School gymnasium at 3 pm on Saturday, the day after the Perryton game, with the Rev. Danny Sanders officiating and Micah Lewis, the father of senior Canadian football player Isaac Lewis, assisting. Kirk Morrow was born February 14, 1967 in Canadian, graduated from Canadian High School in 1985 and attended Texas Tech University. At the time of his death, he was a partner in, and agent for, Canadian Insurance.

The gymnasium was packed with mourners. A site that had hosted many a raucous pep rally that Kirk Marrow had attended over the years was now solemnly quiet, his hometown in shock and mourning over his sudden death.

The coaching staff knew it would be an emotional week ahead for the Wildcats. A funeral of a father of a teammate, who many commented was one of Canadian football's biggest boosters, had now been endured. The tough loss on the football field at Perryton was secondary, but it still stung, leaving many in the community to ask, "When was the last time we lost two games in a row?"

It is often said that one of the main values of high school athletics is that it teaches young people to deal with adversity. Coach Koetting and his staff would now have to deal with a level of adversity that no one, two weeks ago, would have ever envisioned. What was needed now was a steady hand of adult leadership and guidance. Koetting called the week that lie ahead the toughest he had faced in his 20 year coaching career.

Hopefully, several town leaders commented both before and after the Saturday funeral, football will become a rallying point for Canadian, a part of the healing process for the entire community. As small towns will do when tragedy strikes, many after the Saturday service spoke of the strength of their community, pledging to Koetting that they would circle the wagons around "their boys." It would be a mistake, noted many, to write this team off. As Rev. Sanders had said at the funeral for Mr. Morrow, "Time heals all. It is time to move on, time to heal through focus." Ty Morrow told his team-mates, "we got a lot of football yet to play. We got to get back on track and get to Dallas (site of the state finals). That is what my dad would have want-ed."

So on Monday of Week 4, back to work went the former # 1 ranked team in the whole state of Texas, a team now sporting a very un-Canadian like record of 1-2. "I see no panic in anyone's eyes," said Koetting on Sunday. "I still believe in this group. We are going to be OK."

Week 4 had the Wildcats playing their third consecutive road game, as they traveled to Class 2A Sanford-Fritch. Any championship team will tes-tify to the many bumps that lie in the long and winding road that must be traversed to earn a state title, but what a fitting tribute it would be to as big a fan of Canadian Wildcat football as there was, for this group of seniors to right the ship and dedicate the remainder of a championship season to his memory.

Perhaps, but easier said than done, for this is not Hollywood that the Canadian Wildcats find themselves, now in Week 4, moored in. Instead, it's the cruelly demanding world of Texas high school football, where sentiment and self-pity is as about as useful as a deflated football. The wheels of a hoped for dream season had come off in a bitterly cruel fashion that two weeks ago no one could have conjured, even in a worse case nightmarish scenario. Canadian now enters Week 4 as a team in need of a lot of healing; but more importantly, a win on the Sanford-Fritch field Friday night.

The Linton Lions notched a big 14-7 Homecoming win over Milnor. A third quarter TD gave the Lions the lead and a stout defense, just as they did last week, rebuffed a late 4th quarter drive deep into Linton territory, to seal a big regional win. Linton has now knocked off the two teams picked immediately behind them in the regional pre-season coaches' poll. Week 4 will now see the Lions hit the road for the first time this season, traveling to Fargo to take on Oak Grove Lutheran.

Coach Imdieke knew that the last two week's wins, almost identical, could have gone either way. An 0-3 start could have been reality, a first in his 35 years as steward of the Linton program. The wily veteran coach knew that if not for a break here and there, and timely big plays by his defense, a winless start could have been a real possibility. He knew his team had dodged several lethal bullets. "I thought going into the season, we could easily have been 1-2 right now, and I would have taken it," said Imdieke.

First, Imdieke gave props to his defense. Rock solid the last two weeks, was his evaluation. "We made some big plays both weeks. We had big stops in the red zone in the final minute of both games." The offense, according to the coach, in spite of the low point output, is getting better. "This is the third straight year for us to start a senior quarterback. In a small school, proper position placement of personnel is critical. Many times, we will put our best athletes at quarterback and at tailback. In our offense, that gets those two involved in 90% of our plays from scrimmage."

After scoring their second touchdown of the game in the third quarter, the Lions extended a 7-6 halftime lead to 14-6. This would be enough for the Lion win, but barely. Milnor made the homecoming crowd at Lion Field sweat out a last minute Milnor scoring threat. A thirty yard pass completion to the Linton 28 yard line with less than two minutes to go in the game was an eerie reminder of the previous week's game with Oaks. Once again, a worthy visiting opponent was launching a last minute and potentially game winning attack upon the Lion end zone.

The Bulldogs, who had knocked the Lions from the undefeated ranks in last fall's state playoffs, used the next three plays to record another first down, placing the ball at the home team's 17 yard line. Linton then stuffed three straight running plays, and perhaps more importantly, injured the Milnor QB, who had to leave the field for the game's final and climactic play. The Bulldogs attempted an end around reverse play that was snuffed out by the Lion's Clay Jacob, who threw the runner to the ground for a five yard loss, sealing the big win by turning the ball over on downs to the Lions with only ten seconds left on the game clock.

For the second straight week, Linton had dodged defeat by the slimmest of margins, but now stood at 2-0 in the all-important regional standings.

Dan Imdieke admits that he has changed little over the years. At times, he will give hints, as he did after the game with Oakes, of "opening up" the offense, but his conservative bent runs deep in his coaching psyche. When it comes time to pull the trigger on what he considers the most radical play in football, the forward pass, he hesitates.

True to his Northern Plains roots, Imdieke is not a trendy guy- he does not even own a cell phone. He is not a coach to be easily swayed by bells and whistles. Don't try to sell him on the spread offense. He sees it as a fad, and over the years he has seen lots of fads in offensive football schemes come and go. You win football games, according to Imdieke, in the trench- es. Learn your football history, he says. Go all the way back to the days of the leather helmets; it is still the same formula for success: if you want to win football games, you have to block and tackle. "You have got to run the football. Our best plays today are the same ones that were our best plays 35 years ago," the veteran coach says.

The biggest change in his offense over the years, he says, would involve play action passes; setting up pass plays with a fake handoff to a running back. "That helps keep the defense honest," he states. "They have to respect our run, but the play action gives us the opportunity to hit a big play on the pass as well. The run sets up the pass, not the other way around." Imdieke is a bottom line guy. He relishes telling visitors that the two highest yardage passing games in the long and storied history of the Linton Lions occurred in games his team lost. When a coach has won over 82% of his games, as Imdieke has done at Linton, in career that encompasses 35 years, that stat makes you sit up and take notice.

The improvement Imdieke saw in his offensive line play, between weeks on1 and 3, has bolstered his hopes that this team could be a contender come state playoff time in November. "The offensive line play this week was much better. We have three returnees in the line, but we have moved a lot of people around and are playing a lot of young people who are growing each week."

Offensive line play is often viewed on both the collegiate and profession-al levels as the most difficult position to learn, but also the most critical for a team's offense success. Linton places a premium on play in the trenches, on both sides of the ball. "A lot of our kids who play on the offensive line, also fill the spots on the defensive line," said Imdieke. "Defense is a lot about lining up and controlling the man in front of you. We like our defen-sive line to keep blockers off our linebackers, who then can fill the gaps and make a lot of the tackles at the line of scrimmage. On offense, it takes longer for the line to come together. We do a lot of pulling, especially with our guards. We also make a lot of calls for trap blocking at the line with our (offense) lineman, as well. It just takes longer for the offense line to come together."

Imdieke, as a life-long teacher of the game of football, cherishes the feel-ing of satisfaction that, even after three and half decades on the sidelines, he gets, on a Saturday morning after a good win. "Right now, I feel good. Our kids are getting better at the things we have harped on in practice, drilled over and over on. I thought two weeks ago against Oaks, we were lucky to win. They whipped us on the line and that bothers me. Last night (against Milnor), I felt we deserved the win; we outplayed them on the line. We chal-lenged our kids and they responded. As a coach, there is no better feeling than looking back the day after a game and knowing your kids executed what you taught them during the week."

Coach Jeff Gross preached long and hard all week to his undefeated Bison to not take Alliance for granted. A program that the Bison had domi-nated for years, was showing an invigorated posture this fall and would enter the contest with a 2-0 record, playing confident and with nothing to lose to a McCook team that would have to endure another four hour + bus trip to the Western Panhandle. Gross would get his team's attention, but not until halftime.

Clinging to a 10-7 lead, Gross used the half time break to; in so many words, tell his team, "I told you so." Later, several team leaders would admit they had not taken the Coach's preaching about the dangers of Alliance seriously, and had basked far too long in the glory of the big Aurora victory the week before. The eyes of his players at the intermission told Gross that he now had their attention.

"This next half will tell us a lot about the make-up of this team," Gross lectured.

Several lineup adjustments were made. "We got to quit living with Okie," Gross told his defensive coaches. Okie- the standard defense of the Bison in their championship years-was a five player front defense that all but dared teams to run the ball at McCook. "We had kids in those seasons who could dominate in the box," Gross explained after the game. "We could sit five in the box and no matter what you ran at us, we would hold the line. When you can do that, and teams have to throw against what is basically a dime (6 pass defenders) package in the secondary, you aren't going to lose many games. But we just don't have the bulk for a front three (this year), or enough depth at the inside linebackers to be that dominate. We have good solid players in those positions, just not dominant. This year, we have to play the system. We can't let a kid in our defense just cut loose and wreak havoc by free lancing."

Gross repeated the same phrase he had used at halftime of the Aurora game, "do your job." He was in particular, upset about the 80 yard screen pass that had given Alliance their only score of the first half. As he pointed out upon review of the film after the game, "Our defender is there. If he just breaks down rather than going for the interception, that play goes nowhere." He then points to the same play ran in the second half that resulted in a two yard loss. "We have too many people wanting to make the big play on every play, score the touchdown on every play or blow up the ball career with a big hit on every play. We don't need that. We can't do that. We don't have those couple of dominant players who because they are so dominant can wipe out a missed assignment or a missed tackle by a teammate. We don't have that "eraser" this year. I wish we did, but we don't. What we need are people to do their job. That simple, but somehow I am not getting that across to this bunch," Gross said after the game.

Down 10-7 at half time, Alliance marched the ball down the field to start the second half, and to the delight of their large home crowd, took the lead on the mighty Bison of McCook, 14-10. Trading scores the rest of the twelve minute third stanza, the home team led, 20-17, as the 4th quarter began. Gross would point out after the game that he did like the poise his team showed down the home stretch. "It had been a long time since Alliance has led us in the second half, but I sensed no panic in our kids, we just kept playing."

For the second road game in succession, the Bison were hit with double digit penalties. Over the years, competing coaches have been quick to laud the resourcefulness of McCook - Jeff Gross teams do not beat themselves. Like any good program, this reputation has followed the Bison and caused some opposing coaches to also wonder, many times out loud to officials if, similar to Ted Williams' legendary eye for the strike zone which some pitchers felt would give the eagle eyed slugger the benefit of doubt from umpires on border line strikes, didn't give the Bison the same benefit of the doubt on borderline calls. "Not this year," said Gross. "We play at home and we have three penalties. We come to the Panhandle twice and get rung up in double figures. By the way," he said with a wink after the game, "Did you notice we had the same crew (of officials) we had at Scottsbluff?" That is as close to a negative comment on officiating as Gross will come all year. He is widely respected among game officials because he has, over the years, learned to take calls in stride, and is not one for ref baiting. "I can live with the type of penalties we are getting because they are effort flags," he said on the bus ride home from Alliance. "I might change my mind if we continued to get out flagged 2 to 1, but right now I don't want to address it with the team, don't want to take the aggressiveness out of trying to make the extra block, or give the extra support on a tackle at the end of a play away from them. We teach that, and we like that."

The Bison rebounded in the fourth quarter against Alliance with two long drives to put the game away. It was an alpha male type statement to Alliance, driven home with old school smash mouth football: you have improved, you made us work, but when the bell rang, with the game on the line; we answered. We are still McCook - and you ain't there yet.

The only satisfaction Gross found in the long day was in the way his team responded in the 4th quarter. "That was McCook football the last quarter," he said as the two Bluebird school busses hauling his subdued and quiet team rolled east across the late night Nebraska prairie. "Nothing fancy, just do your job. Without that effort and execution in the 4th, this would have been a really long ride home."

Off to a 3-0 start, the Bison are on the road again next week as they travel to Gering, who will also bring an undefeated mark into the week 4 showdown. "Three of our first four games are on the road and if you take away the game with us, our first four opponents have a combined record as of now of 9-0. If we can get Gering next week, well, that would be a pretty good start to the season," Gross deadpanned.

At 4 am on Saturday morning, the team buses, barely ahead of the rising eastern sun, rolled up a deserted Highway 83 into the middle of McCook, made a left on 7th Street and deposited the undefeated Bison at the back door of the school gymnasium.

Week 4 – The "S" word
September 16

As the half-way point in the season approaches – it varies by state association; Texas plays ten regular season games (spread over eleven weeks), Nebraska nine and North Dakota eight – it is still too early to make any solid predications on any of the three Highway 83 team's playoff prospects.

Linton, ND is in the best position of the three. Two big wins against Oaks and Milnor, the two squads picked in the Coaches' regional pre-season poll to finish behind the Lions, have put them in the driver's seat. Week 4's opponent, Fargo Oak Grove, would seem, on paper at least, to not be much of a challenge to the Lions. The Lutheran school has fallen on recent hard times, although they had won a Class B state title as recently as 2007. Since then football at Oak Grove has been a struggle. The team did not win a game in 2010 and has started 2011 with three straight blow-out losses. A drop in classification for this season, from Class AA to Class A, does not seem to have helped their football fortunes. However, Imdieke, after a Wednesday practice that was not up to his expected standards, warned his team, "We are not playing Friday's game on paper."

In an oddity, the game will be played in Morehead, MN, across the Red River from Fargo, ND and game time is set for 4 pm. In the major spring flood of 2007, Oak Grove's field was destroyed. Since then, they have played their "home games" at a fellow Lutheran institution, Concordia University in Fargo's "twin city," Morehead. Since the college had a home game on Saturday, and the field has no lights, the Linton game will require a rare Friday afternoon start.

Imdieke has made plans for his team bus to leave the school at 9:30 am. "It is about a three hour drive to Fargo," he said on Wednesday, "but we like to take our time and stop and get the kids a good meal along the way. We travel well, and will have a good number of parents make the trip, even though they will have to miss a day of work. And we have a lot of former townspeople, alumni and relatives, that sort of thing, that live in Fargo that I think will come out to see us as well."

One group that will not get a day off school to make the road trip to Fargo will be the Linton state ranked volleyball team. In the eyes of their coach, a big home invitational tournament on Saturday trumped an out of town football game. There would be mandatory volleyball practice on Friday after school. "Sucks," commented one of the senior volleyball players when she found out on Wednesday that the Fargo trip would not be on her Friday agenda.

"Western Ho," should be the early season battle cry for McCook, as week 4 will see the Bison hit the road once again for another 500 mile round trip into the Nebraska Panhandle. The northwestern junket to Gering will be their third such lengthy trip in the season's first four weeks. "I sure didn't make this schedule," said Bison Head Coach Jeff Gross.

The state high school association in Nebraska uses a unique scheduling system for football only. The association sets the football schedule for every Class A and Class B team in the state. According to off the record sources, the state took on this chore three years ago because several of the larger schools in the Nebraska's isolated Panhandle, in particular Scottsbluff, Alliance and Gering - the very three away trips McCook has had to endure to start the season – could not find interested foes of their size willing to travel to the remote western part of the state.

Travel or not, "we had better be ready to strap it on," said Gross. "They will have the best receivers we will see all year. Gering is off to a great start and their record (3-0) shows they are dangerous. This is a big game for us. If we can get this one, finish off this murderous stretch to start the season, we got a chance to get on a pretty good roll. But this is a tough one on Friday."

The Canadian, TX Wildcats, the team that can't seem to catch a break, will hope for a change in fortune as they travel to Sanford-Fritch. The Eagles are not off to a strong start, but were the pre-season pick to win their Class 2A district, returning ten starters from a 9-3 playoff team from a year ago, and have returning a QB who missed last year with an injury, but threw for almost 2000 yards as a sophomore. "We need a win," said head coach Chris Koetting of his Canadian team. "We have had a good week of practice, now we need to have that transfer onto the field." Two heartbreaking last minute losses the past two weeks leave the Wildcats with a 1-2 mark for the year.

While not off to the start they had hoped for, Sanford-Fritch has an all-state caliber running back in Colton Valle, who has caught Koetting's, and his staff's, attention. "He's as good of a running back as there is in the area, so we're definitely going to have our hands full."

Over the years the Eagles have developed a reputation as a team that will play a very physical game. "Defensively, they always play tough," Koetting said. "They will hit you. That is one thing you can always count on when you play them."

Koetting hints that there may well be some changes on the Wildcat's offensive line. "We knew our depth was limited there coming into the season. (Quarterback) Braden (Hudson) has got to have time to throw the ball. He can't do it sitting on his butt all night. We have got to improve the protection we are giving him. Some of that has to do with our passing schemes and routes. We need to simplify some things, as a staff. But we also need to do a much better job of pass blocking, and the players have got to execute that on the field," Koetting said.

Linton, ND High School is an athletic power. No one in the world of south central North Dakota high school athletics will dispute that. With a long winning tradition in football, of course, but also volleyball, wrestling, boys and girls basketball; the Lions are almost always state ranked and serious contenders for state titles across the board. A win over the Lions, both boys and girls athletes of Linton will tell you, is greeted with a celebration by the opposition worthy of a state title. "We take that as a back handed compliment," said Linton Head Football Coach and Athletic Director Dan Imdieke.

Remember the Terrell Owens controversy? Ok, there were many with the self-promoting and flamboyant Owens, but his biggest might have been when, as a member of the San Francisco 49'ers, he celebrated a touchdown catch by sprinting to the middle of Texas Stadium to do a celebration dance on the Cowboy star logo, located dead center on the 50 yard line. When Owens repeated his dance after catching a second TD pass, Dallas defensive back George Teague took offense and sprinted to the star - the logo, not the showboating Owens- and with a forearm shiver, leveled the 49er in mid dance move. Surprisingly - in many people's mind commendable- Owens' own coach, Steve Mariucci, suspended Owens. When asked why he would suspend a star like Owens, Mariucci said, "Because I respect the game." To show proof positive that pro sports operate on a short term memory, in a few years, Owens became a member of the Cowboys.

Imdieke knows his history. "We never, and I mean never, celebrate a win on a visitor's field. That is a tradition that we have developed and our kids respect that." Instead, the Lions have created a celebratory routine all their own, one unique to high school victory celebrations- the private celebration.

Having just played a solid, if not spectacular game, to defeat winless Fargo Oak Grove 26-0, the Bison have departed the visitor's field and are on the three and a half hour bus trip back to Linton. The seniors know the drill. Ten minutes into the trip as the bus, driven by Imdieke, heads west on Highway 94, the seniors quiet the underclassmen. That is Imdieke's cue. He releases a deep guttural growl, starting low and growing in volume. When he hits peak pitch, the entire bus erupts in a loud cheer, so strong that the bus literally rocks. It would be interesting to know the comments of travelers who witness this celebration on the busy interstate.

"We never want to give the opposition a reason to have any extra motivation the next time they play us," the wise Imdieke explains.

The solid effort against Oak Grove was just what Imdieke had hoped for. After an opening season loss to a strong Mobridge, SD squad, and two one touchdown wins the next two weeks, with his Lions hanging on for dear life by defending last second passes into their own end zone, the coach knew his team needed a game where "we can have a little fun." The 26-0 win over the Grovers fit the order to a T.

The game began with a scoreless and uninspired first quarter. Hoping to jump ahead early and take advantage of his team's stout defense, Imdieke made the unorthodox decision to kick after winning the coin toss to start the game. That meant Oak Grove would get the ball to start both halves. An interception, one of the few mistakes senior quarterback Tanner Purintun and the offense made on the day, initially slowed the Lions and a lackluster first quarter ended with 0-0 score.

Linton had begun to show signs of life as the first quarter ended. The Lions had recorded two straight first downs and were facing a third and four from just outside of midfield as time ran out on the first quarter.

Imdieke gathered his team at the sideline during the one minute intermission between quarters. "Can we go on two," he asked his assembled offense? All heads nodded in the affirmative. "Stay disciplined," he encouraged, as the team broke the huddle. The hope was that by not going on the first count, as his offense had done the entire first quarter that an overanxious Oak Grove defense would jump off side. It worked to perfection as the

Lions held steady and the entire front five of the Grovers jumped in unison on quarterback Purintun's hard first count.

The bit of trickery seemed to inspire the Lions. The next play was a 48 yard run by junior fullback Brock Nagel on a quick hitting trap play executed to perfection by the offensive line. With the ball sitting first and goal on the two yard line, senior tailback Cody Sehn followed the blocking on the right side of the line to walk into the end zone, giving the visitors a 6-0 lead.

A swarming Linton defense forced Oak Grove into two consecutive punts. Both were poor, low and end over end down the middle of the field, but both times the Linton return men failed to catch the ball, instead letting it roll, each time adding twenty plus yards to the kick. Imdieke was not happy and promised to address the problem at half time. It would be one of only a few complaints the coach could find with his team's second quarter play. Linton drove the ball inexorably down the field on both possessions, mixing well running plays and play action passes. Purintun scored on a one yard sneak on the first possession and then the signal caller hit tight end Jayden Gross wide open in the corner of the end zone for a five yard score on the following possession. One two point conversion pass to Gross made the score at the half 20-0.

At halftime, Imdieke implored his team to do a better job of running the ball inside the tackles. "We got to hammer that thing," he told his linemen as they had not executed, to his satisfaction, the inside trap plays that had over the years been the staple to the run oriented Imdieke offense. He took it as a personal affront that this year's team had not mastered his trademark blocking scheme. At halftime, he lined up his JV into the Oak Grove defense set and walked his varsity line through how he wanted the plays blocked. "We have got to be able to stick it in there and run it, or we are not going very far," he stated, wrapping up his impromptu half time adjustments. "I want to see us dominate the line this third quarter."

A short kickoff and a decent return to start the second half gave the Grovers their first drive of the day to originate inside Linton territory. They quickly drove to a first and goal on the Lion's 5 yard line. The table was set perfectly for what the old school hardnosed head coach wanted his team to accomplish. "They were not going to beat us," Imdieke said after the game. "I am glad we had to stop them and then have the challenge of driving the whole field. It was what we needed."

Three running plays and an incomplete pass gained the home team only four yards and the Lions took over the ball on their own one yard line.

Thirteen plays later - only the last one a pass- Jayden Gross snared a 5 yard lob pass from Purintun, off of a great play fake by the senior signal caller, for the final score of the day. The 99 yard drive ate up over 9 minutes of the third and fourth quarters, greatly pleasing Imdieke. "Now that is winning football," he crowed to everyone on the sideline within ear shot. "You can't win if you can't pound it up in there."

By the fourth quarter, Imdieke was feeling giddy by the display of hard-nosed football from his team. He sent his senior quarterback, Purintun, back onto the field to run the offense after an Oak Grove fumble, but first he pulled him aside and announced, "A few more plays and you are done. From here on in, you call the plays." Even through his face mask, Purintun's delight was evident.

Imdieke is notorious with his players for his refusal to open up the play-book and put an emphasis the pass. The veteran coach subscribes to the old school theory that when you pass the ball three things can happen, and two are bad. He will mix in the play action pass, which had led to two of the team's four touchdowns on this afternoon, just to keep the defense honest, but in the playbook of the Linton Lions, the run always sets up the pass.

As Purintun jogged to the huddle, energized with his freshly anointed power of play calling, Imdieke must have suddenly realized what he had just done and yelled after his departing QB, "That don't mean pass on every down." Four passing plays later, Imdieke could take no more of the aerial circus and sent in the subs, the short lived experiment of site based manage-ment play calling for the Linton Lions, over. After the game, while the play-ers ate a quick meal of sloppy Joes and chips, provided by Oak Grove par-ents, Imdieke told his three assistant coaches, "Tanner does a great job of throwing. Maybe we need to open it up some, what do you think?" The assistants all smiled and one rolled his eyes, a non-verbal message of "we've heard this before."

The Lion's JV and freshman teams manned the field for the rest of the contest. The Linton seniors, with the coach's permission, now "depadded" on the sideline; done for the day. The varsity defense made very clear to their understudies as they took the field, that the shutout was to be main-tained at all costs. The encouragement helped and the clock on the Concordia College scoreboard ran out with the team from Fargo failing for the day to cross the Lion goal line.

As his team gathered in the end zone at the conclusion of the 26-0 white-wash, Imdieke congratulated them. "Very good effort, everyone out there today, I was pleased with the effort. I think we let the fancy field here (a college stadium with an all turf artificial surface), the trip up and the afternoon start, throw us off. But when we decided to play, we got some things done. Next week is going to be tough. We got to practice better next week. We got to be better prepared and we will be. Now let's get out of here."

In his post-game analysis, Imdieke was clearly pleased with his team's performance- after the first quarter. "Once we got it going, I thought we played well," he repeated to his staff as the players showered. One of the few areas that the staff identified as a concern was a failure to field multiple punts, that after they hit the ground, took up to twenty yard rolls in the favor of Oak Grove field position. A Bear Bryant story was told. The Bear, legend has it (what about Bryant isn't legend?), once asked a freshman punt returner who had failed to fair catch a kick that subsequently rolled dead inside the Tide five yard line, "Son," the Bear drawled, "Is there a penalty for not catching a punt inside the twenty?" No, answered the rookie, don't believe so. "There is," corrected Bryant, "Loss of scholarship."

Imdieke had reason to want to get his team showered, changed and on the bus headed back to Linton as quickly as possible. First, it was one of his many duties to drive the bus and he was looking at a sixteen hour work day. Second, the next day, Saturday, he would don his athletic director's hat and supervise the all-day Linton Volleyball Invitational Tournament. His wife had made the drive to the game and would spend the night in Fargo with the couple's three children, all of whom now lived in Fargo. Joining the kids and mom on the field in congratulating the coach after the win were his son-in-law and a future daughter-in-law. "Boy, what a great bunch," Imdieke crowed after the game (Imdieke always had a special glow when he spoke of his family). "I wish I could stay here tonight, but somebody has got to drive the bus, and for 35 years, that has been me. And we got the volleyball tournament tomorrow. We got a pretty good volleyball team, you know?"

Dan Imdieke just looks like a football coach. Thirty five years on the sidelines have left him with the chiseled features of authority. His presence makes up for what he may lack as a speech maker. He needs few words. Jeff Gross, head coach at McCook, NE, sounds like a coach. He is an excellent communicator, capable of adjusting his approach to reach across lines to players, parents and community members alike. Listen to Gross speak on football for only a few minutes and it is obvious he has a solid grip on what it takes to win high school football games. Chris Koetting, head coach at Canadian, TX, on initial introduction, neither looks nor sounds like a football coach. He is quiet and introspective, choosing his words carefully, to friend and stranger alike. But still waters run deep. Koetting's stewardship in guiding the floundering ship Canadian through the troubled waters of the past two weeks shows beyond a doubt, the man can lead.

"We talk a lot about pride and hard work and discipline when we talk about Canadian football," said a smiling Koetting after a 44-6 win over Sanford-Fritch, "But not often do we talk about joy. Tonight we played with joy."

A team that had seen a season begin with the burden of a #1 state ranking, and after three weeks sport an unheard of for Canadian 1-2 mark, compounded by the tragic and sudden death of a popular parent, Koetting admitted, had taken its toll on coaches and players alike. "It has been a long two weeks. You really start to doubt yourself. You don't want to, and we didn't panic, but it really shakes your confidence. I didn't think 7:30 would ever get here tonight. It was like once the game started, the burden of the whole world came off our shoulders. Our kids were running around out there having a great time. We just played football and it was what we needed. You could see it in the players on the field, the players on the bench and the coaches. It was just like little kid Christmas time joy. It was pure. We just wanted to play some football. Man, we needed that."

As Koetting had promised after the Perryton defeat, several personnel changes were made on the offensive line. A 160 pound sophomore was moved up from the JV team to play center, a trouble spot since the first day of summer camp. "In our scheme, the center does not have to be very big. We have won state titles before with 160 pound centers. That young man tonight, well, he did a great job. We got the best quarterback around and when we gave Braden time to throw, you could see tonight what he can do. His numbers are down compared to last year, but there is not a thing wrong with him. He can't throw sitting on his butt all night. We got to protect him and tonight was a much better job by the line of doing just that." Koetting noted that, as also promised, the play book was trimmed down for this game. "We were trying to do too much. When you got the skill people like we have, you have so many options. Maybe a better way to say it would be that we were trying not to do too much, but more like we were trying to do too much too soon. As the season goes on, we will get some of what we took out put back in, but for this week it was important that we mastered what we had in the game plan and I think it showed we did."

The high octane offense was hitting on all cylinders as the Wildcats raced to a 26-0 first quarter lead. Canadian dominated the game from the opening kickoff, putting a total damper on the Sanford-Fritch homecoming. Canadian racked up over 500 yards of total offense. The offensive show could have been even more explosive if Koetting had not taken his foot off the gas late in the first half.

"That is how we want to play all the time," the Cat head coach related after the game. "We are a fast paced team. Our kids like to play that way, and we have the personnel to play that way. But so much is confidence and momentum, and we have had little of either the past couple of weeks. Tonight, we just let it fly and it just snowballed for us and against them. When we play that tempo, we can play with anyone and tonight we showed that. Fritch is a dangerous team, but tonight we were ready."

The Canadian defense was stifling, limiting highly touted running back Colton Valle to being a non-factor in the game.

Three touchdowns and a safety in the first quarter had the Wildcats up 20-0. The Hudson brothers, quarterback Braden and sophomore receiver Boston, hooked up for the first score, a 22 yard pass. Braden and Taylor Schafer also found the end zone in the first period, both via short runs. Schafer also recorded a two point safety on defense when his hard blitz forced Sanford-Fritch quarterback Chris Bryant out of the back of the end zone.

The second quarter saw more of the same: a fast and hard hitting Canadian team on both sides of the ball, frustrating a demoralized Eagles' team. The Canadian offensive line did a much better job, as was well noted by Koetting at half time, of giving Hudson time to throw. He responded with marked precision tosses and the score continued to mount in the second quarter. A one yard run by Hudson and a seven yard effort from Schafer, pushed the lead to 32-0 with still 8 minutes to play in the first half.

An 18 yard touchdown pass from Bryan to Christian Ward got the Eagles on the board before the half but the game, by then, had been long ago decided. Isaac Lewis caught a 27 yard scoring strike from Hudson to finish the first half and Schafer added another rushing TD early in the third period, to push the lead to 44-6 with 8 minutes left in the quarter.

The varsity was now done for the evening. "No injuries now," Koetting told his players and staff in regard to his decision to pull the plug on his sizzling first team offense. "We got it done. We got it done." The relief on the head coaches face was reflected in the satisfied tone of his pronouncement.

Xs and Os, Koetting admitted, was not what had been ailing his Wildcats. "We just hit one of those times all coaches, if you stay in it long enough, are going to hit. It has been hard." All week Koetting and his staff had made it a coaching priority to stay up beat, but demanding. Self-pity was not an option. "The worse thing we as coaches could have done this week would have been to come in and jump all over everybody. But we also knew that we had to challenge this team. Sure, we have had some tough breaks and a great tragedy (occur). But we still have a job to do and in football you get no points for bad breaks. No one is going to feel sorry for you on the other side of the line of scrimmage. They want to stomp your butts as far as they can into the ground. That is just football."

The balance needed for Canadian in week 4 was for Koetting to deliver a combination of a wake up kick, in the seat of the pants, and some empathy for what his team and staff had been through, recognizing the pressure they were all working under.

The conclusion of the Wednesday practice for a high school football team is always a time for reflection. The hard work and preparation for this week's Friday night opponent has been completed. Where are we? Are we ready? Such common reflections and feedback take place on thousands of practice fields across the nations as coaches gather their young warriors for a mid-week, post-practice talk. Koetting knew this team was at a mid-season crossroads and what he said to them at this instance would have a huge effect on the mental direction his team would take.

"We done a lot of talking," Koetting told his team. "We all know what has happened the last two weeks and none of us are happy about it. If you are, you shouldn't be here. But gentlemen, what a chance we have to grow as a team, and as people. When everything goes your way, it is easy to be a leader, be a good teammate. And we all have had a lot of great things happen in our lives because of Canadian football. Me, probably more than anyone here. But when things go bad, that is when you really find your leaders, your solid teammates, your friends who you know you can count on when things go bad. And that is so important. That is the opportunity we have now, so let's embrace that challenge. Let's look around this field and know that we have a field full of people, players and coaches alike, who have not given up on themselves or on you. We have practiced this week like champions and I feel good about where we are. Is my confidence shaken? Sure it is. Am I questioning my own ability as a coach? Sure I am. If I wasn't, there would have to be something wrong with me. I know you feel the same way. But when I look around this room, that is what brings my confidence as a coach back, because I know what kind of people we have in this room. Enough talking, let's just go out there and play Canadian football. Just let it rip. Play FAST. We do that, and we are going to be just fine. Trust me. I trust you."

"If we throw it six to eight times a game," says McCook Head Coach Jeff Gross, "then we are going to be on the right side of the score when the game ends." His approach is not as conservative as it may at first sound. The Bison offense will live and die on the veer belly option play. The attack is a triple option with the ball carrier being the fullback up the middle, the quarterback around end or the tailback on the sweep pitch from the QB. Gross had stated many times that strength of this year's offense was that all phases of the triple option were in the hands of solid, experienced, and most importantly; athletes with speed. Quarterback Matt Chitwood, fullback Jason Terry and tailback Jake Schlager; all three, especially for rural Nebraska standards, can flat out run.

Chitwood had the physical ability to be an outstanding triple option quarterback. Gross had been more concerned recently with the mental aspect of Chitwood's game. He preached patience to the senior. "He has to learn," said Gross, "that he can't score a touchdown on every play. Take what the defense gives you. That is how our offense is structured."

The first phase of the triple option veer series requires Chitwood to stick the ball in the belly of the diving fullback, senior Jason Terry, as he hits the center of the line. Chitwood then reads the defense's commitment to the fullback and either leaves the ball with Terry or pulls it back and continues down the line of scrimmage to next read; the defensive end. Both the fullback and the quarterback, regardless of which has the ball, continue out the play, hopefully committing defenders taken in by the fake ball handling. If Chitwood keeps the ball he then has the option of cutting the ball up field or pitching it to his trailing tailback Schlager.

McCook scored early in the Gering game, with Chitwood tucking the ball and sprinting into the defensive secondary. Once free of the line of scrimmage, using a combination of his speed and several shifty moves, Chitwood out-sprinted the Gering defense into the end zone for a 50 yard touchdown run, giving the visitors an early lead.

The teams then traded punts through most of the first half. With a lead of 7-0, late in the first half, it was decision time for Gross. The scoreboard clock showed 1:40 for his offense to work with. The score could have easily been tied, or even could have shown the Bison behind. Gering had fumbled inside their own five yard line to void an excellent opportunity to score. McCook's offense, other than Chitwood's one long run, had been sporadic, at best.

The Bison's offense would take over now with 100 seconds left in the half. It was 80 yards to the end zone, but with the super strong leg of Chitwood, 50 or so yards would get them to the edge of his field goal range. Either method of putting points on the board, a field goal or a touchdown, would make the Bison lead at halftime two scores, a major momentum factor heading into the half time break. On the other hand, a McCook turnover deep in their own territory would set up Gering for a last second score and the momentum would completely shift to the home team. Be aggressive and put the ball in the air, or conservative by the run and get into halftime with the current 7-0 lead in place?

Gross decided to keep it on the ground, but still hoped for a big play. Since Chitwood's long TD run, Gering's defensive coaches had pinched the ends, telling them to stay home and guard the perimeter, with specific instructions to not let Chitwood get into the open field by outflanking the defense. Much like a "no doubles" defense in baseball, where the first and third baseman are positioned right on the foul lines to take away the extra base hit down the line, Gering was leaving the middle of the field open. Gross instructed Chitwood to "read" the belly play and if the blocking numbers in the box favored fullback Jason Terry, then leave the ball in his belly for a fullback run into the middle of the line.

Gross first, and then Chitwood, read the situation perfectly. The straight dive off the belly veer play resulted in a 68 yard gallop by Terry to the Gering 12 yard line. On the next play, the Bison stuck the ball in the end zone and took a commanding 14-0 lead over a now dispirited undefeated Gering team. The Bison would go on to win by a commanding score that would raise eyebrows around the state when read on the late night internet scoreboards, 31-0.

"We are ready for a home game," Gross said after the Gering win. "I am happy. We played very well tonight. We were much better focused than last week. This team got better this week and that is what we want this time of the year. No looking ahead, one week at a time. Our defense held them to under 30 yards rushing. We do that, we win." For the game, Gering netted only 7 yards on the ground. The Bison multi- faceted running machine rumbled for over 300 yards. Chitwood threw only six passes, but gained 71 yards through the air.

On the bus ride home, Gross gave props to a group that under normal circumstances receives little recognition; the offensive line. The Bison O linemen entered 2011 with a good number of questions to answer. Many close to the program openly stated that the current group, when comparing ability levels to past Bison lines, did not stack up. In August pre-season workouts, their head coach even called them the weak link of the 2011 team. After the Gering game, Gross sang the praises of center Austen Sis, guards Mitch Collicott and Trevor Gleason, tackles Will Burkert and Clint Beguin, plus tight end Matt Collicott.

"This game was won by a bunch of offensive linemen that dug in and created holes," Gross told the McCook Gazette. "We had a bunch of guys in the (defensive) box, most of those same guys, that were able to annihilate Gering's run, and then the rest becomes just playing football, line up and bat balls down and make plays, and this and that."

After the game, a vocal as always Sis, who also plays linebacker, summed up the first half of his senior year. "It's been a very good start to the year. Probably better than we thought back this summer. We expected to be good, but we also knew the first four games were going to be tough, and they have been, but we are sitting 4-0."

Adopting his head coach's motto of one game at a time, Sis assured that the early season success would not go to his or his teammate's heads. "If we lose focus, we can be beaten. We know that. We got to keep working hard and take it to teams."

Sis' teammate Schlager, agreed. Out of the showers and dressing next to Sis in the cramped visitor's locker room, the junior said, "We get big headed now, and we will find out we are not very good. But that is not going to happen. We know we got a lot of work to do, but we also know that we can be a very good team this year, maybe better than any of us had even dreamed going into the year. But we got to keep working and we will."

A Chitwood 28-yard field goal started the second half scoring for McCook, giving the Bison a 17-0 lead.

The Bison put the game away late in the third quarter when Chitwood found a wide open Jake Schlager for a short pass over the middle. The speedy junior then sprinted untouched 43 yards into the end zone.

It was not supposed to be this easy. Gering was 3-0, a mark earned against some decent competition. It would be the third 500 mile trip into the Panhandle in the first four weeks of the season for the travel weary Bison. McCook had not played up to Coach Gross' expectations the week before at Alliance and practices this week had not been sharp. A lot of red flags blowing in the September prairie winds had Gross and his staff concerned. As it turned out, the coaches did a lot of fretting for nothing. The number two ranked team in the Class B Nebraska polls, the McCook Bison, turned in their most complete performance in several years; so good in fact, that no matter how hard the coaching staff picked and dissected on the long bus ride home, they found little to criticize in the performance of their now 4-0 team.

Gross finally saw the offensive balance he had said all summer would be the strength of his team and the reason he felt, going into the season, that the Bison had state championship potential. He was clearly pleased with the 4-0 start. The offense was now clicking. But one area still concerned the coach. "We are as small as we have been ever on the line. Our guys are 200 pounds soaking wet. We get outweighed by 40-60 pounds a man almost every week. Some of that we can make up with technique. Some we can make up with schemes. Our individual technique is improving. Our team schemes are getting there. But we still are going to be small in there."

In the Aurora game, it pained Gross at halftime to admit that his over matched line could not slug it out between the tackles with the bigger and stronger Huskies and hope to win. The strategic decision made that night was to spread the splits in the offensive line and get the ball to the perimeter. This strategy, which created a change in fortune and a thrilling double over-time win in week 2 over Aurora, worked for two reasons. First, it got the ball into the hands of the fastest player on the field, Bison tailback Jake Schlager. Second, it forced the large Aurora line to sprint sideline to sideline on each play. By the games' conclusion, the bigger Aurora players were visibly fatigued and not the dominant factor they were in the first half.

Despite the success of the strategy, it ate at the core belief Gross has in offensive football: he who controls play between the tackles wins the game.

"And Crete," he said, "is bigger than Aurora." The latest Class B state wide poll: 1) Crete, 2) McCook, 3) Aurora.

"We are going to work hard the next two weeks on the power game," Gross said after the shutout of Gering. "We can run the double lead with Schlager carrying off tackle. This will complement the belly series well and gives the defense another look. If Jake gets into the secondary, watch out. Nobody around here is going to catch him. So saying we can't power it up the gut against Aurora and Crete is not right. We don't have everything in yet. When we do get that phase of the offense in, it will open the middle up some and I think our technique and schemes will make up for the bulk disadvantage we obviously do have this year."

Joan Bass quickly ducks from one classroom to the next. The "Para" professional, as her position is known, is attempting to monitor fifteen students working on a computer based program in two different computer labs. She is searching for a way to accomplish the unique American task of having herself in two places at one time. "So much for the easy paced country life in McCook, NE. Isn't that why you are here?" she asks me.

Bass is, according to McCook Head Football Coach Jeff Gross, the driving force behind the McCook Public Schools Alternative School, known as LIFT. "Pretty good name," observes Bass of the school's acronym. "Jeff came up with it himself. It stands for Learning Independently For Tomorrow."

Gross, besides wearing the hat of head football coach at MHS, is also the principal of LIFT. "I would have not gotten the football coaching job here 14 years ago if not for LIFT," Gross says. "When I applied, part of the job description for the head football coach opening here was that the coach would also organize and implement an alternative school. Two coaches before me, more qualified at the time than myself as a head coaching candidate, turned the job down because they didn't want deal with an alternative school. So, yes, I can say that I owe my football coaching success here to the kids here in the alternative school. Without them, I would have never been hired."

An alternative school is a place to educate students who have not fared well in the traditional public school setting. Many have dropped out of school, and then re-enrolled after a couple of frustrating months spent on the streets. McCook's current alternative school curriculum is all computer based. Students work at their own pace, as they earn credits they need for graduation. If successful, they will receive the same diploma as their contemporaries who have taken the more traditional path and attend the regular high school for the customary four years.

"We set this program up to make it tough," says Gross of LIFT. "We still hear it some in the community that we have watered down the curriculum just to try to get these "bad" kids out of the regular school, but that is not true. Kids who go through here must pass the same curriculum that they have at the high school. It is just another setting." Gross emphasizes the validity of his school's curriculum. "If a kid thinks he or she can screw around in regular school for seven semesters, and then come down here and do eight semesters worth of work in one nine week term so they can graduate on time, then they are going to be in for a big surprise when they get here."

The word "setting," according to Gross, is the key. "Many times regular teachers do not understand what an alternative school's role is. This is not some kind of in school suspension, where a student comes over here for punishment and then, in a few days, we send them back to the regular school."

Bass agrees that often times community members view the LIFT program as punitive in nature. "We are not here for punishing kids. Really, we are all about just the opposite. The average student when they come here is 17 years old. We have some as old as 20. We can take them, and get state funding, up until they turn 21. By law, a student can drop out in Nebraska when they are 16. We have a few under a court order that says they have to be here, but most are here because they want to be. They view us as a last chance, so they are pretty well self-motivated when they come here, or they will not last. And we have about a 75% success rate- $^3/_4$ who start our program will earn a diploma."

"Jeff has done a lot with that program," says Superintendent of Schools Grant Norgaard. "The community has not only accepted the program (LIFT), but has come to embrace it. They see the kids who were going to be dropouts and not contributing members of the community, come out of LIFT and hold jobs and make positive contributions to this community That is seen as tax money well spent, and as Superintendent, I like that."

"Our kids are not dumb kids, at all," says Bass. "The opposite is true, most are pretty smart." Adds Bass' fellow LIFT Para-professional Nicole Gomez, "Sometimes they are too smart for their own good."

Gomez brings a unique view to the staff at LIFT; she was once a student. "I screwed up my senior year," she remembers. "I attended a school nearby (to McCook) and was your typical girl on my way to a high school diploma and college. I played sports. I was in the band. I made decent grades. But about age 16 things went bad and I moved in with my great grandma, and that, as it turned out, was a mistake. I just started sleeping in, would not go to school. In February of my senior year I was kicked out of my high school for too many absences. I was only a couple of classes short of graduating. That is how dumb the poor decisions I was making were."

Drifting for a while, Gomez finally moved back in with her single mom, who had relocated to McCook. Nicole says she became a family rehab project. "My mom, my grandparents, aunts and uncles; everyone was on me with the same message: 'get back into school.' I actually enrolled at McCook High School when I was 19 and had been out for a year."

The re-entry to the structure and rigors of public high school, with rules designed for "kids" five years younger than Gomez, just didn't appeal to her. "I stayed about a week," she recalls. "I had been on my own too long."

How you going to keep them on the farm after they have seen Paris? "Exactly," said Gomez. "I went and got my GED (General Equivalency Diploma)."

A GED is better than nothing, but still, as Gomez learned after a series of dead end jobs, not as good as a high school diploma. "I really saw it as a sign of my self-worth to have a diploma and not be labeled a dropout, what with a GED or not, I was. I only needed two classes, and besides, I had decided I wanted to go to college and make something of my life."

LIFT was the perfect fit for where Gomez was in her life. "I loved it. I was not here long and I had my diploma. That short time was life changing for me. Without LIFT, without people like Jeff, I would still be a high school dropout," says Nicole. "I love my job with LIFT. I can tell kids, 'I made it and so can you.' People in town don't realize how many kids' lives have been turned around here, how many have been saved."

One grad of the program that has no hesitance in singing praises of LIFT is 27 year old McCook resident Miranda Spencer. On a hot afternoon, she took a break from helping her mother-in-law paint the inside of a house they were preparing as a new home for a set of grandparents, relocating from a life spent on a family farm. "They need to be in town," said Spencer, "Getting too old for the farm."

Sitting on the open floor between paint rollers and plastic sheeting, the dark haired young lady is more than willing to share her story. "My mom tried, tried really hard to give me a good home, but she had to work all the time and I just had too much freedom. Long story short, by 15, I was pregnant."

"Somehow Jeff found me," she recalls of her first contact with Coach Gross. "I think he had just started the program. It was a perfect fit for me. "

With a child on the way, the teenager had no illusions of living a normal high school social life. "No sports, no clubs, no social life; all the things you look forward to in high school, I had to forget about. I had responsibilities. I needed a job and I needed a high school diploma as soon as possible." LIFT fit the bill for what was a young lady with few other options. "I actually graduated a year ahead of my class," she recalled. "Jeff set it up so I could get my diploma and still take care of my responsibility as a parent. I then got my Associates Degree in two years, all while working and raising a child. I also have some hours towards a Bachelor's Degree over at Kearney State."

LIFT had given her a second chance, Miranda states, a much needed second chance. "I made some poor decisions, no question. But I was only 14, 15 years old when I did. Don't kid yourself, there are kids in McCook doing the same things I was doing 10 to 12 years ago; especially the unprotected sex. I was lucky. I found LIFT and Jeff, or maybe they found me. Doesn't matter, it was a life saver. I am remarried now, raising my son, financially responsible and I like to think a good citizen in this community. Without LIFT, I hate to think where I would be now."

Week 5 – It's all about blocking and tackling
September 23

Entering week 5, Linton knows they are in for a battle. Maple Valley is a veteran team with an explosive offense led by a battle tested and savvy quarterback. Canadian and McCook will face overmatched opponents and both head coaches know it. The hope is that complacency will not set in as both clubs need to continue to build momentum as they head into the second half of the regular season.

Clayton is not a strong team. The Yellow Jackets gave the Wildcats little resistance last season when Canadian made the drive west to Clayton. The visitors are 0-3 on the current season. The past two weeks, they have played out of state games in Kansas and Texas. In those two games they have been outscored 99-0.

McCook will return to Bison Stadium for a much needed home game after spending three of the season's first four weeks on the road. The Bison will entertain Northwest High School of Grand Island. The Vikings will travel to McCook with a 1-3 mark. A two point win over Lexington is the highlight of the year so far. Gross points out to his coaches Sunday evening that NW has been competitive in their three losses to Crete, Alliance and Aurora. Crete and Aurora are ranked one and three, respectively, in the state Class B poll. The McCook Bison are ranked second in the same poll. After Friday, the Vikings will have played all three top ranked Class B teams.

Canadian would appear to have the easiest assignment of the three, but don't tell head coach Chris Koetting that. "We are 2-2, and aren't overlooking anyone. They (Clayton) have some kids who can play and they have nothing to lose coming in here. They have a 6'6, 300 pound lineman who looks like a DI player. But with where we are right now, we just need to take care of ourselves."

Koetting saw many things to like in last week's game at Fritch. "I am telling you, Fritch has some weapons, they just haven't gotten it together yet. But we did what we wanted to do. We played fast. We ran fifty plays in the first half, which might be a record for us. It is how we have to play to be at our best."

The kicking game is still a concern. At Fritch the Cats went a dismal 0-6 on extra point kicking attempts. "We moved a new guy in there last week and he looked great in practice, I mean he was punishing the ball. Then we get over there and we are kicking into the wind in pre-game and he just falls apart." Koetting knows the lack of a kicker could be very problematic down the road. "We already have lost a game at Perryton on the kicking game. We have never had this problem before. It is all comers right now. The tryout door is open."

Jeff Gross spent the week worrying how his McCook Bison would handle the fatigue brought on by their grueling early season road schedule. Entering week 5, with a perfect 4-0 mark, his concern was with the physical toll the travel had taken on his team. For the second consecutive week, his team had arrived back in McCook after a five hour bus ride from the Western Panhandle, pulling into MHS at 4 am on Saturday.

On Monday, the practice was listless. Gross evaluated afterwards that the team was just plain tired. "And why shouldn't they be," he said. "I like our mental focus, but we just didn't have a lot of zip today." Gross had informed his team on Monday that he wanted them in bed by 10 pm each day this week. The Bison would have a much needed home game this Friday. Complicating the week would be that school would not be in session on Thursday and Friday, due to district parent/teacher conferences.

Gross viewed not having school as both a blessing and a potential concern. Young people, he well knew, were creatures of habit and the lack of school for the two days had him concerned that the normal disruption in rhythm of their daily routine could lead to a lackluster effort against Grand Island Northwest. On the other hand, his players could sleep in both days and get some much needed extra rest

At Sunday's coaches' meeting, Gross threw out his concerns to his staff. It was decided to bring the team in by 10 each morning on Thursday and Friday for extra film study. The benefit, Gross explained to his staff assembled in his family room, was not so much the film work itself, although all agreed it wouldn't hurt, but the idea behind the film session was to get his players up and moving, focused on the game. "We don't want them lying in bed all day. On the other hand the extra couple of hours of sleep on both days will help," Gross said.

After Wednesday's practice, Gross was optimistic that the bus lag from the previous two weeks' long trips had been cleared by some quality rest his team had enjoyed the past few days. The day's practice had been sharp. "We are dialed in," he told his team after practice. "I like the maturity we are showing. Our legs are back under us and we are getting everything in we need for Friday, and tonight we practiced at the level of intensity that we want to see on the field Friday night."

Gross read his team's mental state well. The Bison destroyed the Vikings of Grand Island Northwest. The defense was overwhelming in forcing turnovers that were the catalyst to a 49-0 half time lead. Jake Schlager was a dominant force on both sides of the ball, showing the large home crowd why he was receiving so much DI interest. Only a junior, Schlager knew the upcoming summer would be critical in his recruitment. "I went to a lot of camps last summer," Schlager stated. "I got my name out there." What the DI scouts found most intriguing about the Bison RB/LB was his speed. He was a legitimate and consistent 4.5 man in the 40 yard dash, the favored barometer of football people when evaluating speed. "Right now I want to concentrate on the season, but I know I can get bigger, stronger and faster in the off season." Adding bulk to his lean 175 pound frame would help on the collegiate level if Schlager was to play on the defensive side of the ball, a position most college suitors were telling him and his father Russ, the Bison defensive coordinator, would be his best collegiate fit.

"He wants to play, but right now he wants to stay focused on the season," says Russ, a former college player himself. "He will need to add some weight, but that shouldn't be a problem. He has the frame to get up over 200 pounds and still add quickness. Most are projecting him as a free safety (in college)."

At halftime, Gross was almost thoughtless on what to tell his team. He and the coaches gathered outside the team's makeshift locker room, located under the north bleachers, for longer than normal. Adjustments, when you lead 49-0? Not really. Challenge the team to improve? In what areas? The offense, due the domination of the Bison defense and special teams, had hardly been on the field. "We have no (offensive) stats this week," Gross said after the game. "How could we. We never snapped the ball." In reality, the Bison only ran 22 offensive plays in the first half, 10 in the first quarter, never having to punt. Until half way through the second quarter, and the home team already leading 42-0, McCook had not snapped the ball from farther out than the Viking's 21 yard line.

If any game of football proves that statistics are for losers, the NW game did. Throughout the first half, the defense and special teams of McCook either scored by means of forcing a turnover or a long return; or set the offense up in short field situations. To prove Gross' point about his team having "no stats" for the game, an examination of just the first quarter statistics would lead the observer to believe that McCook was probably behind. In the first quarter, McCook ran only 10 plays, compared to 22 for Northwest. The Vikings, while only having 40 total yards offense themselves, held McCook to just 54 total yards of offense. Yet the score at the end of the first 12 minutes of play was McCook 28, Northwest 0.

A bad snap deep in McCook territory on a Northwest punt after a three and out to start the game, set up McCook's first score, an 8 yard TD run by Matt Chitwood. Justin Terry recovered a NW fumble on the next possession and then took the ball 12 yards from his fullback position to the end zone for a 14-0 Bison lead. Next, Jake Schlager returned an intercepted pass for a 40 yard score. Then a poor punt from NW set the Bison up on the Viking 21 yard line. Five plays later Chitwood carried into the end zone from seven yards out. McCook now held a 28-0 lead and still 4:14 was left to play in the first quarter.

Northwest's only sustained drive took place on the next series. From the Bison 36, the visitor's faced a 4th and 15 yards to go for a first down. "Watch the out route," yelled defensive coordinator Schlager from the sidelines. Chitwood must have had his ears tuned in because he timed the throw perfectly, jumping in front of the intended receiver and sprinting 70+ yards untouched into the end zone for another Bison score. McCook 35, NW 0.

After another three and out by the Viking offense, Justin Terry took the handoff in the belly series, read perfectly by Chitwood, and sprinted straight down the middle of the field, 76 yards untouched and into the Viking end zone. The scoreboard read 42-0 McCook.

The last score of the half climaxed a rare Bison drive of any significance, a nine play, 65 yard effort, topped off by a nine yard Kyle Stewart run. Chitwood then booted his seventh consecutive PAT.

When the smoke cleared from the barrage of fireworks shot off behind the east end zone to signal another Bison score, the scoreboard told of a 49-0 halftime lead for the home team.

It was that rare moment, Gross admitted later, that the halftime atmosphere was one that a coach dreams of, almost surreal. His team was in total control. Whatever scheme or play his staff had dialed up in the first 24 minutes of play, had worked to perfection. It was obvious he and his staff were in no hurry to leave the cozy feeling of their half time huddle. The feeling of empowerment felt by the coaches was intoxicating. For this evening, at least, they were on the top of their profession, the master piece of art their team had just spun, proof of their prowess. Northwest was not that bad, but on this night at least, McCook was just that good.

It was finally decided to simply congratulate the first team and turn the second half over to the junior varsity. It was the shortest half time session of the season. "These kids are not dumb," said Gross. "What as coaches could we possible find to be upset about how we played the first half? Let's just be honest with them and move on. There will be half times to come this year when we will need to make adjustments, maybe need to jump in their grill a little, but not this one."

The Viking varsity regrouped at half time and outscored the McCook JV in the second half, 26-0. The Vikings did force one Bison punt in the second half. Because of Gross deciding to rest the varsity the entire second half, the McCook/NW final score, when posted on the many state wide scoreboards, would appear more competitive than what it was. But for those who witnessed the total domination of Gross' team in the first half, they would know that McCook was a team getting better and better each week. "We are in the hunt," said Gross on Saturday morning.

Even Northwest Coach Kevin Stein knew the final score in no way represented how totally dominant McCook had been over his team. In no way was he going to kid himself and not admit that Gross could have named the final score, so complete was the Bison performance. On his radio show after the game, Stein acknowledged the mercy Gross had shown. "I know we scored some in the second half and held them down offensively, but I also know we were not playing against their number 1s. They were a machine the first half."

As Friday night gave way to Saturday morning, several hours after his staff and other team supporters had left the after game party at his house, Gross continued to review the previous night's game film over and over, always evaluating, always looking for improvement. Gross knew his team was making marked improvement each week. On Saturday morning, while watching a downtown parade, Gross was cautious with his midseason assessment of his Bison, but the veteran mentor knew that this year's team gave him all the offensive tools he needed at his disposal to compete at the state's highest level. "I don't see a weak link. If we stay healthy, we got a chance," he said, his thoughts thinking ahead to a game in Lincoln on November 22, taking at least for a moment the liberty of breaking his own rule of "taking it one week at a time."

The Canadian matchup with the visiting Clayton Yellow Jackets proved to be the blow out that many had predicted. The visitors, from the minute they stepped off their bus, were outmanned in every facet of the game. By halftime, Canadian held the ghoulish lead of 61-0. For the second straight week, Coach Koetting sat his first team the entire second half. Final score: Canadian 67, Clayton, NM 6.

When unleashed, the Canadian juggernaut is an awesome display of offensive football. While employing the wide open spread offense and playing their trademark FAST style, the Cats can score points at a head spinning pace. Their skilled offensive players are head and shoulders over anyone the overmatched Yellow Jackets could place on the field. When Canadian is rolling, you get the sense that this offense can score at will. The Wildcat defense, the last two weeks against Fritch and Clayton, has been down-right scary. They will hit you, and you will know it. For a team that plays with such class; no showboating, no taunting, no excessive demonstrative demonstrations of selfishness; the Wildcats can still strike terror in the hearts of less skilled teams like Clayton. On several occasions, for just an instant, after another vicious hit from a human heat seeking missile wearing a Canadian jersey, one expected to see varied body parts come spinning off the unfortunate Clayton player who had the football.

Is Canadian back after two lopsided wins? Were the two last second crushing defeats of weeks 2 and 3, just what the Wildcats needed, a wake-up call? Or was the competition in weeks 4 and 5 just so substandard that any successes the last two weeks are just fool's gold; a temporary reprieve before the monstrous last six weeks of the Canadian regular season schedule?

"We will find out Friday," said Coach Koetting. "Panhandle is a traditional rival and they have a heck of a team this year. But you know what, we are playing really well."

A healthy lineup, especially at a Class 1A school like Canadian, is many times more important going into district play than the team record. If you lose the wrong player to injury, at a school with an enrollment of under 100 boys, the odds of being able to roll out a suitable spare part is slim to none. Koetting was encouraged by the news that two key players who had been out with injures would be returning to game action. Seniors Colton Cates, hurt on the first play of the first game of the season and Chance Walker, out since the second week of the season; were both cleared by doctors to play at 100% speed for Friday's game with Panhandle. Defensive Coordinator Craig Campbell called Cates his team's best linebacker. A pre-season magazine had picked him as the best defensive player in Canadian's district.

"For many people around here," said Koetting, "Panhandle is the game of the year. We will have one heck of a crowd and many will be from down there. For the old-timers, this is the bragging rights game." But other than bragging rights, the Panhandle game held no other meaning. It would be the last non-conference game on the regular season schedule of Canadian. The following Friday would see a road trip to Sunray for the opening district contest.

A recent column in the Amarillo Globe had called Class 1A- Division I District 1, where the Canadian Wildcats resided, the toughest of any in the state. Because of tradition and past successes, area followers expected the

Wildcats and Stratford to battle each year for top district honors. In 2011, the columnist pointed out, the other three schools, Sunray, West Texas and Boys Ranch; all had their strongest team in years. Sunray was the surprise team in the area and undefeated heading into the 6th week of the season.

But first up would be the visitors from Panhandle. Week 6 would be Homecoming week at Canadian High, an occurrence, due to the many hormonal distractions high school homecomings generate, a time always ripe for a potential team let down.

After the Clayton blowout win, a sense of calm prevailed in the Canadian locker room. The return of Cates and Walker buoyed the spirits of the close senior class. For Cates, his return to action was long overdue. "I just want back out there," said Cates. At first, back in week 1, it was feared on the sideline that his injury was a knee ligament tear and that Cates' senior season might be over as soon as it began. "I would die on the spot if that would have happened," he said. The four games he had been forced to miss was like a life sentence. "It has been very hard in practice and games both," Cates said in the locker room after the Clayton win. "I could have gone this week, but not 100%. We knew this should not be a tough game, so we deceived to give it one more week and then be at 100%. It don't matter who we play next week, I just want on the field."

Cates had been a tormented soul in the halftime locker room of the first game, when he feared his senior season, and his career, might be over. "Man, I was scared. I will not play again after this year," he said, his recognition that colleges seldom save scholarships for 170 pound linebackers. "I just couldn't stand the thought I was going to miss this year. I will be so excited next week to step on the field. You don't really think about missing football until you think maybe it's over. Having to sit out the last month has made me realize what I have. I am going to enjoy every last second of the rest of this season."

All week long, leading up to the critical Maple Valley game, on my blog, I had sung the praises of the Linton Lions and their well-earned reputation, built over many years, for heart stopping comebacks. Credit "The Hill" I was told.

Several area enthusiasts told me that Coach Dan Imdieke had somehow, over 35 years, convinced his players, as only the gonzo like Imdieke could, that Linton has some special gear they can reach down for when needed to pull out last second wins. Whatever the reason, you know when you play Linton, I was told by more than one area coach, you had better play all 48 minutes, "cause they don't quit." "Over the years," said another coach whose team now plays 9-man, but for many years prior had butted heads with Linton in the 11 man division, "I have seen some strange endings over there. Makes you wonder if they don't have some kind of special power for comeback wins. You say, no, that's just bull, but then you see it happen over and over, year after year. It does make you wonder, though."

On Friday of week 5, as if right on cue, the Lions delivered again; another chapter to the lore of Imdieke and his never say die teams. The last second win over a very good Maple Valley team should be talked about in the Linton coffee shops along Main Street (Highway 83) for a lot of years to come. It was that good, that unexpected, even by Linton standards. (However, by the end of the season its memory would be reduced to a footnote, not the comeback the 2011 club would be remembered for.) More importantly, according to its coach, the win probably sewed up another regional #1 seed for a Coach Imdieke team.

"We are not there yet," said an exhausted Imdieke after the game. "But this was a big step. Three more to go yet (for an undefeated regional season), but this was big tonight. We are in the driver's seat now (both figuratively and literally as Imdieke still had to drive the bus back to Linton). If we do get beat in these last three games, we have no one to blame but ourselves."

Maple Valley entered the game as the state's 4th ranked team. Linton was unranked. Imdieke had mentioned this slight to his players during the week several times. "We can go up there and play loose. We got nothing to lose," he stated to his team at Tuesday's practice. "We are going to let it all hang out and just have fun," he told a fellow teacher at school on Wednesday.

The team during the week was focused, which pleased the coach to no end. Imdieke was at times, during the early season, frustrated over what he saw as a lack of senior leadership. "They don't lead, they don't follow; I am not sure what this bunch does," he commented after one early season practice that had not lived up to his expectations.

Now, with the season more than one half over, he realized that his 4-1 team could easily be 1-4. The evaluation by Imdieke of the character of his team was evolving to the positive. "We do not have vocal leaders but they have played to the max three times this year with the game on the line. We have had 4th quarter comebacks to win each one. This group responds, and as a coach you appreciate the mental toughness it takes to do that."

Quarterback Tanner Purintun was the team's most obvious physical talent. His ability to use his strength and speed had saved the Lions at Maple Valley. Down 11 with six minutes remaining in the game, Purintun's 80 yard touchdown pass to fellow senior Jayden Gross was the play that turned the game around. As his pass protection broke down, Purintun had scrambled to his left, back to his right, while breaking several tackles in the process, before unloading a 60 yard in the air bomb. Gross, who had broken off his pattern when he saw his friend and QB in trouble, hauled in the perfect spiral and showed his own athleticism by out sprinting the MV defensive backs the last 20 yards into the end zone.

Purintun is a soft spoken but well-mannered young man. "I don't do a lot of yelling and cheering," he said after his heroics at Maple Valley. "I am not a cheerleader. I do my job and expect everyone else to do theirs. I try not to get too excited; stay calm and in control. I try to send that message to the team. We don't panic."

Linton had taken a 6-0 lead on an earlier 20-yard pass play from Purintun to Gross. Maple Valley scored on both of its next two possessions, the second score set up by a rare Linton turnover. A fumbled kickoff gave the home team a short field to work on.

Linton would take lead in this see saw battle 13-12, on its next possession. A Purintun interception return placed the ball inside the Falcons five yard line. From the five, Tailback Cody Sehn punched the ball into the end zone.

Maple Valley responded to the Lion score with another touchdown pass of its own, this one from 21 yards out. Maple Valley went to the locker room with a 19-13 halftime lead.

The Linton coaches were calm at the half. "We can move the ball," said Imdieke. "We can run it or throw it. We got to shut down their big play on defense. (Quarterback) Lund is picking us apart. We got to get pressure on him," Imdieke told his staff at the break. He then addressed his team, his tone still calm. "We got to tackle better," he said. "They can't keep getting those long runs off missed tackles. If we don't stop that, we can't beat them. But we will stop it and don't forget we had a great week of work in practice. We are in better shape. Get us to the 4th quarter and we will see what happens."

A scoreless third quarter, with both teams bogged down in the middle of the field, set the table for the latest in a long line of Linton cardiac comebacks.

In the early minutes of the 4th quarter, Maple Valley seemed to take control of the game by scoring with a QB Lund one yard sneak. "He gave us fits all night," Imdieke said after the game. "We had no answer for him. He is a very good player."

The foiled extra point attempt by the Falcons after taking the 25-13 would prove to be the game changer. Linton blocked the kick and Lund suffered what appeared to be a concussion on the play. The key cog of the Maple Valley offense would not return to the game.

Still, 6:52 was all the time the scoreboard clock allotted Linton, a team trailing by two scores. "Come on men," the always positive Imdieke implored his team. "Two scores, that is all we need, and lots of time to get em."

The coach then got the big play he had been asking for all night, as Purintun and Gross hooked up on their 80 yard scoring pass. But Linton still needed one more score. They also needed the ball back.

Maple Valley drove the ball on the ensuing kickoff into Linton territory and appeared to be threatening to run out the clock. But a defense that had carried the Lions throughout the early season bowed its neck one more time and forced a Falcon punt.

Imdieke had begged all half for a "big play and a break." The Purintun to Gross TD pass had given the Lions the big play and now Maple Valley provided the break. A bad snap on the 4th down punt gave the ball to the Lions at their own 44 yard line.

Purintun once again used his ability to scramble to turn a broken play into a big Linton gainer. He scrambled from sideline to sideline, narrowly avoiding several potential tacklers and found an open Al Gefroh for a 38 yard gain to the home team's 18 yard line. Sehn then finalized the comeback with an 18 yard TD run on the next play, giving Linton a 26-25 lead with two minutes to play. Forced to go with a backup QB, the first Maple Valley pass was intercepted by the hero of the latest of Linton Lion improbable comeback, Tanner Purintun.

Amazingly, even when down by 12 points to a very good Maple Valley team, on the road and half of the fourth quarter gone, there never was a sense of panic on the sideline. Coach Imdieke had pointed out entering the 4th quarter that the Maple Valley tank was empty, their players tired. "Look at em bent over sucking air," he told those on the sideline to start the 4th quarter.

"I felt all along that we could get them if we just stayed close enough," said the coach. "I was still confident and I hope that carries over to the kids. We talk all the time that if we outwork the other team during the week, that the 4th quarter is ours. We did have a great week of practice leading up to this game and I think that had our kids confident. And Tanner and Jayden made a heck of a play."

The Lions had run the ball well all evening and with only four minutes left in the game, began a confident march to the winning score. Coach Imdieke had told his signal caller, as he sent him out on the field for the game deciding drive, "Be calm. We can run it. If we don't stop ourselves, we will score. We got 'em right where we want 'em. Be calm."

"This one was fun," said an elated Imdieke after the game. "I really felt we outplayed them. We would move the ball and then have a sack or a penalty set us back. We just needed a big play and a break and we got both with the 80 yard pass and then the bad snap on their punt to set up our last touchdown."

"This is really fun," concluded the coach as he walked to the bus to drive his cheering team home. A player asked, "Did you think we could do it, coach?" Imdieke gave the same answer he has for 35 years when asked if he expected his team to accomplish the unexpected. "You betcha."

Add another chapter to the book on heroic Linton comebacks, additional lore for the growing legend of The Hill.

Homecoming

I have a friend, whom by any social measurement of her life's accomplishments, would be labeled an unqualified success. Still a few years on the sunny side of 40, she can look back at a life that has displayed across the board achievement. In particular, her school girl days are a resume that would make anyone jealous. A widely decorated athlete and an accomplished scholar, she won it all. All-state on the courts and track, combined with top academic standing in her class, she was the quintessential golden girl every parent dreams of.

One night, in a rare moment of vulnerability – perhaps due to inhibitions loosened by the lubrication of a few malt beverages - she made a startling revelation to me about herself. All of her high school awards and accomplishments, she told me in a whisper, she would have gladly traded for the one honor that eluded her in her high school days of glory. "I always wanted to be Homecoming Queen, ever since I was a little girl" she admitted in a sad voice, little tempered by the passing of 20 years, "I dreamed about it, but I didn't make it. I would gladly have traded every other honor I won in high school to just be Homecoming Queen."

The fall celebration of football homecoming in small town high schools across this vast nation is a community rite of passage and the social event of the school year. It is a time of not only celebration, but of amazing transformation. A farm wagon, used 364 days a year for the mundane chore of hauling hay, on one magic Friday night each fall, becomes –with the generous application of crepe paper - a throne worthy of royalty, a setting for the Queen and her court. A sleepy town square, dusty and empty on most days, is now a "parade route," lined with the town's young and old; those who dream of what will be and those who remember what once was.

The highlight of the week's long celebration, the one moment no one will miss, and the most breathtaking of transformations for the town to witness, occurs during the halftime introduction of the Homecoming Queen candidates. Girls who come to school each day sans makeup, dressed in their normal attire of jeans and tee shirts, or after school in their volleyball practice gear, now take the spotlight. Wow. They are, for that one shining night at least, the best the town has to offer, the fairest maidens in the land. Dressed in total splendor, hair done just right, evening dresses, elaborate makeup and stylish shoes; no expense spared, they command attention. A proud but nervous dad, searching but failing to find the right words to confront what he has long tried to ignore; the reality of his little girl maturing into a woman, will awkwardly offer, "Cleans up nicely, don't she?"

Linton, ND High School crowned its 2011 Homecoming Queen at halftime of the football game on Friday, September 9. The protocol for selecting the Queen varies slightly from school to school, but Linton's method is a very common process found at schools around the country. The Senior, Junior, Sophomore and Freshman classes, plus the athletic and the co-curricular clubs, each choose a candidate from the girls in the senior class; a total of six nominees. The entire student body will then vote for their choice for Homecoming Queen.

The winner in Linton for this year is Miss Samantha Gross, daughter of Sam and Missy Gross. She has found growing up in the small North Dakota town to be a positive experience and would like to raise her family, someday, in a similar nurturing environment. Her large family has deep roots in the area, her father is a second generation farmer and her mother works at the local medical clinic. Samantha is also a valued member of the Lion's volleyball team, who finished last season as the state North Dakota Class B runner-up.

In Canadian, TX, each class, freshman through juniors, choose one of the girls from their class to be a maid of the court. The underclass girls are not eligible for the Queen selection, which must go to a senior. The senior class will then vote for their choice. The top three vote getters will form the Queen's court, with the top vote getter chosen as Queen. The 2011 Homecoming Queen for Canadian High School is Ms. Shelby Paul. Members of her court were fellow senior nominees Carley Knight and Autumn Childester. A class officer for four years, Shelby is also a key contributing member of the basketball and tennis teams. After graduation, she intends to pursue a degree in nursing at Wayland Baptist University.

In McCook, NE; the senior Homecoming Queen candidates were Kalie Kennedy, Amanda Fuchuck, Kelsey Collicott, Elizabeth Wilcox, Betsey Hardin and Emily Tolliver. The MHS student body voted on Friday for their choice of Queen candidates, with the winner announced on the field, in a short ceremony after the completion of that evening's game. A big change in the format at McCook for this fall was the moving of the dance from Friday night after the game to Saturday evening.

The 2011 Homecoming Queen of McCook High School was Ms. Amanda Fuchuck.

Chapter 7

October: Jockeying for Position
Weeks 6-10

People stress the violence. That's the smallest part of it. Football is brutal only from a distance. In the middle of it there's calm, a tranquility. The players accept pain. There's a sense of order even at the end of a running play with bodies strewn everywhere. When the systems interlock, there's a satisfaction to the game that can't be duplicated. There's a harmony. ***Don Delillo***

I just wrap my arms around the whole backfield and peel 'em, one by one, until I get to the ball carrier. Him I keep.
Gene "Big Daddy" Lipscomb

If you see a defensive team with dirt and mud on their backs, they've had a bad day. ***John Madden***

Week 6 - A Blitzkrieg
September 30

Canadian will spend the week preparing for a Friday night showdown with their traditional rival, Panhandle. The game will climax homecoming week at Canadian. The Panthers of Panhandle have been one of the area's surprise teams this fall. Coming off 2010's disappointing two win season, not much was known about what to expect in 2011. Panhandle will march into Canadian Friday night, along with their expected large entourage of fans, sporting a 4-1 mark. Last Friday evening, they defeated Canadian district foe Boys Ranch, 21-19. Although they will be led by a sophomore quarterback, Tyler Hall, who started as a freshman, this is an experienced, but still a young team. Running back Shane Smith is a senior leader on a roster dominated by underclassmen.

Linton and McCook both, on paper, seem to have easier week 6 draws. The Bison of McCook will be home for the second consecutive week and will host a one win Sidney team. It is hard to believe that McCook can play much better than they did against Gering two weeks ago and in the first half against Grand Island Northwest the past Friday. For those six consecutive quarters of play, the Bison held a scoring edge of 80-0.

Linton will travel to Kidder County to take on the one win Pirates. Coach Imdieke would never admit it, but his Lions all but wrapped up the regional title last week with a 26-25 comeback road win over the state's 4th ranked team, Maple Valley. This week's opponent, Kidder County, has made the move this year from the nine man ranks to eleven man, and the transition has had its rough moments. Linton will attempt on Friday night to inflict a few more growing pains on the Pirates.

Football coaches have to have something to worry about. It is in their nature. But when you lead 61-0 at halftime, such as the case for Canadian Wildcat coach Chris Koetting in his team's week 5 home encounter with Clayton, NM, what do you fret about?

"Our extra point kicking has me at a loss," he said Monday. "We have always had someone step up and fill that role. Last year our kicker was 84-88 and he never kicked before his senior year. But this year...," Koetting shook his head in frustration as his thoughts tailed off.

The Canadian PAT kicking results of last week – 4 out of 7 - by the winner of the weekly kicking sweepstakes contest, Salvador Escamilla, was a huge improvement over the 0-6 performance of the previous week against Fritch. "Big Sal gets another chance his week," said Koetting, after Wednesday's practice.

His newly claimed kicking throne aside, Escamilla is perhaps the Wildcat's most formidable lineman. A 6'1, 250 senior, Salvador has attended the Canadian schools since half way through his kindergarten year. Amazingly, he never played football until his sophomore year of high school. "I had to have help and be taught just how to put on my pads. I knew nothing," Escamilla now admits. "But everyone here has been so helpful to me. I am so glad I got the chance to play."

A young man who tips the scales at 250 pounds as a freshman walking the hallways of Canadian High School and is not out for football in a school where football is king? "The coaches were always on me to come out, but my parents didn't want me to play. I had a bad accident to my leg when I was little and they were afraid I would hurt it again."

Salvador gives the majority of credit for his meteorically rapid development as a football player to former teammate and all-state Canadian lineman Kyle Alexander. "He got me in the weight room in the off-season of my freshman year and he really made me work." With Alexander, who is now a cadet and freshman football player at the United States Military Academy Prep School in West Point, NY, serving as the task master, Escamilla's football stock soared. "I weighed the same back then as I do now," Salvador says. "But back then I was fat. I am not fat now."

Escamilla would like to continue his development as a football player somewhere in college next year. The coaching staff feels he is still a work in progress and will become a more complete player as experience helps him grow into the game.

Have mom and dad changed their mind about football, the muscular lineman (and now kicker) was asked? "Oh yeah, they come to every game. They are learning. They grew up in Mexico and know nothing about football. When I get home from the game now, they ask me all kinds of questions about why this and why that."

Escamilla has a nine year old brother. Will he wait until he gets to his sophomore year to put on the pads for the Wildcats? "No way," says Escamilla with a wide grin. "He is already playing. You just wait until he gets to high school. Now he is going to be good!"

Chris Koetting dragged his computer mouse down the menu projected on the large screen attached to the wall in the coaches' meeting room. It is 7 pm on Wednesday and the last long practice before the Panhandle game is in the books. "Let me see if I can find this play," says Koetting.

When it comes to the latest in media technology in the world of high school football, Canadian High School is in the front of the line. Every game is filmed from two angles, from the line of scrimmage and from the end zone. Computer software the district has purchased then sorts each play so that a click of Koetting's computer mouse will show the play back to back from each angle. The coach has stated many times that the computer programs the Wildcats utilize are invaluable as he prepares his team for the weekly wars of Texas high school football.

"It is the time factor," he relays. "With this program, we can have everything ready to go by Monday morning. We have the whole game plan for that week's opponent, plus we have broken down our previous game, graded each of our players on every play and go over that with the team on Monday."

Koetting wants to show me one particular play from last year's thrilling last second win over Albany in the state quarterfinals. "Here it is," he says," you are going to love this." Canadian is driving to the red zone in a tie game. The Wildcats have reached Albany's 20 yard line, but only 12 second remains in regulation time. Koetting decides to take one last shot at the end zone. If that fails, he will then send out his field goal team to attempt a winning kick. "On that last drive, that was the loudest crowd I have ever heard at a high school football game. The whole stadium was in a frenzy," Koetting tells me.

Braden Hudson lays a perfect pass to the back left corner of the end zone where Canadian receiver Jacob Ramirez makes a game winning over the shoulder catch. Koetting is however not focusing on the clutch throw and catch. He barks, "watch the corner of the screen."

As the official in the back of the end zone raises his arms to signal touchdown, a huge man, dressed in Canadian school colors, explodes from the darkness to the middle of the end zone, where he joins in with the on-field celebrating Wildcats. As he repeatedly leaps in the air - no small task for a man whose shoulders appear to be as wide as the goal posts - he triumphantly punches the air with both fists flying. "That," said Koetting, "is how I will always remember Kirk Morrow."

The father of Wildcat star senior lineman, Ty Morrow, Kirk died in a car accident three weeks ago. Morrow was a single parent raising two sons. His house became the favorite hangout for youngest son Ty and his friends. "If we wanted to know where our kids where," Isaac Lewis' dad Micah told me, "we just drove by Kirk's house." For the current group of Senior Canadian players, when they began with organized football in the 5th grade, Kirk was their first coach. For many, he was also a second father figure.

"It did help," Ty says in a low voice when recalling that tragic afternoon, "that I got to the hospital to say goodbye. The nurses said Dad kept asking, 'how far away are they.' I think he was just hanging on, waiting for me to get there. His heart stopped five minutes after I got there."

Two days after his death, a dispirited Canadian team lost on the road to Perryton, 33-32, on a last second field goal. Not playing the game was never even considered. Kirk would not have liked that, said Koetting. The next day, an emotionally spent Canadian team buried Kirk Morrow.

Ty says that his father's death had yet to set in, admitting he still to some degree is in denial. "It is the little things," he said after Wednesday's practice. "My uncle lives in San Angelo and he called me at lunch today to say he had talked to the coach at Angelo State and they really liked the film on me that Coach Koetting sent them. I was really excited. The first thing I thought was, 'I got to call my Dad and tell him.'"

The low point for Ty, he says, was after the Perryton game and the night before his dad's funeral. "My teammates were crushed after we lost that game. They felt like they had let dad down, that they didn't honor him as they should have because we lost. My Uncle Dave came into talk to the team and he told us not to let my dad's death be a burden we had to live up to, but an inspiration to be the best team we can be, win or lose. That helped."

Morrow says that football has been a great release for him and he is grateful that the Canadian community has shown such a great out pouring of support. "I couldn't go on without all the help," he says.

The players have dedicated the remainder of the season to Kirk Morrow's memory. They wear his name printed under their game jerseys. "Even winning a state championship is not going to bring my dad back," says Ty. "But we all want to show him that he has inspired us to play as hard as we can. That is all he would ask, if he was here."

One of Kirk Morrow's favorite duties was carrying the Canadian Wildcat flag for pre-game introductions. As the team lined up, ready to storm the field, Morrow would hand over the flag to a captain, to carry into battle. The day of the Perryton game that same flag had to be retrieved from Kirk Morrow's mangled pickup truck.

Coach Koetting starts off each Friday during the season with a before school meeting with the Wildcat 8th grade team. The young Cats had the night before destroyed a previously undefeated Panhandle 8th grade team, 58-20. Often times, with an 8th grade team, such a scoring explosion in an indication of one athlete, often older and/or more mature for his age than the normal 8th grader, who can singularly dominate a game. Of course, when the other athletes, over the next few years, catch up physically, the dominant 8th grader will come back to the pack as he moves through the high school ranks.

That is not the case with the Canadian 8th graders. "We run the spread offense and we do just that, we spread it around," said Koetting. "The 8th grade has two very good quarterbacks. We had one already here that is pretty darn good and then this summer we had another move in. I told the coaches to prepare them both as quarterbacks, give them equal time. You can never have too many quarterbacks," Koetting says. I ask if we could see a signal caller controversy in the fall of 2014. "Wouldn't be a bad problem to have," he says with a smile. "They are both pretty good."

The JV Wildcats have not lost a game in over two years. Playing after the 8th grade, the Junior Varsity destroyed the previous night what was felt by many area observers to be a pretty good Panhandle team, 58-14. "I would take 58 tonight in the varsity game, that is for sure," a laughing Koetting stated while sitting in his office after his talk with the 8th grade. "Our JV coaches have done a great job. We gutted them, we pulled their QB, best lineman and best receiver up to the varsity, and yet they just seem to plug someone else in and keep rolling."

Texas has a unique rule in that a player can only participate in one football game a week. Most states limit participation to a set number of quarters a player can participate in during a calendar week. Six seems to be the most common, but some allow eight. With this system, a younger player can get the game experience as a regular on the sub-varsity team, but still fill the role of a back-up or special team's player on the varsity.

In Canadian, since the JV and freshman games are always played on Thursday, the day before the varsity game, the coaches are often placed in the precarious position of not knowing who to commit to the JV and who to save as a backup for the Friday night varsity game. There is always a good chance that, as a backup, a player will not be needed in the Friday varsity game. But injuries in a football game cannot be predicted and no varsity coach wants to be caught shorthanded on Friday night because of a key back up's non availability, due to participation in a sub varsity game played earlier in the week.

Koetting has just such a dilemma this season. His sophomore quarterback, Ben Arbuckle, looks like a star in the making. He is tall, 6'2", and has a very strong and accurate arm. He played in the first two JV games this fall, but since week 3 has dressed as the backup on the varsity, insurance for arguably the best Class 1A QB in the state, Canadian senior Braden Hudson.

"We finally got to the point that we just didn't feel comfortable with our early season backup QB situation. If Braden would happen to go down early in a game, we would have been in bad shape," Koetting said.

The insurance of a strong back up, especially as the season progresses and district games begin, Koetting notes, becomes even more crucial. "I worry not only about the number of snaps Ben gets in a varsity game," says Koetting, "but also the quality of those snaps. Last week was a good example. Ben played the whole second half, but we are up 61-0 at the half. We are not going to try and embarrass anyone, so Ben only threw it four times in the second half, and that bothers me. But what bothers me more would be to not have a quality backup at a position that is so critical to our scheme."

Veteran assistant coach and defensive coordinator Craig Campbell is known for his dry wit and pragmatic view. "You know," when the discussion on the wisdom of Texas' one game a week rule was brought up for discussion in the coaches' office, "the rule is not going to change. Everyone has to play by it, so no one gets an advantage. What it does do is give a whole bunch of kids on the JV reps they wouldn't be getting if the varsity backups were down there. So, next year we got more depth on the varsity," he concluded.

Braden Hudson had injured his right hand at practice on Monday of week 6 when he inadvertently hit his throwing hand on a teammate's helmet. Koetting saw the whole season pass right before his eyes. The all-state quarterback, if his throwing hand was broken, would leave a void difficult for Koetting to fill. By Friday morning, sitting in Koetting office, Hudson was more than happy to show everyone how his finger had healed. "No swelling, no pain," said the QB, "I am ready to go." As a precaution, Koetting had not allowed Braden to throw any passes in practice. "I might need to throw a little extra in warm up, but believe me," the young man told those assembled in Koetting's office, "I am ready."

Halfway through his senior season, Hudson was still troubled by the five interception game he had suffered in Week 2 at Meade, KS. "They only rushed three and left eight in the box and I made too many bad reads. Their front three were pretty good, but we have made a lot of gains in the last two weeks with our pass blocking. We are coming on."

Both Koetting and Hudson agreed that the offense was trying to do too much, too early in the season. "Our skilled people," said the coach, "were very experienced and were ready for everything we had put in. But our young line really struggled. As quick as our passing game is, we shouldn't have sacks. We have had some years where we went three straight games with no sacks. But it was problem early and it contributed to Braden throwing more interceptions than normal."

Joining Hudson in the Friday morning conference was the second preseason poster boy of the high octane passing game of the Canadian Wildcats, senior receiver Isaac Lewis. He also graded the first half performance of his team with a mixed evaluation. "We spread the ball around so well," he said, "that trying to just focus on me is a mistake. My numbers are down some and that is from getting more attention this year because of my numbers last year, but we have a lot of football yet to play. We want to be in Cowboy Stadium (site of the state championship game) in December. That is more important to me right now than any personal stats."

Lewis has longed dreamed of attending Texas Tech and playing for the Red Raiders. The Big 12 member's wide open passing game fits the style Lewis has found so appealing at Canadian. "My size has been a concern to some scouts. But Tech has had players similar to me- small (size) and from a small school, (who) will go to Tech and do well. That is my plan now, anyway." If a Tech football career does not pan out, Lewis will more than likely end his career on the high school level. "Then I would probably just go to school. I don't have to play football next year to be happy, but Tech would be special."

Hudson, although on the surface will deny any such concerns, has not seen the avalanche of interest by college suitors lining up to bid for his quarterback skills. After such a great junior year as he had recorded, his hopes were that he would see some Division I interest. That has not as yet happened. "I have heard from a couple of D II schools in Colorado and from Tarleton State here (Texas). I made some visits over the summer."

Although not stated, Hudson knows his lack of height (5'10"), more than the slow statistical start of his senior year- in particular the 5 interception game the second week of the season against Meade, KS – has hurt his stock in the eyes of colleges coaches.

Hudson, who holds the respect of the Canadian community as much for his off the field reputation as he does for the touchdown passes he throws each Friday night, is a mature young man. He is the type a high school girl's parents would love to have over for Sunday dinner. "He is a very good player to interview," says Wesley Hardin, the radio announcer for the Canadian games. "He is well spoken and comes across as a very confident, but also a very humble young man."

His father is the boys' basketball coach at Canadian High School. His mother is a former basketball coach who now is in charge of the dyslexia department in the Canadian schools' special education program. Braden has been raised around athletics and knows what to say and when to speak. "Right now I am feeling good. I am not worried about college until after the season. Our focus right now is that we want to be on the turf at Cowboys Stadium in December. But we got to earn it."

The Schlager family and the Cherry family are bound together tightly by both the local farm economy and McCook Bison football. Both have junior sons who are mainstays on the football team. Jake Schlager is the starting tailback and outside linebacker, while Austin plays wide receiver and defensive back. He is also the quarterback in waiting as he is heir apparent next year to the position held in 2011 by Senior Matt Chitwood. Schlager's dad, Russ, is the Bison Defensive Coordinator.

The elder Schlager has been coaching at McCook since relocating back to the area from Colorado twelve years ago. For the last five years he has held the coordinator's slot for the Bison defense. He had seven previous years of coaching in Colorado, where he made his living in the restaurant business. After growing up in Sacramento, CA; his parents decided to return to their roots and moved the family for Schlager's junior and senior years of high school to nearby Culbertson, NE. After high school, he played football and graduated from Fort Lewis College in Colorado. Schlager's wife is from McCook and teaches at the Junior High. Besides Jake, the couple has two other sons' 14 year old Joe and 12 year old Zach.

When the Schlagers made the decision to move back to McCook, Russ decided to sell his interests in the restaurant business and use the proceeds to buy grazing land for the cattle business he intended to start. Today he runs around 900 cattle on 5,800 combined acres of pasture land he owns and rents. "Most of our profit comes from the yearlings we sell," Schlager explains. "The normal cycle includes 6 months of grazing on pasture land, three months on corn stalks and three months being hand fed grain."

A weak overseas market, coupled with a strong US dollar, has made both farming and ranching up and down Highway 83 for the last few years profitable. The Northern High Plains have been spared the draught that has ravaged the southern region. The abundant rain fall has produced bumper crops of grain from Kansas to the Canadian border. Schlager buys much of the feed needed for his yearlings to conclude the 12 month cycle before he ships the calves to market. He says all is not as rosy as it might first appear. "Grain prices, due to supply and demand, are significantly higher this year. I raise some of my own hay, but most of what we feed we buy. So our costs are going up. But still, all and all, the last couple of years have been good financial times for most of us around here," Schlager states.

The agriculture economy, so important to the financial stability of the McCook area, has been enhanced by new technology, which Schlager says allows locals to stay ahead of the curve. "You have to change with the times. Everything now is so equipment based that we are in constant need of growth. The improved technology allows for increased production, which increases the value of the land. For an operation like mine, which depends on renting large acreage, which drives up another area of our costs; the rent we pay for pasture."

Schlager explains one area he is researching as a means of diversifying and growing his business; breeding. "It is an area of potential growth that I can see being very profitable around here, if you get in early and you are smart about how you use the technology to control the process."

The Cherry family interest is on the economic end that Schlager says now drives the industry, equipment sales. After spending many years employed by the city of McCook, nine years ago Pat Cherry made the decision to leave the safety of a public sector job and cast his lot in sales as a John Deer sales representative. "We spent a lot of late nights discussing the risks against the potential awards," Pat recalls. He and his wife Melanie finally decided the gamble was worth the risk and the timing for the family has proved to be perfect. "The farm economy has really boomed around here and we got in right at the right time," Pat says.

Happily for the Cherrys, selling on commission for 13 state wide franchises that encompass Pat's territory during the recent boom years has proved to be a lucrative venture. "There are always going be up and down years in the farming industry," he says. "But the techniques that farmers use today have improved so much, the land is always going to be profitable. You can't control the weather, that is for sure, but we are still a dry land farming area. We have learned how to use what natural resources we have to maximize the productivity of the land. For example, farmers don't till the ground like they use to. That is why selling sprayers have become so profitable. Also, the government price support programs are a key. It takes some of the gamble out of the business. This country cannot afford to let the farming industry go bad. The ones who are being forced out today are the small operations. The land is worth too much to the big operations that they make offers the little guy can't turn down. Most of the small family farms that have shut down in the area have sold their land for a good price. It is not like the days of the Dust Bowl when broken families were forced off the family farm with nothing to show for it."

The Cherrys are deeply invested in the recent success of the Bison football program. Their oldest son Josh was a quarterback on some very could McCook teams from 2003-2005. After graduation, Josh migrated to Kansas State University where he was the Wildcats number 1 placekicker for four years, concluding an outstanding career in 2010. Amazingly his parents, in four years, missed only one of Josh's college games, both home and away. "We thought he was going to red shirt that first year," his dad recalls, "so even though he traveled with the team, we didn't expect him to play. They had a senior kicker ahead of him and what are the odds of a kicker getting hurt? The first game of the year was at Fresno State and the kicker gets a concussion on a kickoff and Josh is thrown in. We watched it on TV."

Like Wally Pip leaving the Yankees starting lineup with a headache, giving a young Lou Gehrig a chance to play first base, a position he then stayed at for 2,130 straight games; Cherry never was unseated by the former kicking incumbent. "We never missed another game," says Melanie. "Even the bowl games, we saw them all. It took a lot of planning and a lot of late night drives to the airport in Denver to catch a flight to away games, but we managed. We made some great trips and have some great memories. It was fun."

Mrs. Cherry works in a local bank. She sees, firsthand, the advantages of life in a small town. "The bank being local is very important. We can make decisions that are not always what a corporate outsider would consider sound. We work with people all the time to restructure payments, if that is what we need to do. I can't recall any foreclosures by our bank on someone's home. It is rare that we even ever have to reprocess a car. We make smart loans, but still things can happen that can throw the best families into trouble. These people are our neighbors. When the person involved is someone you know, it becomes more than just a business decision, it makes us go that extra mile to help them. That wouldn't happen in the big city."

It is time for a couple of quick history lessons. # 1: On September 1, 1939, Adolph Hitler unleashed his war machine on the world with an invasion of the independent nation of Poland. A startled and suddenly terrified world watched as Hitler's powerful military juggernaut executed a new strategy of war; Blitzkrieg. Translated, lightning war. When perceived world military powers France and England came to the aid of their ally Poland, Hitler turned his armies east and invaded France. Spearheaded by his Panzer tank divisions, and backed by the German Air Force, the Luftwaffe; the new war making technology that Germany now had perfected was no match for the British and French militaries, both still vested in outdated WW I military equipment and methods.

The Maginot Line, a system of fortified French trenches on the common French and German border, was breached by Hitler's tank divisions in days. For 20 years, this line of defense was the pride of the French military, giving its citizens a sense of security against their vanquished WW I foe, the Germans. When Hitler's mechanized Panzers, followed by German infantry divisions, swatted aside the Maginot Line like a fly, the rout was on. Hitler literally drove the French and British armies into the Atlantic Ocean, climaxing with the desperate evacuation across the English Channel of the survivors from the French port of Dunkirk. For the next four years, Hitler would have total control of the main European continent, and as history has recorded, come so ever dangerously close to conquering the world.

Blitzkrieg is the best description of the 12 minutes it took on Friday night for Canadian to blow away Panhandle High. Using the newest in modern football offense- the spread- to perfection, the Wildcats were unstoppable. When the smoke cleared, a 14-7 Canadian lead had in a mere 12 minutes of the first half been stretched to 48 to 7.

#2: From the single wing to the spread, football is a game that can trace its origins to the English sport of rugby. Tight formations and brutal force were the traits needed to be successful in the late 19th century early days of American Football. As the game evolved, offenses began to spread out and an emphasis was placed on speed, quickness and deception. A very predictable pattern in coaching developed. High school football coaches were almost always several years behind their college counterparts as they emulated the newest and most successful offensive strategic innovations being put on Saturday afternoon display at the great collegiate stadiums around the nation.

In the early years of the 20th century, legendary coach Pop Warner developed and fine-tuned the single wing. The name for the formation was derived by the alignment of the four backs, with the tail back five yards directly behind the center and the other three backs aligned on the same side of the center, in a wing between the guard and end line positions. The center would directly snap the ball to the tailback. The tailback would then pass, run or hand the ball off to one of the other three backs. Fakes and deception were critical to keeping the defense off balance.

In the 1920's, Notre Dame, under the leadership of Knute Rockne, took the single wing principles of timing and deception to a new level, developing what became known as the Notre Dame box shift. The backs would be put into movement slightly ahead of the snap of the ball and the precision of the backfield movements made the offense almost impossible to stop. So effective were the Irish with their shift, that overmatched opponents demanded rule changes to counteract the offense's deadly efficiency. Much as the three second and goaltending rules were implemented in basketball to offset the 1950's domination of Wilt Chamberlin, the rules of football were changed to do what no defense could, stymie the Notre Dame box shift. A rule made it mandatory that backs must be set for at least one second before the ball is snapped. With a later modification that allows for one back to be in motion parallel to the line of scrimmage before the ball is snapped, this same rule is still on the books today.

In the 1930's, the next major formation innovation was developed by University of Chicago and later Stanford University head coach Clark Shaughnessy, considered the father of the T- Formation. Shaughnessy brought the quarterback up under center to take the snap from the center directly. A rule change in 1933 helped the popularity of the T-formation. A forward pass could now be thrown anywhere behind the line of scrimmage, instead of only between the ends as had been the previous rule. By 1953, the last team in the NFL to run the single wing, the Pittsburg Steelers, had converted to the T.

In the late 1960's, the University of Texas introduced the wishbone formation. The "Bone" moved the full back up from the T-formation to only a yard behind the quarterback. The QB would then have three options of what to do with the ball: hand it to the full back on a quick dive play, run the ball himself around end or pitch to a trailing halfback. This "triple option" proved lethal for nearly twenty years. By the early 1970's almost all of the great coaches of the college game had embraced the wishbone. Bear Bryant at Alabama, Daryl Royal of Texas, Woody Hayes at Ohio State and Lou Holtz at first Arkansas and later at the University of Notre Dame; won numerous national championships riding the triple option wishbone offense.

Limitations, more so than weaknesses, of the wishbone eventually were identified by defensive coaches. The wishbone quarterback would take a terrible beating as he would be hit by the defensive end every time he slid down the line of scrimmage. In theory, the defensive end was the man that the quarterback would option and was therefore always left unblocked. This allowed the defensive end a free and unabated shot at the quarterback on every option play. Another major detraction of the wishbone was that it made the forward pass almost non-existent in a team's offensive arsenal and therefore made it very difficult for a team to comeback from a deficit. Finally, the wishbone was a high risk offense with so many risky pitches. The result was a large number of fumbles, making developing consistency on offensive an allusive accomplishment. By the mid 1990's, the wishbone had all but disappeared from the college football landscape.

The latest offensive formation to ripple down to the high school level is the spread. It is an off-shoot of the NFL's West Coast offense perfected in the late 80's and early 90's by Bill Walsh, with assistance from quarterback Joe Montana and the San Francisco 49ers. The strategy was based on a series of short, high percentage passes. The quarterback was given great latitude in reading the defense, both before and after the snap of the ball, and making quick decisions based upon defensive responses to the patterns being run by receivers. This offense often initiated the play from the shotgun formation, moving the quarterback out from under center, five yards off the line of scrimmage, in order to take a direct snap from the center. The shotgun allowed the quarterback of less stature – Montana stood barely 6 foot tall – to be more effective through improved sight lines in seeing over large onrushing lineman.

Many football historians note the similarities between the single wing and the spread. Although separated in birth by over 100 years, both initiate with a direct snap to a back situated five yards behind center and both are more dependent on speed, timing and deception than they are on brute strength. The more things change, the more they stay the same.

Each year the senior football players at Canadian develop a slogan. This year's is the acronym: F.A.S.T.; which stands for Faith, Attitude, Strength and Tradition. It also describes the way the Cats like to run their no huddle, spread offense.

In the Week 6 game with the Panhandle Panthers, Canadian showed when they truly play F.A.S.T., just how lethal they can be. With 2:28 seconds left in the first half and his team in the lead 14-7, Coach Chris Koetting called timeout. Canadian faced a 3rd and 12 from the Panhandle 14 yard line. Koetting used the sixty second break to verbally lash into his team. The Cats had driven the ball into the red zone on their last two possessions, but due to costly penalties and a couple of missed blocking assignments had come up empty on both trips.

Koetting both spit out his frustration and laid down a challenge to his team. "Gentleman, we have played around enough," Koetting said. "We are letting them hang around. Right now, from here on in, we play F.A.S.T. We haven't done that yet. We talk about it, now show me you really mean it. I want the tempo jacked up where we like it. Sprint to the line of scrimmage. Get the play called and let's go. We will wear them down."

Fast forward to 2:28 left in the third quarter, and let the scoreboard tell the tale of the 12 minutes of play after Koetting's challenge: Canadian 48, Panhandle 7. Once Koetting put his foot to the gas, the Wildcats were a team in perpetual motion, an unstoppable whirlwind that Panhandle had the misfortune to have encountered at the wrong moment in time, thus incurring the resulting carnage of the Wildcat offensive fury.

As Koetting had predicted, the pace wore down the larger Panhandle players. A Panhandle pass rush that had been problematic for Canadian in the first half was non-existent by the middle of the third quarter. The frenzied pace that Koetting drove his team to, left the Panhandle defenders gasping for air, hands on their knees.

The game was highlighted by several spectacular individual performances by Canadian. Braden Hudson showed that all the worrying during the week over his sore right throwing hand had been for naught. The senior had a great statistical night, hitting on 18-of-24 passing for 224 yards and four touchdowns. Two of his TD tosses were to his little brother Boston, a sophomore. The younger Hudson made a spectacular catch in the left hand corner of the end zone for a 34 yard TD. The catch came with under 30 seconds left in the second quarter, stretched the score to 34-7 and was the last nail in the Panhandle coffin, staking the Wildcats to an insurmountable lead going into half time. Boston stretched every last inch of his slender 6 foot, 145 pound body to wrestle the ball away from a Panhandle defender, who was in perfect position to make the interception.

Perhaps the most spectacular play of the game, and maybe of the season, came with under two minutes remaining in the first half. With Canadian holding a 20-7 lead; and looking for a knockout of the pesky Panthers before half time, Koetting reached into his trick play bag. Running back Taylor Schafer took a handoff from Braden Hudson and started to sweep around his right end. When he reached the area outside the end, Schafer suddenly stopped and launched a pass toward teammate Isaac Lewis, who was running a crossing route at midfield. The Panhandle defender was not fooled, and was in perfect position, to make the interception and perhaps give his team time to drive for a touchdown before the half and cut the Canadian lead to six points. As the ball arrived, Lewis became a defender. The Panhandle player caught the ball and attempted to pin it to his chest as he was losing his balance. Lewis, with perfect timing – lucky, said a smiling Koetting at halftime, when complimenting Lewis' effort – reached across his body and pulled the pigskin from the defender. It was a perfectly executed strip of the ball. What made the play even more dramatic was that Lewis did it while never breaking stride, so when he secured the ball in his possession, he was in full stride, on his way with a 67 yard TD pass.

In addition to the nice pass he threw on the halfback option, Taylor Schafer had another good game running the football. The 5'10,155 lb. senior rushed for 125 yards on only 11 carries. Schafer had been mostly overlooked with the pre-season hype of the powerful Canadian offense, overshadowed by the returning passing duo of Hudson and Lewis. He was, however, putting together a solid senior year. Defensive Coordinator Craig Campbell sung Schafer's praises after the game while clarifying responsibility for the one major goof by the Canadian defense in the first half.

With the game only several minutes old, the Panthers got on the scoreboard first by catching the Canadian defense in a total breakdown. Panhandle ran a double reverse flea flicker pass that found a wide open Tyler Powers in the end zone for a 28 yard touchdown pass. There was not a Wildcat defender within 20 yards of Powers. Upon the snap the ball was pitched to a Panhandle wide out who then flipped the ball to the wide out from the opposite side of the field, cutting behind the ball for the lateral. As the second wide out – with the ball – reached the end, he suddenly stopped and threw the ball backwards across the field to the quarterback Tyler Hall. Since the ball was thrown backwards it was a lateral and not a forward pass, therefore a legal maneuver. Hall then simply lobbed the ball to the embarrassingly wide open Powers for a touchdown.

When the defense returned to the bench, Campbell made it loud and clear that it was Schafer who had blown the assignment, being suckered up from his safety position, sure that the second handoff between the wide receivers was the sign of a running play. He vacated his spot in the middle of the defensive secondary.

Schafer took the dressing down without a word, perhaps knowing that in the world of small town high school football a skilled player would not be on the sidelines long. After the Canadian kickoff return team brought the ball out to their 22 yard line, Schafer strapped on his helmet, and with Coach Campbell's concerns still ringing in his ears, trotted out for the first offensive play of the series. It would prove to be a one play series.

Schafer took the ball from Hudson on a belly read series dive, the most conservative play in the Canadian play book. It is a simple play to test the resolve of the defensive interior and to keep the linebackers honest by knowing that a times Canadian will utilize a simple running play up the middle. Coach Koetting said later he ran the play to give his offense, and in particular Schafer, a nice safe play to help them settle down.

Instead of a small gain, Schafer broke two arm tackles at the line of scrimmage, cut back to his left, picked up several good downfield blocks, and sprinted down the sideline with two purple clad defenders in hot pursuit of a target they could not outrun. Schafer's 78 yard run and Salvador Escamilla's extra point kick tied the game at 7-7.

Being the goat one minute, then a hero the next, is a common occurrence in the life of a small town football star, where the game makers seldom leave the field. Schafer had, in a matter of minutes, redeemed himself.

With a 48-7 lead and several minutes and a whole 4th quarter left to play, Koetting made the decision to take his starters out and insert his 2nd team. Panhandle took advantage of the drop in Canadian personnel, to score 27 unanswered points in the 4th quarter, to make the final score a misleading 48-34.

A discussion took place in the Canadian coaches' office after the game as to the decorum of the Panhandle coaches in leaving their starters in the game to pound on the younger Canadian athletes. "We could have beaten them by 60," one assistant commented. "You think they would have appreciated what Chris did, instead of running double reverse flea flickers. They should have had their 2's in like we did. I thought it was bush league."

Koetting was more concerned about getting out of the game with all of his players healthy. "I would hate to have Braden in there pounding them by 60 and have him get hurt. It is always a tough call as too when to get your 1's out. We do what we need to do for the benefit of our program and let the other coach worry about what is best for his team."

Even the Canadian extra point kicking for the evening was more than adequate. Lineman Salvador Escamilla made 6 of 7 attempts. "Big Sal has settled in," Koetting joked with his coaches after the game. "We are going to need someone we can count on to hit those PATs. Sal looked pretty good tonight." On Thursday, Koetting had toyed with the idea of allowing a sophomore kicker who had lost the varsity job earlier in the year, after going 0-6 at Fritch, to move back into the varsity kicking slot. That didn't sit well with Escamilla, the senior having taken his new job to heart, staying after practice to work with the long snapper and holders. Kicking with his toe, the old fashion way of kicking a football, a style that disappeared from the college and pro fields over 20 years ago, Escamilla, now a kicker/lineman, looked like an old school reincarnation of Lou Groza.

"Sal does not want to give up the kicking job. Somebody told him that in college, kickers get the best looking girls," the coach laughed. "But I do worry about asking him to do so much, that he doesn't wear down."

The only negative to be taken from this game was the re-injury to the knee of senior Chance Walker. The 155 pound WR/DB had been injured in week 2 at Meade. The Panhandle game was his return to action. "We need him back," Koetting had said during the week. "Chance probably could have played last week, but we didn't want to rush him in a game we didn't need him. He really helps us at linebacker, because he likes to hit."

It didn't take long for Walker to make his presence felt. On defense, with Canadian ahead in the second period 14-7 and Panhandle facing a 4th and long, Walker timed perfectly his hit on a would be pass receiver. His blow knocked the ball loose and forced Panhandle to give up the ball on downs. On the first play from scrimmage after the possession exchange, Walker caught a crossing pattern pass in the middle of the field, then broke several tackles as he turned up field. Walker needed to beat only one more Panhandle defender to make it to the end zone. For a moment, it looked like Walker had done just that. But as he ran over the defensive back, the defender managed to get enough of an arm on Walker that he lost his balance and feel awkwardly to the turf, his right knee buckling under the strain. Walker had been ever so tantalizing close to a touchdown, just a matter of inches of being past the last defender and on his way to the end zone. Instead, a shoe string tackle had caused what appeared to be a season ending injury.

No one would say for sure without an MRI on Monday morning to validate the prognosis, but it was pretty well assumed that Walker had torn an ACL in his knee. There is no medical redshirt year in high school. You have four years to play, period. If the injury would prove to be a torn ACL, then Walker's season- and his football career- were over.

If Walker was indeed through as a player, he could take solace into his retirement that his last two plays as a Canadian Wildcat were spectacular.

On the big white board in the coaches office was projected a website's scoreboard of other games around the area. The Stratford vs. Perryton game drew the attention of every Canadian coach. Stratford was considered by many as a serious challenge to Canadian for the district crown. In a couple of weeks Canadian would travel to Stratford for the ninth game of the season. Perryton, who earlier in the year had defeated the Wildcats with a last second field goal, had beaten Stratford this evening by two touchdowns.

Koetting, without saying so, took a lot from that score. After the Perryton loss, his team had been as low as a Canadian team had been in years. In the last three weeks he had watched his team grow. What he had seen tonight, coupled with the Stratford one sided loss, told him his team was back on track and maybe dreams of playing in Cowboy Stadium in December were not as divorced from reality as they had seemed after the Perryton loss. But first, was the opening district game at Sunray next Friday. Opening district play against a team the caliber of Sunray, who was undefeated (6-0) and looking for their first win over Canadian in longer than anyone could remember, the coach knew, would be a challenge. "We will get their "A" game, I promise you that," Koetting told his team after the Panhandle game. "Be here by 10 tomorrow morning for film. From here on in, they all count."

Jeff Gross is a man pushing all the right buttons. His undefeated McCook Bison continue to roll, unchallenged for the last three weeks. Sidney High

School is the latest victim of the Red Wave of McCook, falling 49-7 in week 6.

Gross admits he did not go into the season seeing this team as dominant as what it has so far this fall been. "We have had a few breathers the last two weeks," the coach said. The two home game blowouts were just what his team needed. The first four weeks had been stressful. The schedule was front loaded with most of the top teams his squad would see. The travel was as challenging as the opponents. The Bison traveled over 1,500 miles for their first three away games. They had survived and now were thriving after two consecutive home field blowout wins.

McCook has enjoyed the last two weeks. The home crowds have been energizing. The competition provided by Grand Island Northwest and Sidney was just enough to make the Bison break a sweat, but not strong enough for either to ever mount a serious challenge to the home team. It was a perfect stage for Gross to put his work on display for the appreciation of the home fans. It had almost become too easy.

Similar to the week before against Northwest, the Sidney game was over by half time. Sidney never crossed the Bison 30 yard line in the game's first 24 minutes and trailed at the half, 42-0.

Even in the first quarter, Sidney was trying to shorten the game, taking all the Bison had to give and then getting the heck on the bus; headed home to Sidney. Before every offensive snap, the Sidney quarterback would wait until the 25 second clock was down to five seconds before starting the play. By adhering to this time milking strategy, the visitors could limit the number of plays McCook would run in the game, hopefully keeping the score down. It didn't work. In reality, Gross did more to keep the Bison score down than any stalling strategy by the opposition. By the middle of the second quarter, McCook was liberally subbing for both offensive and defensive starters.

Of the many McCook stars developing as the season played out, Matt Chitwood continued to shine the brightest. The quarterback rushed for four touchdowns in his one half of action against Sidney. Austin Cherry added a fifth ground touchdown for the home team. In the first half alone, McCook rushed for 194 yards on 25 carries. As almost an afterthought, Chitwood threw his only pass of the evening right before the end of the first half. His toss landed in the waiting arms of Alex Broadfoot for a 27 yard touchdown.

Fullback Justin Terry finished the scoring for the Bison with a 3 yard touchdown run on McCook's first possession of the third quarter. For the game, Chitwood lead the Bison with 123 yards rushing on 11 carries. Terry gained 85 yards on 11 rushes.

The biggest story in the coaches' office after the game was the health of Jake Schlager. The star junior had gone down with a dislocated shoulder halfway through the first quarter. Early prognosis was that the speedy tail-back/linebacker would be out for two weeks. Due to a deep bicep bruise suffered the week before in the Northwest game, Schlager had been held out of contact the entire previous week of practice. Gross intends to play it safe in rehabbing Schlager. "We don't get far in the playoffs without Jake. He is so important to us on both sides of the ball."

Even without Schlager, McCook continued to roll. Four of their six first half touchdowns came after Schlager had gone to the sidelines injured. So overwhelming was McCook's offense, that Chitwood only attempted one pass in the Sidney game. The senior QB is one of the best passers, Gross says, he has had at McCook. The Bison also have two speedy and athletic wide outs and a stable of running backs, all who catch the ball well and are dangerous threats for gaining yards after the catch. So why does Gross keep the lid on the passing game?

"If need be, we can pass and I have a lot of confidence in our passing game," says Gross. "But we believe in the running game. Our veer has carried us to a lot of big wins over the years," says the coach who once stated that if his offense is limited to five or six passes a game, he is happy. What sets Gross' offense apart from other ground oriented teams is the ability the Bison have for making the big play. "We have the speed and the skills in our backs this year that gives us confidence we can score from anywhere on the field, at any time," said Gross. The major weakness of teams that do not have productive passing games is the inability to come from behind in a limited period of time. That does not concern Gross. "With our skilled people, we are confident we can score quickly."

McCook is going to run the football, period. Head coach Gross has a very pragmatic reason for not having fallen smitten for the glitz and bright lights of the currently in vogue spread offense, so popular today. The spread, which is a spinoff of the West Coast offense made famous by the San Francisco 49'ers in the 1990's, is often run without a huddle and from the shotgun formation. It is dependent upon precise reads and exact timing. When all the proper stars align, it is a thing of beauty.

Over the last five or so years, the spread has turned many high school football games into a semblance of a track meet. The football is passed all over the field, with little concern for game factors such as down, distance and score. Scoreboards on Friday nights around the country, thanks to the spread, now spin like roulette wheels. This sexy new way to win football games is fine, says Gross, but this is Nebraska.

"Our big games are in November and they are played outdoors," Gross said. "Rain, snow, blistering winds; we have played in some horrible conditions in the state playoffs. No artificial turf, no dome. When its' 10 degrees with a slick grass field and the wind is blowing 40 mph, I will take our veer over more high risk offenses that are committed to passing the football. Let's just say our offense is weather proofed and battle tested for Nebraska winter weather."

The Linton Lions continued their winning ways, capturing their fifth straight after a season opening loss. Linton defeated the Pirates of Kidder County 20-0. Win be damned, Coach Imdieke was not happy with how his state wide 4th ranked squad had prepared or played against Kidder County. "I guess in some ways I should have expected a letdown," the coach said after the game. "The win (last week) at Maple Valley was so big and so emotional in the way we came back, that I knew we were due for a letdown this week. But still, I don't like it."

Most upsetting to the veteran coach was the five turnovers - 2 pass interceptions and 3 lost fumbles - his team coughed up. Five turnovers in a game by a Dan Imdieke coached Linton team is about as likely an occurrence as finding a white running back starring at Grambling.

"You do not win football games turning the ball over five times," said Imdieke. "There were years we would go half a season and not turn the ball over five times. And Friday night four of the five were not forced. We were just sloppy when it came to taking care of the ball. We got to get that corrected."

Linton dominated the game's statistics, but as Imdieke pointed out, shot themselves in the foot with turnovers and untimely penalties. The Lions took their first seven possessions into Pirate territory. Kidder County crossed the 50 yard line into Lion territory only twice in the first half. The second Linton score came on a short field drive after a Kidder fumble deep in their own territory. Imdieke pointed out to his team at half time that if not for that gift score, the game could easily be 7-0 at half time and not the more comfortable 14-0 that the scoreboard showed.

The Lion's first score of the evening came when Cody Sehn capped a 45 yard drive with a 13 yard touchdown run. For the first time all season, Linton chose to kick the extra point instead of going for a two point conversion. Junior Brock Nagel nailed the kick, as he would do after the last two Lion scores. "We were not having much luck going for two so far this year," explained Imdieke, "So we worked on it this week in practice and Brock did a real nice job." The veteran coach knows that accomplished place kickers at small schools in North Dakota are rare and can give a team that extra weapon needed to win close games. "You bet it is big," said Imdieke after the game. "It could easily be the difference between winning and losing when we get to the playoffs."

Senior quarterback Tanner Purintun scored on a 9 yard run in the second period to up the lead to 14-0. Kidder's best chance at scoring came late in the first half, when a fumbled punt gave the home team the ball at the Linton 33 yard line. Three incomplete passes and a sack as time ran out in the first half stopped the threat.

At half time, Imdieke lectured his team about its sloppy play. "This is the worst we have played all year," he told his team, before getting into several tactical changes. The only production the Pirates had in the first half on offense had to do with the Lions not properly defending the triple option that Kidder ran. Imdieke wanted the defensive end to take the quarterback every time he optioned down the line. Twice in the first half, his left end had instead been fooled by the fake to the fullback and had abandoned the containment of the quarterback, who then ran for large gains around the unmanned end position. "Your only job is to hit the quarterback on each play," lectured Imdieke. "How hard can that be? How can you get beat on a fake when you shouldn't even be looking at the fullback?"

The third quarter did nothing to appease Imdieke. The third 12 minute stanza was, in many ways, a continuation of the first half, a major annoyance for Imdieke. On Linton's first two possessions in the second half, they again drove deep into Pirate territory only to turn the ball over both times; first with a fumble on the Kidder 20 and then an intercepted pass at the home team's 22.

Late in the 4th quarter, a Tanner Purintun 23 yard run sealed the win and put Imdieke out of his misery. "I hate to win like this," he told his team after the game. "We do this next week or in the playoffs, we get beat. I saw it coming in how we practiced this week. If we don't focus in practice, you will not focus in games. I hope we learned something tonight."

The win did clinch a playoff berth for the Lions, marking the 16th consecutive year that they have achieved that distinction. That type of consistency is what makes Imdieke so well respected among his coaching peers. The Lions just never have a down year. "I can't explain it," Imdieke said in reference to their consistency, year after year, qualifying for the state playoffs. "If anything causes us to be so consistent it's that we are a stable staff. We are here year after year and we don't change a lot. Our kids learn our system in the junior high. We try not to complicate things any more than we have to. Football is a pretty simple game. If you block and you tackle better than the other guy, then most nights you are going to win."

"Of everything we have accomplished, I am most proud of that playoff streak, even more than the state championships. It shows that we don't take shortcuts for a quick fix and a quick win. We identified the course years ago and we stay the course."

The veteran educator has learned over the years that success is measured by consistency and loyalty. There is nothing shallow about the way the Linton Lion program is run by Imdieke. "We do things the right way, every time, and I think that is a good life lesson for our kids to learn. Winning is never our main objective. Doing things the right way is. The winning will take care of itself," says a coach who has won, over the last 35 years, eight of every nine times he has sent his Lions onto the North Dakota gridirons.

WEEK 7 – 36 inches short of immortality
October 7

Chris Koetting knows that the real race to a Texas high school state championship begins this week. His team's assignment for the first round of district play will be a tough draw. The Canadian Wildcats will travel To Sunray to tangle with an undefeated pack of Bobcats.

While optimism is back in the Canadian camp, Koetting has stressed with his team all week the importance of being prepared when they step off the bus Friday evening. "Sunray will bring it on Friday. This is a high point for their program and they would like nothing better than to silence the doubters by beating Canadian. They are a legitimate team, and their record is no fluke. They will be sky high, but we look forward to the challenge."

Sunray finished at 5-5 in 2010 and were picked 4th in the pre-season district poll. Are they for real, or is their 6-0 mark simply a by-product of a week non-district schedule? The question will be answered on Friday. For

Sunray, this will be the biggest game they have played in years. A win over mighty Canadian would sky rocket their credibility.

The Bobcats are led by senior quarterback Talon Dooley, a very athletic, duel threat signal caller. His 4.6 speed worries Koetting and the defensive preparation time in practice this week is to be devoted to developing schemes to keep him in the pocket. Shawn Lindsey is a hardnosed linebacker who leads an underrated Sunray defense. "They have always had a reputation as a team that will hit hard," said Koetting on Wednesday. "This year they have the offense to back up their defense. It will be a war."

The start to district play brings those front runners, those 6-0 teams like Sunray, back to the rest of the pack. The slate is cleared, and in Texas every team is now 0-0. With district play at hand, all is forgiven and all is forgotten. Every team has a fresh start.

A loss to Sunray, the Canadian coaches know, would be disastrous. Despite the recent success of the team, it is a tense week of preparation in Canadian. A misstep on Friday would sink the Wildcats even lower than they were several weeks ago after the Perryton game. It is district time and every game now counts.

In week 7, McCook travels to Lexington to meet the Minutemen. There was time when Lexington was the game circled on every McCook fan's calendar. Since Jeff Gross arrived at McCook 14 years ago, due mainly to the program Gross has built, the rivalry has diminished. It has been too long since Lexington has beaten the Bison, for today's players to appreciate how intense a McCook/Lexington match up once was. It wasn't always so. Gross will preach over and over during the week that it would make Lexington's season if they could somehow manage to knockoff the high flying team from McCook.

Gross will share with his team his first year at McCook when the roles were reversed. Lexington entered the state playoffs ranked number 1 in the state. McCook, who had been beaten by Lexington earlier in the year by 40 points, managed to sneak into the playoffs with a 4-5 record and the 16th and last seed in the tourney. As every true Bison fan knows, somehow Gross and his over matched crew managed to pull off a stunning upset on the Lexington field, That game has become part of the Bison legend and was the beginning of the incredible successful ride that McCook has been on ever since.

Because of the unique system that Nebraska uses in filling out its playoff bracket, this week will be McCook's first district game, but all six previous games are used in determining not only who qualifies for state play, but also their placement on the bracket. Nebraska uses a point system, taking into account the entire season's schedule, to determine wild card qualifiers.

With the never ending controversy of the BCS system used on the major college level, a fair selection process for awarding post season playoff positioning is always a hot topic. The Nebraska high school system is as good as I have seen around the nation; if you desire the evaluation criteria to be based upon rewarding teams for season long success, but also giving mid-season hope to teams who struggled early in the year but are playing well in the later stages of their schedule. The Nebraska system attempts to address this balance.

Most states use geographical criteria in setting up bracket placement, with no concern if the best teams in the state are all located in the same region. Ranking all 16 teams on the bracket, as Nebraska does, regardless of geographical location, gives the best chance for the best two teams in the state to reach the final title game. To accept the Nebraska process, schools need to expect large travel requirements in the early rounds of the playoffs, but it is the fairest method if a balanced bracket is desired.

Here is how the process is explained in the official football manual of the Nebraska State High School Activities Association:

Evaluation Scale

The following point evaluation scale will determine a team's total points:

A first division team is a team which has won more than 66% of its games played. Examples: 9-0, 8-1, 7-2, 6-3.

A second division team is a team which has won at least 34% but not more than 66% of its games played. Examples: 5-4, 4-5

	First Division	Second Division	Third Division
Victory Over	50	45	40
Loss To	38	33	28

A third division team is a team which has won less than 34% of its games played. Examples: 3-6, 2-7, 1-8, 0-9

In addition to the previous basic points, bonus points are awarded on the following basis:

No points are deducted for playing teams, which are, classified below your classification.

In competition with schools one classification above yours, two bonus points will be awarded.

In competition with schools two classifications above yours, three bonus points will be awarded.

In competition with schools three classifications above yours, four bonus points will be awarded.

A team's point rating will be determined by dividing the total number of points by the number of contests played.

If there is a tie in enrollment for a classification spot, the three-year Nebraska classification tiebreaker will be used to determine that school's exact classification.

The score of a game does not affect the number of points a team receives for a particular game. **Example:** A score of 7-6 will result in the same number of points as a 50-0.

I will not even attempt to explain what happens if there is a tie and the four page tie breaker procedure of the NSHSAA comes into play.

McCook does lead its District after 6 weeks, as they now prepare to play their final regular season games against the three schools in their District. Below are the district standings entering week 7.

McCook (**6-0, 0-0**), 45.8333
Adams Central (**4-2, 0-0**), 40.1667
Lexington (**3-3, 0-0**), 39.0000
Holdrege (**3-3, 0-0**), 37.3333

The top 16 teams qualify for state play and will be bracketed by seed. The seed will also determine the home team. If the playoffs started after week six, based on the standings below, McCook would be the state's top ranked team and would host the 16th seed, Omaha Skutt Catholic in the first round. Interesting is the 17th ranked team, the last man out of the dance, is Lexington. A win over the Bison in week 7 would jump them way up in the standings. Is this another cause for concern for Coach Gross? "There is not an easy team on our schedule. We had better be ready Friday when we go to Lexington," Gross predicted on Wednesday.

McCook (**6-0**), 45.8333 , Elkhorn (**6-0**), 45.0000 , Crete (**6-0**), 44.1667 , Blair (**4-2**), 43.5000 , Gretna (**6-0**), 43.3333, Aurora (**4-2**), 41.8333 , Plattsmouth (**3-3**), 41.5000 , Gering (**3-3**), 41.5000 , Elkhorn South (**5-1**),

40.5000 , Scottsbluff (**4-2**), 40.1667 , Alliance (**4-2**), 40.1667 , Adams Central (**4-2**), 40.1667 , Omaha Gross Catholic (**3-3**), 39.8333 , Beatrice (**3-3**), 39.8333 , Norris (**2-4**), 39.5000 , Omaha Skutt Catholic (**4-2**), 39.3333 , Lexington (**3-3**), 39.0000 , Hastings (**2-4**), 38.6667 , Ralston (**4-2**), 38.5000 , Boys Town (**4-2**), 38.5000 , Waverly (**1-5**), 38.3333 , Northwest (**1-5**), 38.3333 ,Seward (**3-3**), 38.1667 , Lincoln Pius X (**2-4**), 37.8333 , South Sioux City (**3-3**), 37.6667 , Bennington (**1-5**), 37.5000 , Holdrege (**3-3**), 37.3333, Sidney (**1-5**), 36.6667 , Nebraska City (**2-4**), 36.1667 , York (**2-4**), 35.3333 , Schuyler (**0-6**), 33.8333, Mount Michael Benedictine (**0-6**), 33.8333

Linton's objective in week 7 will be to lock up another regional crown for Coach Imdieke. The Lions will host Cass County and celebrate senior night. "This will be our last regular season home game for the seniors," Imdieke says. "This group will go down as special. When they were younger, it was not a strong class. Many of them didn't play much until this year. But they got themselves ready. I still don't know how good we are, but we keep winning. That is what makes this group special, they always find a way. We want to send them out as winners."

Cass County will present a size problem for Linton. Their starting tackles weigh 325 and 250 pounds. Imdieke welcomes the challenge his undersized line will face. "Our line play has gotten better and better each week." The coach singled out seniors Alex Gross and Luke Mosset for praise. "The line was a real question mark coming in to the season. But each week they have gotten better and better. This is nowhere near the most talented line we have had, but I am really pleased with how they have developed. I still don't think we are overly talented as a team of individuals, but as a group, we have found a way all year to win."

Northern Cass County is a tough team for Imdieke to label. "They lost to Milnor early in the year 55-0," Imdieke reports. "Milnor looks now as though they will finish fourth in our region. But then last week, Cass plays Maple Valley to a near draw, and loses 22-19. Talk about a turnaround! We only beat Maple Valley by one, and we had a letdown in focus last week in practice. Coming off such an emotional win like we had at Maple Valley, I guess I should have expected a letdown against Kidder. I still don't like it, but if we had to have a week like that, last week was a good time to get it over with. If we play like that this week against Cass, we will get beat."

It was, to say the least, one crazy night of High School football in Lexington, NE.

McCook defeated Lexington on the road in double overtime, 16-13. The game was eerily similar to the double overtime win by the same score over Aurora earlier in the season. As with Aurora, McCook needed a missed extra point in the first overtime to stay alive, and got it. Lexington also had a chance to win the game in regulation, but a last play field goal was blocked. The Bison returned the blocked kick all the way to their one yard line, before a game saving tackle by Lexington forced overtime. After Lexington fumbled on their first play of the second overtime, Coach Gross, just as he did against Aurora, sent Matt Chitwood in on first down to attempt the game winning 27-yard field goal. Just as he did against Aurora, Chitwood delivered. McCook goes to 7-0.

"If a Bison, like a cat, has nine lives, then we used 8-$1/2$ of them tonight," quipped head coach Jeff Gross, as he limped off the field. (More on Gross' limp later.) "We made enough mistakes to have lost this game five times. Somebody was watching over us, for sure. All I want to do is get on that bus and get back to McCook as quickly as possible before something else crazy happens," said Gross.

The weather all evening in Lexington had been threatening. Prairie lightning storms popped up across the state, forcing several games in western Nebraska to be delayed or even postponed. As Chitwood lined up his game winning field goal in the second overtime, lightning was flashing to the west of the stadium, and moving in. McCook Gazette sports editor Steve Kodad stood on the sideline with double nervousness as he watched Chitwood place his kicking tee at the 17 yard line. "If he misses this, they are liable to go into a lightning delay and we could be here all night," the reporter said out loud, verbalizing everyone's worst fears.

The McCook coaching staff had made the decision to sit star junior running back and safety Jake Schlager. "He bummed up a shoulder last week early in the Sidney game," said his dad. "Maybe he could have played, but we have a lot of big games left and we don't want a player out there right now who is not 100% ready to go." Gross knew Schlager's absence would be tough "We probably missed Jake on defense even more than offense," said Gross. "Kyle (Stewart) stepped in and did a commendable job at tailback in Jake's place. Our offensive stats were great, we just kept shooting ourselves in the foot." Stewart gained 89 yards on 10 rushing attempts. The workhorse in Schlager's absence became quarterback Matt Chitwood. The all-purpose senior carried the ball 32 times for 249 yards.

Senior fullback/linebacker Justin Terry had a sprained right knee and could hardly walk by the game's end, although he stayed on the field. "Justin gutted it out," said Gross, "But every fan in the stands could see he was hurt. With him not a viable threat in the veer option, and with Jake not in, it just limited what we could do. By the end of the game it was Matt right, Matt left and Matt up the middle."

As with the Aurora game, the Bison trailed at the half to Lexington, 7-0. Gross was much more vocal during this intermission than he been a month earlier during intermission of the Aurora game. This time, the coach questioned his team's mental state and their lack of preparation for the game. He was particularly unhappy with the line play, calling out several regulars by name in front of their teammates, something he rarely did, drawing the line in the sand as to their future playing time if their effort and production did not pick up. "If we are going to get whipped up front," Gross said, "then at least give me your best effort. If he (the opponent across the line) is better than you, that is one thing, but when you are getting whipped because of poor effort, that is totally unacceptable."

By Sunday evening's coaches meeting, after Gross had the opportunity to objectively view the game film, he announced that two offensive linemen would be demoted and it would be up to them in practice to earn back their starting spot. "If we can't block a simple dive play this late in the year," he said, "then we are not going very far. It is too late in the season and too close to the playoffs to be screwing around with people who are not giving 100%."

A strong straight on head wind blew throughout the game and had a noticeable effect upon coaching decisions. Gross debated before the game taking the wind and letting Lexington have the ball to start both halves. He decided against this unorthodox strategy, but was second guessing himself after the game. "They had field position the whole first quarter and we got off to a real slow start. The wind played a role in that," Gross said.

With a 7-0 lead at halftime, the Minutemen took the second half kickoff and drove the ball into the red zone. A second score, at this point in the game, could have spelled doom for the Bison, and Gross knew it. As he gathered his shaky defense, he challenged them to "make a play." Chitwood was listening. On the next play he intercepted a Lexington pass in his own end zone to thwart the Minutemen's threat. McCook then completed the big swing in momentum and drove the ball to the end zone on a grinding 11 play 80 yard drive. Chitwood put the final touches on the Bison resurrection with a 13 yard TD run. "That interception by Matt and that drive were huge," Gross said after the game. "We didn't play well but showed that, when we reached down, we responded."

In the 4th quarter, with under two minutes to play and the score still deadlocked at 7-7, Lexington had the ball at the McCook five yard line. The Minutemen had been effective on this drive by getting the ball to the perimeter and challenging the Bison's tiring ends and outside linebackers. Lexington quarterback Jeremy Callahan rolled left and appeared headed for the end zone when he inexplicably decided to execute an unneeded pitch to his trailing back. The ill-advised toss was behind the tailback and resulted in a fumble that was recovered on the two yard line by the Bison. The Bison had been handed their first big break.

After a first down, Lexington stopped McCook setting up a fourth and four for the Bison from their own 17. With 40.5 seconds left on the clock, Gross took advantage of a Lexington time out to try and steal a first down. Regular punter Matt Collicott had injured his knee early in the game and was not able to return. With a backup punter kicking into the wind, Gross knew that he could expect a net gain of 20 to 25 yards from a punt. Lexington had used up its allotment of timeouts and could not stop the clock. With the strong wind at their back, if they could advance the ball inside the 25, they would have a reasonable chance to kick a game winning field goal.

With all those factors running through his head, Gross instructed his quarterback Chitwood to line up as if to run a play and attempt to draw Lexington offside with a "hard count." If the Minutemen did not react and jump offside for a five yard penalty, allowing McCook to keep the ball, then Chitwood was to call time out and Gross would send in his punting team. The head coach was putting his faith in his defense to hold Lexington out of field goal range in the three or four plays they would have time to run. However, as he often did, Chitwood had other ideas.

When he saw the defensive alignment, Chitwood said after the game, "I thought I could get the four yards." When he got under center Austin Sis, Chitwood slapped him on the rump, the universal signal from quarterback to center that says, "snap me the ball." Sis did and Chitwood slipped, his knee touching down behind the line of scrimmage. The sudden turn of events was disastrous for McCook. Chitwood's lack of success had turned the ball over on downs to the Minutemen at the McCook 15 yard line, well within distance for a short game winning wind aided field goal.

Chitwood was lucky that he was required to stay on the field to play defense and did not have to encounter a livid Gross on the sideline. After the game, Gross again lectured his quarterback about "trying to win the game on every play." Chitwood was a riverboat gambler. Gross was a play the percentages type of coach. Often throughout the season, these personalities would collide. After the game, and following Chitwood's heroic game winning kick, Gross threw his arm around his senior leader and told him he hoped that Matt realized how fortunate it was for him that he made the winning kick because it would have been a long walk back across the stormy Nebraska prairie, from Lexington to McCook. It was hard to tell if Gross was kidding or not.

With fourteen seconds left in regulation, Lexington set up for a 28 yard chip shot field goal that, if successful, would derail McCook's hopes for an undefeated season. Gross called timeout and rallied his kick block defensive unit. "I have a feeling, I have a strong feeling we are going to block this kick," he told his players. His intuition was dead on. Senior lineman Spencer Bruntz broke through the center of the line to cleanly block the kick and scoop up the resulting loose ball, setting the stage for a play that was both incredible and comical, and would come within one yard of being miraculous.

After the blocked kick, since the ball had not crossed the line of scrimmage, it was live and could be advanced by either team. The ball Bruntz was holding was still in play. He stood in the middle of the field, for an instant, unsure of what to do. His teammates were celebrating the block while the Lexington players, heads down, retreated to their sideline to regroup for the overtime session. Bruntz stood alone, holding the live ball!

Coach Gross, jumping up and down on the sideline like a man on fire, motioning for Bruntz to run, finally caught the lineman's attention. "So I thought, alright, I will run with it," Bruntz said after the game. With an unexpected once in a lifetime opportunity to be a hero dropped in his lap, into the wind, towards the Lexington end zone, he rambled. Eighty yards to victory!

Doing his best rendition of "run, Forest, run," Bruntz lumbered down the sideline past the Bison bench. Suddenly, he picked up an escort, Gross. Caught up in the moment, adrenaline flowing and perhaps the theme of

"Chariots of Fire" blaring in his head, the coach ran stride for stride with Bruntz. After pacing his would be hero for 40 yards, Gross' brain finally caught up with his body, announcing "you are 43 years old and not in the best of sprinting shape," abruptly grounding the coach in mid stride with what was later diagnosed as a hamstring pull.

Alone now, Bruntz still had 40 yards of open field ahead of him and one alert Lexington player, quarterback Jeremy Callahan, sprinting after him. The Minuteman had an angle on his prey, the tiring Bison lineman dead in his sights, but the pursuer was still a good 10 yards behind. It was going to be close.

Charitably described by his coach after the game as not the fastest guy on the team, Bruntz began to lose steam twenty yards from the end zone and what would be the most unlikely game winning touchdown in the history of Bison football. "I kept thinking I am almost there, keep going," Bruntz said after the game. "When I got to the ten, I thought about diving into the end zone, but then I thought, if I don't make it and land short, everybody will be laughing at me."

As Callahan closed in for the tackle, Bruntz, using his last ounce of energy, lunged for the end zone pylon. At that last possible instant, Callahan caught the McCook lineman's left leg, spinning him off balance and forcing Bruntz out of bounds at the one yard line.

As crazy a play as anyone in the McCook crowd could ever remember witnessing was over. In its' wake lay a hobbled coach forty yards up the field, and an unlikely hero 36 inches short of immortality.

Overtime.

McCook had the ball to start the first extra stanza. Since both teams would operate their offenses in the same direction, for the first time all evening, the wind would not be a factor. Chitwood had attempted only five passes for the evening. His sixth would strike gold. Wide out Cody Wudtke begged Gross on the sideline before the start of the overtime session to let him have a crack at his defender. "I can beat him, just get me the fade in the air and I will out jump him," Wudtke informed his coach. "He is taking the inside away every time. Throw it high to the outside and I got him." The athletic junior, although seldom called on in the Bison run oriented offensive scheme, had made several big catches in the season when the ball came his way. Wudtke was true to his word and the result was a nine yard Bison touchdown pass. However, as he did in the Aurora game after the first overtime TD, Chitwood missed the PAT, wide left. It was only his second miss of the year. McCook clung to a six point lead. It was now Lexington's possession. A matching touchdown and a routine extra point kick was all the Minutemen needed to pull off the monumental upset of the state's top ranked team. But nothing in this game was routine.

On second and ten, the Minutemen caught the Bison by surprise, running to perfection a flea flicker pass from the running back to a wide open quarterback in the end zone. Once again for the Bison, defeat was only one short extra point kick away. But again, due to a low snap from center, Lexington fanned on the PAT kick and a second overtime waited. It was big break number two for the Bison.

With first possession in the second overtime, Lexington committed the last miscue of a mistake filled game, this one fatal. A perfect pitch for a sweep bounced off the halfback's hands and Bison linebacker Sis covered the loose ball. It was big break number three for the gratuitous Bison. They would need no further assistance. As in the Aurora thriller, Gross allowed for no more drama, sending Chitwood on with his kicking tee to boot a 27 yard field goal and allow the Bison to creep out of Lexington with an improbable win.

Five hundred miles south on Highway 83, the Canadian, TX Wildcats suffered a huge setback in the district opener at Sunray, falling in double overtime to the undefeated Bobcats by a score of 20-14. Sunray scored in the second overtime on a 4th down 20 yard pass to win the game. Canadian had missed a potential game winning field goal at the end of regulation. The loss puts the Wildcats' backs squarely against the wall, as they need to run the table in their last three district games, if they are to control their own playoff destiny. If they stumble again, the Wildcats will need help, and lots of it, to get into the post season. The loss drops Canadian to 4-3 overall, 0-1 in district play.

'What is frustrating," said coach Koetting on Saturday morning, after a sleepless Friday night, "is that we are about four plays away from being 7-0." Koetting knew well that his team had not shown yet that they could win a close game. When the game was on the line, in all three losses, it seemed that every break would go against the Wildcats. However, as Koetting pointed out, you win close games by making your own breaks. "We have got to step up and make the big play. We have kids talented enough to do that, but we don't get it done. It just seems we can't catch a break."

As in their previous two losses, breakdowns in the Wildcat pass protection were instrumental in Sunray's success in holding the Canadian passing game in check. "We didn't block well. We didn't pick up stunts and we didn't always make the best reads on where and when to throw the ball," evaluated Koetting.

The Canadian defense was once again solid. "We held them under 200 yards total offense and they came in averaging over 500. Our defense did a great job. They put us in a position to win and the offense didn't come through," said Koetting.

The game began with a weather delay to let a passing storm blow its' way out of the area. For a game that was predicted to be a good old fashion Texas shootout between two high powered offenses, the end of the first quarter score of 0-0 was, for many of the huge crowd in attendance, the biggest surprise of the night.

Canadian finally scored in the second period with a Taylor Schafer 7 yard run. Salvador Escamilla's PAT kick made it 7-0. The teams took that score to the locker room at half time. The Wildcats had one more chance to score before the end of the half, a crucial accomplishment as it would have given some cushion at half time and shaken the confidence of Sunray. The Wildcats, however, turned the ball over with an interception in the red zone.

The feeling in the Canadian locker room was that now was the time to go for a knockout punch and show the upstart Sunray team, which, despite their 6-0 record, that they were not yet in the class of the Wildcats. A stop on defense to start the half, and another score by Canadian, the coaches told the Cats during intermission, and the Bobcats would be finished, their pre-game confidence proven to be nothing but self-bravado. It didn't play out that way. Sunray took the second half kickoff and drove the ball the length of the field to tie the game at 7-7. The drive ate up a majority of the third quarter clock, eight minutes that the Wildcat high powered offense did not have the ball.

Field position became the dominant force in the game the rest of regulation as neither team scored. Canadian did have a chance to win it in regulation as Escamilla attempted a 32 yard field goal with a strong wind at his back. The kick was tipped at the line and fluttered harmlessly to the ground in the Sunray end zone. After the game, Koetting bemoaned the near miss. "Sal hit it square and he hit it straight. With a stiff wind behind him, he had plenty of leg to get it in. The length of a finger cost us the win, but that has been the case now several times this year."

Canadian had the ball to begin the overtime and put the pressure right back on the Bobcats, as they scored on a Marcus Trevino 19 yard touchdown pass from Braden Hudson. Escamilla again converted the point after.

Texas does not follow National High School Federation rules when it comes to overtime. Texas teams are instead governed by NCAA rules. The NF puts the ball in play in overtime on the 10 yard line. In Texas high school football, as in college, all overtime drives start on the 25 yard line.

Sunray faced a 4th down and 20 on their first overtime possession, and the Wildcats were poised for a big win. However, the Bobcats were bailed out on a very questionable pass interference call in the end zone. The call took the win away from Canadian and gave new life to Sunray, and the ball at the 1 yard line, first and goal. Give credit to Koetting. He has a policy of never commenting on the record about officiating. After the game, he stuck to his policy, but under the circumstances, he could not have been blamed to vary his course just this one time. It was a brutal call that decided the game and could possibly ruin Canadian's season. "It should have never come down to overtime," was the coach's post game comment. "We should have won it before it ever got to overtime."

Sunray scored on the next play. The Bobcats converted the PAT, forcing a second overtime.

Sunray had first possession in the second extra stanza and scored on a 20 yard pass. The point after attempt failed. Canadian now needed a touchdown and a conversion kick to get the win. They got neither. Under pressure, as he had been most to the night, Hudson was sacked twice. Facing fourth and long, his desperation pass fell harmlessly incomplete in the end zone and Sunray had a signature win over the mighty Canadian Wildcats, validation for their rebuilding program, 20-14.

On Saturday morning, Koetting complimented his team's efforts. "We played hard, I can't question that. But we are just not making plays when we need them. Right now, nobody is stepping up and making the big play."

The Canadian passing game hit rock bottom at Sunray. Hudson completed only 11 of 24 passes, for a measly 106 yards. Isaac Lewis caught only two throws for an anemic total of 13 yards.

The universal adage in sport is that the breaks will even out. The hitter in baseball who drives a screaming line drive caught for an out knows that, the next time up, lady luck can smile on him with a bloop "Texas Leaguer" base hit to the opposite field. It is hard for Koetting to take much solace in any talk of future breaks; his beleaguered team needs breaks now. But he also knows that the football gods owe him a couple fortuitous bounces and he hopes to cash in those IOUs come playoff time. But first, the Wildcats must make the playoffs.

Koetting told his players at the Saturday morning film session that they had no more room for error. "We need to get into playoff mode right now," he said. "We lose anymore and it is over. We have some loaded teams to face. It is going to take a total effort. No more excuses. We need a great week of practice to get ready for West Texas High."

Koetting knew that by this time next week, if another loss occurred on Friday of week 9, his talented team would be meeting knowing that they were out of the playoff hunt. That is the sense of urgency he was trying so hard to relate to his team.

The Linton Lions rolled over North Cass County 46-13. The game all but clinched home field advantage for the Lions throughout the post- season and raised their record on the year to 6-1. It was the last regular season home game for the seniors and a nice crowd was in attendance to send them off properly. It was also their first home game in a month.

Coach Imdieke told his team after the game that their performance that evening was the best they had played all year. After going into the season not really sure of what to expect, the veteran coach was eyeing another undefeated regional title. If he could have envisioned the level of play his team was now giving him in mid-October, he would have had less sleepless nights in August. "Right now, we are a pretty good football team," he stated as he prepared to oversee his regular Sunday evening coaches' meeting.

Imdieke was especially pleased with the development of his quarterback, Tanner Purintun. "Tanner has waited his turn to be our varsity quarterback. He was a very good tight end for us last year. He is learning to make good decisions and I am getting more and more faith in him and allowing him to audible more at the line. But Tanner knows not to push me too far," laughed Imdieke.

Linton is known for its grind 'em out, ground oriented offense. Imdieke wears his team's conservative reputation as a badge of honor. "Football is a tough game," he said. "And tough teams run the football." Against Cass County, Purintun completed 13 of 16 passes for 245 yards and four touchdowns, maybe, according to Imdieke, one of the more productive passing games in his 35 year tenure with the Lions. Still, Imdieke keep a tight leash on the right arm of Tanner with threats of separation of other vital body parts. When sending in one play in the third quarter, Imdieke gave specific instructions, "You tell Tanner if he doesn't know what castration means, he will if he audibles to a pass this time." For the normally dry witted coach, it was a threat that, when announced in the huddle, drew a smile from everyone. Tanner ran the play the coach sent in.

As a team that normally took the first quarter to get its offense in gear, Friday night was a nice change of pace for the Lions. Linton roared to a season high four touchdowns in the first 12 minutes. Two Northern Cass County turnovers by a team that would drop to 2-5 on the season, contributed to the early scoring onslaught. Two passing scores and two running TDs, including a 64 yarder by Cody Sehn, were highlights for the large home crowd at Lion Field to enjoy. The only downer for the home team was the inability to kick PATs. After going 3 for 3 the week before, this week's kicking effort was a dismal 0-4 The Lions did convert 2 of 3 attempts at two point conversions. "Somewhere down the road," Imdieke said after the game, "we are going to need a big kick. Don't throw the kicking tee away yet."

After Linton had taken a 38-0 lead, half way through the second quarter, Northern Cass did manage a score on a nicely executed screen pass that covered 52 yards to the Lion's end zone. "They caught us napping on that one," Imdieke told his team at half time.

Another regional title could be wrapped up next week with a win over a weak (0-7) Maryville –Portland team. Is this edition of the Lions a state caliber team, Imdieke was asked on Sunday? "I don't know. On a talent level, we have had better teams. But these guys keep getting better and better. I don't even like to bring this up, because I don't want to jinx us, but we have had some really good teams, like last year, that had some key players injured late in the year and we got beat in the playoffs by teams I don't think would have beaten us if we had a full roster. But that is football. This year, we have stayed very healthy."

Addition by subtraction and winning the game of injury attrition, Imdieke knew were factors that, at least so far, were on his side. At this late point in the season, the coach is enjoying the seven week winning streak his team is now on. They have already passed his summer projections and show no signs of slowing down. Just don't audible out of too many running plays to pass the darn ball, and this team just might make it back to the Fargo Dome. "Hot dang, you betcha we'd like that," said Imdieke.

"Surely you have heard about the "Helmet?"' I am asked by McCook, NE superintendent of schools, Grant Norgaard. "I know someone in town, when they found out you were a writer, just had to tell you about the "Helmet," athletic director Darren Nichols informs me. "And then of course, there is the "Helmet," McCook high school Principal Jerry Smith says, with a weary shake of his head. All three of these conversations occurred on the second day I was in McCook back in August and none were initiated by an inquiry from me. That same afternoon, I asked a random student who was still at her locker several minutes after the dismissal bell for the school day had rung, to tell me about this "Helmet." She just rolled her eyes.

It did not take me long to deduce that the "Helmet" was a story within itself and I needed to pry some. When I re-attached with Coach Gross before the afternoon practice, I asked him to fill me in on the "Helmet." Oh, the 'Helmet,'" says Gross as he lets out a mischievous laugh. "Well, let me tell you about the "Helmet.'"

According to official school sources, the "Helmet" was bought without school funding or school knowledge and approval. This object of so much attention is an inflatable balloon blowup replica of the Bison helmet, decked out in the school colors of black and red. When blown up to full size, the Helmet is 12 foot tall and 12 foot wide, highlighted with a two foot long facemask in the front. When fully inflated it weighs approximately 100 lbs. It takes a crew of six about five minutes to fully inflate the Helmet and about the same amount of time to take it down and store it away. The football team, home and away, when they take the field to start a game, will run through the "Helmet" and then into a human tunnel of cheerleaders and students. It has become a town tradition to the point that parents of 5th and 6th grade players in the youth league program in McCook state that their boys are already dreaming of the day when they will run through the "Helmet," onto the green carpet of grass under the bright Friday night lights of Bison Field.

The "Helmet" was bought and paid for by a group of football fans, a combination of parents of football players and longtime team supporters. No school funds or booster club funds, as I was told many times by McCook school officials, were used in the purchase.

Almost every school in Texas whose games I attended, had a similar helmet to run through to take the field. As far as my inquiry went, and I asked administrators at about a dozen schools in Texas, since everyone had one, it was a non-issue. About half the teams in Nebraska, in the games I saw, had a blow up helmet. So, to be fair, in Nebraska it is not a McCook alone "excess." I don't recall seeing any such blow ups helmet replicas in no frills North Dakota.

As I asked people around McCook about the "Helmet," it became clear that the issue was not the inflatable device itself that had caused such a controversy and had become such a lightning rod in the community, but what it represented to some in town; excess for the football program.

McCook Gazette Sports Editor Steve Kodad confirmed my assumption. "A lot of people said 'Why did it have to be a football helmet? Why not get an inflatable Bison and then all the teams could use it?' To me that is dumb," said Kodad. "Is the cross country going to run through it before a meet? Are we going to drag it into the gym for volleyball and basketball? Nobody does that and the kids would feel stupid. It is something that is unique to football."

For school leaders to take a stance that the issue of fairness will not be raised when one sport, such as football at McCook, receives so much more notoriety than other sports, is not facing the issue and is therefore counterproductive. Simple human nature dictates that the issue of fairness will be questioned.

The best answer I received into the fairness issue that the "Helmet" represented, one that was thoughtful, fair and balanced, so to speak, came from an unlikely source, Emilyne Nichols, the daughter of the McCook high school Assistant Principal/Athletic Director Darren Nichols. She is the senior class President, and a three sport athlete herself; participating in cross country, basketball and track. I knew I was putting her in an awkward position by asking her about an issue that was very touchy to the school administration, in particular her dad, the AD. But I also felt as the elected leader of her peers, her thoughts would be a good summation of the view of the students at MHS. So I asked.

"I go to all the games and I support the football team," she told me. "I don't go just to be seen or to socialize. I want to see the boys do well. I know how hard they, and their coaches, work to win as much as they do."

I cut to the heart of the issue: does football receive an unfair amount of attention, credit and support when compared to other sports at MHS? "If I have to answer either yes or no," Emilyne said, "then I would say no. But I also understand why some might feel that they do, especially athletes from other sports. Football gets most of the attention here, nobody can argue against that. But they also bring in most of the money and they are also under a lot more pressure than the rest of us to win all the time. I think you have to consider all that, as well, when saying if a situation is fair or unfair."

Ms. Nichols emphasized the importance of perception in dealing with questions of fairness. "I think the school does a good job of trying to maintain a balance between school, sports and activities, in order to show support to all students. If you run cross country, or are in one of the school plays, it means so much to us to look out and see the teachers and other athletes in the stands to support us. The football players do a good job of going to our basketball games and showing support. That type of thing matters. The football boys are used to having a lot of support and I don't think they appreciate it the way other sports do; they kind of take it for granted because they have always had it. We don't get it as much, but just coming to watch us means so much to us when you talk about support."

It all, Nichols tells me, comes down to that human fallacy that has been around since the beginning of mankind: jealousy. "It is easy to get jealous of what others receive," said Ms. Nichols, "But when is that not true? What makes this such a special school is that we do support each other. What is fair? It will never be where everyone thinks everything is fair. Our teachers and parents tell us all the time that life is not fair, so get over it. I want to see the boys win state this year, and I will be at each game supporting them. I think most of the students here feel the same way, but hey, don't forget about our other sports, we work hard too and we would love to have the same type of support that football gets."

Senior Amanda Fuchuck, a duo sport athlete herself (and Homecoming Queen), agreed with her classmate that the school's athletes do support each other. "It is not that we don't want to see them (football) do well. We all know how hard they work and how much their coaches require of them and we all support that, it is just that sometimes it gets a little old, when all people in town want to talk about is the football team."

Both young ladies praised the school for their support of the entire activities program, not just football and athletics. "I think the school tries hard to be fair," said Amanda. "Coach Gross is good about supporting the other teams and I think his football boys see that and it rubs off on them. The guys on the football team are really good about coming to the volleyball games, but then they tell us the only reason they come is to check out the girls from the other team in their spandex," she says with a laugh.

Senior Elizabeth Wilcox told me, "I am not an athlete myself, but I support my classmates who are. This is a small town. We grew up with the boys on the football team. To cheer against them, or hope they get beat, would be almost like cheering against your own brother."

The family analogy is dead on accurate when analyzing the issue of football support when compared to other activities available to MHS students. Sibling rivalries, back to the days of Cain and Abel, have always been with us. Wilcox summed it up best, "It is like being the younger sister of an overachieving older brother or sister. You are constantly reminded by everyone at home and at school of how perfect they are. Even though you love them and are proud of their successes, it does get a little old hearing about it all the time."

WEEK 8 – Time to stand up and be counted
October 14

The Linton Lions and the McCook Bison are going to the dance. Their tickets to the playoffs have already been punched. The only question left unanswered for the pair is where they will be placed on the bracket. So while the Lions and Bison jockey for the prettiest girl they can land for their date to the dance, the Canadian Wildcats are desperately clawing to simply earn an invitation. At this point, the Wildcats will take any suitor available, they just want a date.

Canadian knows that their playoff hopes are hanging in the balance of the result of this week's big home game with West Texas High.

Linton will wrap up the regular season with a road game at winless Maryville-Portland, a team with no playoff hopes. Coach Imdieke knows that M-P is just the kind of team that can be dangerous, depending on their mindset coming into the game. Will they mail it in and put up little resistance to an obviously more talented team? Or will their seniors realize this is the last time they will pad up for the school and decide to make a spirited Alamo like last stand, playing with reckless abandon, a team with nothing to lose?

Off the record, Coach Imdieke admits the Patriots are not very good. "They have had a rough couple of years. We would have to really be flat for them to beat us." Imdieke's approach to his team at practice was one of maturity. He challenged them to look to the playoffs and not just take the week off. "We need to realize that, at this time, of the year we cannot regress. We have to practice with a purpose this week and not allow an opponent who is maybe not that talented pull us down to their level. If we do, then that will hurt us in the playoffs next week."

The McCook Bison will have a tough matchup with Adams Central, a team ranked 5th in the state Class B poll. Despite a 5-2 record, this is a team that is well respected by state coaches, and, says McCook Coach Gross, well deserved. Interestingly Adams Central's two losses have gained them as much respect as their five wins. The Patriots have lost to the state's top ranked team in the state wide newspaper polls, Crete and third ranked team in the same poll, Aurora, by one and five points, respectfully.

Adams Central will be the first team that McCook has seen this season that does not employ a spread offense. Gross told his team after practice on Wednesday that they had better be prepared for a good old fashion street fight, because Central would come to McCook determined to take a physical game right at the Bison. "They are a lot like us in that they believe you win football games by controlling the line of scrimmage. If they establish control early, we are in trouble. We can't let that happen. I am looking forward to seeing how we react to a physical team, a team that is going to try and punch you in the mouth on the first play and then keep on punching."

Jake Schlager was back in the lineup for the Bison and his presence was felt immediately on both sides of the ball. "With Jake in there," said Coach Gross, "we can do a lot more blitzing. We move him around and the offense has to adjust." Schlager is often the fastest athlete on the field and against AC, the Bison take advantage of his skills. After sitting out the previous week's double overtime win at Lexington, while running the ball against Adams Central, Schlager looked fresh; his legs "alive".

Justin Terry was nursing an injured groin he had suffered in the Lexington game. The decision was made on Wednesday to hold Terry out on offense in the hopes of being able to get a full game out of him from his linebacker position on defense. A groin injury, as the McCook coaching staff well knew, is an aggravating injury that never seems to heal up. Long term rest is the best remedy, but as senior, Terry had no intention of missing any of his dwindling days left as a Bison.

With Terry out of the offense, the feared Bison veer option offense would be one cog short of its normal triple threat potential. With Schlager's absence at Lexington the week before, the outside speed threat to the triple option was noticeably missing. McCook had regressed to, by the end of the game, having quarterback Matt Chitwood take the snap from the shotgun formation and try and pick an opening in the line to run through. That type of freelancing went well against the sophisticated and precise schemes that Gross had for years conjured up for his offense, but as Gross said at the time, "we did what we had to do to win the game."

With Schlager back in the lineup, the Bison could return to their favored I formation, with Chitwood under center to take the snap and Schlager at tailback. Starting seven yards deep in the backfield, Jake could take a hand off with a full head of steam and find his hole in the middle of the line, or he could serve as an option for a pitch from Chitwood as he slid down the line. The duo was deadly. With Terry at the fullback position, giving Gross a third option, the trio became unstoppable. Gross knew it was imperative to have all three healthy for the rapidly approaching playoffs.

When all were 100%, against Gering, Northwest and Sidney for three weeks, the Bison veer option offense was unstoppable. Against Adams Central, without Terry, the offense would at times look very average. Terry's job at fullback was to allow for Chitwood to stick the ball in his belly immediately after he took the snap, read the defensive tackle and make a split second decision as to leave the ball with Terry, running off tackle, or pull the ball back out and continue with it down the line, with a trailing Schlager as the third option for a pitch from Chitwood. But with the several backs Gross would employ for the Adams Central game to take the place of Terry, the exchange was noticeably not as smooth. When not run properly, the veer option exchange between the quarterback and the fullback can be a risky one, often leading to a fumble due to hesitation and miscommunication.

Early, it appeared that Adams Central would be another casualty of the fast starting Bison. McCook built a quick 14-0 lead, thanks mainly to two outstanding individual efforts by Matt Chitwood. On a quarterback keeper four minutes into the game, Chitwood broke several arm tackles at the line of scrimmage, twisted and stutter stepped his way past a AC safety and raced 65 yards for a touchdown. In the second period, Chitwood, now on defense, perfectly timed a Patriot pass play, jumping the out pattern by stepping in front of the would be receiver and then sprinting untouched down the home team sideline for a 49 yard interception return for a touchdown.

On the next possession, Chitwood almost pulled off another piece of thievery as he positioned himself perfectly in front of an Adams Central receiver for another interception. This time, Chitwood's timing was off as he leaped too early, the ball tipped off his fingers and settled into arms of the Patriot receiver, who then turned and sprinted to inside the Bison 10 yard line. The Adams Central QB, two plays later, snuck the ball from the one yard line into the McCook end zone to cut the lead to 14-7. Inches away from a three touchdown lead, the Bison now found AC back in the game, only one possession down.

The game's momentum had noticeably shifted to the AC sideline. Chitwood would kick a 42- yard field goal late in the second quarter to put the Bison on top, 17-7. Adams Central would respond, scoring just before the half on a two yard run by Tyson Fowler, to cut the lead to the half time score of 17-14. Chitwood had a 65 yard touchdown run in the second half called back due to a holding penalty. Schlager would suffer the same fate on a 50 yard fourth quarter TD dash.

McCook would be on its heels for much of the second half, due primarily to the talents of Fowler. Gross, during the week, had told his team that Fowler would be the best back they would see all year. Fowler lived up to the billing. During the second and third quarters, time after time, he would get ten yards or more on simple dive plays off tackle. He also was a very disruptive influence from his linebacker/defensive back position on defense. He was a very good Class B player, one who could keep his team in a game against a more talented opponent like McCook.

The Bison took the second half kickoff and marched to the AC 13 yard line. On a 4th down play Gross opted for a bit of trickery. Chitwood lined up for a 30 yard field goal attempt. The fake that the Bison executed did not fool Fowler, who threw Tyson Karr for a 7 yard loss.

A ten play, 74 yard subsequent Adams Central drive, climaxing with a one yard Fowler TD run, gave the Pats their first lead of the night, 21-17.

After another holding penalty negated a 50 yard kickoff return by Cherry, McCook took over the ball on their own 10 yard line. It was just the setting Gross was looking for, time to once again show that football is still a pretty simple game. If you out block and you out tackle your opponent, then most likely you will win the game was a philosophy Gross often espoused to his team. Momentum, and the score, has swung to the favor of AC. It was time for what Gross liked to call "Bison football."

When an inspired Adams Central now holding a 21-17 lead, with three minutes remaining in the third stanza, Coach Gross' crew grabbed its lunch pail and went to work, putting together the type of grind it out, stop us if you can, drive this blue collar program has become known for.

On this perfect weather night in a perfect setting to watch a high school football game, the Bison put together a perfect 16 play, 85 yard drive, in the process eating up over 8 minutes of the second half clock to overtake Adams Central 24-21. Call it a signature drive. Call it Bison football. Call it one step closer to a perfect season.

It was now up to Gross' defense and special teams to close out the game.

The efforts of Chitwood and Schlager would be well documented by the media after the game, but the Bison had one more hero ready to make a big play. Senior back up punter Tyson Karr was pressed into duty by the injury of regular punter Matt Collicott the previous week against Lexington. For a team that emphasizes field position as McCook does, the punting game is paramount. Karr had three 4th quarter punts all between 42 and 47 yards. His last, the 47 yarder, was his best effort. His high spinning kick forced Fowler to fair catch the ball at his own 10 yard line. The kick pinned the Pats 90 yards from a winning score. As it would turn out, the Bison needed every yard of the 90 yard cushion Karr's effort gave them.

AC methodically drove the length of the field, using two clutch fourth down pass completions, to sit on the Bison 8 yard line with under a minute left. With no time outs remaining, Adams Central spiked the ball on first down to stop the clock. On second down, Chitwood came within a finger-tip of capping off a once in a lifetime night; even by Chitwood's standards. He had the game winning interception of the second down pass in his hands and he simply dropped it. It was his only noticeable miscue of the evening. Mister Everything for the Bison, he scored 17 of McCook's 24 points. For good measure, after the game, Chitwood was crowned Homecoming King.

After Chitwood's near miss, junior Austin Cherry finished the job on the next play, intercepting a third down pass, with a diving effort at the goal line. There would be no game tying field goal attempt by Adams Central. No overtime would be needed tonight. The Bison had once again pulled out a heart stopper.

Gross told his players after the game that their grit had won the game. He was right. Against Aurora earlier in the year, on this same field, even the Bison faithful had to admit, they had been lucky to win. This evening, though, was different. The Bison had overcome a number of bad bounces. Back breaking holding penalties had taken two touchdowns off the board and took away a 50 yard kickoff return. At times the momentum, especially in the second half, had been in favor of the visiting Patriots. Yet somehow, McCook had found a way, as it had all season, to win. Was this a team of destiny? Gross did not even want to entertain such thoughts. "We made our breaks tonight," he said in his office after the game. "With this team, I never sense any panic. I don't know if that is good or bad, but so far, they find a way."

Adams Central fell to 5-3 on the year. AC's three losses were by a total of ten points to the state's number 1, 2 and 3rd ranked teams. Adams Central was a team that any upcoming playoff opponent should be leery of.

Now only a week 9 trip to Holdrege stood in the way of another perfect regular season for Gross and the McCook Bison.

The Canadian, TX Wildcats got back on the winning track with a convincing 48-14 week 8 home field win over West Texas. The Wildcats went into the contest fighting for their playoff lives against a dangerous WT team, whom the Amarillo paper had projected as that night's winner. The Wildcats showed from the opening kickoff that any predictions of their demise were premature as they raced to a 35-7 half time lead.

The enigmatic Canadian team resoundingly demonstrated that they are still an eleven that is not to be taken lightly. Next Friday night, for week 9, they will travel to Stratford for a district showdown with the Elks. It has been, to this point, a difficult season for the proud Canadian program. But every time coach Koetting's team seems to be down for the count, they bounce up off the canvas, like they did this evening, and put on an eye opening show of explosive football. This is still a very talented team and you have got to like the resiliency they have shown.

Chris Koetting has had enough drama the last eight weeks to last him a lifetime. As a second year head coach, despite guiding his first Wildcat team to a 13-1 mark, he knew many in the community felt the jury was still out on his ability to lead the Canadian program. Great coordinator, not such a great head coach, would be the town's take if his team stumbled in year two of his tenure.

Koetting, to his credit, never shied away from such subjective concerns. In August he had said, "In this job, evaluations come both from the long haul, and the recent. Success and longevity go hand in hand, but so does the question always out there hanging, 'what did you do for me today?' In many ways last year was still Kyle's team (Kyle Lynch, Koetting's predecessor as head coach and now Canadian's superintendent). I am putting my mark on this program, but I am also very aware that we had a lot of success while I was the offensive coordinator, so there was no need to come in and start tearing everything down and start over from scratch. Everything last year just fell in place. We won the big games, the close games. When we needed a bounce, it bounced our way. But I also know that if we get a few bad breaks this year, lose a few games, the doubters will come out. That is when I will be called on to be a leader, and then you can judge me as a head coach."

Koetting had no idea, when stating those thoughts in August, how soon he would be called upon to show just such leadership, his mettle tested to the max. A preseason number one state ranking had put the bull's-eye square on his team's back. The high preseason ranking created an ominous task. There was nowhere for this team to go but down. When the Wildcats suffered two straight last second losses in weeks 2 and 3, eyebrows were raised. A Canadian team 1-2! Koetting showed no sign of panic. He regrouped his team and did a masterful job of steadying his ship in practice the week of the Sanford-Fritch game, rebuilding individual player's confidence and making several personnel decisions that proved to be the right moves. He and his team were also dealing with the emotional trauma of the death of lineman Ty Morrow's father, Kirk. The result of Koetting's work that week was a retooled and reinvigorated Wildcat team who went on the road to Sanford-Fritch and destroyed a dangerous opponent.

Two weeks later came the hard fought double overtime loss at Sunray in the district opener. Suddenly, it was time to face facts. Going into the West Texas game, the cold reality of Texas high school football playoffs was that a loss to an up and coming West Texas team would probably be fatal to Canadian's playoff hopes. From a #1 pre-season state wide ranking to not even making the 48 team post season field to compete for a state title! It was the all too real nightmare that Koetting and his team had to deal with every day in practice the week leading up to the WT game.

"I have been a nervous wreck all week," Koetting said on Thursday. "But we have had our best three days of practice (Monday through Wednesday) that we have had all year." Did his players realize how close they were to becoming maybe the biggest flop in the history of Canadian football, not the type of legacy the talented senior class had discussed leaving behind when they had set team goals back in the heady days of summer? Is the sense of urgency there? "I believe it is," Koetting said. "They are smart kids. They know what is at stake here. I can hardly imagine the mood around here the last two weeks, if we get beat Friday night, and have to simply play out the season with no playoffs to compete in. I don't even want to think about it."

It was obvious the normally even keel coach was feeling the pressure. So was his team. Would the pressure overwhelm the 16 to 18 year olds who knew they carried the pride and hopes of the whole community on their shoulders? Or would Koetting once again find the right words to rebuild their shaken confidence?

To his credit, Koetting never took out his frustration on his team. "They are good kids," he said on Thursday. "We have to keep in mind that they are just kids. But as we told them on Monday to start the practice week, we all signed up for this. We knew what we were getting into. We get a lot of back slaps when we win, and if you are going to accept the praise for wins you got to take the criticism for losses. That is just the way it is. Football is very important in Canadian. It was time for us to stand up and be counted."

Stand up and be counted Friday night the men from Canadian did, with an empathic pounding of West Texas, a team good enough to win many of the Class 1 districts around the state, but now in definite danger of not even qualifying out of the top heavy District 1. Many area coaches agreed that all five teams in Canadian's district were talented enough to win a majority of districts around the state. The reality was, when the five week death march through the district schedule was complete, two very good teams would be staying home, not invited to the playoffs.

West Texas entered the game with a rock solid record of 5-1. The Comanche had their own marquee offensive player in quarterback Alex Ramirez. The senior was an ideal fit to run the triple option offense favored by West Texas. This throwback look had Koetting worried before the game. "We don't see much triple option these days," he said. "It is a look back at what we use to see every week in Texas 20 years ago. We had to dust off some old schemes on defense to get ready for it. Ramirez scares us. It is not so much the offense itself (the triple option) it is a combination of we don't see it that often these days and he is pretty darn good at running it."

In the Comanche previous week win over Boys Ranch, Ramirez passed for only 44 yards, but ran for 163 on 22 carries. "He could have turned those numbers around this week. He has that kind of versatility. He is a good one." Ramirez also operated behind one of the bigger 1A lines in the state. West Texas averaged over 250 pounds a man across the front. "Our defense did a great job, again," said Koetting after the West Texas win. "Looking back over the year, the only time we came out of a game without a real good feeling about our defense was Perryton. And we didn't play poorly that night, we just didn't make the big stops when we had to. But overall, the defense has been our strength this year."

Just as they had done earlier in the rebound game at Fritch, the Wildcats took all the drama out the contest early, scoring at will, proving beyond a doubt to everyone in attendance, believer and doubter both, that they were clearly the better team. It was a tense Canadian crowd fearing the worse that stood for the game opening 7:30 pm kickoff. By 8:30 pm and halftime, the Black and Gold faithful could be seen taking a huge collective sigh of relief, asking each other 'what were we so worried about?'

The Wildcats scored early as they took the opening kickoff and drove the field with a precision drive that gave the large home crowd a preview of the offensive display that was to come. A Tyler Schafer one yard touchdown run capped off the drive. After a defensive stop, the Wildcats stuck quickly as Schafer and QB Braden Hudson executed a perfectly timed crossing pattern for a 49 yard catch and run score. WT cut into the lead in the first minute of the second quarter as Quarterback Alex Ramirez broke away from the Wildcat defense for one of the few times on the evening, scampering 25 yards for a score and cutting the Canadian lead to 13-7.

The Wildcats then found the FAST pace they wanted, gearing into their deadly and feared blitzkrieg attack. Using a pair of WT turnovers and a forced punt by the defense, Hudson and his mates went to work. In an eight minute stretch, they found the West Texas end zone three times to build a 35-7 half time lead, much to the appreciation of their nervous fans. Budding offensive star junior Chris Marquez scored the first of his three touchdowns on the evening on a one yard run. Schafer then went 61 yards on a broken field sprint and Marquez teamed with Hudson for a 16 yard TD pass, in effect driving the last nail into the coffin of any Comanche comeback hopes.

Koetting noted that the Canadian defensive stats, for two reasons, were often skewed and not a fair evaluation of Coach Campbell and his defensive squad's efforts. "Sometimes when you play the fast offensive style we like to play, you increase the number of snaps in the game for both teams and that can increase the number of yards you give up. And a lot of the points we have given up this year have come in the second half of games where we had blown the other team out in the first half and we played our JV defense in the second half against the opponents' first team offense. Our defense has been great this year. That is a big reason why I am very optimistic about our chances in the playoffs. We just got first to get there."

Koetting admitted it had been a tough week. "Our confidence was in question. I know mine was," he said after Friday's game. "It is times like this that you grow as a team. The adversity and the way our kids handled it makes me really appreciate the quality of young men we have in this program. We stuck together; you could see it on the field."

Koetting said after the game that he knew that if his team had played cautious, without passion, not placing trust in each other, then last Friday evening could have easily been a low point in the history of Canadian football. "That is the sense of urgency we had all week," Koetting said. "It was nerve wracking, but I think the tension set the tone for tonight and we used it in a positive way in preparing this week. We were focused all week and it showed (in the game) on offense and defense both. We played with a purpose, a big purpose, we were fighting for our lives."

Admitting he did not know how his team would react when taking the field against West Texas, Koetting said, "I will just say this was the most nervous I have ever been before a game. I knew what was at stake, and how devastating a loss would have been."

Twice in the first eight weeks of the season the Canadian Wildcats have, coming off of potentially season wrecking losses, faced a stiff test against a worthy opponent capable of driving a stake right through the heart of their season's hopes. Twice now, Canadian has answered the challenge by administering a beating worthy of a red headed step child. That gives Koetting confidence heading into the week 9 showdown at Stratford.

For the last two regular season district games, can the Wildcats play the type of football they are capable of and still pull off a district championship? Maybe. What Friday night's demolishing of a good West Texas team did was dramatically improve Canadian's chances of, at a minimum at least, making the playoffs. Despite a resume that is now diminished by three losses, Canadian is not a team other 1A teams would want opposite them on the state bracket.

According to Brothers Bill and Sam Gross, they are farmers who raise three commodities: grain, cattle and Linton Lion football players. Also, according to both, this season has seen a banner crop of all three.

The 2011 Linton roster is dependent upon four of the Gross sons; Bob and Patty's 17 year old Alex and 14 year old Logan and their cousins, 17 year old Jayden and 15 year old Jordan, the sons of Sam and Missy. Two years ago, Sam and Missy's eldest son, 20 year old Justin, was a two year starter for Coach Imdieke's team. Justin is a recent graduate of a community college in Bismarck and is working as a carpenter in the area, now living on his own. But, says mom, he hasn't forgot where the laundry is free and the food home cooked. "We see him a lot," his mom Missy says.

The Gross brothers have adjoining farms, 16 miles east of Linton. Sam and Missy have two daughters, both very involved in athletics; Jayden's 17 year old twin Samantha and 10 year old Shalee. Bill and Patty have a younger daughter Billie Jo, who is 11; and the youngest of the Gross cousins, a 10 year old son, Lane.

Both men earn their living on approximately 1,000 acre farms each owns. They also rent pasture land in the area. Both men raise some grain and a large volume of hay, mostly for consumption by their cattle herds. "If it is a good year, we might sell some hay," says Sam, "But we both make our living with our cattle."

Both Missy and Patty hold down full time jobs outside the home. "Every morning, we have got two car loads heading to town," says Missy. "Then depending on everyone's schedule, we get everybody picked up from practices, games and whatever else is going on, and we've got two car loads headed home."

With so many kids involved in so many activities, the gasoline bill gets quite high, but worth the expense. Patti says it keeps the kids out of trouble. "We support our kids in activities, and I think most around here feel the same way, because it keeps them out of trouble. Sure, it is hectic, but you do it for the kids."

All four parents point with pride to the farm work ethic that has been, since a young age, instilled in their off spring. "When you are a farm kid," says Bill, "you learn that the work gets done first, then the other stuff. Our kids stay busy. They earn the right to play on the teams. It was the same way when Sam and I were in school. We got the chores done first. It is something you learn at a young age."

Sam says he would support any of his sons wanting to get into the family farming business. "It is a hard life, but if it is what they want, then I would not stand in their way or discourage them. It is up to them." He does recognize the important role his children play in keeping his herd of a thousand head of cattle operating. "The boys have always been good help. And when they are not around, Samantha will jump right in and help me." Missy admits that she keeps her two daughters busy running the inside of the home. "I have always worked outside the home and with seven of us; there will always be a lot of laundry to do, meals to cook and such jobs. Samantha has always been great help, since she was little. She never complains. Shalee is only 10, but she has her jobs as well. Often, I think she would rather be outside working with the boys."

Patti recognizes the importance of sports for the social well-being of the area's young. "Both Missy and I grew up in this area and we know that it can be all work if you let it be. Outside of school activities, there was not much to do around here when we were kids and that has not changed. The kid's lives, and to a degree, since we spend so much time driving and cheering, the parents as well, is wrapped up in ball games at the school."

All four parents recognize that the long time winning tradition at Linton, in all sports, makes the commitment from the families even more deeply rooted. "If we are going to go," says Patty, "then we might as well win."

Bill and his brother both admit that farming to support a large family is a stressful endeavor. "We always have to fight the weather," says Sam. "If it is not a drought, then it is storms. We have crop insurance, but still it is always a gamble. That is just the nature of farming. Been like that for as long as people have farmed this area. This has been a good year, the right amount of rain, and we are doing well. But who knows what might happen next year? You learn to live with all the risks, but that doesn't make it any easier."

The increasing cost of buying the new and improved equipment and the high price of fuel are the two biggest worries, both men agree, that the farmers of the area face. "Sam and I own a couple of pieces of equipment that we share," says Bill. "The technology has increased the amount of production each farmer can put out in an hour, say in the hay field. But it does not increase the amount of production from each field, just shortens the amount of time to work that field. So to afford the new equipment by increasing your production, we are always looking for more land to rent, and that gets expensive as there is a real shortage of good pasture land." Sam points out that they hire a combine each harvest season because neither brother's operation is big enough to afford to buy a one. "It would not be cost effective. We don't have enough acres between us to make it cost efficient. It is cheaper to hire it out."

The above factors, both farmers point out, is what is driving young people away from farming. "In some ways," says Sam, "the economy has almost been too good for the big grain farmers up here. They need more and more land to increase production to pay for the new equipment, which is why production and profits are up. But it also drives up the cost of renting pasture land and that hurts the cattle farmers like us. It is just one big cycle and it makes those who can get control of the land very rich. But it also means we need less and less farmers to do the work, even though production is up. It all comes down to improved technology and who can afford to buy it. There are smaller operations that have been bought out by the bigger ones. Many multi- generation family farmers around her have been squeezed out in just this past generation."

Both couples can give clear quantitative facts that show how the population of the Linton area is shrinking. "Sam and I both went to a Catholic high school down in Strasburg in the early 80's," says Bill. "We each graduated with about thirty in our class. A lot of Linton kids went down there, and yet Strasburg and Linton both had good size (public) schools in each town back then. (Up until the early 1960's, Linton also had a Catholic High School) Linton at the time had about 180 kids in their high school, and remember you need to add in a lot of kids who lived in Linton but went to the Catholic high school. Now the Catholic school is closed, and Linton is down to less than 120 kids. Where have all the kids gone? How long can we keep this up?"

The shrinking pool of young families with school age children, Sam says, is the biggest challenge facing this slice of the North Dakota plains, a once hostile land his ancestors tamed over 100 years ago. "I think our generation is set," he says, "we can hold on for the rest of our days. But I don't know about the kids. Things are really changing up here. But our families have been here a long time and we have always found a way. But things are changing in a lot of areas up here that is for sure."

The Linton, ND Lions, a 39-12 winner in week 8, capped an undefeated regional season by running early, long, and often, over a winless

Sophomore Boston Hudson makes a circus catch for a touchdown.

A picture perfect night for high school football in the Texas Panhandle.

A slew of Wildcats gang tackle a West Texas High ball carrier.

Canadian Junior
Running Back
Chris Marquez
breaks away for a
long gain.

Canadian Senior stand out Braden Hudson carries Fritch
defenders (top) as he crosses the goal line. He finds paydirt again
against Perryton (below) as Junior Morgan Shrader (50) signals touchdown.

Canadian Senior Running Back Taylor Schafer.

Canadian Receivers celebrate another Touchdown.

Do it all Senior Isaac Lewis, on his way to the end zone, leaps over a would-be Boys Ranch tackler.

The pride of Canadian, TX takes the field.

Ready for Homecoming action to begin.

Canadian cheerleaders and mascot entertain the home crowd.

McCook Bison Defensive Line digs in against Adams Central.

McCook Senior Fullback Justin Terry divides for the goal line.

The McCook offensive line demonstrates effective wedge blocking.

McCook Senior All State Quarterback, Defensive Back and Place Kicker; Matt Chitwood.

Senior All District Defensive Lineman Clint Beguin puts the clamps on a Adams Central ball carrier.

McCook's Matt Chitwood breaks away for another long run.

Bison Junior Tailback Jake Schlager runs through a huge hole.

The Bison and Head Coach Jeff Gross celebrate another home win.

The infamous Bison Helmet.

The McCook offense poised for a play against Adams Central.

Injured lineman Trevor Gleason is attended to by Bison Medical Staff.

Under a boiling August sun, Bison lineman prepare on the Practice field for the rigors of the upcoming season.

Canadian, TX

McCook, NE

Linton, ND

The Linton Mystequie.

Linton Senior All State End, Jayden Gross (right), leaps for a pass against Kidder County.

Part of the huge Linton crowd that packed the Fargo Dome for the state title game.

Linton Junior Lineman Ethen Roemmich's pregame introduction.

Senior running back Cody Sehn is off to the races.

Coach Imdieke supervises a work out on the legendary Linton practice field "Hill."

The Miracle state semifinal game with Maple Valley.

Gerard Jacob (left), father of Lion player Clay Jacob; and Randy Meidinger, father of Lion player Nolan Meidinger, held the good luck sign for the bus to drive through on the way to Fargo and the state title game.

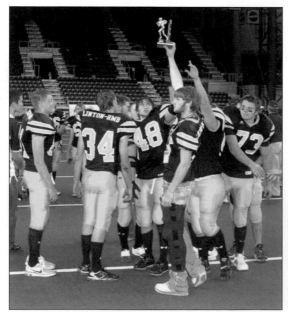

All State Senior Center, Nolan Meidinger.

Injured all State QB and Defensive Back Tanner Purintun lifts the state second place trophy as a salute to the huge crowd of Lion supporters. To the far right is All State Senior Lineman Alex Gross (73).

Jeff Gross, McCook, NE

Chris Koetting, Canadian, TX.

Dan Imdieke, Linton, ND

2011 Linton, ND Lions

Back row, (L to R), Clay Jacob, Brock Nagel, Dillon Doolittle, Nolan Meidinger, Cody Sehn, Ryan Olafson, Alex Gross, Tanner Purintun, Jayden Gross, Lukas Holzer, Luke Mosset, Theo Naaden, Ethen Roemmich and Travis Baumiller; middle row, Head Coach Dan Imdieke, assistant coach Tim Dockter, Chase Jacob, Andrew Leier, Tayler Wetzsteon, Mike Oien, Trevor Martin, Cody Schlosser, Brooks Flyberg, Al Gefroh, Garrick Voigt, Jon Oien, Tanner Bosch, Tyrell Kalberer, assistant coach Paul Keeney and assistant coach Wade Huber; front row, Lee Vetsch, Austin Bernhardt, Ryan Schneider, Rylan Jacob, Jon Purintun, Bradyn Burgad, Austin Schell, Logan Gross, Jade Schumacher and Jordan Gross. Missing from the photo are Mike Rohrich, Kendra Grossman (camera), and statisticians Hannah Jangula, Brittni Brandner and Samantha Jochim.

2011 Canadian, TX Wildcats

Front Row: (L – R) Aaron Avalos, David Morales, Cameron Pearson, Julio Sandoval, Marcos Trevino, Chris Marquez, Tyler Lynch, Cole Banister, Taylor Thompson. **Middle Row:** (L – R) Coach Ronel, Sanez, Coach Tim Fletcher, Chance Walker, Paxton Gallaway, Andrew Ezzell, Braden Hudson, Taylor Schafer, Ben Martinez, Deven Carson, Bo Dickinson, Caden Cleveland, Coach Jeff Isom, Coach Chris Koetting. **Back Row:** (L – R) Coach Kolt Kittley, Coach Hayden Merket, Jose Vigil, Matt Thomsay, Jessie Sandoval, Salvador Escamillia, Ben Arbuckle, Ty Morrow, Morgan Shrader, Johnny Swires, Boston Hudson, Colton Cates, Coach Craig Campbell, Coach Johnny Hudson

2011 McCook, NE Bison

Front Row (L-R) Alex Broadfoot, Tyson Karr, Will Burkert, Justin Terry, Clint Beguin, Nick Albers, Austin Sis, Matt Chitwood, Spencer Bruntz, Shane Buck, Spencer Skolout, Gabe Martentes. **Second Row (L – R)** Morgan Schilling, Cade Hiatt, Matt Collicott, Manny Rodriguez, Brett Guerra, Gavin Harsh,Colt McClonnell, Mitch Collicott, Trevor Gleason, Jake Schlager, Austin Cherry, Cody Wudtke, Javier Beltran, Jacob Riemann, Danile Best Zayne Gillen. **Third Row (L – R)** Irvan Gamboa, Seth Koetter, Trenten Bruntz, Ethan Loibl, Wes Burkert, Dylan Samway, Vince Lyons, Brock Scott, Ian Pearson, Kolton Stone, Clayton Skolout, David Durner, Conner Stamm, Mauro Bueno, Jesse Detty, William Flanagan, Zach Glaze, Dakota Hutchinson, Chandler Wagner, Drew Meissner. **Coaches:** Jeff Gross, Chad Lynons, Russ Schlager, Scott Mollring, Jeremy Yilk, Nick Umscheid, Jeff Ellis, Tom Lentz, Bill Ramsay, Eric Ramsay, Tim Garcia, Clint Coleman, Not Pictured: John Gumb, Barry Schaeffer, Taylor Liess   Student Managers: Bret Baumbach, Cameryn Berry, Alex Bunger, Logan Bunger, DJ Gross, Ethan Hays, Joe Schlager, Zach Schlager, Kaleb Taylor, Not Pictured: Morgan Fawver

Maryville/Portland team. The Lions have drawn Westhope as a first round opponent in next week's Class A state playoff opener. The game will be played at Linton on Saturday afternoon.

The win over Maryville/Portland capped the third consecutive undefeated regional season for the Lions. Head coach Dan Imdieke takes pride in the consistency of his program. "That is our goal every year," he said after the MP game. "If we can go farther and higher than that in the playoffs, then great, that is just a little extra topping to a good year. If we win the region, then it was a good year."

For the Patriots, it was their 25th consecutive loss, going back over three seasons. The MP juniors have never played for the winning side in a high school football game. Such ineptness Imdieke had no frame of reference for, having won over 82% of his games at Linton over the last 35 years, with 4-5 the only losing record of his tenure; but he could sympathize. "That is tough, the situation they are in. I don't know how you turn it around at a school that has little tradition. It has to be hard for the coaches and the players to go out their every week, day after day, and have no payback for their efforts on Friday night. I guess you have to really love the game to keep doing that. I respect that and that is why you saw our JV play most of the last three quarters."

Linton scored four touchdowns in the first 12 minutes of the game and never looked back from a 25-0 first quarter lead. Senior running back Cody Sehn reached the end zone 3 times in the period on a pair of seven yard runs and 32 yard effort. QB Tanner Purintun continued building a solid senior season, connecting with tight end Lukas Holzer for a 29 yard touchdown pass. Brock Nagel added one extra point.

Backup running back Mike Oien raised the Lion lead to 31-0 with a 1-yard touchdown run late in the second period, right before intermission.

In the second half, Purintun re-entered the game and hit Nagel with a 27 yard touchdown pass. He then found Holzer for a two point conversion toss. Those two points would prove to be the final ones of Linton's 39 point evening.

The game against the overmatched opponent was a good way to end the regular season. It gave Imdieke the chance to get many of his reserves some action and get their names in the final statistical summation for the evening. Linton hammered out 374 total yards, including a season-best 246 on the ground.

Sehn led the way on the stat sheet, despite playing less than half of the game, with 88 yards rushing on a dozen attempts, a nice compliment to his three rushing touchdowns. From his quarterback position Purintun gained 42 yards on 2 carries. Nagel netted 35 yards on only four attempts. There was plenty of statistical largesse left over for the JV running backs. Reserves Rylan Jacob and Tayler Wetzsteon added 38 and 34 yards on the ground, respectively, for the Lions. "Those guys will need to play next year, so picking up varsity time like they did tonight will help their confidence and get them ready for next year," Imdieke noted.

The passing attack, showing promising signs over the three previous games, was not needed, and the final stats reflected such. Purintun threw the ball only nine times, connecting on four throws for 101 yards and a pair of touchdowns. Nagel gained 72 yards, and a touchdown, on 3 receptions, while Holzer (29-yd. TD) and Al Gefroh caught one pass apiece for the Lions.

On the defensive side of the stat sheet ledger, Nolan Meidinger and Clay Jacob each picked up sacks; Wetzsteon and Jon Oien were each credited with a fumble recovery. Purintun picked off a pair of passes, while Holzer tallied one interception.

A key to this year's success, said Imdieke after the game, was the ability for his team to stay injury free. "I hate to even mention it," he said, "But we are as healthy as we have been for years going into the playoffs. The last two years, week after week, it was one injury after another to key players."

For a small school, if you are healthy going into the playoffs, you have a big leg up. Imdieke points out that for a school like Linton, with only sixty boys in the school, any injury is magnified. "We not only don't have the backups to run in when a starter goes down, but remember, most of our kids play both ways, so when one of our better players gets hurt, it is like losing two players, one on offense and one on defense. At big schools, many times there is not much of a drop off when a second teamer goes in. In a small school, our backups are often sophomores, or in some cases even freshmen, and there is normally going to be a drop off in talent when you sub a freshman in for a senior."

The Lions did lose a starter over the weekend to a non-football injury. Sophomore tight end and defensive end Al Gefroh lost the tip of his middle finger on his right hand to a farming accident. "He was combining on Saturday," said Imdieke, "And he got his hand caught in a belt. It tore the top tip of his finger clean off. They got the finger sewed back together and now it is just a matter of time to wait and see if it takes to the rest of the finger and heals. He will not play this week for sure."

By the middle of the week, Gefroh was back in school and attending practices. "I can't go this week, but I think by next week I can. We just need to keep winning and I will get back." Gefroh confirmed that the accident had torn the fingertip clean off. "They said it was better that way and would sew back on better than if it had been left dangling. When I saw my hand was caught in the belt, I jumped off the grain truck because I panicked. I went down, and my finger stayed up there," he said, in about as nonchalant fashion as possible when speaking of one's own appendage amputation.

In many ways the 2011 Lions have been one of the more satisfying groups Imdieke has coached in his long tenure. "This group had definitely overachieved. We had some real weaknesses coming in," he says, "especially in the line." Imdieke reinforces again the importance on line play to his basic formula for winning high school football games. "I thought coming into the season our defense would be solid, but I knew it would take some time to rebuild the offensive line. That is the position that is most key to how we play football. We want to dominate on the ground. We want to play field position and we want to always win (the statistic of) time of possession. That is what our program is built upon and you can't do those things if you do not have an offensive line that can control the line of scrimmage."

As the season wore on, and after winning the first two regional games in the last minute of each, Imdieke saw his teaching and mentoring of his offensive line begin to show itself in tangible results on the field. "We are a lot better team (now) than we were in August," he said. "Our kids have grown into their positions. As the line play got better, that helped Tanner establish himself at quarterback and he has really done a nice job for us. I have a lot of confidence in him."

Leadership from within the ranks of the players is always a critical component for any successful football team, but leadership can be hard to define, even harder to identify. "We don't really have a holler, rah-rah, guy this year," said Imdieke. "And sometimes that can be good. What we have is a bunch of guys who lead by example. This is a quiet bunch, but every time this season we needed to get the job done, to have someone step up and make a big play, someone has. That is what I will always remember about this team; they know how to win."

Imdieke gives a lot of credit, for not only this year's edition of the Linton Lions success on the gridiron, but for the past 35 years of his Hall of Fame quality career, to the parents of his players. "We don't have very many kids go on and play football after high school. We have had a few, but not many. For most of our kids, when they take off that uniform after the final game of their senior year, that is it. Football is not life or death here, like I hear it is in some areas of the country. Most of our kids are farm and ranch kids. They learn early in life to work. Very seldom do I have to deal with a kid who has a sense of entitlement, you know, 'you owe me,' type of attitude. Our kids know that you have to work for things you want. Many have to get up before the sun is up to do chores before they come to school and will have more chores to do after the sun goes down and they get home from football practice."

Football for many of the Linton Lions is a welcome diversion. "We don't have the year round programs up here that you find in so many areas of the country," says Imdieke. "These kids just don't have the time. They have to contribute their share of the labor to the family farm. You don't see that much anymore, but it is really important that we make football fun. It has to be or there would be no reason for these kids to be out for the team. Understanding that early on as a head coach in Linton was important for me."

A Lion team that back in August was labeled as not talented enough to garner hardly even a mention in pre-season talk around the state has used a rock solid defense and a developing and balanced offense to exceed veteran Coach Imdieke's pre-season hopes. Could this unheralded group produce a fifth state title winner for Imdieke? Linton will not tip its hand. The Lions are not a flashy crew, which blends well with their "play it close to the vest" coach.

As the winds of November approach on the high plains of North Dakota, the old coach has a hint of a smile on his face. Imdieke likes this team and it is playoff time. That fact alone should cause grave concerns for future Lion playoff opponents.

WEEK 9 – Never dance on our field
October 21

Tim Fletcher is the coach on the Canadian staff who has taken the path less traveled to the isolated plains of the Texas Panhandle. Born in Vietnam to a native mother and an American soldier father, he was adopted by a couple in Gruver, Texas and migrated to the panhandle in 1971.

"I went back (to Vietnam) two years ago and got to see where I came from. I was adopted out of a Catholic orphanage and several of the Sisters (nuns) who were there when I was taken at two years of age are still there today. They survived the communist takeover (in 1975) and all the upheaval that went with it. My home was near Saigon in the south and when the Viet Cong took over, many things changed and many people suffered, but by that time, I had been in the United States for four years. I was lucky."

Fletcher teaches Texas History at the junior high. "We have good kids here. It is a good place to grow up and a good place to teach. I am very content." Fletcher and his wife are raising three children of their own; Mason, a 22 year old senior at West Texas A&M in Amarillo, 18 year old Landon, a senior at CHS, and an 11 year old daughter, Reilly.

Other than a one year stint right out of college at West Texas High School, Fletcher has spent his whole teaching career at Canadian. He acknowledges the slow but steady changes taken place in his adopted hometown. "We are changing, but you have to look close to see it," he says. "The changes here are slow, but they are steady."

Fletcher has witnessed, first hand, the important role that athletics play in small town high schools like Canadian. He validates that sports bring diverse cultures together by providing a common grounds for cooperative success. "The Hispanic population is increasing here, and has been for a number of years. Activities, like football, are very important in getting these outside kids involved. We don't really have an ethnic split here. The split we have is based on language. The Hispanic kids who come here, especially if they are in high school and can't speak English, are the ones who never seem to get into step with the social aspect of being in school here. It has always been a problem."

Fletcher concludes, "I think our school's diversity is a strength for us all because we are able to get kids, through football for example, to all pull together. It is a great lesson for these kids. People from different backgrounds can have common goals and can work together to achieve them. That is the beauty of Canadian Wildcats football."

Canadian at Stratford

Canadian will travel to Stratford to play the game many were predicting before the season began to be the top regular season matchup in all of Texas Class 1A. Both teams will enter the game with several blemishes on their record, but still on the short lists of most experts of teams with a chance to be playing for a state title in Cowboy Stadium come December.

"When we play Stratford, throw the records out the window," said Chris Koetting. The Wildcat coach knows his team will be in for a battle when they travel to the Elk's home field. "Kind of strange, but until we beat them by two touchdowns over here last year, the visitor had won five years in a row. The game had taken on a sidelight that the visitor should always be the favorite. Let's hope that trend re-establishes itself on Friday," said Koetting.

"I expect a close game on Friday," said Koetting. "Somebody will need to make a big play for us to win." Koetting is aware that his team has blown out five opponents this fall, but has fallen in all three close games it has played, two on last second plays. "Those things will even out over the course of time. Still, you can't just sit back and wait for the breaks to come your way. If it is a close game on Friday, and it will be, we will need our playmakers to make plays."

Because every year the matchup with Stratford holds such huge post season implications, the two teams have a great deal of respect for each other. Canadian expects to see the standard Stratford game plan on Friday: play great defense and establish the running game on offense. "They pride themselves on running the football, and they do have a size advantage over us on the line, so I am sure they are going to attack us there. But we have some feisty little guys in there who are not going to back down on defense. It will be a key battle and I think it will be won or lost early."

Canadian entered the year with one of the more highly publicized Class 1 passing games of recent years. The senior duo of Braden Hudson and Isaac Lewis have not matched last year's statistical output. A combination of several critical losses on the offensive line to graduation, and week after week of an opponent placing high priority on stopping the Canadian passing circus, has diminished the number of passing yards the Wildcats have logged this fall. Always a marked man, often double covered, Lewis has still found a way to almost weekly produce some jaw dropping, highlight reel efforts. The problem has been getting the ball in his hands enough. The attention paid the speedy senior, though, has opened other options, especially on the ground for the blitzkrieg (lightning war) style Koetting likes to play. "We got to give time for Braden to throw. When we do, he has been very accurate. In games we have run for a lot of yards, we haven't seen the picks (interceptions) because if the defense has to respect the run, they can't just be getting in a three point sprinters stance each play and coming after

Braden. Right now I like our balance. We are becoming multi-dimensional on offense, and our defense has been rock solid all year."

The Canadian Wildcats are still a work in progress, a team fitting the pieces together, but a team with a huge upside heading into post season play. Friday's game at Stratford, on top of being what should be a delight to watch, by giving fans the spectacle of two contrasting styles of play, by two well coached and proud teams, should also answer a wide spectrum of questions about just how good is Canadian. An enigma the entire season, with last week's convincing win over a very good West Texas team, Koetting has his pack of Cats poised for a break out game at Stratford. Which Wildcat team will take the field on Friday?

McCook at Holdrege

There will be much riding on the game at Holdrege on Friday night Holdrege is battling for a playoff spot. The Bison are in the playoffs, but need a win for improved seeding purposes and to clinch a district championship. A win would also earn the Bison a perfect mark of 9-0 for the regular season.

Holdrege enters the game 4-4 overall, but 1-1 in the district, having knocked off Lexington last week in a come from behind, 25-22 win. The previous week the Dusters had fallen to Adams Central 14-10. A win over McCook, coupled with a Lexington win over Adams Central would leave both McCook and Holdrege with 2-1 district marks, but would give the district crown to Holdrege, based on the Dusters defeating the Bison in head to head play. An Adams Central win and a McCook loss would throw the district race into a three way tie and a tie breaker based on among other factors, comparative scores, would kick in.

McCook head coach Jeff Gross knows how to simplify the whole mess, "If we win, we are district champs."

Immediately after the double overtime win over Adams Central in week 8, Gross and his coaches turned their eye to the next week's opponent, Holdredge. As Gross addressed his team in the east end zone after the thrilling double overtime AC win, he brought up unfinished business. "I still remember last year when they came over here and beat us," he told his team. "I can still see Holdrege dancing on our "M," our school symbol. They had their celebration right there," he said, motioning with his right arm to the mid field logo. "That shows no respect for you, for me and for all the people who have worn the McCook uniform in years past, the same uniform that you wear right now. I said then, put it in the back of your minds. There was nothing we could do about it then. But I told you that there would be a time when we will pull it out and we will remember. That time is now."

In the Coaches office after the game, Gross told his staff, "We will have no problem getting them focused for Holdrege. I think we will kick their ass," he predicted.

When you are a coach, you will find that an infinite number of people with good intentions are willing to help you with your job. If you coach in a small town, such generosity of others will multiply. Advice is never a shortage in demand for the coach of a struggling team. It often will start out low-key and light hearted. As the losses mount, along with the frustration of the local boosters, the "advice" can take on a stinging edge. Unsolicited "advice" on where to find the best realtor is normally not a good sign for the coach.

I once had a mother of a young man who had just failed to make the cut for the varsity basketball team come to my office and inform me that she was a "certified and licensed" witch. She even had a business card announcing her professional services. Cutting her son had earned me "a curse for life." I recommended instead that her talents would be put to better use if she concocted a spell that would make her son taller, stronger, quicker and smarter, since he was deficient in all those areas. I have gotten a lot of mileage – and a lot of laughs - from this "curse" story at speaking engagements over the years. Still, when I hit a run of bad luck, sometimes I do wonder.

Chris Koetting has had his share of advice from well-meaning Canadian Wildcat fans this fall. "After the Meade and Perryton losses, people were very sympathetic and supportive. We had gone through the ordeal of Kirk Morrow's death, and people in town really had empathy for what we were going through."

The mood began to change after the district opening double overtime loss to Sunray. "It never got angry, but after a district loss, the concern level was much higher. Early, it was like 'we need to get this straightened out and we will.' When we lost a district game it became more like, 'we have got to get this turned around now.' But really, I have not heard any negative comments from the town's fans, but then again, I don't listen real close."

What the Wildcats, players and coaches alike, needed to do, says Koetting, was simply get back to playing football. That was why the game with Stratford on Friday is so big, he says. The win over West Texas the previous week was the key win. Unless the Wildcats were to lose to the district doormat, Boys Ranch, the next week at home, even with a loss to Stratford, the Cats were in the playoffs. Still, the Stratford game was in many ways the most important contest on Canadian's regular season schedule. Despite the season Sunray was putting together, the winner of the Canadian vs. Stratford game would be considered by most fans as the best Class 1 team from the Panhandle entering the state playoffs. Sunray needed more than just one good season to break the Canadian/Stratford stranglehold on Class 1A Panhandle football superiority.

The style that Stratford would bring to the field was also of symbolic importance to the mental makeup of the Wildcats. The Elks were a grind 'em out, old school type of team. It was a reputation that had been well earned over the years. "They will hit us," Koetting told his team at a weekday practice, "but we will hit them back."

Many times, fair or unfair, teams such as Canadian, who utilize a wide open offense built around the forward pass, will be given the label of a "finesse" team, or even more damning in the manly world of football, a soft team; one that does not like contact. Koetting knew that in, regard to his team, nothing could be farther from the truth. He knew his defense was a fearless hitting machine. Their team pursuit when flying to the ball – only Cinderella's step-sisters got to the ball faster than the Wildcat Secondary - was a real strength that would be invaluable as the playoffs progressed. Even though his line was often out sized, on both sides of the line of scrimmage, Koetting grew more confident as the season progressed that they were capable of succeeding on the highest levels of Class 1A play. His young line was coming together on the offensive side, while the defense anchored in the middle by seniors Ty Morrow and Salvador Escambia, now reinforced by the return from an early season injury of senior linebacker Colton Cades, had performed well all season.

Still, the Wildcats had lost three times when, in each game, they had not taken advantage of last second opportunities to win. Late minute letdowns, on both offense and defense, had proved fatal in all three losses. Koetting harped all week to his team that he needed someone to step up when the game was on the line and make the big play, make a statement. We have playmakers, so let's see those play makers make plays, was the challenge he issued.

"We need that opportunity, with the game on the line, to show that we have people that we can play physical when we need to," the coach said on Wednesday. "Show people that we will slug it out with any takers." That opportunity, in perfect fashion, would present itself against the Elks, and the Canadian player to lay down the hammer would be an unlikely candidate.

With 2:02 left to play in the game and Canadian nursing a precarious 3 point lead, Stratford faced a 4th and 1 at the Canadian 25 yard line. A little long for a game tying field goal attempt, the Elks, a macho self-styled team who had for years prided themselves on winning the battle in the trenches, had the Canadian defense on its heels, methodically picking up 5 to 8 yards per pop, inexorably moving down the field for what they intended to be a game winning touchdown . There was no doubt what their choice for a 4th down play would be.

The script was playing out eerily in the same scenario that had seen the Wildcats lose earlier to both Perryton and Sunray: the offense had been inside the red zone with the lead and under five minutes to play. A score in either situation would have given Canadian a two possession lead and probably sealed the win. In both games, the offense failed to produce points. In both games, the defense then allowed the opposition to march down the field for the winning score. Here we go again.

But tonight would be different. Coach Campbell had his defense in a short yardage alignment and had inserted an extra lineman, Camron Pearson, a 5'7, 225 pound senior fire plug. Having seen little playing time early in the season on defense, Pearson made the most of this opportunity, meeting Elk's running back Alex Chavoya square in the hole at the line of scrimmage and emphatically pile driving him backwards for a classic "pancake" take down tackle.

Game Canadian.

It was a signature play, a season defining effort. The Cats had shown they could go toe to toe with a physical team, slug it out for 48 minutes, and come out the victor.

Taking over on downs, with 2:02 left in the game, the Wildcats then sealed the big road win with a four play - all rushing attempts – drive, climaxing with a 12 yard touchdown run by Tyler Schafer.

The huge road win for the Wildcats had them now back in the district race. They would need some help, most likely a Stratford win over Sunray, but Canadian was picking up steam at just the right time, a long run into the state playoffs, for the first time since August, seemed a doable goal.

"It was about being physical," said Ty Morrow, "we showed we can run the ball when we have to against a good team."

Quarterback Braden Hudson complete only eight passes for 143 yards, both season lows. For Hudson it was something of a homecoming as he had attended Stratford during his 8th grade year, his dad employed as the head girls' basketball coach for the Elks, before enrolling at Canadian as a freshman. "I know all those guys," he said after the game. "We did what we needed to do. I am just glad to get out of here with a win. We are back where we need to be, and I couldn't be more excited."

Koetting noted on the bus ride home that Canadian had run a season low 50 offensive plays from scrimmage, only 14 in the first half. "Stratford is so physical, if you let them they will run it down your throat. They can eat up a lot of time off the clock with all those runs and it really slows the pace of a game, which we knew they would want to do." That, according to Koetting, made the win over the Elks even more satisfying. "It has been an up and down last couple of months for us, but I feel tonight we turned the corner. We are healthy and this win drives our confidence sky high. Stratford has not had the season they had hoped for, but still, anytime we beat them, it is a big win."

The Wildcats had taken a season full of body shots and were still standing. They were survivors. It was now time to go on the offensive.

Bittersweet is the best description of Jeff Gross' week 9 bus ride back to McCook. His Bison had just knocked off Holdrege in a dominating fashion, 35-0. The performance was so overwhelming by Gross' team that Holdrege lodged only 69 yards of total offense for the night, 2/3 of that coming on one drive in the second half against the Bison JV defense. The win sealed not only a district crown for McCook, but also their first undefeated regular season since 2008.

The anxiety felt by Gross, and the pall thrown over the trip home for everyone in the large contingent from McCook who had made the 60 mile trip to see the game, was the broken leg suffered in the second period by Jake Schlager. On a sweep around end, Schlager was rolled up by two

Duster defenders as he went out of bounds in front of the Bison bench. The injury would knock the talented junior from the lineup for the rest of the season.

Several weeks earlier, Gross was musing about how important it was for his team to stay healthy, especially his three headed monster that ran his veer option offense so efficiently: quarterback Matt Chitwood, fullback Justin Terry and Schlager. Since then, Terry was injured with a groin pull in the Lexington game and for the past two weeks had played only on defense. Now Schlager was out for the season.

Gross stated then that the one of the three he would have the hardest time replacing would be Schlager. "If Matt went down at quarterback, we would go with (junior Austin) Cherry. He has always been a QB until this year and he will be our QB next year. He would do fine. But Jake, that would be tough. Not only on offense, but he is so important to our defense because he can play all over the field and he closes on the ball so well. A lot of times he occupies two blockers or they have to run away from him. That is how good he is on defense."

Now, on a night when his team had played the kind of in your face, dominating game he preached, Gross was confronted with his worst case injury scenario. "I don't know yet," when asked after the game as to how he would compensate for the huge hole he now had on both sides of the line of scrimmage. "Jake gives us the speed that sets us apart from a lot of the teams we see. There are not too many 4.4 guys in West Nebraska. Especially ones that will stick their nose in like Jake will. He is just a very good football player and we can't replace what he gives us. What we are going to have to do is compensate the best we can. That is what we will be doing all weekend, figuring how to plug a very big hole."

The Bison led 35-0 at halftime and played their most complete game of the season. No second half let downs after a big half time lead tonight. Perhaps remembering the Holdrege celebration on the McCook logo at Bison stadium the previous year, Gross did not, as he had against Grand Island Northwest and Sidney, call off the dogs with a 35-0 halftime lead. (Northwest and Sidney had not taking celebratory pictures on the the the McCook Stadium 50 yard line logo.) Maintaining the shutout of the Dusters was a way for Gross to settle an old score. Consider the ledger now balanced.

After the game, when speaking with the media, Gross bit his lip and looked to the positive. "We challenged our kids to play extremely hard on every play. We got in a rut the last few weeks. When you hit on all cylinders and play hard, good things are going to happen," Gross said.

Matt Chitwood was once again the unflappable catalyst for the Bison. He threw a season high four touchdown passes and rushed for the fifth first half Bison TD. The senior completed 9-11 passes, and for good measure, ran for 48 yards. "They were determined to not let me run," Chitwood said after the game. "So, I took what they gave me, and that was the pass. If we would have had to play all four quarters I would have thrown for a lot more." All of Chitwood's passing attempts came in the first half.

"They loaded the box and dared us to throw," said Gross after the game. "I know, I know; everyone thinks we should throw more. Without Jake, we may have to."

Chitwood was his usual lassie faire self after the game. "It's too bad about Jake, but we got to do what we got to do. Its playoff time and we just have to take what they give us. That is what we did tonight. We have got to have everyone now, including me, do just a little more to make up for Jake not being in there," Chitwood said.

It is hard to believe that Chitwood can do much more on a football field than he already has. Watching him dominate games week after week is a real head scratcher. As Gross will attest to, Chitwood himself is a real head scratcher. The senior is a hard young man to get a read on. He is uncanny in his ability to make the big play, when the big play is needed. He is a young man at the zenith of a high school career; but he seems unfazed and unconcerned by anything tomorrow may bring. He is clearly basking in the present, and for the star quarterback of an undefeated small town high school, for now, Matt Chitwood is the darling of McCook, NB.

Gross has a love-hate relationship with his unpretentious marquee player. "I have never coached anyone like him," says Gross. "One minute he will pull some stunt that is just crazy and before I can get my hands on him he will turn around and make one of the greatest plays you have ever seen. He is fearless on the football field." There are times though, that Gross feels Chitwood's on field risks display more guts than brains. "I just wish he would use a little better judgment on the field, but if he did, that might take away from how effective he is. I am learning to live with him. Matt is Matt. He is unique."

On top of being arguably the state's top rated quarterback, Chitwood is a ball hawking defender from his corner back position. He may also be the state's best kicker. "It would be interesting to see how good (a kicker) he could be," said veteran assistant coach John Gumb, while watching Chitwood boom one 50 yard field goal after another during a pre practice workout, "if all he did was kick. Think about it, he never leaves the field and he plays positions where he is constantly running. By the end of the game his legs have got to be dead."

Despite the fatigue, Chitwood has won McCook's two overtime games with walk off field goals. His ability to put 75% of his kickoffs in the end zone is critical for a team like McCook which stresses field position. "I have never seen anything like him," Gumb says with a smile and a shake of his head, uttering the same assessment as Gross. The veteran coach then quickly rethinks his proposal of Matt Chitwood, kicking specialist. "It would never work. Matt would get real bored, real quick, just kicking."

With such a stellar senior season and with so many varied gridiron talents, one would assume that Chitwood's phone must be ringing off the hook with college suitors. Don't waste your time, is Chitwood's advice to college coaches. "I got a 1.8 grade point average," the senior states in a matter of fact tone. "I don't like school and I will probably just go to work. I like sports and I have got basketball and track yet this year, but I don't like them enough to go to college just so I can play sports."

On a school day, during his third hour morning English class, an interview of Matt during the period was requested. The teacher of the class he was assigned to, when asked if he could be excused ten minutes early responded, "He is not here yet and I don't know if he is going to bother to show up today or not, but if he does, you can have him."

By nature, Gross is an enabler. He prides himself on his ability to reach out to a young person, confront their risky behavior, and guide them down a less self-destructive path. Those who work with him at LIFT- the district alternative school- say that he has great natural rapport with kids in need of guidance. Perhaps that is what frustrates the veteran educator about the way his star quarterback is planning for his future, or more accurately, not planning for his future.

Like a wild Mustang that will not be broken, the best approach to dealing with the talented but unpredictable and erratic Chitwood, his coaches have learned, is to just stand back, and while he still has a stage to perform on, enjoy the show.

Youth is wasted on the young. Oh, the folly of youth.

Week 10 – The hunted becomes the hunter

October 28, 2011

Craig Campbell is in his 16th season on the Canadian staff. Canadian is the only teaching stop on Campbell's professional resume. The native of Perryton came to Canadian as basketball, football and track coach, starting in all three sports on the junior high level. Former Canadian head coach and current superintendent Kyle Lynch made Campbell his varsity Defensive Coordinator eight years ago. For the time being, Campbell is content in his role as a coordinator. "Someday, maybe, I would be interested in a head coaching position. For now, I am content. My son (Quentin) is in 8th grade and I can't see any changes for me until he is out of school."

Campbell feels that the autonomy that Head Coach Koetting gives him in running the defense fulfills his creativity needs as a coach. "I feel respected here. I run the defense. In many ways I feel I have the responsibilities of a head coach, at least on the defensive side of things."

Campbell is also in charge of the team's strength and conditioning program. Canadian is well known for the speed and strength of its teams and Campbell is well recognized for his role in developing his athletes' physical skills. "We work very hard on core strength. Everything comes from the core. We work at it year round. That is a big change from when I came here. Kids back then did not make the year round commitment to football they do now. It seemed like there was always something else more important; jobs, rodeo, something. That changed when we started winning. Or, maybe we started winning because that changed. Whichever, but I know it has changed."

Canadian, over the years has never had the biggest of athletes to fill out its roster and Campbell says that has required a good job of teaching for the Wildcats to be as effective of hitters on defense that they are. "It is all about physics," he says. "Look at me. I am not the tallest of guys. You have to know how to use your body to tackle bigger players. We teach kids to put their head through the hips. If you go pad to pad against a bigger player, he will win."

Campbell is no longer involved in the basketball program, but he is now the head high school track coach. For a school that does not offer baseball, Campbell says the football athletes know it is important that they be out for track, even if just for the conditioning.

Boys Ranch will travel to Canadian to finish up the regular season. Boys Ranch is winless in District 1 play, but according to Chris Koetting, dangerous. "They might be the most athletic team we will see all year. They always have a player or two. The circumstances there are just so different."

Koetting was referring to the set-up of Boys Ranch. The school was established in 1941 through legislative action. It is classified as an independent school district, but is considered a "special purpose" district of Texas. Most students board at the school. BR was founded in the 1930's, at the height of the Great Depression, by the legendary Cal Farley. The school served as a home for the many homeless orphan boys in the area. Farley's deep pockets keep the school financially afloat through hard times, to where it today is housed on a state of the art campus. It is also now a coed institution. With the classification as an Independent School District, and with most of its students coming from poverty backgrounds, the state and federal money flows freely, thus the nice facilities.

"They have a lot of things going for them with facilities and funding being good, but you never know week to week who is going to be there. Most of their kids were placed there," says Koetting. "It would be a challenging place to coach and build a program. The lack of student stability would be a problem." Although Koetting refuses to breech the subject, it can be assumed that most young men at Boys Ranch were not sent to the special school for singing off key in church.

The one thing that Boys Ranch does not have in its favor is the brutal district the UIL placed them in, District 1. The Roughriders started the year at 5-1, but then hit district play. With the top two teams in the district yet to play, Sunray and Canadian, Boys Ranch is looking at a 5-5 season overall mark, but a goose egg 0-4 district record.

It was a festive crowd that packed the Canadian Stadium to bid farewell to the senior class. Last week's big win at Stratford had allowed everyone to exhale. If Sunray were to stumble when Stratford comes to visit this evening, then the Wildcats would have the inside track for the tie breaker and the district title. If Sunray was to continue on their surprising winning ways and knock off the Elks, then Sunray would be the district winners. Even an unlikely loss by Sunray to Boys Ranch the final week of the season, leaving Sunray and Canadian each at 3-1 in the district, would still give the title to Sunray as they had defeated Canadian in the head to head matchup, the first tie breaker criteria.

As Koetting vowed, his team did not take Boys Ranch lightly, steam-rolling the Roughriders 44-8. On senior night, it was senior wide receiver/running back Isaac Lewis who stole the show. After Taylor Schafer got the Cats on the board early, Lewis scored the next four TDs for the Wildcats on rushing efforts of 3, 4 and 5 yards; and a 34 yard TD toss from Braden Hudson. Lewis ran for 101 yards on 13 carries and caught 8 passes for 108 yards. Hudson also had a stellar night on the stat sheets, completing 16 passes in 25 attempts for 178 yards. It was a good way for the two senior pass and catch buddies to close their home careers as Wildcats.

Koetting liked the balance of the pass/run performance. "I just thought we played real well, he said after the game. "Braden and Isaac have both been under a lot of pressure this year. After the junior years both had, that was expected. It took our offensive line a bit of time to mature and that put even more pressure on both, especially Braden. Both handled it very well. It was good to see both go out with such good performances tonight.

The Wildcats totally bottled up the Boys Ranch offense. The only score the visitors could muster was a late game kickoff return for a TD, after Canadian had taken a 44-0 lead, and against the second line kick coverage team. "Our defense was great tonight and has been all year," Koetting said, echoing the compliments he gave to his defense after almost every game in the regular season. "And now the offense is starting to click." Koetting noted with pleasure the balance in the BR win between his running and passing games. "Two hundred and sixty eight on the ground, two hundred and seventy seven in the air,' he read from the stat sheet. "You can't get much more balanced than that," he said.

For the last week of the season, the Wildcats would get a bye before starting the playoffs. Koetting said his team needed the break, probably more mentally than physically. "It has been a grind," he admitted. "We started off with two scrimmage games and then ten regular season games in a row. That is a lot of football for high school kids." And, he might have added, high school coaches.

After the Boys Ranch win, Koetting and his coaches gathered in their offices at the stadium to find out how the other teams in the area had done. Of particular interest was the District 1 game between Sunray and Stratford and the results from District 2. District 1 would be placed on the state bracket opposite District 2. The winner of District 1 would receive a bye.

When the coaches were informed that Sunray had continued its winning ways by defeating Stratford, Canadian knew they would now most likely be the 2nd seed from District 1 and would be matched up with the number three team in District 2, most likely Clarendon, when the state playoff bracket was released in eight days. Panhandle, the team that Canadian had destroyed in week 6, seemed to be a lock for the top spot in District 2; giving further credence to what Koetting had said several weeks prior, "if we can just get in the playoffs, we can play with anybody, but this district is so tough, two good teams are going to be sitting home."

After the completion of week 10, the district 1 and district 2 standings were:

District 1	Record	District	PF	PA
Sunray	9-0	3-0	346	141
Canadian	7-3	3-1	388	176
West Texas	6-3	1-2	256	164
Stratford	4-4	1-2	215	191
Boys Ranch	5-4	0-3	146	147

District 2	Record	District	PF	PA
Panhandle	7-2	2-0	360	206
Quanah	6-3	1-1	242	261
Clarendon	5-4	1-1	225	188
Lockney	2-7	0-2	113	254

It now appeared, after dropping two consecutive games, first to Canadian last week and now Sunray, that one of those teams staying home could be Stratford. The Elks would meet West Texas next Friday with the winner advancing to the playoffs and the loser storing away the equipment until next year. "None of us would have thought back in August there was any way that Stratford would come down to the last week and need a win to get in. They are in the same situation we were before the West Texas game, a have to win situation," said Koetting.

If the Wildcats, already with a bye the final week of the regular season, would have won the district title, they would have been given another bye in the first round of the playoffs, creating the unusual scheduling situation of two straight weeks without a game. "We had to do that last year," remembered Koetting," because we drew the bye for week 11 and then we won the district. It was different for sure, but I would rather have the first round bye, because you are never going to lose that one," he laughed.

(I know of a beer league level coed softball team in St. Louis who were never very good, but would pick up a couple of forfeit wins each year due to their name, "Bye Week." One of the players told me, "A couple of times a year, the other team would see bye week on the schedule and not show up. We would win by forfeit. Those were about the only games we won.")

Before leaving the football offices after the Boys Ranch game, the Canadian staff had the bye week schedule laid out. "We will bring them in for film on Monday," said Koetting. "Tuesday, Wednesday and Thursday, we will treat like any other week. Friday, we will get out and do some scouting. Saturday morning, we will meet back here like any other week, knowing who we have in the first round and get to work."

It had been a tough ten week regular season for the Canadian Wildcats, but now that the hay is in the barn in terms of the regular season, one could sense, due to the mood around the football Fieldhouse, a high level of confidence in both the players and the coaches. There was a bounce in their collective step that was not there a month ago.

Hard times in this life, that do not kill you will, only make you stronger. Be warned; the pulse of the Canadian Wildcats, heading into the playoffs, is beating strong and fast.

Landon Landry is a recent transplant to Canadian, but no one could speak in any more glowing terms about his hometown than the investment specialist who hung out his shingle in Canadian in 2007. "I coached high school football down in the southern part of the Panhandle, so I was quite aware of the reputation of the entire community, but for sure the dominant football program in Canadian."

Landry and his wife, who is a Canadian native, were attracted to area for relocation by the solid school system as much as they were by the booming local economy. "There is no doubt that oil plays a major role in the economy here and that you are going to have ups and downs, that just is a given in a local economy dependent upon oil. But what I have seen transpire here, even in the short time we have lived here, is that there are so many people here that are moving in that are self-employed. People who want the small town life style that is so unique to Canadian, but have also found a way to make a good living. Driving this, no question, is the internet. The other interesting part of the people moving in, from what I have seen, is how many of them grew up and went to school in Canadian and are now coming home and putting their kids in the local schools."

But the real drawing card says Landry is the strong local schools. "Our kids are now in school and the quality of their education is top priority with us. That is the main reason we relocated here, the solid education we feel that Canadian can provide to our kids."

Landry lists the same universal concern about potential growth in Canadian as most every business leader in the north panhandle town I spoke with: lack of housing. "It is so unusual at a time the national housing market is in such a free fall that you can drive around this town and not find one house for sale. There was one on the market for a while, but the price was so high, even in Canadian, no one was going to bite. There is a subdivision now going up on the south side of town and some government subsidized apartments on the planning board for the north side, and they are both well needed."

Pride in the community, according to Landry, is crystal clear, to any newcomer. "Just use your eyes, look around," he offers. "Everything is clean, everything is well kept; even the older areas of town. That just gets passed on. If I fix up my place and you are next door to me, then you fix up yours. Look at the businesses downtown. What a pretty area. It shows local pride and that is what makes Canadian special."

Even the Women are Pissed

The date is a little hazy and so is the location. In fact, they can't even all agree if it was an 11 man game or a 6 man contest. What they do agree on is that the ole boy was big, dressed like he just got off a tractor; and he was clearly not happy.

I am having 7 am coffee with seven veteran high school football officials. The group represents 70% of the high school officials in the McCook, NE area. There are two five man crews, located out of McCook, that have worked high school games together for years. Between the seven men, they have 209 years of high school football officiating experience. Arthur Skinner is the long tooth of the gang, with 40 years of blowing his whistle on Friday nights. Nick Johanson is the pup, with a mere 12 years in stripes. The others are Bob Elder (31 years), Brian Esch (26 years), Jim Hall (31 years), Paul Wood (24 years) and Darren Esch (25 years).

The unhappy farmer approached the crew as they departed the field for the halftime break, and gave them the line that would become their mantra, of sorts, for future self-evaluations of their craft: "You guys are so bad," the farmer said, "even the women are pissed off."

Since then, I was told by the group, "We now evaluate ourselves after each game by comparing notes and seeing if we had pissed off the women."

That type of camaraderie is why both crews go out in every type of weather imaginable for the privilege of being the target of outrage from half of the crowd, almost every Friday night, from August to November. All agreed they got into officiating because they loved playing the game in high school and wanted to stay involved. The pay, about $75 a night is, for certain, not a driving motivating factor.

Several mentioned they had considered coaching, but for various reasons, had gone into other lines of work. Sometimes, their occupations can overlap with their officiating duties. Paul Wood is the County Prosecutor. He recalls a time, "years ago," when the star of one high school team was in jail. Wood was scheduled to work the "big game" that Friday night. "I worked the game. He stayed in jail," laughed Wood. Bob Elder owns several successful sporting goods stores throughout southwest Nebraska and northwest Kansas areas. He is chided by his partners, "we always got to go find Elder to get the game started. He's always over on the sideline somewhere trying to sell a coach some shoes."

With so many years of officiating experience at this impromptu breakfast, as can be expected, the anecdotal stories flowed like the early morning coffee: A coach in 6 man that still wore his high school letter jacket on the sideline's during games; a mismarked field that when the first down chains were placed on the 10 yard line and stretched to the goal line, went three yards deep into the end zone; a contest interrupted by two dogs on the field during the game "making puppies;" an official with a medically implanted penis pump that for some reason malfunctioned during the game; and so on.

Both crews are highly regarded around the state and are often given the assignment of working the biggest games in the area, including several state championship contests. "We don't ever have them," says McCook Coach Jeff Gross, "Because they are all from McCook, but I know both crews are well respected by coaches around the state. They are two of the better crews."

The relationship with coaches, all present agreed, was important. Brian and Darren Esch both recognized that the roles of both officials and coaches were interwoven in that both were in service to the young people on the field. "Football is a great learning experience and that is why we are out there, for the kids," Darren Esch said, while recognizing that the role of the coach is more deep and committed, - a coach is involved in a vocation that is his livelihood; while an official takes a couple hours a week to follow an avocation that caring for his family is not dependent upon. "Coaches are under a lot of pressure," said Brian Esch, "We know that and respect that."

Arthur Skinner, with his 40 years of experience, was asked about the changes he has seen over the last four decades. "The players are so much bigger, so much faster and so much stronger than they were when I started," said Skinner. Credit the upgrade to weight training, says Skinner. "In the old days a 250 pound lineman was often just a kid who was way overweight, fat. Today, that 250 pounder is likely (to) be nothing but solid muscle. The collisions on the field now are so much more physical than they use to be. And then of course, the issues with using the head as a weapon, the big concern today with concussions. The game today is just so much more physical, so much faster than when I started."

All agreed that the lack of younger officials entering the trade is a concern, especially for McCook. "These guys have been together so long," says Nick Johansson, speaking of 12 years prior, when he first picked up his whistle, "It is hard to break someone new in." The problem with getting new people involved, says Elder, is timing. "Every game counts," he says. "There really is no place for a guy to learn without the pressure of making a call that might be the wrong call and cost a team a game." That, all agreed, is a problem in a job that you are expected to be perfect your first game, and then improve as you become more experienced.

Jim Hall noted the watershed effect that is going to hit the area in the not too distant future. "Most of us got started about the same time and for a lot of years we have taken care of the schools and they know we are here. When we get out, it will be around the same time for all of us and it is going to take a lot of new people to take our place, or there will be a big void. And that day is not that far off. We really need to start training some younger guys, the next wave, so to speak."

Football officials execute their duties, when compared to their basketball brethren, in relative obscurity. With the exception of a pass interference call (or no call), most often a football official will not be in the sight lines of the spectators or participants. "We like it that way," Johanson said. If after the game, no one can remember who the officials were, then they have done a good job. Johanson is the only one of the group who currently officiates basketball. "In basketball," he said, "the officials get a lot more notice. Sometimes that can lead to guys in basketball who are out there with big egos. That can cause problems. People did not come to watch the officials. We need to remember that," he said.

So why do they do it? To get it right, says Skinner. "That is a good feeling after the game, when we know we did the best we could. We hustled, we were in position and we gave the players a good effort. We are a part of the game, a part that, without us, couldn't take place." Elder concurred, "We take pride in doing our job with the best effort we can give. That is why we go out there each Friday night."

How long will they continue? All seven answered, with non-committal laughs and shoulder shrugs, inconclusively. My best guess; as long as there are women to piss off, these guys, for as long as they can will, every Friday night in the fall, don the stripes, warm up the whistle and do their duty.

Chapter 8
November: Survive and Advance
State Playoffs

All species capable of grasping this fact manage better in the struggle for existence than those which rely upon their own strength alone: the wolf, which hunts in a pack, has a greater chance of survival than the lion, which hunts alone. *Christian Lous Lange*

Moderation is the secret of survival. *Manly Hall*

Survival is nothing more than recovery. *Dianne Feinstein*

Survival is triumph enough. *Harry Crews*

Victory at all costs, victory in spite of all terror, victory however long and hard the road may be; for without victory, there is no survival. *Winston Churchill*

There's nothing like being involved with a team that can go the distance. *Chuck Daly*

October 22 – One more beer
Westhope at Linton
Round 1 Class A North Dakota State Playoffs

Ironically, Linton's first round opponent represented the school the farthest north, and thus closest to the Canadian border on Highway 83. Westhope, ND high school is located a scant seven miles from the Canadian province of Manitoba and only 15 miles southeast of the province of Saskatchewan.

Lion Head Coach Dan Imdieke knows his team will be challenged by the Sioux. Sporting a 5-3 record, Westhope has played well the last four weeks. "They have two very good linemen. One, Josh Farmer, weighs 300 pounds and he moves well for his size." While reviewing game film of the Sioux, it became obvious to Imdieke that the huge tackle was good enough to take up two players. "They try and have him fill both the A and the B gap on his side, which is mostly the right. If he can do that, then it frees up any extra unblocked linemen for them on the opposite side, and if you try and run away from Farmer's side, you are playing right into their hands."

During the week of preparation, Imdieke devised several blocking schemes where his linemen would double team Farmer. "We can't let him fill two gaps," the coach told his team on Monday. "We can double team him and still have enough people to block if we run right at him. That is what we have to do early, go right at him and make them move the extra man over to Farmer's side, and play us straight up. When that happens, then we can run away from him and they will not have the extra defender on that side."

Much like Linton, Westhope head coach Tom Nesvold is a proponent of running the football, making who can establish control of the line of scrimmage early in the game critical. "They have a sophomore quarterback," said Imdieke, "And I don't think he is as good as ours. We can throw on them and, I think, have some success. On the other hand, we want to make them have to throw the ball. First down is a key down. If we can force them into some third and long passing situations, I think we will be in real good shape with defending their passing game."

The Sioux are on somewhat of a roll, having won blow out games the last four weeks of the regular season, scoring 40+ points each week. The biggest adjustment for Coach Nesvold's team was moving up this fall to the 11 man game from the nine man game they had played for years. The top 80 enrollment schools in North Dakota play the standard 11 man game. The rest of the remaining teams play a hybrid form of the game with 9 players on each side. "We had to make the change once," says Imdieke. "It really is not that big of a deal." Westhope Coach Nesvold commented on the move, "It is still football. You still block and you still tackle. You just have two less people standing on the sideline."

"Our goal this year," said Nesvold, "was to get in the playoffs. We did that. Now our goal is to be the last team standing."

The first team standing in their way would be the Linton Lions.

As the Lions waited for the arrival of the Sioux from Westhope, the day broke warm and clear on the High Plains of southern North Dakota. Once the playoffs start in North Dakota, all games are played on Saturday after-noon. During the regular season, games are always contested on Friday nights, under the lights. A big factor, come playoff time, is the daytime strong winds that almost always blow across the open prairie during the daylight hours.

Thirty-five years of experience had taught Coach Imdieke to expect a strong wind for a playoff game. "When the sun goes down around here, the wind, unless we are having a storm, almost always will die down. But in the afternoons in October and November, oh boy, get ready." For a ball control team such as Linton, field position would be affected greatly by whether a team was punting into the wind or with the wind. Same with a team's pass-ing game.

Linton won the pre-game coin toss. They deferred their option to the sec-ond half. Westhope took the ball to open the game. Linton took the wind for the first quarter. It was another subtle, but astute decision by the Lion's skipper. With the wind at its back, Linton played with a short field the entire first 12 minutes, keeping the Sioux on their heels, pinned on their own end of the field. By the end of the first quarter, Linton had raced to an 12-0 lead. As Imdieke liked to say, "This ain't my first rodeo."

Imdieke's new blocking schemes, to offset the size advantage Westhope would bring with them from up north, were effective from Linton's first offensive snap. "I think those big boys were not quite ready for the after-noon heat we had down here," Imdieke said after the game. "We took the wind right out of their sails early and they just never seemed to get back into the game. Their linemen were good, but I think we had a good scheme for them, and more importantly our kids executed the schemes we put in for them. You can have the best plan in the world on the blackboard on Monday, but if that is where it stays, it will not do you much good."

Using the wind, Linton scored on its first two possessions of the game and had a 12-0 lead before the Sioux would record their initial first down. The first touchdown drive of the day would prove to be the Lion's most impressive. The nine-play, 65 yard march was highlighted by a balanced attack as QB Tanner Purintun continued to earn his coach's gradual confi-dence in his passing abilities. The senior completed 3 of 5 passes on the drive, the big strike being a 16 yard completion to Jayden Gross to give the Lions a first and goal from the 10 yard line. Running back Brock Nagel then bulled his way the last ten yards on the next play to give Linton a 6-0 lead.

Linton's defense was once again stellar. Westhope had come into the game averaging 44 points in the last three games of the regular season, all wins. They had no answer for the swarming Lion defenders. The Sioux second possession was also a three and out. The subsequent short punt into the wind gave the ball to Linton at the 50 yard line. This time the Lions needed only four plays to break the Westhope goal line. The scoring play was an 8 yard pass from Purintun to wide receiver Dillon Doolittle, who hauled down the strike in the right corner of the end zone. With 3:34 still to play in the first quarter, the Lions already held a 12-0 lead.

Midway through the second quarter, Linton put the game on ice with a 46 yard drive for their third and final score of the day. Purintun overruled none of the nine consecutive running plays by an audible that Imdieke sent in as the offense went on a nine play drive to establish a half time lead of 18-0.

The first half played by Linton was almost flawless on both sides of the ball. The offense was showing the type of late season versatility that all good teams need for a deep playoff run. Imdieke's team had passed for 76 yards and ran for 87. The stingy Linton defense held the much heralded Sioux offense to a total of only 55 first half yards.

The second half saw a conservative Linton team never allow Westhope to seriously challenge for a come from behind win. The visitors did score late, but Linton was in total control and coasted to an 18-8 victory. Imdieke said afterwards it was the most solid effort his team had turned in this season. No turnovers, only three penalties and no serious blown assignments. "We looked good," was his assessment to his staff, after the game. "And we got no one hurt. Now we need to find out who is next."

Linton advances to next week's quarterfinal for the 5th time in six years.

I always want my ledger balanced. I don't like to owe anything to anyone. So I was very happy this fall to chip away 5 yards of a 15 yard debt I owed.

Let me explain: At the Linton vs. Milnor, North Dakota State Quarterfinal game last month, while standing next to the line judge on the sideline and just before the ball was snapped, I commented loudly (for him to hear), "hey, their end is lined up in the neutral zone." The official blew his whistle immediately after my observation: five yard penalty, Milnor.

"Nice call," said Linton Assistant Coach Tim Dockter to me, "you got us five yards." Yeah, but I am still 10 yards in the hole, I thought.

In the time I spent covering St. Louis Roosevelt High School in 2008, which was the background for our first book, _Riding the Storm Out_, I cost the Roughriders an untimely 15 yard penalty. During the crucial Gateway Tech game, I got Roosevelt flagged by an official for unsportsmanlike conduct. Roosevelt's Coach Campbell is a big guy who I knew could become very emotional during a game. The official's response to Campbell's inquiry of the responsible party doomed me, "it's on the white guy," he told Campbell. Wow, that for sure narrowed the list of suspects. Once Campbell learned the identity of the culprit responsible for the untimely penalty flag, I knew he would come looking for me with blood in his eyes.

Despite my best attempt to practice my claim of invisibility by hiding on the sidelines behind the 310 pound Rene "Man-Child" Faulk, it didn't take Campbell long to locate my white face. Before I could express my innocence, claiming reverse discrimination - I threatened so often to invoke the race card defense, that one Roosevelt assistant coach nicknamed me Johnny Cochran - while explaining the referee's total over-reaction to my suggestions for improving his craft; Campbell grabbed me by the shoulders and said, "Dave, you are one of us. You can tell the refs anything you want. Give 'em hell! I don't care, just wait until we get the game a little more under control before you do it again, OK?"

I still need to get those other 10 yards back.

October 28 – Why does McCook win?
Alliance at McCook
First Round Nebraska Class B State Playoffs

The process for seeding the Nebraska Class B state football playoff bracket had undergone a major policy change for the 2011 season. In prior years, the two districts in the west, each containing four teams, would have the 8 entries seeded 1through 8 by use of the state points system. The same process would be repeated in the east and the two winners of the 8 team East and West brackets would meet for the state championship game in Lincoln.

The problem with that setup, said coach Jeff Gross, was that you would most always see the same teams in the playoffs that you had played in the regular season and if one side of the state was disproportionately stronger than the other, the best two teams would, some years, meet in the semifinals and not the final game. "We were a real driving force behind getting the process changed," Gross stated.

For 2011, the geographic split would be eliminated and the top 16 teams in the state would be placed on the bracket based solely on the point standings. As the number one ranked team in Class B, McCook would play the 16 seed. Opposite the Bison would be the 8 and the 9th seed. The irony was that when the final standings were calculated and released by the state on Saturday morning, McCook learned it would host the 16 the seed, Alliance, who the Bison had played in September. The winner of that match would take on the winner of the 8 and 9 seed game, Gering and Adams Central, both also regular season victims of the Bison.

The top 16 ranked teams and their points: McCook (9-0), 45.0000, Gretna (9-0), 44.4444, Crete (9-0), 43.8889, Elkhorn (8-1), 43.1111, Blair (7-2), 42.8889, Scottsbluff (7-2), 41.2222, Aurora (7-2), 41.2222, Adams Central (6-3), 41.0000, Gering (5-4), 40.7778, Ralston (7-2), 40.6667, Norris (5-4), 40.2222, Beatrice (5-4), 40.2222, Omaha Skutt Catholic (6-3), 39.8889, Elkhorn South (6-3), 39.8889, Plattsmouth (5-4), 39.6667, Alliance (5-4), 39.1111

Gross, on Saturday morning, laughed at the irony. "That is how the formula worked out, so we can live with that. We always like our playoff draw because it means we are playing in the post season. We don't ever want to take that for granted. With all that being said, we still like ranking all the teams 1 through 16, and feel it is the best way to reward teams for a good regular season. This setup gives the best chance of getting the best two teams to Lincoln (for) the championship game."

The first round game with Alliance would be played in McCook. "Hey, remember, we trailed Alliance in the 4th quarter," Gross warned his players on Monday about the September 4th quarter rally his team had to launch to stay unbeaten. "No matter what the process, no matter who or where you play, you still got to get it done on the field. Our focus right now is 100% on Alliance. We will have our hands full with them."

"We will show them some new looks that they didn't see up there is September," Gross said.

"We going to have to compensate for not having Jake. They know that and it is no secret we are going to pass it a little more."

By Sunday morning, Gross was already playing the chess game in his head. "I can put (Austin) Cherry in place of Jake, move him to a wide out and we still have three pretty athletic kids out wide. It also takes one more defender out of the box, which opens things up even more if we want to run Chitwood from a Wildcat set."

Gross then cut to the bone when analyzing the post-season, "We have had a great year, but Alliance could end it all here Friday night. There are no do overs from here on in. We got to make sure we have this team 100% prepared when we take the field. For here on in, we play for keeps."

Alliance made the 250 mile one way trip from the Panhandle intent upon not falling victim to what their coach called the "McCook Mystique." Before the game, the underdog's head coach, Travis Hawk, made it clear his team was not making the long trip to be intimidated before the game even began. "We can't get caught up in all the non-football stuff," he said. "The inflatable helmet, the music, the smoke, the fireworks; we are going to ignore all of that and just play football. They have had some great teams at McCook, but we are not playing those teams from 10 years ago, we are playing only this year's team and we proved back in September we can play with them. We moved the ball and we feel we should have won that game." Earlier in the season, September 9, in week 3 of the season, McCook had made the trip to Alliance and had to rally in the 4th quarter for a 31-20 win.

Hawk's moxie is admirable, but quicker than you can say 'humble pie," the Bison had both hands around the neck of Alliance, performing a death grip choke hold on the visitors to the tune of a 21-0 first quarter lead. No drama tonight. For all practical purposes, the game was over by the end of the first quarter. Matt Chitwood added a field goal in the second quarter for good measure and the Bison took a 24-0 lead to the half time locker room. McCook went into second half cruise control, as Gross took his foot off the gas – Alliance has never danced on the McCook "M" – coasting to a 37-14 win.

The Wildcats forced the Alliance offense to go three and out - three plays and a punt - the first three times they touched the ball. McCook's first two scores were set up by long Matt Chitwood to Cody Wudtke pass completions, the first 36 yards in length and the second 41, both giving the Bison first and goal on the Alliance three yard line. Justin Terry took the first trip into the visitor's end zone on a straight dive and Chitwood snuck over from the one on a quarterback sneak for the second. In between, Bison Defensive lineman Trevor Gleason recovered a midfield fumble.

Chitwood thrilled the huge home crowd with a 62 yard broken field touchdown run on the Bison's third possession, only to have the play nullified by a questionable blocking in the back penalty. The Bison shook off the ill-timed flag and scored two plays later on an 8 yard run by Terry.

Down 21-0, now Coach Hawk found his squad in the early hole he had preached so sternly in the pre-game talk to his team that they must avoid at all costs. It required he go away from what his team does best, handing the ball to talented senior tailback Mitch Pancost. Forced into more of a passing game, many times run from a no back offensive set, the Wildcats threw a blanket over the Bulldog receivers in an effort that Gross after the game would call the defensive's best all-around effort of the season.

Gross labeled the win as a good springboard into what was a hoped for trip to Lincoln and the Class B state title game. "We took care of business," the coach said. "We forced them away from Pancost and kept a lid on everyone else. On offense, it was good to have Terry back in the game. You could see how well he and Matt worked together on the veer option, and that was a very productive part of our game. We knew without Schlager, we would have to open up some other areas and I thought we did that. Our offensive line blocked better than they have all year."

As I departed the Bison Stadium after McCook's first round district game with Alliance, I was stopped by a blue windbreaker wearing gentleman I assumed to be an Alliance supporter, perhaps a parent. Our conversation went as such: Him: Aren't you that writer guy I read about in the paper? Me: Yes. Him: Then you must be pretty smart. Me: Depends on who you ask. Him: Then I have a question. Me: Ok. Him: Why does McCook always win? Me: I don't know. Maybe it was just their night. Him: It is always their night. We have just as good of players as them and we are just as big. I don't get it. Me: I don't know what else to tell you. Him: I think they are just darn lucky.

He spun on his heels and left, obviously dissatisfied with the non-answer he got from the smart writer.

I was due in Linton, ND the next afternoon for a Class A state playoff game and was faced with an all-night, eight hour drive to get there. I was not looking forward to the lonely passage through the Sand Hills on a dark, moonless and cold night.

North of North Platte, NE and south of Pierre, SD, Highway 83 hits a stretch where no over the air radio stations are available to the bored traveler, with the exception of National Public Radio. As a card carrying Democrat, I whole heartily endorse NPR and hope that their funding, which has become an election year political football exploited by those dastardly Republicans, stays intact. However, there is only so much Hungarian Peasant Folk Dance music a body needs in one day.

So imagine my delighted surprise when I discovered that, due to the evening airwaves carrying a stronger signal, I could pick up one commercial AM station, the 50,000 watt giant KMOX, directly from my hometown of St. Louis, MO. Due to this stroke of good luck, I was able to listen to Mike Shannon butcher the English language as only the lovable "Moon Man" can, as he described the last three innings of the Cardinals historic 7th game World Series win over the Texas Rangers.

In between Shannon's malapropos, as he told an elated home town audience of the Redbirds unlikely march to their 11th world title, I contemplated the gentleman in blue's question: "Why does McCook always win?"

By the time I crossed the border from Nebraska into South Dakota, with the Sioux Nation's Rosebud Casino on my left, the question had gnawed at me enough that I spent the next 3-1/2 hours of driving through South Dakota formulating an answer in my mind. When I reached the North Dakota boarder, having cheated a 45 mile detour of Highway 83 by taking a gravel road route that a weather-worn farmer had shown me back in August, usurping those cursed "government" barriers that, if obeyed, would have added close to an hour to my already long enough trip, I had the answer. The Bison do not beat themselves. It is that simple to label, but much more complex to understand. I next needed to break down and examine each detailed plank coach Gross has laid in building his powerhouse program.

Gross' long term success is built upon preparation. The formula for another Friday night win begins each proceeding Sunday evening in the Gross family/rec room, as the Bison coaching staff gathers to formulate the upcoming week's practice schedule that will, they hope, come to fruition with a well-executed game field performance on Friday night.

Many coaches can create a great game plan on the chalk board during a Sunday night meeting, but are unable to transfer the plan to the playing field on Friday night because they either do not understand, or will not accept, the number one rule of good teaching: accountability. If the student fails to master the task, then the teacher has failed, not the student. McCook players master their football tasks so well that many times they collaborate with the coaches to make game field adjustments.

During halftime of one game, Gross was not happy with defensive end Matt Collicott for allowing the opposing quarterback to get to the sideline for a long gain. "You got to have containment on the naked boot, what happened?" Gross barked. "Their end scraped and I went with him," the lineman answered. "Why can't you do that?" an animated Gross demanded. "Cause Javier has the receiver on the drag pattern and nobody else is back there," correctly answered the player. "So what do you do this half?" Gross quizzed. "Stay home and contain," the player said. "Then do it, dammit," Gross concluded, the correction of the mistake completed.

On the first possession of the second half, the same misdirection roll out by the quarterback was again attempted. This time though, the opposing signal caller was met head on by a "stay at home" Collicott and dropped, dammit, for a five yard loss.

The Bison gather for their pre-game and halftime instruction on home game nights in the area below the north grandstands of their stadium. For five to seven Friday nights a year, the location serves as a makeshift command center for the battle planning of the town's teenage heroes. The other 360 or so days of the year it is a storage area for the grounds crew who takes care of the stadium. Amid tractors, lawn mowers, hoses, crescent wrenches and other assorted tools; the team will assemble.

The second plank of the formula for Bison success, which builds on the back of plank one, is the organization of the large coaching staff Gross oversees, and how they contribute to both preparation and the game night execution of the team. For any given game, six to eight assistant coaches will join Gross on the sideline, another three to four in the press box, communicating to the coaches on the sideline through radio headsets. The efficiency and the success of the instruction given to the Bison players is because the McCook coaches, when it comes to teaching football skills, are all on the same page. With many teams, when a player, either in practice or a game, receives instruction from more than one coach, the frustration of the athlete becomes apparent due to contradicting instruction given by multiple coaches. I have never once, either in practice or a game, seen that happen at McCook. The instruction is rapid fire in its delivery, and to the point. It is, most importantly, consistent from one coach to the next. The correction is made, the grasp of the athlete's understanding validated and the practice or game continues without interruption or delay.

The third plank is that Gross has an uncanny ability to place his players in positions where their skills will allow them to be successful. Gross does not ask his players to do things they can't do. Bob Elder, a longtime local booster of the team, told me, on my first trip to McCook, that over the years he has seen Gross time and time again make personnel moves that have proven to be just the right assignment for both the player and the team. When Jake Schlager, arguably the Bison's most irreplaceable player, broke his leg in week 9, Gross adjusted his playbook to accommodate Schlager's replacement at tailback, Kyle Stewart. The junior is a talented hard runner, but he does not have Schlager's speed. "We are not going to ask him to be Jake," said Gross, the week before the Alliance playoff game, the first game plan that would not include Schlager. "You don't replace that speed. We can adjust."

The next plank is Gross' loyalty to his upperclassmen. Players growing up in McCook know that if they stick with the sport, training on the sub varsity levels as they are required too, that when they are juniors and seniors there will be a spot for them on the varsity stage. They will have the chance to run through the Bison helmet onto the green game field under the bright Friday night lights; before a packed and cheering stadium. It is the main reason that McCook will dress, on game night, 50 to 60 varsity players.

Next, Gross will listen to his trusted and able assistants. He loves to tell the self-deprecating story of his first year in McCook and his attempt to instill a "Mouse Davis" Portland State style wide open offensive passing game. It didn't fit. "Wouldn't have blamed them if they would have fired me right then for that stunt," he says now, 14 years later. That off- season, Gross sat down with his assistants and created the more vanilla, veer style option offense, that has become the trademark of the McCook dynasty.

Finally, the consistency of Gross' conservative approach to the game plan does not vary. McCook will run the football. If the Bison cannot control both lines of scrimmage, then Gross feels they cannot win. His defensive philosophy mirrors that of the offense, also conservative in nature. Gross says that his defense will bend but not break. "We dink you to death," is how he once described it to me.

For the McCook conservative approach to be successful, field position is an absolute for the Bison. They must be able to impose their conservative will on the flow of the game. Paramount to their ability to dictating game pace, year in and year out, lies with McCook having the best special teams play in the area. That is not just a happenstance of luck, but a cause and effect result of long term planning.

McCook begins training punters and kickers in junior high. From a list of fifteen or so kicking hopeful candidates in 7th grade, the group will be pared to two or three survivors by the time a class reaches the varsity level.

Voluntary summer training sessions with professional kicking instructors develop the skills of the McCook specialists, not only kickers, but also long snappers and holders. The depth of the kicking ranks in this small high school speaks of the emphasis the coaching staff places on the importance of dominating the kicking game. In pregame warm-up, the Bison will have three place kickers blasting 40 yard plus field goals, while on the other sideline will be a couple of punters launching 50 yard spirals.

Twice this season, Matt Chitwood, whom Gross calls the best placekicker in the state, has won double overtime games for the Bison with walk off field goals. Gross, in August, also labeled his punter, junior Matt Collicott, as the best punter in the state. When Collicott was injured against Lexington, his back up, senior Tyson Karr, stepped in and for his first varsity game against Adams Central as the #1 punter, hit three critical 4th quarter punts, ranging from 43 to 47 yards with zero return yards, to keep Adams Central mostly pinned in their own end of the field for the decisive late minutes of a three point win. If Collicott is the best punter in the state, then his back up, Karr, is number 1A.

The importance of field position for a defense built on the principle of bending but not breaking was on display in the first round playoff game with Alliance. Twice in the first half, the visitors from the Panhandle broke 50 yard plays. However, both efforts began with the ball deep in Alliance territory, 80 to 85 yards from the McCook end zone. Eventually, neither long gain led to any points for Alliance, despite twice covering over half the field on one snap of the ball. The first ended with an Austin Cherry interception, the second on a missed field goal attempt. Due in large part to winning the field position battle, McCook raced from the gate to a dominating 21-0 first quarter lead.

As the sun rose over a breaking perfect weather day for high school playoff football in Linton, ND, I felt satisfaction in that I had unlocked the secret of the long term success on the gridiron of the McCook Bison: they don't beat themselves and, with all due respect to the man from Alliance whose inquiry stimulated me to make constructive use of my time on an all-night drive through the Sand Hills; Gross is riding a 14 year lucky streak.

October 29: Time for a second half beat down
Milnor @ Linton
Second Round North Dakota Class A State Playoffs

After a satisfying and convincing first round win over Westhope, the Linton Lion's coaches, their spouses and other well-wishers, retreated to the town's favorite bar for some post- game levity. As Coach Imdieke and his happy entourage dissected the Lion's recently completed 18-6 win over the Sioux, talk naturally turned to gathering scores of the state's other seven first round games, all played that afternoon. Of particular interest were the final scores from the other three games on the Lions' side of the playoff bracket.

In North Dakota Class A football, 32 teams are assigned to 4 regions, based on their geographical location. The last seven weeks of the regular season, a round robin regional schedule is played. At the end of week seven, the top four teams in each region are ranked, based on the seven game round robin schedule, and assigned according positions on the state bracket. The other 16 teams are eliminated. Linton is in Region 1. The bracket will have region 1 teams cross bracketed with Region 2. The higher seeded team is the home team. As the champions of Region 1, Linton played at home against the #4 seed from Region 2, Westhope. The Lions would play the winner of the game between the #2 seed in Region 2, Larimore; and the #3 seed from their own Region 1, Milnor.

In the bottom half of the right side of the bracket would be the #1 seed from Region 2, Harvey-Wells County, a team that had been ranked #1 all season. Harvey, who had won the 2010 Class A title, had over the offseason- too conveniently thought some- cooped with Wells County, the defending state nine man champion, to hatch what appeared to be an unbeatable powerhouse. Their first round opponent would be the #4 seed from Linton's regional, Maple Park. The other game in the lower bracket would pit the #3 team from Regional 2, Park River against the Region 1 #3 finisher, Oaks.

As the Class A scores started to slowly trickle in and be posted on the state wide website, the good news for Linton flowed as freely as the complimentary beers bought for the coaches by the grateful town boosters. Milnor had upset Larimore, 42-30, and would be traveling to Linton next Saturday for a rematch of the 7 point win by Linton in September.

Next, better news, Oaks had beaten Park River 14-8. 3-0 so far, for Region 1 teams.

But the real shocker, the state's #1 ranked team all season and the overwhelming favorite to hoist the state champion trophy in the Fargo Dome in three weeks, Harvey-Wells CO, had been shocked by Maple Valley, 16-15. A clean 4-0 sweep for Region 1.

The Lions, due to the success of their Region 1 brothers, were now guaranteed home field advantage all the way to the final game. To get to Fargo and the state championship game, they now knew, would require wins over two teams, Milnor next week and either Maple Valley or Oaks the following week, whom they had already during the regular season beaten. Coach Imdieke could not have drawn the bracket himself more advantageous for the benefit of his Lions. The road to the Fargo Dome was wide open. The biggest hindrance, Harvey, had been removed and prematurely sent home.

Ironically, on the other side of the bracket, matching Regions 3 and 4, the higher seeded team won all four games.

As any coach would, under similar circumstances, Imdieke attempted to convince the Lion backers that there was a lot of football yet to play on the road to Fargo. He accurately pointed out last season, when one of the strongest Linton teams he had fielded in 35 years, one he openly admitted was more talented than this year's team, advanced to the second round only to be upset on their own field, 17-14, by the same Milnor team that would show up at Lion Field on Saturday. "I am sure," he told the faithful, "they will show up here on Saturday with a lot of confidence they can pull it off again." He also noted that, yes; his team had defeated all three of the teams left on their side of the tournament bracket, but only by a total of 13 points. "You know he said, "We could have just as easily lost to all three."

Okay coach, he was told by the celebratory crowd, you can worry about that tomorrow, but for now sit down and have another beer. It did not take much arm twisting for Imdieke to agree to that game plan.

"Hot dang boys, is this not fun?" The game his Linton Lions have in the state quarterfinals with Milnor had not yet begun, in fact, it was still 48 hours away, but Imdieke could not contain his enthusiasm as he drove the team bus on Thursday to the Lions' practice field at Seaman Park, just south of town. "You know what is really great," he yelled over his left shoulder at his team, wisely keeping his eyes on the road. "Since we don't play until

Saturday we get an extra day of practice. That means hills today for conditioning." The veteran coach laughed at the uniformed groans of his team. "Oh man,' Imdieke gushed, "you can't beat it, playoff football in North Dakota."

In 48 hours, Imdieke would see his team play their most complete game of the year and defeat a very good Milnor team, 28-14. "They knocked us out last year," said senior Lion quarterback Tanner Purintun after the game, "and we were going to make sure that didn't happen again. The seniors decided at halftime that this would not be our last game."

The effort earns Purintun and his Lion mates' one more home game, next Saturday in a semifinal matchup with Maple Valley. The winner of that match-up will advance to the Fargo Dome for the state championship contest. "All year long, we said our goal was to get to the Dome," said senior tailback Cody Sehn. "Now we got our chance. We need another effort like we had today in the second half and nobody can beat us." Sehn certainly did his part against Milnor with an afternoon of work that saw him carry the ball a workhorse 24 times for a career high 182 yards. He found the end zone three times.

After a scoreless first quarter, that saw each team punt the football twice in a battle for field position, the Lions put together an 80 yard drive, highlighted by a third down 48 yard run by Sehn.

Linton got on the board first, as Sehn carried the ball in from the five yard line. Purintun ran around his right end for the two point conversation and Linton was staked to an 8-0 lead. Milnor used a kickoff return to start a drive that would end with 41 seconds left in the first half on a 14 yard touchdown pass and the subsequent two point conversion to tie the game. Linton made a strong attempt to retake the lead in the closing seconds of the half, but ran out of time on the Milnor 19 yard line. The Lions even went to a trick play, a phenomena seldom seen in the tenure of the conservative Coach Imdieke. Tight end Jayden Gross went in motion and took a lateral from Purintun, stopping as he neared the sideline and hurled a pass back across the field to an open teammate, Brock Nagel. Gross' passing effort was caught in what was becoming a stiffening wind, fluttering just long enough in the air for the Milnor defensive secondary to react and knock the pass to the ground.

A unique feature of the stadium at Linton is that both teams' benches reside on the south side of the field. A chalk line at each 45 yard line represents the far edge of each team's bench zone, with a 10 yard buffer - a sort of demilitarized zone - separating the two teams. After the failure of Linton's end around reverse pass in the closing seconds of the half, Milnor head coach Eric Olson, standing not twenty yards from Imdieke, shot a good natured barb in the direction of his counterpart. "Hey Imdieke, how long did it take you to draw that one up in the dirt?" he yelled. "Stole it from the JV," Imdieke countered.

Imdieke spent the halftime break restructuring his blocking scheme. The prior week, against Westhope in the first round playoff game, the Lions had successfully executed several screen passes. It was obvious the Milnor coaches had studied the game film. Twice Imdieke had called for the screen pass and the Milnor defensive line had not fallen for the ploy by rushing the quarterback, who would then lob the ball over the heads of the defenders to a waiting back with a convoy of linemen to escort him, and the football, down the field. Instead of falling for the rouge, the well-schooled and prepared Milnor line man simply peeled off and blanketed the waiting receiver.

"We can't throw the screen, but we can run it down their throats," the coach said as he rubbed his hands together in anticipation of a second 24 minutes of football just the way he liked it, in the trenches. "Give me the JV defensive... line up here," Imdieke ordered. He then used the remaining ten minutes of the half time break to show his linemen the changes he wanted to make on their blocking schemes to take advantage of the interior of the line that he felt Milnor was ignoring. "Hot dang, boys," Imdieke said as he finished up his halftime adjustments, "this is going to be fun. It's time for a good old fashion Linton Lions football beat down."

He was right. Linton scored on its first two possessions of the second half to take a lead which they would not relinquish. A 67 yard drive on 11 plays started the half for the Lions. A key play was when Purintun kept the drive alive with a 16-yard run on a 3rd and 10, giving the Lions a first down at the Bulldog 38. Two plays and a Lion penalty later, Sehn broke free for a 36-yard run to the Milnor 7 yard line. On third down, Purintun pushed into the end zone from a yard out. After a failed PAT, the Lions, with 7:34 left in the third quarter, held a 14-8 lead.

The first Milnor drive of the second half ended with perhaps the momentum changer of the day. Facing a 4th and 1 from their 31 yard line, trailing only by six points, Milnor unexpectedly gambled and went for the first down. A quick out pass was on the money to the open receiver, but a hard hit on the Minor player by Jayden Gross dislodged the ball from the receiver's grasp and Linton took over on downs.

After the game Imdieke paid Gross his due. "Jayden is a terrible practice player, I mean the worst," said a happy Imdieke. "He probably has run more hills than anyone that has ever played here. But on Friday nights, he shows up to play. That was a big hit he made and really turned the momentum of the game. After our third score, we were able to run the ball and eat up clock. I thought we controlled the game from there on in and were never again in real danger."

On the first play after the turnover on downs, Purintun found an open Dillon Doolittle who made a diving catch at the Bulldog five yard line. Sehn got his second TD of the day on the next play as he barreled into the end zone standing up.

Now down two scores, Milnor answered. On 4th and one from the 50 yard line, QB Hansana found an opening on a sneak play, busted through the line and raced untouched for the touchdown. It would be Linton's only real breakdown on defense. 1:52 remained in the third quarter. It was time for the Linton running game to go to work.

Imdieke called all running plays for the remainder of the game and his ground attacked churned up the yards and ate up the clock. So effective was the Lions ball control offense that Milnor only snapped the ball nine times in the 4th quarter. Sehn notched his third touchdown of the day on an eight yard, third down and goal rush, which upped the Linton lead to 28-14. A stingy defense would let Milnor nowhere near the Lion end zone for the remaining five minutes of the game.

After the game, Imdieke was all smiles as he addressed his team in the winning locker room. "Great job today, men. Oh boy, that was fun," he told his, fresh from the showers, team. "The best we have looked all year. Well seniors, we got one more here (at home). We need a good week of practice, everybody focused and then we head to the Dome. What do you think? I told you, hot dang, isn't this fun?"

The win over Milnor was the 297th in the illustrious and long tenure of Imdieke at Linton. To reach the magic number of 300, his Lions would need to win next week's semifinal game, the state title game to be held in two weeks at the Fargo Dome, and next year's season opener. It is doubtful that the longtime coach is even aware of the possible milestone achievement in his near future; he is having too much fun living in the present.

Casey Stengel was an often quoted and loveable manager of the New York Yankees; as well known for his eccentric quotes as he was for the seven World Series titles his Bronx Bombers won, under his care, in the post war 1950's and early 1960's. Standing next to Imdieke on the sidelines is akin to spending the afternoon at a baseball game in the dugout with the late Stengel - on steroids.

Imdieke keeps up a non-stop chatter with anyone on the sidelines who will listen. His enthusiasm is contagious. His quarterback Tanner Purintun, says it is hard to have a bad day with the coach around. "That is what coach is known for, making football fun. Sometimes I think I take it more seriously than he does, but he just has a way of having you ready to play. A lot of times I will think before a game, well, maybe we aren't as ready as we should be, and then the game will start, and everything he said all week that the other team would do on defense, they do. But yeah, it is obvious that he knows what he is doing and also that he really enjoys what he is doing."

Having one of the best coaching years of his career - Imdieke's team was not even mentioned in the pre-season projections as a top 10 club - but are still standing after the Milnor win, one of only four Class A team's left in the state of North Dakota.

Stengel once said, "When you are younger you get blamed for crimes you never committed, and when you're older you begin to get credit for virtues you never possessed. It evens itself out." Imdieke is enjoying the same elder statesman stature now, earned by his years of success. "I like this team because of the chemistry," he says. "They all bring things to the team with their different personalities, that when you put them all together, they make a strong group. We have had better individual talent on a lot of our teams here, but this group is a strong team and that is why we have won a lot of the close games we have this year. They know they can count on each other."

Imdieke's strength as a coach, and what he will tell you is the base rock his offense has always been built upon, is that he is a master at teaching the art of line blocking, a skill that has eroded over the last twenty years. Two amazing stories: the University of Alabama, under Coach Bear Bryant, in 1965 won the national championship with an offensive line that averaged 180 pounds per man. Story two: there was not one player listed on an NFL roster in 1976 that weighed over 300 pounds. Today, most small colleges have lines that, on the average, weigh over 300 pounds. The causes are many, but mainly lie in a major rule change, on all levels of the game –high school, college and pro – that was implemented in the late 1970's. The rules on blocking were liberalized so that offensive linemen could now extend their arms, as long as they stayed in a triangle that was formed roughly by the defender's two shoulders and his sternum. This increased the importance of raw strength and decreased the importance of technique and quickness. In other words, under the new rules, size now trumped quickness.

Due to the increasing size of linemen, most teams have today gone to a "zone" blocking technique on the offensive line, occupying or "locking up" a defender and letting the running back use his vision to cut away from the defender. This has eliminated many of the intricate blocking schemes based on pulling guards and trap blocking tackles which were, for years, a staple in the playbook of every football team that employed a run oriented offense; but not at Linton. Imdieke, in another nose thumbing gesture of his to the changing times (the man does not own a cell phone), the Lion linemen pull and trap, and they do it with a mastery not often seen in the 21st century football world.

"We are not as big as a lot of teams this year on the line," Imdieke says the night before the second round playoff game, "so our trap plays are even more important this year." The system is dependent upon timing, with an offensive lineman leaving his side of the field, pulling behind the center, but ahead of the running back, and blocking an unexpecting defensive lineman who has been left unblocked and allowed to penetrate to the offensive backfield where the pulling offensive lineman will then execute a blind side "kick out" block. When watched from the end zone, when the timing of the lineman and the back are in tune, the choreographed movements are a thing of beauty, a form of football ballet and, hot dang, fun to watch.

The man on the hot seat for the Milnor game was Linton defensive coordinator Paul Keeney, now in his fifth season of calling the defensive signals for the Lions. He needed to develop a game plan to stop the two- time Milnor all-state quarterback, Josh Hansana. "I felt we shut him down as well as anyone the first time we played," Keeney said in alluding to a September 9th 12-7 Linton win over the Bulldogs. "But this is the third year and fifth game I have had to get a defense ready for him, and I tell you what; I will be glad to see him graduate. He can hurt you so many ways. He can run, he can pass and he is smart," evaluated Keeney.

Several long nights of watching film until past midnight on Sunday and Monday nights, had the coach feeling that he had a good plan of attack. "We are going to rush four, maybe only three, linemen. Our ends have got to keep him contained. We can't rush him hard from the end and then let him get around our containment and to the sideline. We are going to have to let him have time to throw, and our coverage people are going to have a tough assignment, because he is going to have a lot of time to look for receivers. But I would rather have him throwing than running all over the field on us, and he is capable of doing just that."

Keeney wears several unique hats in earning his monthly paycheck. In addition to his duties as a coach at Linton, he serves as the secondary school (grades 7-12) principal at Hazelton High School, located 12 miles north on Highway 83 from Linton. He is also the district's athletic director, and he teaches all the secondary level science classes. At 3 pm, he loads a school bus with the ten Hazelton students (four are junior high players) who play football at Linton and drives south on Highway 83 for daily football practice.

Since the early 1980's, Hazelton has "cooped" with Linton's football program. This arrangement, which is very typical of North Dakota, with so many small districts not having the enrollment to support an athletic program on their own, allows a small school like Hazelton to give its male students the opportunity to play high school football. With an enrollment of 31 high school students, only 12 of whom were boys, the school is much too small to field even a 9 man football team; 11 men being out of the question.

While Hazelton had been sending its football players and wrestlers to Linton for almost a generation, the past school year, 2010-11, was the first year that Hazelton had not fielded its own basketball teams. All Hazelton athletes were now Linton Lions. The Hazelton Tigers, after over 70 years of play, are now a footnote in history.

Keeney says the school had no choice than to give up the identity that the basketball teams brought to the school and community. He points out that over the past five school years the Hazelton enrollment figures for grades kindergarten through high school had dropped from 144 to 99.

The declining enrollment of the Hazelton schools sent a clear message - if you want our kids to have a team to play on, we have to send them to Linton. Despite the numerical necessity, the decision to permanently mothball the Hazelton basketball jerseys was met with much community resistance. "It was a much harder sell to the community than it was to the kids," says Keeney, who had served as the Hazelton Tigers last boys' basketball coach. "And I understand why, but we just didn't have a choice. We didn't have enough students interested to fill out a roster."

Keeney, who hails from the small town of Melba, ID, found the transition to small town North Dakota, a smooth one. "I played baseball and football at Mary University here in North Dakota and I met my wife there. She is from Hazelton and really liked the area. It has been a good fit for our family."

Most small schools in North Dakota, especially in a sport like football- which requires at least a 30 man roster to be competitive even on the small school level- have been cooping for years. The current Hazelton schools itself is a product of consolidation. The small towns of Moffit and Braddock had closed their own schools years before and sent their students to Hazelton, creating the hyphened school district of Hazelton-Moffit-Braddock.

The Hazelton school district in 1998 saw the educational god's smile upon them with a much needed infusing of funds that came from an unlikely donor- a home town boy who had moved away 40 years prior to seek and find his fortune in the proverbial land of milk and honey; California. Dennis Farrey is the quintessential American rags to riches success story. In the mold of a modern day Horatio Alger, Farrey graduated from high school in North Dakota on May 25, 1964 and departed on a west bound airplane for the promised land of California on May 26, 1964. He has never looked back.

Tired of working weekends bagging groceries, his first gig in the Golden State, Farrey signed on in the mid 1960's with an Electronics company repairing radar on US ships coming back from Vietnam. He then started a company in the infant stage of electronic circuits. "Everything in the field was so new back then that it did not hurt me not to have a college education. There was no one to teach any such thing anyway. We were buying and selling new components coming into the field as we went along and I learned by doing, as I went along. I was fascinated with the whole concept and the potential that the industry held. My timing was perfect and it was pure luck. I was in the heart of the industry when the computer boom hit in the 70's," remembers Farrey.

In 1974, anchored smack in the infant computer industry's holy land of Silicon Valley, Farrey founded Jameco Electronics, a mail order electronics component distributor. In 2004 the company introduced its own product line. Today, Jameco Electronics offers, through its mail order business to its customers, more than 40,000 of the industry's most popular name brand components. The company is one of the best run stocking distributors in the United States. "We're privately held, debt-free and financially strong," said Farrey. "This, combined with good management and employees, means we can negotiate great deals and be on the front end of technology with the products our customers need and have stock when they need them."

Today, living in the glittering world of Northern California, Farrey is far removed from the harsh and remote regions of his native state; but he has not forgotten his roots on the northern high plains. With his son now taking responsibility for most of the day to day operations of Jameco, the senior Farrey has turned his attentions to more philanthropically motivated endeavors. In 1998 he paid back, in many fold, to the home town that raised him through his sophomore year of high school; Hazelton ND.

"My family ran a bar in Hazelton," Farrey recalls. "In 1962, right after the end of my sophomore year at Hazelton High School, my Dad became very ill. We sold the bar and moved to Jamestown. Two weeks into my junior year, my Dad died. It was that quick. He was 36 years old. I finished high school in Jamestown. I hated that I couldn't play sports like I did in Hazelton. With Dad gone, I had to get a job, and I worked at a grocery store from 4 to 8 pm every day after school and all day on Saturdays. I made one dollar an hour, but we needed every penny of it for the simple necessities. I had three younger siblings to help support. I didn't graduate from Hazelton High School, but I always considered Hazelton my home town."

In 1998, word reached Farrey in California that his hometown's school was at a cross roads. The district's building, circa 1920, was in desperate need of upgrading, but cost estimates to modernizing the decaying facility were more than the cost of building new. The other option open to the patrons of Hazelton was to let their students be bussed to a nearby district, probably Linton, and shutter their own school. According to Farrey, the community was not going to allow that to happen. "If the school closes, the town dies. That has happened all over North Dakota, and a number of us were not going to let that happen to Hazelton."

Saddled for a number of years with a declining enrollment, the district was limited in the amount of capital they could devote to the project. Still, the citizens of the district voted 72% in favor of building the new school with a budget of 1.1 to 1.3 million dollars to complete the project. That same spring, seven small towns in south central North Dakota held bond elections for their local school. Only Hazelton's passed; and with a whopping

72% in favor. "That told me something," said Farrey. "We had to get this done."

A bare bones proposal was drawn up and Farrey flew back to North Dakota to attend an all-important Hazelton Board of Education meeting where the district, and the communities' future, would be debated.

At the meeting, Farrey was very outspoken in challenging his former hometown. "If you are going to do it, then you need to do it right." He knew the resources for the district were limited, but he was not satisfied with the district's proposed finished product, especially the gymnasium. "The gym that had been drawn up in the original proposal was worse than what we had; about three rows of bleachers on each side, with a tile floor. The cost of building a modern building and doing it right, creating something for the long term use of the community, was above what the district could afford. That was clear. But why build something that is not going to meet either your current or your future goals? I told the community at the meeting that night, 'this is not acceptable and a waste of your money if you build it.'"

Farrey put his money where his mouth was. He will not disclose amounts or figures, but sources say that the original bill for what the district felt it could afford was 1.1 to 1.3 million dollars and Farrey tripled that amount, in dollars of his own, to create the educational state of the art facility that today's Hazelton students have enjoyed for the past decade. The gym seats 2,000 and, when it was built, was the biggest high school gymnasium in the state. Even now, with Hazelton cooping their basketball and volleyball teams with Linton, the facility is still used to host the more important state events and contests held in the area. The school itself was designed with all the modern educational technology available in 1998. All rooms have closed circuit TV, an 80 seat movie theater room and a 150 seat cafeteria. The entire campus has wireless internet. The gymnasium area is highlighted with a modern weight room, equipped with a hot tub sauna that is open to the community with no advertising ever allowed in it.

The new Hazelton School, with much fanfare and local chest swelling, was dedicated on February 16, 1999.

One of the few strings Farrey tied to the building project was that he wanted the gymnasium named after a late local farmer, Ben Kalberer. Many people in the Hazelton area were surprised when the benefactor's name was made public. Kalberer had been dead for over 30 years, the community had either forgotten of the unassuming late farmer, or were not old enough to have even heard of him.

"He was a handsome bachelor who farmed outside of town here when I was growing up," Farrey recalled. "He was successful and had some resources. He did so much to help the kids in town. I, like a lot of kids, didn't have much in the way of material things growing up. He was a big sports fan of the Hazelton teams. For years he bought the uniforms, the ball gloves, shoes; anything that a kid who couldn't afford but needed to play on the baseball or basketball teams, he took care of it. At Christmas, he would have the hardware store owner in town have every kid go in and pick out anything in there; sleighs, bats, balls, any one item they wanted for a Christmas present. I never forgot that and I have tried to give back to the community like he did. One year the Minneapolis Tribune got a hold of the Christmas story and ran a big article. They say old Ben had over 1,000 people contact him after that story was written, and a couple were women who asked about if he needed a wife!"

Room for expansion, wishful thinking for most small rural schools like Hazelton, was considered and built into the school construction plan Farrey had developed and dug into his own pocket to see become reality. "The kids that graduated high school last spring (2011) were the first group that started Kindergarten in the new building. That was special," Farrey says.

Farrey has been instrumental in seeing that the dozen or so graduates, each year, of Hazelton High School have a unique college opportunity. In 2000, with Farrey and other's financial support, the district started the Millennium Endowment Fund. About $40,000 is available each year for graduates to help defer the cost of college.

In 2011, perhaps the most ambitious scholarship endowment available to any small town high school grad in the nation was initiated; the Myron Jahner Academic Memorial Scholarship. (Myron Jahner was a local man who donated hours of his time to oversee the construction of the new school. His willingness, and skills, in serving as the project manager was instrumental in completing the project.) Any four year attendee of the Hazelton school district who graduates from the high school with the credentials to gain admittance to one of the nation's top 10 universities: Harvard, Princeton, Yale, Columbia, Stanford, Penn, Cal Tech, MIT, Dartmouth or Duke; will receive $80,000 of tuition assistance to cover their four years of education.

Hazelton Class of 2011 grad Lindsey Marie Voller entered Stanford University in the fall of 2011 to embark on a studies course she hopes will lead to a career in medicine. Voller said in a press release from the Hazelton schools, "This scholarship has not only humbled me, but has also given me the confidence to know I can succeed at a larger university. It has allowed me to fulfill my dream of attending a top 10 university. I intend to work hard at Stanford and meet the responsibilities and expectations that accompany this tremendous opportunity. I will always remember this life-changing award and how it contributes to the success of others."

His motives, Farrey says, are grounded in the pragmatic view of survival so needed by those who have survived and flourished in the harsh environment of the High Plains of North Dakota. "I have found over the years that success is a matter of opportunity and I want to see every worthy kid in Hazelton have the opportunity to fulfill their potential," Farrey says. "I have built my business and run my company on this formula: 55 % of people go along and do their jobs (nothing more, nothing less) 40% are the complainers (gripe about everything but do nothing to change anything) than we have the 5%, they are the ones who get things done, they inspire people, they are the doers (and) you have got to have them in your company to survive. Your community finds most of their problems because of these statistics. I have found that these statistics are the same in business as they are in communities- look around, you see and hear it every day. This country needs these people and we, as a nation, cannot let schools like Hazelton die of simple neglect."

Facilities and Scholarships are great, but the commodity most needed for a school is students, and Hazelton has been steadily losing student population for over two generations. "We have a long range goal in place," said Keeney. "We think we have seen the worst of the dropping enrollments. Out elementary grades are stable and we feel that we can maintain an enrollment of about 30 in the high school over the next 10 years. If we can do that, then we should survive."

Keeney takes an "if you build it they will come," attitude, in regard to the student drain problem faced by his district. He says that the students in Hazelton get a good education. He points to the 21 average score on the ACT of the class of 2011. "We think, as parents see what we can give their child in terms of an education, we will see people moving in to take advantage of the good schools. We are not planning on going anywhere."

November 4, 2011 – Life is not an undefeated proposition
Adams Central @ McCook
Second Round Nebraska Class B State Playoffs

When I first started this project, I was told by an acquaintance that I was taking a big gamble, rolling the dice and banking on the three schools I had chosen to cover, to have the type of seasons that would be worth chronicling. I was asked what would be the worst possible scenario in regard to my plans. My answer was that all three teams having losing seasons would be disastrous. However, I pointed out, considering the historical success and the quality of coaching in each program that result was about as likely to occur as a royal flush on a one armed casino bandit.

My second biggest fear, I added, would be if all three teams went through the season undefeated. That result I didn't consider a likely occurrence, but it wouldn't be a total shocker if it did come to be.

Call me a voyeur of discord, discontent and disappointment, if you wish, but I believed that the group dynamic that would prove most fascinating in the story I intended to write was how players and coaches would handle the adversity that almost every team, every year, is faced with. True human spirit and character is best laid open for inspection by the brutal pressure created by failure in competitive endeavors like high school football.

Until Friday evening, the McCook Bison had lived a charmed life this fall, rolling to a perfect undefeated mark. Every button head coach Jeff Gross pushed proved to be the right one. When misfortune finally found the Bison, as it did Friday night, it came unforeseen, swiftly and painfully; very painfully.

McCook entered the state quarterfinal game with Adams Central on Friday night with a perfect 10-0 record. However, even the most die-hard McCook fan would not call the 2011 edition of the Bison an overpowering team. In four of their ten wins, McCook had to overcome a 4th quarter deficit; three game outcomes had come down to the last play of the game, two in double overtime. Coach Gross' team had successfully zigzagged through mine fields all season long.

In the quarterfinal game against Adams Central, when they needed to zig, they instead zagged, landing them square in the cross hairs of the football gods of fate. The result was a very un-McCook like loss.

All season long, the Bison had lived off the big play; in particular, the heroic efforts of senior quarterback Matt Chitwood. With the teams other main playmaker, speedster Jake Schlager lost for the season with a broken leg, even more of the spotlight for the playoffs fell on Chitwood. The quarterfinal game would prove to be the only game all season that the shake and bake Chitwood could not break loose. "They did a good job on Matt," said Gross after the game. "They just said 'he will not beat us', and they committed the defensive resources to stop him. But we still had enough offense to win the game."

McCook seemed in control late in the game, when they completed a masterful 15 play drive that covered 68 yards, putting them ahead by 11 points. The drive ate up over seven minutes of the fourth quarter clock, and was just the kind of clutch, mistake free football that had secured so many Bison wins during the Gross years. "We executed on offense tonight about as well, at times, as we have ever done. That is what is so frustrating about losing this game. In hindsight, we played well enough to win. Several times this year we have escaped with wins when maybe we had been outplayed, but capitalized when the other team made a big mistake. Tonight, we got some of our own medicine."

With an 11 point lead and only 5:53 left in the game, all the Bison needed to advance to the semifinal round was one stop on defense and a couple of first downs. They got the stop, but not the couple of first downs.

The Patriots used a 50 yard quarterback run to take the ball deep into McCook territory, but two plays later, Bison DB Zayne Gillen picked off his second interception of the night, and most of the standing room only crowd felt the McCook ticket to the next round had been punched.

In a play that will long be remembered with groans in McCook, the Bison did what they hardly ever do, fumbled the ball. "The only way we lose this game is to give them one score and let them earn the other," said assistant coach Russ Schlager after the game. "They didn't have time to earn a score twice, we had to give them one, and we did."

On the first down play, to start the drive that was supposed to eat up the clock and move the Bison on to the semifinals, quarterback Matt Chitwood and fullback Justin Terry, on a maneuver the two seniors had successfully executed thousands of times since junior high, mishandled the ball on the veer hand off. AC fell on the fumble at the three yard line. The Patriots needed only one play and a two point conversation to pull within three points of the Bison.

The McCook offense had rolled all night, primarily running the football. A couple of first downs now, despite the costly turnover, and the Bison would again have escaped with a close win. Instead, the Bison offense went three and out. With four minutes to play, after a clutch 55 yard Bison punt by Tyson Karr, the Patriots took control of the football on their own thirty yard line. It took the visitors only two minutes and three plays to march down the field and take their first lead of the night, 28-24.

All-everything Adams Central running back Josh Fowler caught a short pass over the middle and raced untouched for 40 yards to the McCook 34 yard line. On the next play, fullback Kyle Cuddeford caught a swing pass and sprinted around the right end for a 15 yard gain. Quarterback Blake Overmiller then finished off the three play drive by outrunning a Bison defense that was uncharacteristically on its heels for the decisive drive of the game. Overmiller's effort covered the final 23 yards needed to reach the Bison end zone on a way too easy, three play, 66 yard drive. "We were much too soft on that last drive," said Gross. "We let the momentum slip away with the three and out on offense and then they just ran through us for that last score."

McCook still had one last gasp of breath left. They came close. With the help of a 15 yard unsportsmanlike conduct penalty on AC, Chitwood led his team to the Patriot's 23 yard line. But there would be no magic tonight. A third down Chitwood pass to the left sideline was intercepted by Adams Central at the 6 yard line.

That quickly, the Bison dream season was over, crashing on the hallowed ground of Bison Field, a stage that had seen this senior class perform so well all year long. The twelve senior players, who only minutes before had been at the apex of their careers, cashing in on all the years of hard work in perfecting their skills, cheered on by another packed stadium of home town fans, now had suddenly joined the ranks of former Bison players. In less time that it would take to go to the concession stand for a bag of popcorn, they found their careers over. Most, if not all, will never play football again.

The stunned large Bison crowd sat in stone silence, as if not believing what they had just seen, waiting for a reprieve from the football gods. None would be forthcoming. Many McCook players lay on the field in disbelief as the Adams Central players danced and hugged in celebration.

Later that evening, Gross would pay the senior class their dues. Sitting in his office, exhausted and still visibly disappointed to have a perfect season come crashing down so suddenly, he called the class of 2011 one of his fondest. "They laid it on the line all year. It was a small class and they weren't one of our more successful groups on the lower levels, but they kept working, kept getting better and willed themselves into a very solid unit. They will be missed."

On the only night of the 2011 season that saw his team on the field pull up short, Gross stood his tallest. His heartfelt, and emotional, post-game address to his devastated team was the perfect blend of the adult educator who keeps the priorities of his young players in perspective- "you might not think so now, but the sun will come up in the morning" – to the heart-broken coach who knows his team should have won the game –"you seniors will always be special to me. But they made plays tonight and we didn't. Give them credit, shake their hand and hold your head high. Tonight, they were the better team. But never forget what a great senior season you had. Don't let one game dictate the whole year or your career. The record book will say 10-1, and that is pretty darn good."

A choked up Matt Chitwood and his stunned teammate Justin Terry could not believe they had disconnected on the fumbled handoff that doomed the Bison fate. "I just wish we could have that play back. We haven't fumbled that handoff all year," said Chitwood. "And then it happens now," added Terry.

It is appropriate that that there is a second capital letter in the name McCook. Coach Gross runs a class program, with a capital C. If his team must lose, then the coach was not going to pass up one last opportunity to teach the youngsters entrusted to his care one last life lesson. Gross told his assembled team in concluding his post-game comments, "there are no do overs in life guys, or in playoff football games. It is time to move on."

November 5, 2011 – More guts than a fish market
Maple Valley @ Linton
Semifinals North Dakota Class A State Playoffs

Six week old Lane Otto is the first grandchild of Linton head football coach Dan Imdieke and his wife Cathy. The young man was in attendance for his first football game as Maple Valley traveled to Linton to take on his Grandpa's Lions in a state semifinal game. The winner would advance to the North Dakota Class A state title game, to be played the next weekend in the Fargo Dome.

It young Lane lives to the ripe old age of 100, witnessing multiple games weekly every fall for a century, it is quite possible he will never see a more improbable comeback than he did on the day of his first game.

The Linton Lions, on a windy and cold North Dakota day, displayed more guts than a fish market in executing what the 35 year veteran Imdieke called the greatest comeback he had ever seen. In Linton, a school known for 4th quarter heroics, that is quite a statement. "We have had some great comebacks here," said an emotional Imdieke, postgame, while sitting in his office drying his hair after a player induced Gatorade bath, "but nothing ever like this, not even close. How these kids pulled together today, and did what they did, is unbelievable. I can't express how proud I am right now."

Down 20-0 and forced to play the second half without their injured all-state quarterback, the win was a true Linton team effort, but the lead actors of the second half miracle were as follows: 1) A tight end turned quarterback, a role he last played in 7th grade, eagerly jumping into his new position with a moxie induced swagger worthy of Captain Morgan, leading his team out of what seemed an insurmountable half time hole. 2) A center that – since the new quarterback did not know the plays – resorted to the old backyard two hand touch strategy of drawing the plays up in the dirt as the team huddled around him. 3) An injured fullback, conscripted to become a kicker, booting the decisive last second winning kick, but only after a time out, so he could have his dislocated shoulder popped back into its socket.

What started as a promising day for Linton and its huge fan following, quickly went south. After forcing a Maple Valley punt following a three and out on their initial possession, the Lions took over on the 50 yard line. Lion quarterback Tanner Purintun, having an all-state caliber senior season, scrambled down the north sideline for a gain of 20 yards. As he was tackled out of bounds, he grabbed his right knee, letting out a loud scream, heard even above the roar of the cheering Linton crowd.

After Purintun left the field, his replacement, a sophomore, who in his defense had not taken a meaningful snap on the varsity level all season, promptly fumbled the ball on a fullback exchange. The ball was recovered by the Falcons. A sub was put in to play Purintun's defensive position of corner back. The Maple Valley coaches, smelling blood in the water, on the first play called for a streak pass pattern to be run at Purintun's defensive replacement. The perfectly laid pass resulted in a 76 yard touchdown. Maple Valley had taken a 7-0 lead.

Purintun gamely attempted to re-enter the battle. With his QB reduced to hopping on his injured leg, Imdieke decided to run everything from the shotgun formation, limiting the amount of movement required of Purintun. It was a bad decision. The pain in the gritty senior signal caller was overbearing. In his junior year, on the same knee, he had torn his MCL (medial collateral ligament). He was sure he had suffered the same injury again. Between tears of pain and frustration, he told his Dad, who had come down to the bench area, "it feels just the same as last year." A short time later, a doctor examined the injury and confirmed Tanner's worse fears, torn MCL. Purintun would contribute no more on the field this day, but he still would play an instrumental half time leadership role.

The rest of the first half was a nightmare for the Lions. Halfway through the second quarter, Imdieke saddled up to me on the sideline and said, "we are in big trouble, this could get real ugly."

It was obvious that his young sophomore quarterback was in over his head. In the first round of the playoffs, Maple Valley had knocked out the QB of the state's number one ranked team, Harvey. The injury led to a 15-14 upset win. The Falcons readily promoted their reputation of a tough, hard hitting and edgy team. The image was enhanced by a large number of MV players sporting Mohawk haircuts. Now was the perfect time to play the bully, and the visitors gladly accepted the role. Demonstrative displays of emotion, accompanied by shouts and chest pounding after almost every tackle, were meant to unnerve the Linton players, and it seemed to be working. The large visiting crowd joined in with several taunting chants. The barbarians had broken down the city gates and the Lions seemed to not have the fight needed to defend their own field. The visitors kept pounding away as the Linton players, both on the field and on the sidelines, hung their heads. The feeling on the Linton sideline was one of hopelessness.

Halfway through the second quarter, down now 14-0 and the season slipping away before his eyes, Imdieke was desperate. "We can't move the ball if we can't throw it," he said to an assistant, an admission that the Falcons were simply lining up to stop the run with all 11 defenders packed tight in the box between the ends, daring Linton to throw the ball. A lineman had a suggestion, "Coach, Jayden can play quarterback." Label it as a suggestion for the ages.

Jayden Gross was a senior tight end having a good season, leading the team with nine touchdown pass receptions. "Jayden" asked Imdieke, "Can you play quarterback?" "I did in 7th grade," Gross confirmed. Imdieke, in an almost pleading voice asked, "Want to give it a try?" Why not, was Gross' shoulder shrugging response. Like Paul Newman's character in the movie "Cool Hand Luke," it was Gross' cavalier way of saying, "whatever you say, boss man."

Gross promptly fumbled his first game snap from center in four years. Imdieke raised his eyes to the heavens, seemingly out of miracle solutions, stowing himself for a long second half. Maple Valley took a 20-0 lead into the halftime intermission.

Imdieke, during the first part of the break, huddled with his offense and Gross. "How many plays do you know from the quarterback position?" the coach asked. "None," said Gross. "Coach, I know the quarterback plays, I can tell him and he can just do what I say. We can do it. I will make it work," said center Nolan Meidinger.

With no other option available, Imdieke agreed to the arrangement that led to the strange site of each time the team huddled for an offensive play in the second half, number 50 could be seen crouching like a baseball catcher in the middle of the huddle, intensely scratching out diagrams in the dirt. "In case you couldn't tell," Imdieke said with a wink after the game, "Nolan is our smartest kid."

The talk amongst the players and coaches at halftime was of pride, determination and holding on to some sort of dignity as they accepted their bad luck and dismal fate. The word "winning" was not mentioned until Purintun, assisted to the team's meeting area on the shoulder of his brother, through tears of more frustration than pain, lit into his teammates. "You guy have quit. Hear that word, quit. I will say it again, quit." His tone was one more of disgust than anger, as he spit out the word seldom associated with a Linton team; quit. "I can't be out there with you, I wish I could, but I am only one guy. I mean nothing to our defense and you lay down for 20 points to these guys? We are Linton. We are known for great comebacks, the team that never quits. I will not see my senior class remembered as the team that quit. That is not going to happen. We can win this game. All we need is one score. Then we are back in it. We got to shut them down and we can. We can. You just got to believe, just like we always have. Trust each other. We still got time."

On their second play from scrimmage in the third quarter, Maple Valley appeared to salt the game away with a 64 yard untouched run to the end zone by Ethan Preston. The sobering tally was posted on the new Linton scoreboard: Home 0, Visitors 26. The only question left to answer would be could the Lions fight off the embarrassment of a mercy rule running clock that would kick in if the score reached 35-0? But don't close the casket and start shoveling dirt on the Lion carcass just yet. A small yellow flag lay up the field, unseen by the chest pumping celebrating MV players. Holding penalty, the official signaled, bring it back.

The penalty seemed at the time to be just a minor delay to the inevitable thrashing that was to come Linton's way, but it turned out to be the play of the game. "If they score there and go up four touchdowns, even as hard as our kids fought, I don't think we could have come back," said Imdieke after the game.

The confidence builder, just as Purintun had predicted with his emotional half time plea, came with the Lions first score. With 5:45 left in the third quarter, Brock Nagel found the end zone, Gross ran in the two point conversion and the deficit was now a doable 12 points. The play of the drive was a 30 yard pass from Gross to Dillon Doolittle, converting a 3rd and 7 to a first down. It was Gross' first completion on the day. As the game wore on, the Linton passing game was reduced to Gross taking the snap and simply running in the backfield as his receivers freelanced, running arbitrary patterns, looking for an area not containing a defensive back. It was back yard touch football at its best.

After the first score, Gross said he and his teammates knew they had a chance. "That touchdown took a lot off our shoulders. After we scored, we now had to depend on the defense. We needed the ball back at least two more times."

Maple Valley drove deep into Linton territory on the next possession, but this time, the Lions did not break. Led by Jayden's first cousin, All-State lineman Alex Gross, the Lions were now beginning to shut down the MV offense, fatigue setting in on the larger Falcon lineman. Remember the Hill, the Lions reminded each other. "The Hill" was the legendary conditioning program the Linton teams had followed for years, running up and down a steep incline located next to their practice field. Over the years, many friend and foe alike, credited the training routine with the uncanny ability Linton had for staging 4th quarter comebacks.

Forcing a change of possession on downs at their own 24, the ball was back in the hands of Gross and the offense. He promptly led the Lions 76 yards to their second touchdown, scoring himself on a 3-yard run. With 10:59 left to play, the lead was now down to 6, 20-14. Gross accounted for 69 of the 76 yards on the drive, rushing for 27 yards and initiating the long distance play of the day, hitting Doolittle with a 42-yard pass that set up the Lions first and goal at the MV 6.

Now, said Gross to his defensive teammates, we need one more stop. Get me the ball just one more time.

With 8:02 left in the game, the Falcons had driven into Linton territory, when Gross (who else) picked off an errant Falcon pass at the Lion's 44 yard line. It was now make or break time for the Linton season.

Imdieke huddled his offense on the sideline before sending them out for the decisive drive. In an excited voice he told his team exactly what they needed to do. "Look, we are going to run it down their throats, you hear me, right down them. 56 yards is what we need. We are going to block and we are going on an 8 minute drive to win this game. We will leave them no time to come back. This is it, right now. What we work all year for. This is Linton football. This is how you play football. This is fun. It is right there for the taking; a chance of a lifetime and we will not be stopped."

The old coach is a pretty good prophet. But it was not easy. The Lions had to convert on 4th down twice as they drove to the west end zone. The 14 play drive, culminating in a one yard sneak by Gross, left only 39 seconds on the clock and tied the game at 20-20. The stage was now set for one more hero in a maroon jersey to step forward.

As the Lions inexorably drove down the field for the winning score, Imdieke played his hand; one last trick up his sleeve. "Get the extra point team ready," he told an assistant, "when we score, we are kicking it." The reaction of those who heard the coach's directive was dead silence. Finally someone spoke up and reminded the coach that the team had not attempted a kick in over a month, and for good reason. Their kicker, junior fullback Brock Nagel, was a great blocker but a terrible kicker. He had missed his last six tries. And one further problem, Imdieke was told, Nagel had left the game early in the 4th quarter with a dislocated shoulder. But Imdieke had made up his mind. "We are kicking," he insisted. "Put his shoulder back in and find the kicking tee," he ordered.

Nagel's winning kick, into the setting High Plains afternoon sun, will go down in Linton lore as an end over end blast, a rocket shot that finally grounded somewhere west of the city limits. Let it be so, but in reality, the kicked ball fluttered like a wing shot North Dakota pheasant, as it crawled over the cross bar and between the uprights with all of several feet, at the most, to spare. To the Linton crowd, the injured Nagel's effort was a masterpiece, a fitting end to as improbable a comeback as anyone could ever remember seeing.

Assistant Coach Tim Dockter kidded me after the game that I had brought the Lions "St. Louis Cardinals good luck." My hometown Cardinals had, the week before, pulled off a very improbable run to the World Series championship. "Doc" was referring to the sixth game of the Series when, on the brink of elimination, the Cardinals had twice used two out, two strike base hits by David Freese and Lance Berkman to tie a game they would eventually win in twelve innings. Many had since labeled the game as the greatest comeback in the history of the World Series. I told Doc that the Cardinals win had been improbable and very exciting, but the Linton win was much more spectacular. I based this on the fact that Freese and Berkman were paid millions of dollars to do their specialty, hit a baseball. For the Cardinal effort to rival that of what we had just witnessed in Linton, the Cardinals would have had to be three runs down with the bases loaded and two outs in the bottom of the 9th inning, with no bench players left, thus having no other options than to send to the plate a relief pitcher who has not batted since the 7th grade, but who somehow manages to hit a walk off grand slam home run. That would be the magnitude unlikeliness of we had had just witnessed on the playing field of Lions Stadium.

Rebounding from a 20-0 deficit in high school football is a great accomplishment, but it does happen. But to pull off that type of a comeback with a makeshift offense built around a quarterback who does not even know the plays, is simply amazing. To their credit, the Linton coaches all admitted they did not believe at half time they could win the game. "I just hoped we could hold them down better the second half," said defensive coordinator Paul Keeney. "I thought no way," admitted Imdieke. "I just wanted to not get embarrassed by the score. I was really down at the half. I mean we couldn't even move the ball. It is still unbelievable that our kids pulled this off."

Gross' was unfazed by his sudden Saturday's Hero status. "I was always wanted to play quarterback," he said tying his shoes in the hectic and celebratory Lion locker room. "I was glad I could help out." Was he nervous? "Not really," he said.

Imdieke graciously admitted after the game that Gross was not the best of practice players. "He has run a lot of hills over the years," Imdieke joked. "But maybe that helped today. I don't think that kid ever gets nervous. He just takes it as it comes."

Lion assistants, after the game, laughed as they traded stories of Gross, the non-interested practice player, turned unlikely quarterback hero. "Have you ever known him to not to show up on game day? Did you see him out there today? We are dying from the stress and he is having the time of his life. On that last drive, and you know how intense that was, we are driving for a chance to play in the state championship game, to go to the Dome and Jayden is up to the line acting like he is calling an audible, clowning around, just calling out numbers and colors. Our guys are looking at him like 'WTF.' He doesn't even know the audible calls! Nolan looked like he was laughing so hard he almost couldn't snap the ball. This is crazy, just crazy." No, it is small town high school football at its best.

November 11, 2011- Dooms day at the Dakota Dome
Canadian vs. Clarendon @ Pampa
Texas Class 1 D-1 First Round Playoff

Many football coaches believe that the most two important possessions of any game are the last of the first half, and the first of the second half. Canadian's first round game with a dangerous Clarendon team is a great example of this old maxim. Both possessions in the Canadian first round victory played out to be major momentum swings for the Wildcats.

Fast out of the gate, Canadian took an immediate 21-0 lead, and seemed to be poised for a blowout. "We came out just like we wanted to," said coach Koetting, on the start of his Wildcats. "I thought we were real close to putting them away, and then those darn turnovers and we give up two long runs. Give them credit, they didn't quit."

In the first half Canadian, twice inside the Broncos 10 yard line, coughed up the ball, once on a fumble and once on a contested interception. The Wildcats also fumbled the ball at the Clarendon 40 yard line.

"I couldn't tell you the last time we fumbled the dang ball, and we do it twice in the first half," moaned Koetting after the game. "That is just not us. We don't fumble the ball. We got to get that out of our system."

Canadian used three rushing touchdowns to take a 21-0 lead with 8 minutes remaining in the first half. On the evening the Cats rushed for a season high 325 yards.

Clarendon, though, fought its way back into the game with two long TD runs; one a 64 yard effort by speedy Charleston Harris and a 78 yard gallop by a hard running Wes Williams. "I told you going in, how good those two guys are, and was I not right?" Koetting asked rhetorically after the game.

"But other than those two long runs, our defense did another great job. I don't think they completed a pass until our second group was in, late in the fourth quarter."

With their lead cut to one touchdown, the Wildcats drove the field only to have Braden Hudson's pass picked off at the one yard line by Bronco defensive back Trevor Cobb. The play sparked some controversy as it appeared that Canadian's Isaac Lewis had come to the ground in possession of the ball only to have it taken away on the ground by Cobb.

The Wildcat's then forced a Clarendon punt from their own 5 yard line and the ball was returned to the Clarendon 25 yard line. The ensuing four play drive was climaxed with six seconds showing on the scoreboard clock with a 9 yard TD strike from Hudson to his sophomore brother Boston. "That was a big score," said Koetting. "It gave us some breathing room at the half."

The only sustained drive the Broncos mounted the entire game came to start the second half. Using their two strong running backs, Clarendon marched down the field on a drive that ate up more than six minutes of the third quarter, only to be rebuffed by an Isaac Lewis interception at the Canadian five yard line.

The remainder of the game featured a solid defensive performance, and three touchdown passes from the senior duo of Hudson to Lewis.

Survive and advance is all that matters when a team enters the end of the season playoff football.

"We did some good things," said a pleased Koetting after the game. "Now we get ready for the next round. They are all tough from here on in, but we are still alive, still playing and that is all that counts right now."

Stanley- Powers Lake vs. Linton @ Fargo Dome
November 11, 2011
Championship North Dakota Class A State Playoffs

In the perpetual upbeat world of Dan Imdieke, if the dawning day finds breath in his lungs and air in the football, then it is going to be a great day. Accordingly, a 42-6 spanking by Stanley of his Linton Lions in the Class A North Dakota state championship game is just something to be endured; it doesn't have to ruin the day. "We got beat today by a very good football team," he said after the game's completion, "pretty simple."

The Linton Lions, one week off of a Cinderella type, 21-20 comeback in a semifinal win, saw the clock in the Fargo Dome strike high noon as Stanley kicker Chase Ladwig toed the ball into play. Midnight would have been more appropriate. It was obvious from the first possession of each team that the magical coach Linton had rode to the state finals had returned to a pumpkin. Even the star of the previous week's miracle, emergency quarterback Jayden Gross, looked more like a tight end- his normal position- as he spent most of the afternoon running for his life from a relentless and physical Stanley defense. "I bet Jayden would have been glad today to go back to tight end," said Imdieke with a chuckle, after the game.

Stanley entered the game undefeated and with a bushel full of accolades, split equally, between their defense and offense. "They have no weaknesses. It is going to be tough," an honest Imdieke had stated after Tuesday's practice.

The Bluejays defense did not allow a rushing touchdown during the regular season and only one – entering the championship game - during the playoffs. Their offense was led by two punishing running backs, Abe Roehrich and Landon Smith. The two entered the game with a combined 2,303 yards rushing in 11 games. Their combined average per carry was a ghoulish 8+ yards per rush.

In the championship game, Roehrich and Smith combined for 327 rushing. Roehrich gained 227 yards on 20 carries. His running mate, Smith, ran for an even 100 yards on 13 carries. The Bluejays finished the year with a 12-0 mark, winning their first state title since 2002.

"We never had an answer for either of those backs," said Imdieke after the game. "They were so strong, even when we met them in the hole at the line of scrimmage, they could still fall forward after the hit for a couple more yards. Very few backs over the years have been able to do that to us."

The highlight for the Lions came in the second quarter when Nolan Meidinger recovered a fumbled punt return on the Stanley 20 yard line. Cody Sehn capped the short drive with a 3-yard touchdown run, pulling Linton to within one point, 7-6, with 41 seconds left in the first quarter.

The confidence Sehn's touchdown brought to the Linton sideline was short lived; the Linton score seemed to irritate a slumbering Stanley monster, as the team from the northwest part of the state, exploded with 21 unanswered points in a span of seven minutes.

Just 24 seconds after the Lion's score, Roehrich sprinted for a 62-yard touchdown run. After a three and out by the Linton offense, Stanley quarterback Sam Footh found a wide open Seth Leupp for a 34 yard touchdown pass, raising the score to 21-6. On the Lions third play of their next possession, Smith gobbled up a Jayden Gross fumble and strode 34 yards to the Lions end zone. Suddenly, Stanley had a commanding 28-6 lead.

"That was pretty much the game right there," Imdieke said. "You can't give a team that good that many easy points, and expect to have a chance to beat them. There really was not a whole lot to say at halftime."

It was pointed out to Imdieke after the game that the halftime deficit of 28-6 was only two points more than his team had overcome the week before. "Yeah," he said with a smile, "But this was a different team we were playing this week. They are pretty darn good. I don't know if our best effort would have been enough today, and we sure didn't give our best effort."

The Lions ran the ball 34 for times for a puny 48 yards. "That hurts," said Imdieke after the game. "I don't know if anyone has ever held us for that low of a run average. Today, we were are a running team that could not run the ball."

As the 2011 schedule unfolded, and his team squeaked out one close win after another, it was clear that Imdieke was enjoying the season. After the state final loss, he paid his team one final compliment. "This is a special group. They were fun to coach, not always easy, because we had some weaknesses, but fun. Yeah, I would have to say this group was special."

Imdieke often states that his team's consistency over the years is what he is most proud of, even more than the five state titles and 298 victories he has achieved at Linton. "This was our 12th appearance in the state championship game. It averages out to about one trip every three years. Almost all of our four year kids over the last 35 years have had the opportunity, at least once, to play in this game. That is what I am proud of, the opportunities our kids have had because of being in our program. Playing in a state championship game is special, something you never forget."

What does the future hold? "We will be back," the coach said. "I liked in the fourth quarter how (sophomore) Michael (Oien) ran the ball and (sophomore) Brooks (Flyberg) ran the team from the quarterback spot."

Before going off to socialize with a large number of immediate and extended family members who had made the trip to Fargo, Imdieke promised, at least for one night, to enjoy the moment by reflecting on a team that received little pre-season respect, but fought its way to a state runner-up finish. "But hey," he said, "We start wrestling on Monday, and I don't know if I have told you, but we are going to be pretty good this year, we have…

Chris Koetting is a rational man caught in the irrational world of coaching Texas high school football. To keep one's sanity, especially come November and playoff time, a head coach learns that logic has to be applied in ways that often appear as an illogical application.

Friday, Canadian will travel to Lubbock to take on an undefeated Albany juggernaut, a team ranked as high as second in some state wide polls. Koetting and his Wildcats will, for the first time this year, enter a game as the underdog. Logic would dictate that apprehension and stress, with such a Goliath as next man up, would be running rampant this week in a panicked Wildcat camp.

Nothing could be further from the truth. Koetting and his team can finally take a deep breath and loosen the death grip on the survival rope they have grasped all year long. Not release, but loosen.

Since a week 2 loss to Meade, KS, the Wildcats have teetered on the cliff's edge of disaster. A #1 pre-season state wide ranking put the bull's eye squarely on his team's back. Koetting never asked for that type of pre-season pressure, but he did the best he could to keep his team on a level plain as they prepared for the season.

Losses in the second and third weeks, combined with the tragic death of a player's father in a car wreck, sent Canadian reeling. "We were in bad shape for a while," Koetting now admits. "It was a blur at times, but, each time we seemed to be on the edge and ready to fall, we have come together. Every time, we found a way."

In week 7, a one point double overtime district opening game loss to the 2011 surprise team of the Panhandle, Sunray, sent the Wildcats into the second district game, against a very good West Texas team, with their backs against the wall. With a trip to Stratford still on the schedule, a loss to West Texas would have dropped the Wildcats to a 3-4 record and probably eliminated them from the playoff hunt. True sacrilege in Panhandle high school football would be a Canadian team with a losing record and not in the playoffs. Unheard of and most certainly unacceptable from a team that entered the season with such high hopes. His team, and Koetting knew it, was 48 minutes on the scoreboard from an eternal place of infamy in the proud annals of Canadian football.

Canadian methodically pounded West Texas and then went to Stratford the following Friday and delivered a knockout punch to the Elks' season.

An impressive round one playoff win over Clarendon has the Cats purring and looking forward to their role of underdog.

"The pressure is off now," said Koetting on Monday, following a spirited practice. "We are not relaxed, by any means, but we now think we can play with anyone. We know Albany is a great team, but now, we just go out and play football. Let someone else wear the favorite label for a while."

Since the win over West Texas a month ago, the mood around the Canadian Fieldhouse has been one of growing confidence. Restrained and low key - the only way their coach will have it - but in the air is a sense of a confident team that has ridden an emotional roller coaster all fall.

These two giants in small town Texas high school football have a recent history. Albany brought a 12-0 team into the quarterfinal round last year to challenge the Canadian Wildcats, only to be eliminated by a last second Canadian touchdown pass.

Koetting calls his cohort at Albany, Coach Denny Faith, one of the best and smartest coaches in the state. If so, Faith must be cursing his fate, angry with the Texas football gods for giving him such an early round lurking giant to contend with. Take away a total of five or six plays in the three Wildcat losses, and Canadian could easily now be sitting on a 11-0 record, still holding onto that state #1 ranking.

Down in the Texas Panhandle, in the jungle of Region 1 playoff football, the hunted has become the hunter.

If, as a society, we want to go beyond the often shallow evaluation of a high school coach based strictly on data derived from the Friday scoreboard, in other words, beyond the final win and loss tally; then we must practice patience. Often times lessons learned on the high school athletic field are not fully appreciated until years later, when the recipient is deeply embedded in the up-hill fight of the adult dog eat dog world.

John Malpert lives in Toledo, OH. He holds a Ph. D in Organic Chemistry and is decades removed from the rock hard high school football practice field at Seeman Park in Linton, ND; but he has not forgotten the important life lessons he learned there, or the man who taught them. From 1983-1986 Malpert was a mediocre end for the Linton Lions. In his own words, "I was never a great athlete, just a skinny science geek who loved to play sports. All through junior high and junior varsity, I was never in the starting line-up, but I was always running and lifting weights during the offseason, which eventually caught Coach Imdieke's eye, even though I wasn't that talented."

I had deduced long before I heard from Malpert that Imdieke was loyal to his seniors. Pay your dues and you will get your chance. Malpert's experience validates my assumption. "I remember thinking that he (Imdieke) was nuts when he told me during the summer after my junior year to keep working hard because he planned on starting me at right end on offense," Malpert remembered. "I kept working hard, and he kept his word. Not only did I start on offense my senior year, but Imdieke made sure that I had my 'moment in the sun'. (About) two-thirds of the way through the season in a game that Linton had well in hand, he called for a pass play to me on the one yard line so I could score a touchdown. He never specifically said 'this is for all your hard work,' but I knew the minute that the play came into the huddle why Imdieke was calling it."

Malpert is still touched to this day by Imdieke's gracious act. "In all my years of football, I only scored that one touchdown. To this day, some twenty-five years later, I can remember clearly every detail of that play. That one touchdown was very special to me in more ways than one because my father was in the stands that night. My folks were divorced, and my father lived in another town, four or five hours away. In all my years of junior high, JV and varsity football, I am certain that my dad was only able to come to three or four games at the most. And yet he was there on the night that I scored my only touchdown. I am positive that Imdieke didn't know that my dad was going to be there that night, as I had only found out myself a few hours before game time. It was just a case of Imdieke being Imdieke. He was going to do the right thing and give one of his least talented players a moment in the sun. In the end, his small payback of recognition turned out to be an extra special moment that I never will forget. That's just typical Imdieke, taking something good and turning it into something great."

Malpert remembers few details about winning and losing in high school. He says he would be hard pressed to remember a season's final win/loss record; let alone a score to a particular game. "What I do remember," the scientist says, "are the life lessons I learned just watching how Imdieke lived his life."

Malpert readily concedes that he was a pretty unremarkable player and that his old coach, having coached so many players over the last 35 years, might have a hard time even recalling his face. But the coaches' influence on this former "science geek" end was indelible. Malpert remembers one specific demand Imdieke made. "He always insisted that the players on the left side of the line block just as hard when a sweep was being run around the right side because 'you just never know when our running back might break one, and the blocking on the back side might be the difference between a touchdown and the pursuit catching up,' he would say. Do the right thing, do it all the time and more often than not, good things will happen - that was one of the many lessons I still use today that I learned from Imdieke. I think that one of the reasons that Imdieke is such a success is that he lives his life very much like the lessons that he teaches on the football field."

November 18, 2011- Foxhole buddies to the bitter end
Canadian vs. Albany @ Lubbock Cooper HS
Second Round Class 1 Texas State Playoffs

An injury to his starting quarterback in the first game of the season last year forced Albany Coach Denney Faith to go with sophomore signal caller Jake Bumguardner. If the young man who played ahead of Bumguardner is a better player, then I hope that today finds him fast tracked to the National Football League, for the young Bumgaurdner is one outstanding high school football player.

In round two of the Class 1A Texas state playoffs, he threw the Lions on his back and delivered a 56-27 pounding to the Canadian Wildcats that had locals asking the head scratching question after the game, "who remembers when was the last time a player did this to us?" It has been a long time, was the general consensus of the more shocked than angry Canadian backers.

Bumgaurdner ran over, around and through a stunned Wildcat defense. So dominant was his performance, that if need be, he probably could have found a shovel and tunneled under the clawless Cat defense. Bumgaurdner ran for 374 on 21carries. His efforts resulted in five rushing touchdowns. To share the wealth, or maybe just to rest his legs, Bumguardner - who was seven for seven kicking extra points and performed punting duties on the only punt the Lions were forced into on the night- completed 4 of 5 passes for 56 yards and a touchdown. He also plays a very solid free safety. I hope he was given a choice seat on the charter bus ride back to Albany; he for sure earned it.

Coach Koetting was philosophical after the game, telling his team, with special note to a distraught group of seniors, to remember the good times. "Seniors, I cannot tell you how special you are to me and how much you have meant to this program," Koetting said to his team huddled in the south end zone. "I didn't want it to end like this. None of us did. But you know what? This season is a lot like life, all the ups and downs we have been through, you are going to find the same thing happens to you in real life, and if you fight and bounce back when the hard times hit, like you did this year, then you are going to be all right."

The night began with promise for the large Canadian following that had made the four hour drive to witness the contest played at the 8.7 million dollar, two year old Lubbock Cooper High School stadium. Taking the opening kickoff, the Canadian offense marched efficiently down the field. The Cats took a 7-0 lead as a wide open Boston Hudson caught a 22 yard touchdown pass from big brother Braden.

Koetting and his staff had thought during the week of preparations for the game that they had found a flaw in the Albany defense. "When we catch them in cover three we can beat the corners, you just have to look off the safety and go to the side where he gives you the one on one coverage," the coach had told Hudson during the week. When a Lion free safety broke to the right, Hudson found his brother on the left flank beating the one on one defensive pass coverage like a drum, launching a perfect throw to give Canadian what would prove to be their only lead of the night.

Like the two heavyweight programs they are, the teams traded touchdowns through the first quarter and the first four minutes into the second stanza, only to see Albany use the last half of the second quarter and the first five minutes of the second half to go on a 28-0 scoring run. For Canadian, the hole they had now dug themselves was too deep to climb out of.

After the game Canadian coach Chris Koetting said his club knew what needed to be done against the 11-0 Lions, but knowing and doing proved to be two completely different tasks. "We knew coming in the key to the whole deal was slowing down their quarterback and you can see we didn't get that done," Koetting said.

The Hudson brothers teamed up one more time in the second period to tie the game with a 37 yard touchdown strike. From then on it was the Bumguardner show. Once the talented signal caller broke through the line, he was not to be caught. With a blazing 48 second 400 meter time turned in for the track Lions last spring, once in the open field, Bumguardner would not be caught.

The game, and the Canadian season, hinged on two critical plays at the end of the first half. Albany took a 28-14 lead with under two minutes to play in the second quarter. However, on the play before Bumgaurdner had appeared to fumble the ball before his knee touched the ground. The ensuing loose ball rolled into the end zone and then out of bounds before either team could recover. By rule, the play should have been ruled a touchback and the ball awarded to Canadian at their own 20 yard line, first and ten. The official on the sideline at first offered no signal, then motioned that the ball had rolled out of bounds at the one yard line. He later told the head official that he thought Bumgaurder's knee was down before the fumble. Both of his versions were countered by the replay on the stadium's scoreboard Jumbo-Tron.

Canadian took the kickoff and drove down the field until they were faced with a 4th down and the ball at the Albany six yard line. The scoreboard clock showed three seconds left to play. Isaac Lewis caught a swing pass but was brought down at the Albany one yard line. The half ended with a 14-point deficit for Canadian. "We had our opportunities on offense but we didn't always cash in," Koetting said. "We'd just shot ourselves in the foot."

As the second half unfolded, it became obvious that the adjustments and changes made at halftime by Canadian defensive coordinator Craig Campbell had not slowed down the Bumguardner led Lion offense. Most of the second half, on the Canadian sideline, the intense Campbell, well respected for his defense intellect and his ability to make game speed adjustments, was beside himself.

In larger high schools and in all college and pro programs, the offense and defense are separate units, with defensive coaches able to gather their troops on the sidelines, while the offense has the ball. This is crucial time needed to make in game adjustments. However, in small Class 1A football, almost all players play both ways, leaving a defensive coach like Campbell to stew on the sidelines alone while his team has the ball. Campbell spent a great part of the second half by himself, muttering under his breath. Campbell would later admit he has never had such a hopeless feeling as he had this game, no answer from the vivid defensive mind of the successful coach for slowing down Bumguardner. His defense gave up an unheard of, for Canadian, 554 yards of total offense and 56 points. For the proud Campbell, it was looking like a long off-season.

The win moved Bumguardner's record as a starting quarterback to 23-1. The lone setback came in last year's regional final game, a last second loss to the Canadian Wildcats. Consider the ledger now balanced.

Koetting says he and his staff would love to see a rubber match contest next year. 'That would mean we are deep into the playoffs and that is where we intend to be next year. We are losing a great senior bunch, but we have a strong nucleus coming back. We need to get to work."

Chapter 9

Epilogue

The most unfair thing about life is the way it ends. I mean, life is tough. It takes up a lot of your time. What do you get at the end of it? A Death! What's that, a bonus? I think the life cycle is all backwards. You should die first; get it out of the way. Then you live in an old age home. You get kicked out when you're too young, you get a gold watch, you go to work. You work forty years until you're young enough to enjoy your retirement. You do drugs, alcohol, you party, you get ready for high school. You go to grade school, you become a kid, you play, you have no responsibilities, you become a little baby, you go back into the womb, you spend your last nine months floating......and you finish off as an orgasm. *George Carlin*

Moving on is simple. It's what we leave behind that's hard.
Author Unknown

Many activities and team play participation will give you a training that will prove invaluable later on in life. *Walter Annenberg*

I wanted the players to feel like they were part of a family, to be conscious of that controlled togetherness as they made that slow entrance onto the field. It had a great psychological effect on the opposing team, too. They'd never seen anything like it. *Hayden Fry*

I don't care how I got here. In the books, when you look at it 10 or 20 years from now, it's not going to say how he got here, it's going to say he's here and he represented the team. *Vince Carter*

Freedom is just another word for nothing left to lose. *Janis Joplin*

I refuse to live in the past, but I do enjoy an occasional visit.

I have never attended a high school reunion of my graduating class, and I probably never will. It is not that I have deeply troubling unresolved issues with my almost four decades ago high school years, nor that I collectively dislike my classmates. In reality, my feelings are quite to the contrary. As I look back, my experience was pretty much in line with what everyone goes through: a lot of firsts, a few downs and a lot of ups. I have at times, over the years, run into a former classmate and I have always found the spontaneity of the reminiscing to be enjoyable. I just see no need to force the issue with a planned and artificial rendezvous where everyone can dress up, put on airs and tell lies. If former classmates want to know what has become of me, they can look me up on Facebook.

Living in the past can be dangerous. The human brain has a way, as time passes, of filtering out the bad and embellishing the good. We all have the "one that got away." Why temp fate? If we are honest with ourselves, there is always a good reason why "the one that got away;" got away. If you are smart, you leave it at that.

High school years are challenging ones for all. We are thrown in, ready or not, at the most awkward of age, into a whirlwind of change. Then we are expected to be delivered four years later to the far side, once again ready or not, on the brim of adulthood. What happened to each of us over the four years in between are the defining events that will shape us for the ages.

I will not try to out semantically glib Dickens, so I will quote directly: "It was the best of times, it was the worst of times, it was the age of wisdom, it was the age of foolishness, it was the epoch of belief, it was the epoch of incredulity, it was the season of light, it was the season of darkness, it was the spring of hope, it was the winter of despair, we had everything before us, we had nothing before us."

I know of no better or concise descriptive verse to describe the both agonizing and joyful four years we call high school.

Mandatory and public education for all is a very unique American phenomenon. We, with some assistance and guidance from the ancient Greeks, invented the idea. Compulsory education is the populist plank our democracy was founded upon. Despite many trials and errors – a half century later we still struggle with finding the proper interpretation and application of the 1954 Brown vs. Board of Education Supreme Court mandate – we take this solemn promise to our next generation serious. In spite of all the political posturing over education, meant in many cases to inflame public perception through fear and half-truths, aside, we as a nation still support our local schools like no other people in the world today. Education in America, now more so than any other time in our history, is considered an entitled birth right, a leveling – in theory, at least - of the playing field giving access to hope for even the most poverty bound child.

American communities, urban, suburban and rural, are defined by their local public schools. Let the school die and the town will follow. Bus the communities' young to a nearby bigger school and soon the town square will be empty of all but the weeds of neglect, store front windows boarded up and doors locked.

Gather as many educational, societal and economical school consolidation experts as you can fit in your hat of demigods, let them spout their expert findings, plan their innovative strategies for rural renewal and disaggregate their data to their little bureaucratic heart's desire; bottom line is: lose the school, lost the town. Drive Highway 83 back and forth between Mexico and Canada, as I have for the last three months, and your eyes will deliver to your brain the economic reality of dying high plains communities: every dead town I passed through contained a dead school.

So why is football the one activity in almost all small towns that takes front and center stage, demanding a complete and total town loyalty every fall Friday night? Why not basketball or baseball or tennis? On the surface, this seems to be a very good question with many possible explanations.

Based on my experiences this fall, here a couple of possible reasons:

Football is very militaristic in nature. All sports in our modern society, to some degree, can trace its origins to some type of military connection. Olympic track events - running, jumping and throwing contests - were all tied by the ancient Greeks to the military training of the day. The same is true with ancient boxing and wrestling contests. But football seems to take it over the top. This has been a well-documented and controversial phenomena in our society dating back to the days of the Vietnam Anti- War Movement and the then President Nixon's fascination with football. Just look at some of the common terminology used in the sport of football:

defending the red zone, blitzing, our territory, the bomb, shock troops, reinforcements, battle of the trenches, attacking offenses and containment defenses; I could go on and on.

When it comes to town pride, football and its subliminal militaristic themes appeal to basic human survival needs. Football is a very physical game, and no matter how hard educational leaders try to temper the violence with the enforcement of on field safety rules, it will always be a very physical game, and to some degree, a violent game. We are sending forth the best of our young men to battle the best of the nearby tribe (town). Our city boundaries must not be breeched. Community pride is deep rooted in community survival. The enemy is at the town gates and we must be protected, entrusting our young men to give it their all in fulfilling their sacred duty. Think of this the next time your team runs on the field with the school flag in tow.

There is something that appeals to our primal alpha male instincts that the bragging rights of "we kicked your ass in football," transfers so much better than, and appeals to civic survival so much deeper than; "our girls doubles tennis team smoked yours."

Couple the above with the fact that football has no Title IX counterpart; and I think the reason for football commanding the community's emotional loyalty comes more into focus. Title IX has, over 40 years, dramatically with federal judicial backing, transformed one half of our society – females – from spectators to participants. Basketball, volleyball, softball, track, cross country, tennis, golf, swimming and, to an ever increasing degree, even wrestling; every high school sport with the exception of football, has an alternative outlet for females that demands as much, and at times even exceeds, the attention and resources given to the male counterpart sport. This, for good reason is called progress.

But somewhere, maybe buried deep in our subliminal thoughts, chivalry still lives. Our daughters play a role in the Friday night lights pageantry carried out with such religious fervor in small towns across this nation; but their role is minor and more in line with the plantation mentality of the long ago past. The role of girls in this fall Friday night weekly festival is relegated to subservient tasks: cheerleaders, drum majors, flag girls, marching band members, managers and statistic keepers.

I found the above to be true the farther south I traveled; i.e.: Texas. Football is the one stage the hated feds have not been able to touch; either through legislative or judicial mandates. For many years the guardians of

Title IX tried and every once in a while you will still read of a female high school football player- the homecoming queen who kicked the winning field goal - but it has been relegated to more of a man bites dog abnormal interest level story than one of the norm.

I know the above is far out of step with acceptable modern liberal social thinking. So be it, for in the second decade of the 21st century a sort of truce seems to have been declared between the political correctness watchdogs and small town high school football; it's almost sacred chauvinistic and outdated place on society's mantle for the time being, safe.

Although an elusive state championship eluded all three of my Highway 83 teams in 2011, what I was able to record, and what I was the most interested in, was how each dealt with misfortune, and there was enough for each this fall to go around. The total win loss record for all three teams for 2011was a sterling 28-7, a .800 winning percentage. This success rate for a long career would land most coaches in the Hall of Fame. But at Linton, McCook and Canadian; success on the football field is expected. All three coaches know this and, in many ways, embrace the high expectations for their teams; as all good coaches do. Each head coach ended the season acknowledging the many high points of achievement that each program reached in 2011; but each, as coaches will, wanted that one more victory, to take that next step towards grasping the brass ring of a high school state football title. All three head coaches have state champion engraved multiple times already on their resumes and my prediction is that there will be more added in the future. All three of these programs are led by outstanding high school football coaches.

Now that I have had the time to step back and review the season of each of the three teams, what comes into focus is a good continuum between success and failure, ecstasy and heart ache. Linton achieved beyond pre-season expectations, McCook had a stellar regular season but prematurely departed in the second round of the playoffs and Canadian struggled all year to live up to the pre-season hype fueled by their 2010 success.

Over the years, while observing human nature under the bright searing lights of high school athletic competition, I have learned to look for character. Wins will happen. Losses will occur. What is lasting is the character forged equally from both exhilarating triumphs and heart crushing setbacks. As an educator, I much prefer the term setback to defeat. As long as the heart of a competitor beats, there will always be another day.

Teams will take on the personalities of their coaches. If the head coach of a losing team throws a pity party, his or her players will gladly take a seat at the table. If, conversely, the head coach has the fortitude and the vision procured by the mature poise needed to seize a time of disappointment to hammer home a life's lesson to his or her disappointed students, then the coach has succeeded in his or hers' most important assignment; transcending from the role of coach to that of teacher. If high school athletics are truly an educational stage upon which to showcase the best of what our public schools produce, as we proponents claim, then we should demand that our coaches and athletic leaders keep this task – always a teacher first - as their primary focus.

I look for coaches who stand their tallest on days when their teams come up short.

After an 8-4 season, Canadian head coach Chris Koetting, in his own way, apologized to me. "I feel like we ruined your book," he told me. Nothing could be farther from the truth, I responded. "But this was not one of our best seasons," the coach commented about a four loss year that is almost unheard of for a program that has become the measuring stick for consistent winning high school football in the Texas Panhandle.

"Not in the book I am writing," I assured Koetting.

Koetting in his own sincere way, after the season, did not want the burden of his players feeling they had let him down. "In many ways this was a great season," he told me. "We always want to win and we are always disappointed when we do not, but I want these kids to know how proud of them I am. Their efforts in fighting through tough times all year is how I will remember them; as winners."

In the fall of 2011, Koetting had, dropped in his lap, one crisis after another. Starting in the blistering hot pre-season days of August, forced to operate under the burden of unrealistic expectations created by a state wide #1 ranking, many of the challenges his Wildcats faced were neither of their making, nor within their control. Yet Koetting and his staff never allowed the team to wallow in self-pity. Until the final whistle, the Canadian Wildcats never lost hope, believing to a man to the end that they could battle and overcome any on field opponent. I felt this aura of self-empowerment every time I attended a Canadian practice. I always walked away reenergized with the optimism of a group of young men who never lost faith; in themselves, their teammates or their goals.

The 2011 Canadian team, no matter how severe the on and off field disappointments thrown in their path, were a group that never splintered into finger pointing cliques. To the contrary, the Wildcats were one of the more close knit teams I have seen. They were foxhole buddies to the bitter end, as was so very emotionally apparent in the team's post game gathering after the second round playoff loss.

A season that ended on a cold windy November night in Lubbock, with a lopsided loss to an obviously superior Albany team, was as disappointing to me as it was to any of the loyal Canadian faithful. This program has played into December so consistently the last decade that a run deep into the playoffs has become almost expected by the locals. Too outsiders, not having had the chance to see behind the senses of the 2011 season, I am sure, this unceremonious premature thud of an ending defined the Wildcat's year, one of disappointment. I disagree.

In the fashion begetting of a second hand lion; an aging warrior not quite yet ready to bid the glory of the battlefield good bye, Dan Imdieke, in the twilight of a storied career, coached this past season what was perhaps the most enjoyable of his 35 autumns as the head of the Linton Lions football team. When pressed to call his 2011 squad his favorite group, out of respect to all of his former great players and teams – I presumed – Imdieke wouldn't confirm; but nor would he deny.

Imdieke's team always found a way to win. Despite all the logic I attempted to apply, I could never quite figure out how. When the final gun was fired, week after week, Linton was on the winning side of the scoreboard, often when late in the game their cause appeared to be lost, their chance for victory hopeless.

At first, after hearing from Linton friend and foe alike about the legendary ability of Imdieke's teams to pull off miraculous come from behind wins, with the comeback win in week 2 against Oaks, I found it uncanny, maybe even quirky. Week 3's come from behind win over Milnor, with its similarity to the win the week before, I found eerie. When the Lions came from two scores down with less than five minutes to play to beat Maple Valley on the road in week 6, the improbability of the rally cast a surreal fog over the post- game celebration. But the subsequent state playoff semifinal win against the same Maple Valley team a month later beat all I have ever seen- one for the ages- and felt impossible, a denial by my brain of what my eyes had just witnessed. It was so remarkable, divine intervention is the only plausible explanation I can conjure up for the most unlikely and improbable comeback I have witnessed in fifty years as a high school sports fan.

Coach Jeff Gross and the McCook Bison in 2011 lived through a dream season for ten weeks. Game after game, one shining Friday night after another, the Bison confidently rolled through each and every opponent. Most impressively, they did it the 'McCook Way": impeccable preparation with a focus on the most minute of details, and a hardnosed brand of old fashion football that placed a premium on winning the war in the trenches.

When the football gods finally changed allegiance, the downfall for the Bison was cruelly swift. In a matter of minutes – the last five of the state quarterfinal loss to Adams Central – the McCook dream season fell apart. What made the disappointment almost unbearable to the Bison was that their demise unfolded on their own field. One disastrous turnover and a couple of missed tackles doomed a team that, all year long, had managed to dodge potential disaster, logging four wins with 4th quarter rallies in their first ten games. But the eleventh was not to be. For the twelve seniors to end their careers in this unexpected and atypical fashion was heartbreaking.

A week 9 injury to Jake Schlager proved to be too much for McCook to overcome. During the first six weeks of the season when tailback Schlager, fullback Justin Terry and quarterback Matt Chitwood were all healthy, the triple option veer offense of McCook was unstoppable. The trio would not play together healthy again (after week 6) for the rest of the year. Although Gross would not attribute his team's abrupt departure from the playoffs, a tournament they entered having earned the number one state wide ranking, to Schlager's injury, it was obvious it made a difference in the performance level of the Bison's play on offense. However, defense is the area where Schlager's absence was felt the most. With him in the game, and his 4.4 speed at the ready, McCook knew that most teams would choose to run away from Schlager, to the opposite side of the field. It severely limited the opposition's offensive options and gave the McCook defensive coaches a watered downed opponent's offensive package to prepare for.

Injuries are a part of the game, Gross liked to point out, both before and after the playoff loss; no sense in dwelling on someone who can't play, let's get those ready that can, he announced after the break to Schlager's right leg was confirmed, the week before the first round playoff game with Alliance.

How far would McCook have gotten in the playoffs with a healthy Schlager? We will never know. It is what it is: Adams Central advanced and McCook went home, the seniors' place in history now entrenched, the underclassmen free to dream of next year. The speculation on "what if" among local enthusiasts as the years pass is, in many ways, both the cruelty and the beauty of small town high school football.

It was a study in contrast to watch for three months the work of Dan Imdieke, Jeff Gross and Chris Koetting. As a lifetime educator myself, I found the ability of all three to interact with their athletes, inspiring. All three are unique and conduct themselves in the execution of their coaching duties in very diverse ways. What they have in common is that all are excellent leaders, albeit with different styles. Leave coaching prowess out of the equation for a moment, and all three receive top marks for their genuine and heartfelt concern for their players. I have two children, both now grown. I would have felt blessed to have them fall under the guidance of any of the above three. As a parent, there is no higher endorsement of an educator I can give.

Football in Linton, ND was a 180 degree cultural change from what I found at McCook and Canadian. In many ways, where football was life and death in Nebraska and Texas, it was more of a diversion for Imdieke's players. Most were farm and ranch kids who had learned at an early age a strong work ethic that only 5 am daily chores – cows don't know it is Christmas - can teach. Imdieke told me the first time I met him that football had to be fun or there would be no reason for the kids of Linton to make the sacrifices they did to free up the time needed to play.

Imdieke is the perfect picture of a throwback coach, conjuring up images of a militaristic task master in the mold of a Bear Bryant or a more modern example, a Mike Ditka. In surprising reality, I found Imdieke to oversee a very loose ship. At halftime of games, when Imdieke, as good a master of making in game adjustments as I have seen in any sport, would address his varsity, the younger sophomore and freshman players who never played unless the game became a one sided affair, would break into spontaneous foolishness. Wrestling, play slapping and other such horse play is how they would spend the break while, mere yards away, Imdieke would be intently instructing his varsity players. It would have driven many coaches into a rage at the silliness, but Imdieke never seemed to even notice.

I believe I would have been hard pressed, even if I could have somehow gained access to every young man who Imdieke has coached over the last

35 years, to find any of his former charges who would use the word "fear" when discussing the dynamics of their relationship with the longtime coach. Respect, I am sure, would pop up often. It is simply hard not to like the man.

Imdieke's sincerity is a virtue he makes no effort to cover or stifle. In the state semifinal game against Maple Valley, I arrived at the field just in time to see the opening kickoff. Within minutes, Imdieke saw the fortunes of his team make as far of an about face turn south as was possible. In the game's early moments, his all-state quarterback/defensive back Tanner Purintun, tore up his knee, out for the season, and the opposition quickly pounced on the situation to throw an 80 yard touchdown pass over the head of Purintun's replacement. The week prior, I had mentioned to Imdieke's wife that my wife had been sick. With his season unraveling right before his eyes, Imdieke spotted me standing on the sideline and made a bee line to me. "How is your wife?" he asked me. I couldn't believe it. I said, "Coach she is fine. Thanks for asking, but you have got a game to win here." Many times, while hearing Linton backers recite their favorite similar Imdieke story, they would say at the conclusion of their narrative, "well, that is just Imdieke being Imdieke."

Imdieke had an uncanny ability of knowing when to push and when to back off. A former player from the 1980's related to me how as a player for the Lions he was insecure and did not handle criticism well. John Malpert now lives outside of Toledo, OH, where he is employed by Master Chemical as an analytical chemist, putting to go use a Ph. D in Organic Chemistry he earned at Iowa State University. "Once coach was getting on me pretty good at practice and he must have seen it was upsetting me," Malpert shared. "He stopped and said what I will never forget, 'John, when I stop pushing you it means I don't care, and that is when you better worry 'cause it means I have given up on you.' When I was in grad school, and my advisors were riding me hard, I remembered what coach said, and just buckled down and got the job done. I learned not to feel sorry for myself. Coach taught me that on the football field and I really don't think I would have made it through my Ph. D work without it."

Spend much time with Jeff Gross and it becomes obvious that he is both comfortable and excited about his job as head mentor of the McCook Bison. He is also supremely confident in his own ability to build and maintain a championship level high school football program. In no way does Gross come across as arrogant, but he clearly wears his belief in himself in a very transparent way. Setbacks, he once told me, he has learned over the years, are not an occurrence necessitating self-doubt, but an opportunity for self-improvement. A Charlie Weiss look alike with the contagious optimism of a young Lou Holtz, Gross is simply a master teacher of the game of football. As well as any coach I have ever been around, Gross has a philosophy of what it takes to win football games that he clearly understands and believes in, thus he does not, and will not, vary the prescribed course.

Football, as much as any sport, is a "program" sport and Gross is a program coach. He always had a plan B. Bad bounces did not seem to disrupt his focus and his plan. His players feed off of his confidence and his impeccable planning. In either good or bad times, I never once felt a sense of panic on the Bison sideline. Everyone, from the top down, knew what needed to be done and what their role was in securing another Bison win. The question being, will we do it? That is a result of good planning by a good coach.

Gross has mastered the balance between a control freak and a warm and caring people person, and make no mistake, he is both. When around his staff and his players, be it either on the practice field or in the middle of a game, I never saw Gross pull rank to establish his authority as head coach, but there was also never a doubt of who had the steering wheel on this bus firmly in his grip. Gross is an excellent manager of his assistant coaching talent, never micro managing, but always in a position of assertive over sight. As a former administrator, with much training in the application of human resources, I always walked away from a Bison practice impressed at the organization of personnel and the efficiency of task completion. Gross had at his disposal outstanding coaches, like Defensive Coordinator Russ Schlager and to Gross' credit; he let his assistant coaches to their jobs.

All three coaches were resilient, as anyone who intends to stay in a profession as chaotic as coaching must be; but Gross took it to another level. When things did not go right for his Bison, he had the uncanny knack of being able to quickly identify the problem, those responsible for it and the corrective adjustments needed to right the fault. Adams Central cut through his defense like a sharp knife through warm butter; driving over 70 yards in three plays to knock his undefeated Bison from the state playoffs and end their season. Within an hour of the game's disappointing completion, Gross had viewed the film and could detail the total breakdown to the extent that he could identify those who did not execute their duties. It was not the system that broke down, it was the players, and that could be fixed. The program, in Gross' eyes, remained as always, unscathed.

Gross is the one of the three who I could see someday moving on to another coaching job. He has at times spoken of in the future becoming a full time school administrator. With his organizational skills, he would be a very good one. But I don't see that happening. Jeff Gross, as I see it, is a coaching "lifer." He identifies his self-image with his coaching. He is also too good at the craft, and enjoys it too much to ever walk away by his own free choice. I predict that Gross' retirement gig, decades from now, will be as a color commentary on some high school game radio broadcast.

His personality would make Gross an instant success as a college recruiter. However, I would question if Gross would be willing to become an assistant coach again, a role he would, for most certain, have to endure by beginning on the collegiate level.

I don't see the family farm back in Hays, KS in Jeff Gross' future. I do however, when looking into the crystal ball of the future, see a Nebraska bushel basket full of wins and a Hall of Fame plaque with his name inscribed. What Hall of Fame, and where to build the monument, remains to be determined.

Chris Koetting had the toughest job of any of the three. In only his second year of occupying a position that had been held previously by the widely respected Kyle Lynch, for many in the community of Canadian, TX, the jury was still out on Koetting. If that bothered him, he never showed it. Simply put, Koetting is one of the nicest people I have ever met within the ranks of football coaches.

They say you can judge character by observing a person under stress. If that is the case, then Koetting proved beyond any doubt this fall that he has a wheel barrow full of character. It seemed that weekly, all season long, his mettle was tested. If something could go wrong and disrupt the harmony of the Canadian program; inevitably it did. Koetting had to deal with everything from untimely injuries to the tragic death of a popular father of one of his players.

Through it all, Koetting never flinched. When his team was moored in the dire straits of Texas high school football, Koetting's steady hand was paramount in righting the Canadian ship and steering it back into the path of the trade winds of gridiron success. Seeing him labor under those conditions was – because of my personal like and professional respect for the man – for me, difficult. But I always found his calm approach inspiring. Koetting proved as the offensive coordinator for two state championship teams that he can coach. He proved this year, at the helm of an 8-4 team, that he can lead. There is a big difference between the two traits and any long term successful coach must master both. Koetting has.

Koetting, to his credit, never took out his frustration on his players, but when the line in the sand needed to be drawn, he drew it in an unquestioning assertive manner, challenging his dispirited team to grow up. After a district opening loss to Sunray, the Wildcats, a team picked in a pre-season poll to win a state title, were facing disaster. A loss the following Friday to a very good West Texas High team would have all but eliminated the Cats from a spot on the post season playoff bracket; a totally unacceptable proposition for the proud Canadian program.

Koetting is not a great orator. His talks to his team throughout the year were heartfelt, but not passionate. Emotional pleading is just not his way – Koetting will never challenge Knute Rockne on the stump of public speaking, but on the Saturday morning following the Sunray loss, he delivered his own version of "win one for The Gipper," and it was masterful. Koetting hit on just the right blend of sympathy, and a good swift kick in the hind end to his team. At the time, as he astutely measured, they needed both. He challenged his room full of boys to grow up and be men. John Steinbeck in Grapes of Wrath wrote that a boy becomes a man when a man is needed. That is just the message Koetting hammered home to his team at that critical meeting. It is time to man up. Football players in Canadian are treated like gods, the praise unending, he reminded his team. Along with that glory, the coach explained, comes responsibility. "We knew what we were getting into when we signed up for this," he told them.

"Football in Canadian is very important to the community," Koetting continued in his lecture to his team, "And it is time that we stand up and be counted."

Giving the option to cut and run or stand and fight, his team responded with a total dominating win over West Texas, saving their season and catapulting the Wildcats to four solid wins as they qualified for the playoffs, advancing to the second round before tasting post-season defeat.

This was a transitional year for Canadian football. The pre-season state wide ranking of number one was a kiss of death. The Wildcats possessed a very talented roster, but not of state championship caliber. When a Class 1A team losses two linemen to graduation who move on to Division I college football, like Canadian did last year, then you have to expect some downturn in fortune. Small schools just do not, in one year, replace that type of lost talent.

In due time, I am certain, Koetting will put his own stamp on the Canadian program. One hour after the season ending playoff loss to Albany, Koetting was already scheming for 2012. He loses a very good senior class and most in the area feel that next year will be a rebuilding one for Canadian. Koetting is already looking forward to preparing a team that will fly under the radar screen of projectionists. There will be no number one ranking burden in 2012. But the cupboard is not bare, far from it, in fact. The Canadian 8th grade team was outstanding, maybe the best in recent memory.

The Canadian season teetered most of the fall on disaster, one foot figuratively in the grave and the other on a banana peel. Koetting's quiet but sincere style of leadership held the team together. In my opinion, he has now passed his most difficult exam. I can't imagine a more trying year to endure, than what the Canadian coaches faced this year. I, in the future, look for Koetting to carve out his own niche in the rich history of Wildcat football, having a long and successful run as head football coach of the mighty Canadian Wildcats.

All three coaches –Imdieke, Gross and Koetting - are successful because they understand people, know how to motivate kids, and have earned a level of respect status in their respective communities that allows each to practice his craft in a comfort zone not often found in small town/coach relationships. All three have a sincere desire to see their players grow as people, with the ultimate goal of depositing, within the ranks of society, fully functioning and contributing adults.

All three have learned over the years, they told me, to adjust to their particular communities' expectations. Imdieke's low-key good old boy approach would not have sold well in football crazy Canadian, TX, but fits like a glove in Linton, ND. Gross' intensity and task master approach to practice, is embraced by the community of McCook as the commitment needed to build a winner, but would have raised eyebrows in Linton, ND and could well have driven many players back to the chores of the farm, football be damned. Within their own little kingdoms, each was the unquestioned master of his town's football fortunes, an outside gunslinger brought into a closed community and entrusted by a small prairie town with the best of its sons, given the knee shaking responsibility of leading them to gridiron glory.

Over the years, each proved by trial and fire that the trust was well placed. Over time, each would see the mercenary tag of an outsider removed, settling into an accepting community where each either has, or is, in the process of raising their own families; having earned the hard sought small town label of "one of us".

America is not burdened with a lack of educational heroes; we just do not know where to look for them. They are out there. In the fall of 2011, I found them in abundance in three thriving communities I chronicled along US Highway 83.

So why are the communities of Linton, ND, McCook, NE and Canadian, TX thriving at a time when many of their contemporaries are withering and dying? I saw several common denominators in the equation that drives each town's successful and thriving existence; the most obvious being outstanding high school football programs that each community takes great pride in

Each town has a viable, successful and well respected local newspaper. Since the invention of the printing press, now may be the most chaotic and unpredictable time in the history of the print media. Digital is the word for the future. Are we really headed to becoming a paperless society? Is the day of the printed hard copy journal doomed? Adaptation is the key phrase for today's survival of the printed newspaper. The landscape has become so topsy-turvy that an edition of the Emmons County Record in the town of Linton, ND – population 1200 - contains more pages than any daily edition of the St. Louis Post-Dispatch, with the exception of Sunday. That is crazy.

The strong local and independent press is a key for the binding and cohesiveness of all three communities. Each has a unique role to play in the community. The McCook Gazette is a daily paper (Monday through Friday), quite an accomplishment today for a town with a population of only 8,000. In line with the area being an economic hub for southwest Nebraska and northwest Kansas, the Gazette is a regional paper, covering, for example, twenty plus high schools. Sports editor Steve Kodad might be the most overworked guy in town, but somehow he provides each town with outstanding coverage of all sports; both major and minor.

In some ways, due to the close intimate and personal nature of a small town weekly, the rural papers have a brighter future than their big city daily brethren.

Small town papers are scrapbooks for the community, is how Allen Burke, of Linton's Emmons County Journal described to me his paper's responsibility to the community: recording the everyday accomplishments of the lives of the local citizenry. That role will not change in the future and I cannot see scrapbooks ever becoming totally digital in format, eliminating the paper edition of the small town newspaper.

Newspapers, built on the bedrock freedom of the press our democracy has always enjoyed and treasured, are often a community's watchdog. They uncover and report on misuse of power by elected officials. In small towns this is often a slippery slope for a newspaper editor to traverse. The local prey they have in the cross hairs of their keyboard may well be a personal acquaintance of many years. They may often also control or influence the spending of commercial advertising dollars, the lifeline of any small town paper. I discussed this potential dilemma with all three editors and all made it clear that they took their responsibility as reporters seriously and would not compromise it by basing editorial decisions on advertising dollars. That type of civic service is a key role that a local paper plays in maintaining honest government, an absolute in a thriving community.

Laurie Ezzell Brown is editor of the Canadian, TX Record. She was practically raised in the paper's Main Street Office, her dad being the long time respected editor and owner of the Record. For her, the small paper is more than a business proposition, it is her family legacy and she intends to see it not only succeed, but flourish. She knows her town needs her and her weekly source of all that is good in the isolated Panhandle town of Canadian. "Advertising dollars drive us. Most people don't understand that. They think we live on subscription sales. Very untrue! Our income from subscription sales and over the counter sales wouldn't pay the bills to keep the doors open," she told me. But she is insistent that the Record will not compromise her trusted role as the town's watchdog. "My father established that tradition and everyone around here, friend and critic alike, and he had plenty of both, respected him for it. I will not let that public trust down; no matter how much advertisement it may cost me. It would be a slap at my dad's memory if I did."

All three towns have working and viable hospitals. In a day and age where many small towns cannot even keep one doctor in the community, for towns this small to each provide a cornerstone for local health care that a local hospital provides, is amazing. All three towns have leadership, not only within the hospital administration, but also in the local elected offices; that understands how the economic world of 21st century medical care is wired. In no way can any small town medical entity in today's economy be self-sustaining. Without government support through grants, every small town hospital in the nation would close its doors in a matter of weeks. Staying on top of the trends, and funding changes in an industry, health care, that has become a political football of the worst kind for the warring Democrats and Republicans, both on the state and federal level, is paramount to keeping the health care lights on in small communities such as Linton, McCook and Canadian. It takes leaders with vision to make this happen.

However, from my experience, the key that holds all three towns together are the excellent school systems all three have built and maintained. The long time success on the Friday night gridirons that all three have, for years, enjoyed are the extension of solid planning and implementation of high academic standards. All three towns demand success of their schools and will settle for nothing less. Football is the most visible of the output of the local schools, but all three have deep and well balanced academic and activities programs for their students. Football does not create a successful school district, and as an extension, a strong community. Just the opposite is true: strong communities develop strong public schools who then in turn demand winning and successful activities, with football being the most visible in the public eye. Most see this process backwards, with football as the driving source, which is very untrue.

Football is on the center stage most often, no argument from me there, but solid academics, I found, was the bedrock that each town's educational success was built on. Schools are the anchor for progressive rural communities. Lose the school, bury the town; it has happened all over the High Plains, the sad and slow death of rural communities. Linton, McCook and Canadian have outfoxed the economic grim reaper that has consumed so many of their neighbors, because they are led by civic minded citizens with vision for tackling, head on, the challenges of an evolving world economy.

George Lynn Cross, the University of Oklahoma's president from 1943 to 1968, once told the Oklahoma State Senate "I want a university the football team can be proud of." He said this tongue in cheek, but at a time when the Sooners were known for the great football dynasty that Coach Bud Wilkinson had built in Norman. His attempt at humor aside, Cross' statement has become cannon fodder over the years for those critics of the priority put on athletics in our schools.

I have often said, show me a strong athletic program and I will show you a strong academic school. The tail does not wag the dog, as many times critics of high school athletics will claim. The opposite is true. We often see the cause and effect dynamic backwards because of the high visibility of high school sports; especially football. But make no mistake of the order on the educational food chain; a win on the football field on Friday night is the end of the process, not the beginning. It starts with the community itself and its pride driven demands for excellence in return for their education dollar.

The trail's end for my 25,000+ mile, three month journey through the back country of the High Plains came to be in Lubbock, TX, 100 miles to the west of Highway 83.

On the windy and cold Friday night of November 18, 2011, at Cooper High School, the Canadian Wildcats were eliminated from the Class A Texas state playoffs and the football seasons for all three of my adopted teams were now complete. I had an empty feeling knowing that my journey was finished.

It was a sad ending, as almost all final games of the season are, climaxing in a loss that would leave most of the Canadian senior players in tears. My class of 2012 football playing friends of McCook, NE; Linton, ND and Canadian, TX can now add their names to the long roll call of former high school football players. Most will never play football again.

A note of advice to the all too soon graduating players of all three teams: you are only a high school football player once. I am glad I had the opportunity to witness this, unique to America, phenomena you have lived this fall: the life and times of the small town football hero. I watched each of you, the "Boys of Fall" and the pride of three towns, strut your stuff, while living the dream role of every adolescent male. I hope you enjoyed your moment in the sun. It is, my friends, as good as it gets. Now move on. You will never be able to duplicate this magical feeling of empowerment again, and it will be sheer folly should you try.

College, marriage, children, careers; you have a full life in front of you, but those days when your mere presence on the football field held the total attention and adulation of your hometown - no more. Savor the memories, then move on with grace and a warm feeling of pride and accomplishment, but please, move on.

I started my journey in August, 2011 wanting to make connections with those who could provide insight to me, and help me, validate answers to the following questions: Is the economic existence of the rural American small town as endangered as the media tells us? What is the connection between winning high school football programs and economically thriving small rural towns? Why do some small towns grow and prosper while many of their neighbors die from a slow economical strangulation?

My conclusion is that it all comes back to the quality of the local public school system. I have tried, in this writing, to connect the dots; using three successful small towns as documentation of my findings.

Citizens throughout rural America have dug in their heels and chosen to collectively fight all attempts to consolidate and close their small local schools, bussing their young to a nearby larger school. Let the learned experts present all the data to the locals they wish, quantitatively showing the absolute wisdom of the economic and educational advantages of a consolidation; the local response will still be one of an emotional howl of disapproval with a promise to fight. Who is to say they are not right?

But how can small rural schools be kept educational viable and economically solvent, with the dwindling enrollments that have plagued rural America for the last two generations? The answer, in my mind, crystalized into clearer focus as I spent more and more time in Linton, ND, McCook, NE and Canadian, TX. The stabilizing of school enrollments in rural communities is dependent upon jobs. Towns that are surviving, even thriving, on the High Plains, such as Linton, McCook and Canadian, have attracted solid industries that are welcome economic partners, providing well-paying jobs. They are not quick fix carpet baggers, opportunists who provide short term minimum wage jobs while destroying the local environment.

The positive results of economic development and the recruitment of legitimate business partners that has occurred in all three towns, did not just happen by lucky happenstance, but is the result of civic leaders with vision who were able to reach across political and social lines to embrace all sectors of the community. This cohesion and civic cooperation through inclusion is an absolute if a rural small town is to survive in today's world-wide economy. A dictatorship, even if benevolent in nature, will not suffice.

But what in a small town can create the type of cooperation and hometown pride that I found in abundance in all three I studied? The success formula that Linton, McCook and Canadian have concocted to stimulate their local economies varied to some degree in each; but the longer I poked around - kicking the town tires and peeking under the civic hood - the more I became convinced that the strong local schools are the anchor, pulling together the diverse sectors of population found in each. Reputable businesses, when conducting searches for future communities to set up shop in, will view a strong school system as a must. Parents will also consider the level of education available for their children when considering the merits of a job induced change of residency.

In all three towns, the school was the community treasure that produced the kind of civic pride that is all so necessary in creating the cohesion I found so abundant in each. I very seldom heard the word I or me in these towns, it was always us and we.

As the hot summer of 2011 gave way to the cool High Plains breezes of fall, I began to realize that what I heard so often in regard to the ancestors of each town, those who homesteaded the area 125 years prior – of their indomitable pioneering spirit; their toughness, their grit and their sense of community - traits so paramount in learning to survive the harshness of their chosen homeland; was also deeply instilled in the bloodline of their off spring, still present in abundance in the current local leadership. As I heard over and over again from the inhabitants of all three towns, spoken with a deep sense of heritage pride; "we come from tough stock." When discussing current challenges facing the High Plains, I was told on numerous occasions, "we will find a way."

The High Plains will never be conquered or tamed. What the citizens of Linton, McCook and Canadian have done is to learn to respectfully co-exist with nature in this harsh but beautiful land. Continued growth in a rural High Plains community will always be a challenge for those who chose to live there. Yesterday's problems were isolation, locust and lawlessness. Today they are more economic in nature, deep rooted in a global economy, often out of the reach and the understanding of the locals. Tomorrow's challenges, who can say?

On the High Plains, I was told by one long time rancher south of Canadian, TX, you either grow or you die, but you never just stay the same. It is imperative for future growth that those who call the area home remain vigilant and proactive, collectively open minded while continuing to seek answers to evolving problems.

I would suggest that the nation's leading rural sociologists and academia experts visit Linton, ND, McCook, NE and Canadian, TX and use the community development and educational excellence I found in each as a template for future rural reclamation projects.

We as a nation cannot afford to turn our backs on small town America. So much of who we are today, of what makes our country strong and defines our national consciousness, has evolved from the contributions of those whose foundations were laid, whose character was molded, whose innovative ideas were germinated in safe and nurturing small rural hamlets like the three I found to still flourish, in 2011, along US Highway 83; America's true 50 yard line.

Appendix

Box Scores

WEEK 1

August 27, 2011						
River Road @ Canadian						
Teams	1st Quarter	2nd Quarter	3rd Quarter	4th Quarter	OT	Final
River Road	0	0	0	13	--	13
Canadian	35	13	0	0		48

Scoring Summary
C—Taylor Schafer 1 run (Marcos Trevino kick)
C Isaac Lewis 68 punt return (Chance Walker run)
C—Trevino 24 pass from Braden Hudson (Trevino kick)
C—Lewis 11 pass from Hudson (Trevino kick)
C Dvston Hudson 12 pass from Braden Hudson (kick failed)
C—Boston Hudson 13 pass from Braden Hudson (kick failed)
C—Lewis 48 run (Trevino kick)
RR—Trey Bookout 2 run (run failed)
RR—Tristan Beezley 37 fumble return (Matt Marrs kick)

Individual Stats
Receiving: Isaac Lewis 3-76, Taylor Schafer 5-30, Chris Marquez 3-36, Jesse Sandoval 5-10, Taylor Thompson 5-56.
Passing: Braden Hudson 10-13-0—167; Sandoval 1-1-0—7.
Rushing: Isaac Lewis 3-76, Taylor Schafer 5-30, Chris Marquez 3-36, Jesse Sandoval 5-10, Taylor Thompson 5-56.

Team Stats

Stat	River Road	Canadian
Rushing	88	182
Passing	56	174
Total Yards	144	356
First Downs	10	21
Penalties	2-10	6-45
Turnovers	2	1
Punts	4-41.0	0-0

August 27, 2011						
MoBridge, SD @ Linton						
Teams	1st Quarter	2nd Quarter	3rd Quarter	4th Quarter	OT	Final
MoBridge	13	0	13	0	--	26
Linton	6	0	0	6	--	12

Scoring Summary
M: Bailey Friesz 39 yd. run (kick failed)
L: Tanner Purintun 1 yd. run (pass failed)
M: Payton Friesz 57 yd. pass from B. Friesz (Zack Hoven kick)
M: B. Friesz 59 yd. run (Hoven Kick)
B. Friesz 6 yd. run (kick failed)
L: Jayden Gross 1 yd. pass from Purintun (pass failed)

Individual Stats:
Rushing Tanner Purintun 8-76; Cody Sehn 11-38; Brock Nagel 8-31; Mike Oien 1-2; Dillon Doolittle 2- (-10)
Passing: Tanner Purintun 17-27-209-1.

Receiving: Jayden Gross 8-55, Al Gefroh 4-78, Lukas Holzer 2-30, Doolittle 1-54, Sehn 1-(-4), Nagel 1-(-4).

Team Stats

Stat	MoBridge	Linton
Rushing	34-213	30-137
Passing	83	209
Total Yards	296	346
Return Yards	102	8
First Downs	10	15
Penalties	4-37	2-10
Turnovers	2	2
Punts	3-32.7	4-21.0
Sacks	0-0	2-9

August 27, 2011

McCook @ Scottsbluff

Teams	1st Quarter	2nd Quarter	3rd Quarter	4th Quarter	OT	Final
McCook	14	7	0	7	--	28
Scottsbluff	0	0	7	0	--	7

Scoring Summary
M:Matt Chitwood 37 yd. run (Chitwood kick)
M: Justin Terry 30 yd. run (Chitwood kick)
M: Jake Schagler 7 yd. run (Chitwood kick)
S: Seth Roher 7 yd. run (Randy Wentz kick)
M: Jake Schagler 4 yd. run (Chitwood kick)

Individual Stats
Rushing: Jake Schlager 12-62, Justin Terry 12-144, Matt Chitwood 11-101, Austin Cherry 2-6, Kolton Stone 2-9, Shane Buck 5-21
Passing: Matt Chitwood 2-6-22
Receiving: Cody Wudtke 1-16, Matt Collicott 1-11

Team Stats

Stat	McCook	Scottsbluff
Rushing	250	13
Passing	83	124
Total Yards	333	254
Return Yards	185	28
First Downs	18	10
Penalties	8-65	4-30
Turnovers	2	2
Punts	1/40.0	7/32.3
Sacks	4	1

WEEK 2

September 2, 2011

Canadian @ Meade, KS

Teams	1st Quarter	2nd Quarter	3rd Quarter	4th Quarter	OT	Final
Canadian	12	0	6	0	--	18
Meade, KS	12	6	0	6	--	24

Scoring Summary
M: Jeff Little 90 yd. kickoff return (kick failed)
C: Taylor Schafer 2 yd. run (kick failed)
M: Trevin Wiens 80 yd. run (run failed)
C: Braden Hudson 1 yd. run (pass failed)
M: Little 45 yd. run (pass failed)

C: Schafer 2 yd. run (run failed)
M: Chris Hardaway 1 yd. (run failed)

Individual Stats
Passing: Braden Hudson 20-32-0-5
Rushing: Taylor Schafer 15-72, Isaac Lewis 3-21, Chris Marquez 4-16,
Receiving: Chance Walker 1-20, Isaac Lewis 8-114Matt Trevino 2-19, Taylor Schafer 2-14, Boston Hudson 3-24

Team Stats

Stat	Canadian	Meade
Rushing	151	232
Passing	262	39
Total Yards	413	271
First Downs	21	12
Penalties	10-85	6-32
Turnovers	5	2
Punts	3-37.0	6-22.0

September 2, 2011

Oaks @ Linton

Teams	1st Quarter	2nd Quarter	3rd Quarter	4th Quarter	OT	Final
Oaks	0	0	7	0	--	7
Linton	0	6	0	6	--	12

Scoring Summary
L: Jayden Gross 11 pass from Tanner Purintun (run failed)
O: Trent Ptacek 1 yd. run (Bryce Meehl kick)
L: Gross 2 yd. pass from Purintun (run failed)

Individual Stats
Rushing: Cody Sehn 13-33, Tanner, Purintun 14-15, Brock Nagel 5-3.
Passing: Purintun 9-20-127-2.
Receiving: Jayden Gross 6-100, Nagel 2-6, Al Gefroh 1-21.

Team Stats

Stat	Oaks	Linton
Rushing	39-125	32-51
Passing	78	127
Total Yards	203	178
Return Yards	89	41
First Downs	11	7
Penalties	5-35	1-10
Turnovers	4	3
Punts	5-30.6	6-32.7
Sacks	3-30	3-16

September 2, 2011

Aurora @ McCook

Teams	1st Quarter	2nd Quarter	3rd Quarter	4th Quarter	OT	Final
Aurora	0	7	0	0	6	13
McCook	0	0	7	0	9	16

Scoring Summary
A: Trey Allen 34 pass from Seth Schnakenberg (Austin Barth kick).
M: Jake Schlager 80 run (Matt Chitwood kick).
M: Chitwood 5 run (kick failed).
A: Nate Bell 10 pass from Schnakenberg (kick failed).
M: FG Chitwood 27.

Individual Stats
Rushing - Jake Schlager 6-114, Matt Chitwood 17-38, Justin Terry 6-11, Austin Cherry 4-(-5).
Passing - Matt Chitwood 7-13-1-103 yards.
Receiving - Cody Wudtke 3-38, Jake Schlager 2-65

Team Stats

Stat	Aurora	McCook
Rushing	201	158
Passing	154	103
Total Yards	355	261
Return Yards	30	43
First Downs	15	12
Penalties	8-40	1-5
Turnovers	4	1
Punts	3-31.3	5-37.0
Sacks	1	3

WEEK 3

September 9, 2011

Canadian @ Perryton

Teams	1st Quarter	2nd Quarter	3rd Quarter	4th Quarter	OT	Final
Canadian	6	6	13	7	--	32
Perryton	14	10	0	9	--	33

C: Taylor Schafer 26 pass from Braden Hudson (Kick blocked)
P: Kade Keeth 9 pass from Blake Turner (Heriberto Romero kick)
P: Calum Townsend 24 interception return (Romero kick)
C: Hudson 9 run (run failed)d)
P: Romero 27 field goal
C: Isaac Lewis 6 run (Hudson kick)
C: Hudson 7 run (run failed)
C: Schafer 3 run (Hudson kick)
P: Heath Dorman 10 pass from Turner
P: Romero 23 field goal

Individual Stats
Passing: Braden Hudson 17-26175-1
Rushing: Tyler Schafer 10-36, Isaac Lewis 4-21, Chris Marquez 1-6, Braden Hudson 23-36
Receiving: Isaac Lewis 5-17, Marcos Trevino 5-59, Tyler Schafer 4-82, Boston Hudson 1-7

Team Stats

Stat	Canadian	Perryton
Rushing	90	209
Passing	183	149
Total Yards	273	358
First Downs	22	19
Penalties	2-10	5-65
Turnovers	1	3
Punts	6-28.0	5-42.0

September 9, 2011

Milnor @ Linton

Teams	1st Quarter	2nd Quarter	3rd Quarter	4th Quarter	OT	Final
Milnor	7	0	0	0	--	7
Linton	6	0	8	0	--	14

L: Brock Nagel 1 run (Nagel pass from Purintun)
M:: Josh Hansana 21 run (Hansana kick)
L: Purintun 30 run (pass failed)

Individual Stats
Rushing: Cody Sehn, 19-58, Brock Nagel 11-47, Tanner Purintun 13-46.
Passing: Purintun 6-18-125-2.
Receiving: Dillon Doolittle 2-56, Sehn 2-33, Jayden Gross 1-25, Nagel 1-11.

Team Stats

Stat	Milnor	Linton
Rushing	35-98	43-151
Passing	130	125
Total Yards	228	276
Return Yards	32	56
First Downs	10	12
Penalties	5-47	4-20
Turnovers	1	4
Punts	4.36.8	3-27.7
Sacks	2-18	3-36

September 9, 2011

McCook @ Alliance

Teams	1st Quarter	2nd Quarter	3rd Quarter	4th Quarter	OT	Final
McCook	7	7	7	10		31
Alliance	3	0	17	0	--	20

Scoring Summary
A: Kyle Sanders 37 yd. FG
M: Cody Wudtke 6 pass from Matt Chitwood (Chitwood kick)
M: Matt Chitwood 42 yd. FG
A: Mitch Pancost 15 yd. run (Sanders kick)
A: Kyle Sanders 37 yd. FG
M: Matt Chitwood 60 yd. run (Chitwood kick)
A: Kyle Hooper 80 yd. pass from Alex Burnham (Sanders kick)
M: Matt Collicott 6 yd. pass from Matt Chitwood (Chitwood kick)
M: Cody Wudtke 41 yd. pass from Matt Chitwood (Chitwood kick)

Individual Stats
Rushing: Matt Chitwood 11-109, Jake Schlager 15-79, Justin Terry 15-69
Passing: Matt Chitwood 6-11-83
Receiving Cody Wudtke 3-55, Matt Collicott 2-18, Jake Schlager 1-10

Team Stats

Stat	McCook	Alliance
Rushing	250	89
Passing	83	267
Total Yards	333	356
Return Yards	41	81
First Downs	11	13
Turnovers	2	4
Punts	3/40.7	4/26.8

WEEK 4

September 16, 2011

Canadian @ Sanford Fritch

Teams	1st Quarter	2nd Quarter	3rd Quarter	4th Quarter	OT	Final
Canadian	20	18	6	0	--	44
Sanford Fritch	0	0	6	0	--	6

Scoring Summary
C- Boston Hudson 26 yd. pass from Braden Hudson (kick no failed)
C-Taylor Schafer 1 yd. run (kick failed)
C-Taylor Schafer Safety

C- Braden Hudson 1 yd. run (pass failed)
C- Braden Hudson 1 yd. run (kick failed)
C- Taylor Schafer 7 yd. run (kick failed)
S- Christian Ward 18 yard pass from Chris Brown (kick failed)
C- Isaac Lewis 10 yd. pass from Braden Hudson (kick failed)
C- Taylor Schafer 39 yd. run (kick failed)

Individual Stats
Passing: Braden Hudson 21-28-216; Isaac Lewis 1-1-4; Ben Arbuckle 3-4-32
Rushing: Isaac Lewis 6-90; Braden Hudson 9-83; Taylor Schafer 10-69; Devon Carson 1- (-5); Taylor Thompson 6-18; Ben Arbuckle 2-1; Chris Marquez 7-3
Receiving: Braden Hudson 1-4; Isaac Lewis 7-87; Taylor Schafer 2-23

Team Stats

Stat	Canadian	Sanford Fritch
Rushing	41-259	185
Passing	25-33-252	41
Total Yards	511	226
First Downs	25	11
Penalties	7-50	5-42
Turnovers	3	5
Punts	1-32	3-28

September 16, 2011
Linton @ Fargo Oak Grove

Teams	1st Quarter	2nd Quarter	3rd Quarter	4th Quarter	OT	Final
Linton	0	20	6	0	--	26
Fargo Oak Grove	0	0	0	0	--	0

Scoring Summary
L: Cody Sehn 3 run (run failed)
L: Tanner Purintun 1 run (Jayden Gross pass from Purintun)
L: Gross 5 pass from Purintun (run failed)
L: Gross 8 pass from Purintun (run failed)

Individual Stats
Rushing: Brock Nagel 10-70, Cody Sehn 17-51,Tanner Purintun 6-42, Mike Oien, 3-17, Taylor Wetzsteon 1-15, Rylan Jacob 1-3, Bradyn Burgad, 1-0, Andrew Leier 1-(-3), Austin Bernhardt 1-(-11)
Passing: Purintun 7-10-99-2.
Receiving: Jayden Gross 4-43, Lukas Holzer 2-48, Nagel 1-8

Team Stats

Stat	Linton	Fargo-Oak Grove
Rushing	41-184	39-87
Passing	99	42
Total Yards	283	129
Return Yards	0	71
First Downs	16	5
Penalties	1-10	6-40
Turnovers	2	1
Punts	3-46.3	5-36.6
Sacks	3-13	0-0

September 16, 2011
McCook @ Gering

Teams	1st Quarter	2nd Quarter	3rd Quarter	4th Quarter	OT	Final
McCook	7	7	10	0	--	24
Gering	0	0	0	0	--	0

Scoring Summary
M: Matt Chitwood 1 yd. run (Chitwood kick)
M: Matt Chitwood 1 yd. run (Chitwood kick)
M: Chitwood 28 yd. FG
M: Jake Schlager 48 yd. pass from Chitwood (Chitwood kick)

Individual Stats
Rushing: Jake Schlager 8-37, Justin Terry 15-151, Matt Chitwood 9-65, Austin Cherry 2-4, Kolton Stone 4-40, Cade Hiatt 1-4, Kyle Stewart 1-4, Trenton Bruntz 1-2, Shane Buck 5-8
Passing: Matt Chitwood 2-6-67
Receiving: Cody Wudtke 1-24, Jake Schlager 1-43

Team Stats

Stat	McCook	Gering
Rushing	315	7
Passing	67	161
Total Yards	382	168
Return Yards	70	27
First Downs	12	5
Turnovers	0	1
Punts	2 38	5-40
Sacks	5	0

WEEK 5

September 23, 2011

Clayton, NM @ Canadian

Teams	1st Quarter	2nd Quarter	3rd Quarter	4th Quarter	OT	Final
Clayton, NM	0	0	0	7	--	7
Canadian	34	27	0	6	--	67

Scoring Summary
C- Taylor Schafer 41 yd. pass from Braden Hudson (Salvador Escamilla Kick)
C- Isaac Lewis 6 yd. run (Braden Hudson PAT run)
C- Isaac Lewis 41 yd. pass from Braden Hudson (kick failed)
C- Isaac Lewis 21 yd. pass from Braden Hudson (kick failed)
C- Taylor Schafer 2 yd. fumble recovery return (Salvador Escamilla Kick)
C- Isaac Lewis 9 yd. pass from Braden Hudson (Salvador Escamilla Kick)
C- Boston Hudson 42 yd. pass from Braden Hudson (Escamilla Kick)
C- Taylor Schafer 32 yd. run (kick failed)
C- Matt Thomasy 4 yd. run (Escamilla Kick)
Cl – Wiseman 91 yd. run (Kick good)
C- Jess Sandavol 65 yd. pass from Ben Arbuckle (kick failed)

Individual Stats
Passing: Braden Hudson 10-16-221-5, Ben Arbuckle 2-2-97-1
Rushing: Taylor Schafer 2-43, Isaac Lewis 4-49, Chris Marquez 3-30,
Receiving: Taylor Schafer 2-43, Isaac Lewis 4-49, Chris Marquez 3-30, Jess Sandavol 1-65,

Team Stats

Stat	Clayton, NM	Canadian
Rushing	51	193
Passing	0	318
Total Yards	51	511
First Downs	1	18
Penalties	5-30	6-55
Turnovers	2	0
Punts	5-38	1-34

September 23, 2011							
Linton @ Maple Valley							
Teams	1st Quarter	2nd Quarter	3rd Quarter	4th Quarter	OT	Final	
Linton	6	8	0	12	--	26	
Maple Valley	6	13	0	6	--	25	

L- Jayden Gross 20 pass from Tanner Purintun (run failed)
M- Ty Smith 34 pass from Dylan Lerud (kick failed)
M- Jesse Bielke 2 run (Smith kick)
L- Cody Sehn 3 run (Lukas Holzer pass from Purintun)
M- Smith 21 pass from Lerud (kick failed)
M- Lerud 1 run (kick blocked)
L- Gross 61 pass from Purintun (pass failed)
L- Sehn 18 run (pass failed)

Individual Stats
Rushing: Cody Sehn, 19-128, Tanner Purintun 12-45,, Jayden Gross 2-23, Brock Nagel 10-22.
Passing: Purintun 9-12-190-0. 9-15-164-1, Haseleu 0-1-0-1.
Receiving: Gross3-105, Al Gefroh 3-46, Nagel 1-20, Dillon Doolittle 1-11, Lukas Holzer 1-8.

Team Stats

Stat	Linton	Maple Valley
Rushing	43-218	37-167
Passing	190	164
Total Yards	408	331
Return Yards	47	49
First Downs	13	11
Penalties	1-5	6-35
Turnovers	1	2
Punts	1-20	2-38.5
Sacks	3-15	3-12

September 23, 2011							
Grand Island NW @ McCook							
Teams	1st Quarter	2nd Quarter	3rd Quarter	4th Quarter	OT	Final	
Grand Island NW	0	0	12	13	--	26	
McCook	28	21	0	0	--	49	

Scoring Summary
M- Matt Chitwood 1 yd. run (Chitwood Kick)
M- Jake Schlager 1 yd. run (Chitwood Kick)
M- Jake Schlager 45 yd. Interception Return (Chitwood Kick)
M- Chitwood 75 yd. Interception return (Chitwood Kick)
M –Chitwood 8 yd. run (Chitwood Kick)
M- Justin Terry 60 yd. run (Chitwood Kick)
M- Kyle Stewart 8 yd. run. (Chitwood Kick)
N- Keutz 1 yd. run (kick failed)
N- Lawson 14 yd. pass from Rouzee (Bachle kick)
N- Johnson 17 yd. pass from Rouzee (Blanche kick)
N- Larson 16 yd. pass from Rouzee (kick failed)

Individual Stats
Receiving: Cade Hiatt 1-22
Passing: Matt Chitwood 1-1-22-0
Rushing: Jake Schlager 5-35, Justin Terry 4-81, Matt Chitwood 6-68, Austin Cherry 4-14, Kolton Stone 4-38, Cade Hiatt 1-8, Kyle Stewart 6-20, Tyson Karr 1-4, Shane Buck 2-0

Stat	Grand Island NW	McCook
Rushing	70	268
Passing	138	22
Total Yards	238	488
Return Yards	2-20	3-58
First Downs	12	8
Turnovers	8	0
Punts	4-33.0	3-40.0
Sacks	0	4

WEEK 6

September 30, 2011						
Panhandle @ Canadian						
Teams	1st Quarter	2nd Quarter	3rd Quarter	4th Quarter	OT	Final
Panhandle	7	0	0	27	--	34
Canadian	14	20	14	0	--	48

Scoring Summary
P — Lighe Powers 28 pass from Tyler Hall (Travis Hammer kick)
C — Taylor Schafer 82 run (Salvador Escamilla kick)
C — Isaac Lewis 7 pass from Braden Hudson (Escamilla kick)
C — Taylor Schafer 5 run (kick failed)
C — Lewis 67 pass from Taylor Schafer (Escamilla kick)
C — Boston Hudson 33 pass from Braden Hudson (Escamilla kick)
C — Chris Marquez 10 pass from Braden Hudson (Escamilla kick)
C — Boston Hudson 10 pass from Braden Hudson (Escamilla kick)
P — John Hopkins 10 pass from Tyler Hall (pass failed)
P — Shane Smith 20 pass from Hall (Travis Hammer kick)
p — Zac Berry 20 pass from Hall (Hammer kick)
P — Bradley Powers 45 interception return (Hammer kick)

Individual Stats
Passing: Braden Hudson 21-27-270-4, Ben Arbuckle 4-5-21-0
Rushing: Travis Schafer 11-125, Isaac Lewis 1- (-12), Chris Marquez 4-50, Taylor Thompson 1-2
Receiving: Chance 1-41, Chris Marquez 2-34, Isaac Lewis 9-119, Travis Schafer 3-0, Paxton Galloway 1-3, Taylor Thompson 1-14, Brandon Hudson 4-114, Tyler Lynch 1-10

Team Stats

Stat	Panhandle	Canadian
Rushing	72	223
Passing	235	312
Total Yards	307	535
First Downs	16	21
Penalties	11-110	10-85
Turnovers	4	4
Punts	5-36.0	2-25.0
Sacks	0	2

September 30, 2011						
Linton @ Kidder County						
Teams	1st Quarter	2nd Quarter	3rd Quarter	4th Quarter	OT	Final
Linton	7	7	0	7	--	21
Kidder County	0	0	0	0	--	0

Scoring Summary
L - Cody Sehn 13 run (Brock Nagel kick)
L -Tanner Purintun 9 run (Nagel kick)
L -Purintun 21 run (Nagel kick)

Individual Stats
Rushing: Cody Sehn 23-97, Tanner Purintun 6-40, Brock Nagel 7-25, Mike Oien 2-6.
Passing: Tanner Purintun 8-15-107-2.
Receiving: Jayden Gross 2-20, Lukas Holzer 2-15, Sehn 2-14, Dillon Doolittle 1-32, Al Gefroh 1-26.

Team Stats

Stat	Linton	Kidder County
Rushing	38-168	40-141
Passing	107	13
Total Yards	275	154
Return Yards	32	73

First Downs	12	9
Penalties	4-40	4-30
Turnovers	5	6
Punts	3-27.7	3-24.7
Sacks	4-19	0

September 30, 2011

Sidney @ McCook

Teams	1st Quarter	2nd Quarter	3rd Quarter	4th Quarter	OT	Final
Sidney	0	0	0	6	--	6
McCook	21	21	7	0	--	49

Scoring Summary

M- Matt Chitwood 25 run (Chitwood kick).

M- Chitwood 45 run (Chitwood kick).

M- Chitwood 2 run (Chitwood kick).

M- Austin Cherry 4 run (Chitwood kick).

M-- Chitwood 8 run (Chitwood kick).

M - Alex Broadfoot 27 pass from Chitwood (Chitwood kick).

M- Justin Terry 3 run (Chitwood kick).

S- Chance Anglin 1 run (kick blocked).

Individual Stats

Rushing: Jake Schlager 5-35, Justin Terry 4-81, Matt Chitwood, 6-68, Austin Cherry 4-14, Kolton Stone 4-38, Cade Hiatt 1-8, Kyle Stewart 6-20, Tyson Karr 1-4, Shane Buck 2-0

Passing: Matt Chitwood 1-1-22, Tyson Karr 0-1-0

Receiving: Cade Hiatt 1-22

Team Stats

Stat	McCook	Sidney
Rushing	314	90
Passing	27	-2
Total Yards	341	88
Return Yards	58	676
First Downs	16	6
Turnovers	0	3
Punts	2-42.5	7-24.3
Sacks	4	1

WEEK 7

October 7, 2011

Canadian @ Sunray

Teams	1st Quarter	2nd Quarter	3rd Quarter	4th Quarter	OT	Final
Canadian	0	7	0	0	7	14
Sunray	0	0	7	0	13	20

Scoring Summary

C: Taylor Schafer 7 run (Salvador Escamilla kick)

S: Christian Axelsen 19 run (Talon Dooley kick)

C: Marcus Trevino 19 pass from Braden Hudson (Escamilla kick)

S: Axelsen 2 run (Dooley kick)

S: Shay Wilkins 20 pass from Dooley (run failed)

Individual Stats

Rushing: Hudson 18-48, Isaac Lewis 3-15, Taylor Schafer 13-41, Chris Marquez 6-36

Passing: Hudson 11-24-1—106. Sunray: Dooley 4-10-1—63.

Receiving: Marcus Trevino 4-47, Boston Hudson 2-17, Schafer 2-14, Lewis 2-13, Tyler Lynch 1-14.

Team Stats

	Canadian	Sunray
Rushing	143	136
Passing	106	63
Total Yards	249	199
First Downs	14	12
Penalties	5-35	4-25
Turnovers	1	1
Punts	4-33.0	4-25
Sacks	2-9	4-23

October 7, 2011

North Cass @ Linton

Teams	1st Quarter	2nd Quarter	3rd Quarter	4th Quarter	OT	Final
North Cass	0	6	0	7	--	13
Linton	24	14	8	0	--	46

Scoring Summary

L: Tanner Purintun 3 run (kick blocked)

L: Jayden Gross 16 pass from Purintun (kick failed)

L: Cody Sehn 64 run (pass failed)

L: Jayden Gross 1 pass from Purintun (kick blocked)

L: Brock Nagel 1 run (kick blocked)

L: Al Gefroh 10 pass from Purintun (Lukas Holzer pass from Purintun)

N: McKenzie Cargile 52 pass from Taylor Kyllo (pass failed)

L: Brock Nagel 75 pass from Purintun (Gross pass from Purintun)

N: Adam Teegarden 10 pass from Kyllo (Jed Hansen kick)

Individual Stats

Rushing: Cody Sehn 11-87, Brock Nagel 6-49, Tanner Purintun, 6-15, Taylor Wetzsteon 5-12, Chase Jacob 2-11, Brooks Flyberg 1-0,, Austin Schell 1-0.

Passing: L: Purintun 13-16-245-0.

Receiving: L: Jayden Gross 6-72, Al Gefroh 4-48, Nagel 2-113, Sehn 1-12.

Team Stats

Stat	North Cass	Linton
Rushing	30-98	32-174
Passing	93	245
Total Yards	191	419
Return Yards	122	58
First Downs	10	18
Penalties	2-5	4-40
Turnovers	4	1
Punts	4-28.8	3-28.3
Sacks	1-5	3-23

October 7, 2011

McCook @ Lexington

Teams	1st Quarter	2nd Quarter	3rd Quarter	4th Quarter	OT	Final
McCook	0	0	0	7	9	16
Lexington	0	7	0	0	6	13

Scoring Summary

L: Ryan Reynolds 24-yard pass from Jeremy Callahan (Jeremy Callahan Kick).

M: Matt Chitwood 14-yard run (Matt Chitwood Kick).

M: Cody Wudtke 9-yard pass from Matt Chitwood (Kick failed).

L: Jeremy Callahan Pass from Joe Walker (Kick failed).

M: Matt Chitwood 27-yard field goal.

Individual Stats
Rushing: Justin Terry 6-37, Matt Chitwood 32-249, Austin Cherry 3-12, Kyle Stewart 10-89
Passing Matt Chitwood 2-6-15
Receiving: Cody Wudtke 2-15

Team Stats

Stat	McCook	Lexington
Rushing	402	250
Passing	15	83
Total Yards	387	167
Return Yards	11	35
First Downs	16	10
Turnovers	1	4
Punts	2-21.5	4-54.5
Sacks	3	1

WEEK 8

October 14,, 2011

West Texas @ Canadian

Teams	1st Quarter	2nd Quarter	3rd Quarter	4th Quarter	OT	Final
West Texas	0	7	7	0	--	14
Canadian	13	22	7	6	--	48

C: Tyler Schafer 1 yard run (Salvador Escamillo kick)
C: Tyler Schafer 49 pass from Braden Hudson (kick failed)
W: Alex Ramirez 25 run (Ramirez kick)
C: Chris Marquez 1 run (Boston Hudson pass from Braden Hudson)
C: Tyler Schafer 61 run (Escamillo kick)
C: Chris Marquez 16 pass from Braden Hudson (Escamillo kick)
C: Boston Hudson 8 pass from Braden Hudson (Escamillo kick)
W: Chase Elliot 2 run (Rameriz kick)
C: Chris Marquez 18 run (kick failed)

Individual Stats
Passing: Braden Hudson 15-25-233-3-0
Rushing: Tyler Schafer 10-133, Isaac Lewis 5-65, Chris Marquez 7-63
Receiving: Chris Marquez 2-33, Isaac Lewis 5-70, Matt Traveno 2-31, Tyler Schafer 1-41, Hedge 2-21, Boston Hudson 3-22, Tyler Lynch 1-16

Team Stats

Stat	West Texas	Canadian
Rushing	232	299
Passing	4-11-54	18-28-234
Total Yards	286	533
First Downs	14	24
Penalties	6-60	6-50
Turnovers	2	0
Punts	7-26	1-46
Sacks	0	1

October 14, 2011

Linton @ Maryville

Teams	1st Quarter	2nd Quarter	3rd Quarter	4th Quarter	OT	Final
Linton	25	6	8	0	--	39
Maryville	0	0	6	6	--	12

Scoring Summary
L: Cody Sehn 7 run (kick failed)
L: Lukas Holzer 29 pass from Tanner Purintun (kick failed)

L: Sehn 7 run (Brock Nagel kick)
L: Sehn 32 run (kick failed)
L: Mike Oien 1 run (kick failed)
M: Ryan Ust 77 kick-off return (run failed)
L-HMB: Nagel 27 pass from Purintun (Al Gefroh pass from Purintun)
M: Hunter Torgeson 2 run (pass failed)

Individual Stats
Rushing: Linton: Cody Sehn, 12-88, Tanner Purintun 2-42, Rylan, Jacob 4-38, Brock Nagel 4-35, Taylor Wetzsteon 5-34, Austin Schell 1-18, Mike Oien 3-2, Chase Jacob 1-1, Austin, Bernhardt 2-(-2
Passing: Purintun, 4-9-101-0, Brooks Flyberg 1-5-17-1.
Receiving: Nagel, 3-72, Lukas Holzer 1-29, Al Gefroh 1-17.

Team Stats

Stat	Linton	Maryville
Rushing	34-256	43-125
Passing	118	23
Total Yards	371	148
Return Yards	101	187
First Downs	19	9
Penalties	2-10	3-20
Turnovers	1	5
Punts	0	5-28.6
Sacks	2-8	0-0

October 14, 2011

Adams Central @ McCook

Teams	1st Quarter	2nd Quarter	3rd Quarter	4th Quarter	OT	Final
Adams Central	7	7	7	0	--	21
McCook	14	3	0	7	--	24

Scoring summary
M: Matt Chitwood 65-yard run (Matt Chitwood Kick).
M: Matt Chitwood 49-yard interception (Matt Chitwood Kick).
A: Kyle Goldenstein 1-yard run (Chance Vorderstrasse Kick).
M: Matt Chitwood 42-yard field goal.
A: Jake Fowler 2-yard field goal (Chance Vorderstrasse Kick).
A: Jake Fowler 1-yard run (Chance Vorderstrasse Kick).
M: Jake Schlager 2-yard run (Matt Chitwood Kick).

Individual Stats
Rushing: Jake Schlager 20-106, Matt Chitwood 18-142, Kolton Stone, 6-18, Cade Hiatt 1-5, Tyson Karr 1-0
Passing: Matt Chitwood 2-26-22
Receiving: Austin Cherry 1-8, Jake Schlager 1-14

WEEK 9

October 21, 2011

Canadian @ Strafford

Teams	1st Quarter	2nd Quarter	3rd Quarter	4th Quarter	OT	Final
Canadian	7	7	6	7	--	27
Stratford	3	7	0	7	--	17

Scoring Summary
C: Isaac Lewis 4 pass from Braden Hudson (Salvador Escamilla kick)
S: Nicolas Eizmendi 30 FG
S: Braiden Palmer 1 run (Eizmendi kick)
C: Boston Hudson 5 pass from Braden Hudson (Escamilla kick)
C: Taylor Schafer 20 run (kick blocked)

S: Alex Chavoya 3 run (Eizmendi kick)
C: Isaac Lewis 11 run (Escamilla kick)

Individual Stats
Rushing—Canadian: Braden Hudson 11-44, Isaac Lewis 3-27, Taylor Schafer 9-68, Chris Marquez 2-20.
Passing—Canadian: Br. Hudson 7-17-0—143. Stratford, 3-3-0—31, Palmer 3-7-0—44.
Receiving—Canadian: Lewis 2-41, Marcos Trevino 4-97, Boston Hudson 1-5

Team Stats

Stat	Canadian	Stafford
Rushing	159	200
Passing	143	75
Total Yards	302	275
First Downs	12	14
Penalties	6-45	5-30
Turnovers	0	0
Punts	3-34	3-30

October 22, 2011

Westhope @ Linton First Round Playoffs

Teams	1st Quarter	2nd Quarter	3rd Quarter	4th Quarter	OT	Final
Westhope	0	0	0	8	--	8
Linton	12	6	0	0	--	18

Scoring Summary
L: Brock Nagel 10 run (kick failed)
L: Dillon Doolittle 8 pass from Tanner Purintun (pass failed)
L: Purintun 3 run (pass failed)
W: Karlie Hancock 4 run (Hunter Braaten run)

Individual Statistics
Rushing: : Cody Sehn 20-86, Tanner Purintun, 9-42, Brock Nagel 10-40
Passing: Purintun 8-18-96-0.
Receiving: Sehn 2-44, Dillon, Doolittle 2-16, Nagel 2-4, Jayden Gross 1-16, Jordan Gross 1-16.

Team Stats

Stat	Westhope	Linton
Rushing	32-131	39-168
Passing	70	96
Total Yards	201	264
Return Yards	59	84
First Downs	8	14
Penalties	3-30	3-20
Turnovers	2	0
Punts	5-24.8	6-28.8
Sacks	1-5	2-27

October 21, 2011

McCook @ Holdrege

Teams	1st Quarter	2nd Quarter	3rd Quarter	4th Quarter	OT	Final
McCook	13	22	0	0	--	35
Holdrege	0	0	0	0	--	0

Scoring Summary
M: Zane Gillen 46 pass from Matt Chitwood (Chitwood kick)
M: Chitwood 2 run (kick failed)
M: Cody Wudtke 7 pass from Chitwood (Chitwood run)
M: Wudtke 6 pass from Chitwood (Chitwood kick)
M: Austin Cherry 65 pass from Chitwood (Chitwood kick)

Individual Stats
RUSHING: Kyle Stewart 8-54, Matt Chitwood 9-48, Jake Schlager 6-32, Kolton Stone 7-16, Shane Buck 3-8, Cade Hiatt 3-6, Vince Lyons 1-2, Team 1-(-6).
PASSING: Matt Chitwood 9-11-0, 219 yds.
RECEIVING : Austin Cherry 3-89, Matt Collicott 2-58, Zane Gillen 2-51, Cody Wudtke 2-51.

Team Stats

Stat	McCook	Holdrege
Rushing	38-160	24-43
Passing	9-11-219	5-10-26
Total Yards	379	69
Return Yards	74	98
First Downs	14	3
Penalties	2-20	4-30
Turnovers	0	2
Punts	2-39	7-37.8
Sacks	4	0

WEEK 10

October 28, 2011

Boys Ranch @ Canadian

Teams	1st Quarter	2nd Quarter	3rd Quarter	4th Quarter	OT	Final
Boys Ranch	0	0	0	8	--	8
Canadian	7	14	7	14	--	42

Scoring Summary
C: Taylor Schafer 5 run (Salvador Escamilla kick)
C: Isaac Lewis 3 run (Escamilla kick)
C: Lewis 34 pass from Braden Hudson (Escamilla kick)
C: Lewis 5 run (Escamilla kick)
C: Lewis 4 run (Escamilla kick)
C: Ben Arbuckle 3 run (Escamilla kick)
B: Taylor Robinson 70 kickoff return (Devin Kaiteis pass from Robinson)

Individual Stats
Passing: Braden Hudson: 16-25-178-1-1, Ben Arbuckle 3-3-20-0-0
Rushing: Taylor Schafer 8-34, Isaac Lewis 13-101, Chris Marquez 6-39, Taylor Thompson 2-2
Receiving: Chris Marquez 2-16, Isaac Lewis 8-108, Taylor Schafer 2-27, Boston Hudson 2-17, Taylor Thompson 3-20, Brock Hedgecoke 2-2

Team Stats

Stat	Boys Ranch	Canadian
Rushing	268	268
Passing	9	145
Total Yards	4-6-0-277	17-26-1-1453
First Downs	13	24
Penalties	7-68	6-55
Turnovers	2	2
Punts	3-23	1-30

October 29, 2011

Milnor @ Linton State Quarterfinals

Teams	1st Quarter	2nd Quarter	3rd Quarter	4th Quarter	OT	Final
Milnor	0	8	6	0	--	14
Linton	0	8	12	8	--	28

Scoring Summary
L: Cody Sehn 5 run (Tanner Purintun run)
M: Jacob Greenmyer 14 pass from Josh Hansana (Hansana run)
L: Purintun 1 run (run failed)

L: Sehn 5 run (pass failed)
M: Hansana 50 run (run failed)
L: Sehn 11 run (Purintun run)

Individual Statistics
Rushing: Cody Sehn 24-189,, Brock Nagel 14-55, Tanner Purintun 9-45.
Passing: Purintun 4-12-79-2, Jayden Gross, 1-2-(-1)-0.
Receiving: Dillon Doolittle 2-50, Sehn 1-25, Gross, 1-4, Lukas Holzer 1-(-1).

Team Stats

Stat	Milnor	Linton
Rushing	26-117	47-289
Passing	160	78
Total Yards	277	367
Return Yards	144	38
First Downs	11	18
Penalties	2-15	3-15
Turnovers	3	2
Punts	2-42.5	4-25.8
Sacks	0-0	1-8

October 28, 2011

Alliance @ McCook First Round Playoffs

Teams	1st Quarter	2nd Quarter	3rd Quarter	4th Quarter	OT	Final
Alliance	0	0	6	8	--	14
McCook	21	3	7	6	--	37

Scoring Summary
M: Justin Terry 3-yard run (Matt Chitwood Kick).
M: Matt Chitwood 3-yard run (Matt Chitwood Kick).
M: Justin Terry 7-yard run (Matt Chitwood Kick).
M: Matt Chitwood 21-yard field goal.
A: Isaac Burnham 11-yard run (Pass failed).
M: Justin Terry 3-yard run (Matt Chitwood Kick).
M: Matt Chitwood 1-yard run (Kick failed).
A: Andrew Garza 1-yard run (Isaac Burnham Run).

Individual Stats
Rushing: Justin Terry 17-92, Matt Chitwood 12-94, Kolton Stone 2-12, Cade Hiatt 1-0, Kyle Stewart 6-28
Shane Buck 1-0, Mitch Collicott 1-0
Passing: Matt Chitwood 6-11-114, Vince Lyons 0-1-0
Receiving: Cody Wudtke 3-89, Austin Cherry 2-20, Zayne Gillen 1-5

Team Stats

Stat	Alliance	McCook
Rushing	148	226
Passing	178	114
Total Yards	340	326
Return Yards	70	29
First Downs	16	13
Turnovers	3	0
Punts	2-42	1-36
Sacks	3	1

WEEK 11

November 5, 2011

Adams Central @ McCook Class B Quarterfinal

Teams	1st Quarter	2nd Quarter	3rd Quarter	4th Quarter	OT	Final
Adams Central	0	7	6	15	--	28
McCook	0	10	7	7	--	24

M: Matt Chitwood 1-yard run (Matt Chitwood Kick).
A: Jake Fowler 4-yard run (Chance Vorderstrasse Kick).
M: Matt Chitwood 37-yard field goal (Kick).
M: Cody Wudtke 40-yard pass from Matt Chitwood (Matt Chitwood Kick).
A: Jesse Ackerman 4-yard pass from Kyle Goldenstein (Kick failed).
M: Matt Chitwood 2-yard run (Matt Chitwood Kick).
A: Jake Fowler 3-yard run (Jake Fowler Run).
A: Blake Overmiller 22-yard pass from Kyle Goldenstein (Chance Vorderstrasse Kick).

Individual Stats
Rushing: Justin Terry 18-91, Matt Chitwood, 20-69, Kyle Stewart 13-78
Passing; Matt Chitwood 9-24-139, Austin Cherry 1-1-22
Receiving: Cody Wudtke 6-126, Matt Collicott, 3-13, Matt Chitwood 1-22

Team Stats

Stat	Adams Central	McCook
Rushing	202	238
Passing	155	168
Total Yards	357	399
Return Yards	30	75
First Downs	24	13
Turnovers	2	3
Punts	2-39.0	4-37.4
Sacks	2	3

November 6, 2011

Maple Valley @ Linton State Quarterfinals

Teams	1st Quarter	2nd Quarter	3rd Quarter	4th Quarter	OT	Final
Maple Valley	6	14	0	0	--	20
Linton	0	0	8	13	--	21

Scoring Summary
 M: Jordan Haseleu 78 pass from Dylan Lerud (kick blocked)
M: Lerud 12 run (run failed)
M: Lerud 13 run (Wade Steidl pass from Lerud)
L: Brock Nagel 9 run (Jayden Gross run)
L: Gross 3 run (run failed)
L: Gross 1 run (Nagel kick)

Individual Stats
Rushing: Cody Sehn 22-98, Jayden Gross 20-84, Brock Nagel 7-35, Tanner Purintun 2-19, Mike Oien 1-1.
Passing: Jayden Gross 3-5-0, 85 yards; Purintun 3-5-0, 11 yards; Brooks Flyberg 1-2-0, 4 yards.
Receiving: Dillon Doolittle 3-85, Jayden Gross 2-11, Jordan Gross 1-7, Sehn 1-(-)3.

Team Stats

Stat	Maple Valley	Linton
Rushing	27-167	52-237
Passing	7-14-144	7-12-100
Total Yards	311	337
Return Yards	56	92
First Downs	11	17
Penalties	5-40	3-30
Turnovers	3	1
Punts	2-33	3-17
Sacks	1-2	2-12

WEEK 12

November 11, 2011						
Linton vs. Stanley Powers Lake @ Fargo Dome Class C North Dakota State Championship						
Teams	1st Quarter	2nd Quarter	3rd Quarter	4th Quarter	OT	Final
Stanley	14	14	7	7	--	42
Linton	6	0	0	0	--	6

Scoring:
S: Landon Smith 1 run (Eduardo Salgado kick)
L: Cody Sehn 3 run (pass failed)
S: Abe Roehrich 62 run (Salgado kick)
S: Seth Leupp 40 pass from Sam Footh (Salgado kick)
S: Smith 34 fumble recovery (Salgado kick)
S: Roehrich 8 run (Salgado kick)
S: Smith 19 run (Salgado kick)

Individual Stats
Rushing: Michael Oien 6-20, Cody Sehn 12-14, Jayden Gross 8-8, Brock Nagel 3-5, Taylor Wetzsteon 3-3, Chase Jacob 1-(minus-1), Austin Schell 1-(minus-1).
Passing: J. Gross 8-19-2, 99 yards; Brooks Flyberg 1-2-1, 3 yards.
Receiving: Sehn 3-41, Dillon Doolittle 2-31, Brock Nagel 2-24, Ryan Schneider 1-3, Lukas Holzer 1-3.

Team Stats

Stat	Stanley	Linton
Rushing	43-358	34-48
Passing	4-12-60	9-21-102
Total Yards	418	150
Return Yards	74	178
First Downs	20	10
Penalties	7-58	1-10
Turnovers	4	4
Punts	2-31.0	6-27.1
Sacks	2-11	0-0

November 11, 2011						
Canadian vs. Clarendon @ Pampa First Round Texas Class 1 D-1 Playoffs						
Teams	1st Quarter	2nd Quarter	3rd Quarter	4th Quarter	OT	Final
Canadian	14	14	7	13	--	48
Clarendon	0	13	0	7	--	20

Scoring
Ca: Braden Hudson 9 run (Salvador Escamilla kick)
Ca: Hudson 21 run (Escamilla kick)
Ca: Chris Marquez 17 run (Escamilla kick)
Cl: Charleston Harris 64 run (Cole Ward kick)
Cl: Wes Williams 78 run (kick failed)
Ca: Boston Hudson 9 pass from Braden Hudson (Escamilla kick)
Ca: Isaac Lewis 24 pass from Braden Hudson (Escamilla kick)
Ca: Lewis 14 pass from Braden Hudson (kick failed)
Ca: Lewis 51 pass from Braden Hudson (Escamilla kick)
Cl: Williams 15 pass from Chance McAnear (Cole Ward kick)

Individual Stats
Rushing—Canadian: Br. Hudson 13-124, Taylor Schafer 11-96, Lewis 7-57, Marquez 6-50, Braiden Gala 1-(-)2.
Passing: Braden Hudson 11-18-1—185
Receiving: Lewis 4-85, Boston .Hudson 4-41, Marcos Trevino 1-28, Schafer 1-12, Marquez 1-19.

Team Stats

Stat	Canadian	Clarendon
Rushing	325	162
Passing	11-18-185	5-14-58
Total Yards	510	220
First Downs	21	9
Penalties	3-25	7-80
Turnovers	3	3
Punts	3-46.0	7-29.1

WEEK 13

November 18, 2011

Canadian vs. Albany @ Lubbock Second Round Texas Class 1 State Playoffs

Teams	1st Quarter	2nd Quarter	3rd Quarter	4th Quarter	OT	Final
Albany	7	21	28	0		56
Canadian	7	7	7	6		27

Scoring:
C: Boston Hudson 30 pass from Braden Hudson (Salvador Escamilla kick)
A: Hudman 4 run (Bumguardner kick)
A: Bumguardner 43 run (Bumguardner kick)
C: Boston Hudson 37 pass from Braden Hudson (Escamilla kick)
A: Bumguardner 77 run (Bumguardner kick)
A: Bumguardner 1 run (Bumguardner kick)
A: Cody Petree 27 pass from Bumguardner (Bumguardner kick)
A: Bumguardner 63 run (Bumguardner kick)
C: Marcos Trevino 11 pass from Braden Hudson (Escamilla kick)
A: Sam Raymond 35 run (Bumguardner kick)
A: Bumguardner 43 run (Bumguardner kick)
C:Braden Hudson 1 run (kick failed)

Individual Stats:
Rushing: Isaac Lewis 6-7, Braden Hudson 19-118, Taylor Schafer 6-50, Chris Marquez 1-2.
Passing: Braden Hudson 17-32-1-244.
Receiving: Boston Hudson 4-100, Brock Hedgecoke 1-12, Schafer 1-0, Braiden Galla 3-65, Lewis 6-55, Trevino 2-12.

Team Stats

Stat	Albany	Canadian
Rushing	492	177
Passing	4-5-0-59	17-32-244
Total Yards	551	421
First Downs	20	21
Penalties	2-10	4-35
Turnovers	0	1
Punts	1-31.0	2-30.0

II. Schedules/Results
2011 Season

Linton, ND Lions (10-2)

Date	Opponent	Score	W/L	Record
August 26	MoBridge, SD	12-26	Loss	0-1
September 2	Oaks	12-7	Win	1-1
September 9	Milnor	14-7	Win	2-1
September 16	@Fargo Oak Grove	26-0	Win	3-1
September 23	@Maple Valley-Enderlin	26-25	Win	4-1
September 30	@Kidder County	21-0	Win	5-1
October 7	Northern Cass	46-13	Win	6-1
October 14	@Maryville-Portland	39-12	Win	7-1
October 22	1st Round Playoffs Westhope	18-8	Win	8-1
October 29	2nd Round Playoffs Milnor	28-14	Win	9-1
November 6	Semifinal Playoffs Maple Valley-Enderlin	21-20	Win	10-1
November 12	State Championship Stanley-Powers Lake	6-41	Win	10-2

McCook, NE Bison (10-1)

Date	Opponent	Score	W/L	Record
August 26	@ Scottsbluff	28-7	Win	1-0
September 2	Aurora	16-13(2OT)	Win	2-0
September 9	@Alliance	31-20	Win	3-0
September 16	@Gering	31-0	Win	4-0
September 23	Grand Island NW	49-26	Win	5-0
September 30	Sidney	49-7	Win	6-0
October 7	@Lexington	16-13 (2OT)	Win	7-0
October 14	Adams County	24-21	Win	8-0
October 21	@Holdrege	35-0	Win	9-0
October 28	1st Round Playoffs Alliance	37-14	Win	10-0
November 5	2nd Round Playoffs Adams Central	24-28	Loss	10-1

Canadian, TX Wildcats (8-4)

Date	Opponent	Score	W/L	Record
August 26	River Road	48-13	Win	1-0
September 2	@Meade, KS	18-24	Loss	1-1
September 9	@Perryton	32-33	Loss	1-2
September 16	@Sanford Fritch	44-6	Win	2-2
September 23	Clayton, NM	67-7	Win	3-2
September 30	Panhandle	48-34	Win	4-2
October 7	@Sunray	20-14 (2OT)	Loss	4-3
October 14	West Texas	48-14	Win	5-3
October 21	@Strafford	27-17	Win	6-3
October 28	Boys Ranch	48-8	Win	7-3
November 11	1st Round Playoffs Clarendon @ Pampa	48-20	Win	8-3
November 18	2nd Round Playoffs Albany @ Lubbock	27-56	Loss	8-4

III. Rosters

McCook Bison

No.	Name	YR	Position	Ht.	Wt.
1	Jake Schlager	11	RB/LB	6'1	185
2	Ian Pearson	10	RB/LB	5'11	160
3	Cody Wudtke	11	WR/LB	6'2	165
4	Vince Lyons	10	QB/LB	6'1	135
5	Austin Cherry	11	QB/DB	5'11	160
7	Jacob Riemann	11	WR/DB	5'11	155
8	Conner Stem	10	TE/LB	6'0	145
9	Zane Gillen	11	WR/DB	5'10	160
10	Matt Chitwood	12	QB/DB	6'3	175
13	Zach Glaze	10	WR/LB	5'11	130
14	Jesse Ditty	10	TE/DL	6'4	160
15	Tyson Karr	12	WR/DB	5'8	135
16	Shane Buck	12	RB/LB	5'9	130
17	Dylan Samway	10	WR/DB	6'1	130
18	Wes Burked	10	WR/DB	6'2	160
19	Cade Hiatt	11	RB/LB	5'10	155
20	Miguel Navarro	10	RB/DB	5'4	145
22	Javier Deltran	11	WR/LB	5'8	160
23	William Flannigan	10	WR/DB	5'8	120
25	Brock Scott	10	RB/LB	5'11	180
29	Brett Guerra	11	WR/DB	5'10	130
31	Mauro Buenos	10	WR/DB	5'9	130
32	Kyle Stewart	11	RB/LB	6'1	175
33	Drew Meissen	10	RB/LB	6'1	155
34	Ethan Loeb	10	RB/DB	5'8	140
35	Gavin Harsh	11	RB/LB	5'8	160
36	Trenton Bruntz	10	RB/LB	5'8	185
40	Justin Terry	12	RB/LB	6'1	210
45	Kolton Stone	10	RB/LB	5'11	200
52	Gabe Marinates	12	OL/DL	6'	220
54	Clayton Skolt	10	OL/DL	6'1	220
55	Austen Sis	12	OL/DL	6'2	195
56	Mitch Collicott	11	OL/DL	5'11	250
57	Morgan Schilling	11	OL/DL	6'1	205
58	Seth Katter	10	OL/DL	5'10	255
60	Nick Albert's	12	OL/DL	6'3	205
62	Clint Beguin	12	OL/DL	6'2	240
63	Will Burkert	12	OL/DL	6'3	195
65	Trevor Gleason	11	OL/DL	6'	220
66	Daniel Best	11	OL/DL	5'8	205
70	Spencer Skolt	12	OL/DL	6'2	230
72	David Darner	10	OL/DL	5'11	200
73	Dakota Hutchins	10	OL/DL	5'10	185
76	Colt McConnell	11	OL/DL	6'2	280
77	Chandler Wagner	10	OL/DL	6'2	265
82	Irvin Gambia	10	WR/DB	5'6	115
83	Alex Broadfoot	12	WR/DB	5'10	160
84	Spenser Bruntz	12	TE/LB	5'11	190
85	Manny Rodriquez	11	TE/DL	6'	180
89	Matt Collicott	11	TE/DL	6'4	185

Head Coach: Jeff Gross
Assistant Coaches: John Gumb, Chad Lyons, Scott Moll ring
Russ Schlager, Jeremy Yolk Freshman/JH Coaches: Bill Ramsay,
Jeff Ellis, Tim Garcia, Clint Coleman, Nick Mushed, Berry
Schaeffer, Tom Lentz, Eric Ramsay, Taylor Liess

Canadian Wildcats

No.	Name	YR	Position	Ht.	Wt.
2	David Morales	SR	WR/DB	5'6	130
3	Braden Hudson	SR	QB/DB	5'11	175
4	Chance Walker	SR	QB/DB	5'9	155
5	Isaac Lewis	SR	WR/DB	5'8	165
6	Jessie Sandoval	JR	WR/DB	5'10	160
7	Taylor Schafer	SR	RB/OLB	5'10	155
8	Ben Arbuckle	SO	QB/DB	6'2	15
9	Chris Marquez	JR	RB/OLB	5'8	165
10	Caden Cleveland	SR	WR/DB	5'8	145
11	Colton Cates	SR	WR/LB	5'11	170
12	Marcos Trevino	JR	WR/DB	5'9	160
14	Deven Carson	SR	WR/LB	5'9	165
15	Paxton Gallaway	JR	WR/DB	5'9	150
19	Tyler Lynch	JR	WR/LB	5'10	170
20	Andrew Ezzell	FR	WR/LB	5'10	170
21	Boston Hudson	SO	WR/LB	5'11	145
22	Taylor Thompson	JR	WR/DB	5'9	160
25	Matt Thomasy	SO	RB/LB	5'10	170
30	Julio Sandoval	SR	WR/DB	5'9	160
50	Morgan Shrader	JR	OL/DL	6'2	200
51	Camron Pearson	SR	OL/DL	5'7	225
55	Johnny Swires	SO	OL/DL	6'2	215
56	Salvador Escamilla	SR	OL/DL	6'0	240
60	Ty Morrow	SR	OL/DL	6'3	275
62	Alex Martinez	SO	OL/DL	5'8	185
64	Bo Dickinson	SO	OL/DL	5'9	185
66	Ben Martinez	SR	OL/DL	5'9	165
70	Tucker Brown	SO	OL/DL	5'10	160
71	Cole Banister	SR	OL/LB	5'9	190
75	Jose Vigil	SO	OL/DL	5'9	180
80	Brock Hedgecoke	SO	WR/DB	5'9	150

Head Coach: Chris Koetting   Assistant Coaches: Craig Campbell, Hayden Merket, Tim Fletcher, Jeff Isom, Kolt Kittley, Johnny Hudson, Ronel Saenz

Linton Lions

NO	Name	YR	Position	Wt.
10	Jon Purintun	FR	QB/DB	125
12	Tanner Purintun	SR	QB/DB	170
15	Travis Baumiller	JR	WR/DB	150
19	Brooks Flyberg	SO	QB/DB	135
20	Rylan Jacob	FR	RB/LB	135
21	Trevor Martin	SO	WR/DB	125
25	Brock Nagel	JR	RB/LB	160
26	Taylor Wetzsteon	SO	RB/LB	155
29	Mike Oien	SO	RB/LB	175
30	Chase Jacob	SO	RB/LB	120
34	Jayden Gross	SR	TE/LB	160
37	Austin Bernhardt	FR	RB/LB	170
40	Bradyn Burgad	FR	RB/LB	145
41	Andrew Leier	SO	RB/LB	130
48	Cody Sehn	SR	RB/LB	160
50	Nolan Meidinger	SR	OL/DL	225
53	Jade Svhumacher	FR	OL/DL	175
56	Jon Oien	SO	OL/DL	170
60	Mike Rohrich	SR	OL/DL	170
61	Cody Schlosser	SO	OL/DL	205

63	Luke Mosset	SR	OL/DL	210
65	Lee Vetsch	FR	OL/DL	160
66	Theo Naaden	JR	OL/DL	200
68	Tanner Bosch	SO	OL/DL	175
70	Ethan Roemmich	JR	OL/DL	180
71	Clay Jacob	JR	OL/DL	180
72	Tyrell Kalberer	SO	OL/DL	145
73	Alex Gross	SR	OL/DL	215
74	Ryan Olufson	SR	OL/DL	160
75	Garrick Voigt	SO	OL/DL	170
77	Logan Gross	FR	OL/DL	140
80	Austin Schell	FR	WR/DE	140
81	Lukas Holzer	SR	TE/DE	165
82	Ryan Schneider	FR	TE/DB	150
83	Jordan Gross	SO	TE/DE	145
84	Al Gefroh	SO	TE/DE	160
86	Dillon Doolittle	SR	WR/DB	140
88	Tom Lauinger	FR	OL/DL	125

Head Coach, Dan Imdicke Assistant Coaches. Tim Dockter,
Paul Keeney, Wade Huber, James Haak, Bob Weber

IV. Playoff Brackets
North Dakota
Class A State Football Playoffs
2011

October 22   *October 29*   *November 5*   *November 11*

| Linton-H-M-B 18 | Linton 28 |
| Westhope-N-G 8 | |

Linton 21

Larimore 30	Milnor –N.
	Sargent 14
Milnor-North	
Sargent 42	

Linton 6

Harvey-Wells Co	Enderlin-Maple
14	Valley 12
Enderlin-Maple	
Valley 15	

Enderlin-Maple Valley 20

| Oakes 14 | Oakes 7 |
| Park River 8 | |

Dakota Bowl @ Fargo
Stanley-Powers Lake

Stanley-Powers Lake	Stanley-Powers
20	Lake 35
Killdeer 0	

Stanley-Powers Lake 28

| Heart River 61 | Heart River 0 |
| Lewis & Clark-OR 20 | |

Stanley-Powers Lake 42

| Hazen 42 | Hazen 37 |
| Williams County 0 | |

Hazen 27

Velva 26	Velva 19
New Salem-Glen	
Ullin 16	

Nebraska
Class B State Football Playoffs
2011

October 28   *November 4*   *November 11*   *November 22*

McCook (9-0) 37 | McCook 24
Alliance (5-4) 14

Adams Central 7

Gering (3-4) 13 | Adams Central 28
Adams Central (6-3) 49

Elkhorn 28

Blair (7-2) 23 | Blair 7
Beatrice (6-4) 13

Elkhorn 41

Omaha Skutt Catholic (6-3) 21 | Elkhorn 14
Elkhorn (8-1) 48

@ Memorial Stadium, Lincoln
Elkhorn

Crete (9-0) 36 | Crete 14
Elkhorn South (6-3) 0

Crete 20

Norris (5-4) 31 | Aurora 13
Aurora (7-2) 40

Crete 17

Scottsbluff (7-2) 12 | Ralston 9
Ralston (7-2) 14

Gretna 15

Plattsmouth (5-4) 3 | Gretna 38
Gretna (9-0) 35

Texas Class 1A D-1
Regional I Football Playoffs
2011

November 11   *November 18*   *November 25*   *December 2*

Sunray	Sunray 18
Bye	

Seymour 24

Seymour 20	Seymour 35
New Deal 6	

Seymour 20

Sundown	Sundown 55
Bye	

Sundown 20

Quanah 32	Quanah 12
Stinnett 26	

**Region 1 Winner Advances
to State Semifinals
December 9**

Stamford

Albany	Albany 56
Bye	

Albany 21

Canadian 48	Canadian 27
Clarendon 20	

Stamford 49

Panhandle	Panhandle 3
Bye	

Stamford 28

Olton 32	Stamford 56
Stamford 35	

V. SEASON STATISTICS

McCook

Rushing

Name	Attempts	Total Yards	Average per Attempt
Matt Chitwood	144	1114	7.74
Justin Terry	94	730	7.77
Jake Schlager	75	487	6.49
Kyle Stewart	48	311	6.48
Kolton Stone	28	153	5.46
Shane Buck	22	59	2.68
Austin Cherry	17	28	1.65
Cade Hiatt	7	22	3.14
Tyson Karr	6	15	2.50
Trenton Bruntz	1	2	2.00
Vince Lyons	1	2	2.00
Ethan Loibl	2	1	0.50
Drew Meissner	1	1	1.00
Mitch Collicott	1	0	0.00
Total	**447**	**2,925**	**6.54**

Passing

Name	Att	Comp	Yds	Comp %	Int.	TD
Matt Chitwood	99	48	846	48%	4	11
Austin Cherry	1	1	22	100%	0	0
Vince Lyons	1	0	0	0%	0	0
Tyson Karr	1	1	0	100%	0	0
Total	**102**	**50**	**868**	**49%**	**4**	**11**

Receiving

Name	#	Total Yds	Avg per Catch
Cody Wudtke	24	391	16.29
Austin Cherry	6	120	20.00
Matt Collicott	8	102	12.75
Jake Schlager	5	94	18.80
Zayne Gillen	4	90	22.50
Alex Broadfoot	1	27	27.00
Matt Chitwood	1	22	22.00
Cade Hiatt	1	22	22.00
Total	**50**	**868**	**17.36**

Scoring

Name	TD	XP	FG	2XP	Safety	Total Pts
Matt Chitwood	20	40-44	7-9	1		183
Jake Schlager	7					42
Justin Terry	6					36
Cody Wudtke	6					36
Austin Cherry	2					12
Matt Collicott	1					6
Alex Broadfoot	1					6
Zayne Gillen	1					6
Kyle Stewart	1					6
Totals	**45**	**40-44**	**7-9**	**1**	**0**	**333**

Punting

Name	#	Total Yds	Avg.	Long
Matt Collicott	16	620	38.75	58
Tyson Karr	14	502	35.86	45
Total	**30**	**1122**	**37.4**	**58**

Returns

Name	#	Total Yds	Avg. Yards
Austin Cherry	15	322	21.47
Jake Schlager	13	283	21.77
Matt Chitwood	2	123	61.50
Spencer Bruntz	1	68	68.00
Cody Wudtke	4	63	15.75
Tyson Karr	2	49	24.50
Zayne Gillen	2	34	17.00
Alex Broadfoot	1	10	10.00
Jacob Riemann	1	8	8.00
Total	**41**	**960**	**23.41**

Defensive Stats

Name	Tackles	Assists	Fumble Rec.	Int.
Austin Cherry	58	23	1	2
Mitch Collicott	56	29	1	1
Clint Beguin	48	28	1	
Austin Sis	48	26	2	
Javier Beltran	43	23		1
Austin Cherry	42	33	1	
Jake Schlager	36	24		2
Matt Chitwood	35	11		7
Alex Broadfoot	25	13	1	
Zayne Gillen	20	7		2
Matt Collicott	19	16		

Tyson Karr	16	4		2
Trevor Gleasonh	15	10	1	
Nick Alberts	12	6		
Kolton Stone	9	5		
Kyle Stewart	9	2		
Cade Hiatt	9	4		
Spencer Bruntz	8	7		
Gavin Harsh	7	2		
Cody Wudtke	4	3		1
Manny Rodriguez	4	0		
Will Burkett	3	4	1	
Ian Pearson	1			
Drew Meissner	1			
Vince Lyons	1			
Jacob Riemann	1			

Team Defense

	Total	Average per Game
Rushing Yards Given Up	1166	106.0
Passing Yards Given Up	1142	103.8
Total Yards Given Up	2308	209.8
Points Allowed	148	13.46

Linton

Rushing

Name	Attempts	Total Yards	Average/TD
Cody Shen	204	968	4.7/12
Tanner Purintun	76	497	6.5/8
Brock Nagel	95	417	4.4/4
Jayden Gross	29	122	4.2/2
Tayler Wetzsteon	13	60	4.6/0
Mike Oien	17	52	3.1/1
Rylan Jacob	5	41	8.2/0
Austin Schell	3	18	6.0/0
Chase Jacob	4	12	3.0/0
Bradyn Burgad	1	0	0/0
Brooks Flyberg	1	0	0/0
Andrew Leier	1	3	3.0/0
Dillon Doolittle	2	-10	-5.0/0
Austin Bernhardt	3	-13	-4.3/0
Sacks	13	-86	-6.6/0
Totals	**468**	**2,075**	**4.4/27**

Passing

Name	Att	Comp	Yds	Int.	TD
Tanner Purintun	161	88	1,388	11	14
Jayden Gross	25	12	181	2	0
Brooks Flyberg	10	3	23	2	0
Totals	**196**	**103**	**1,592**	**15**	**14**

Receiving

Name	#	Total Yds	TDs	Avg Per Catch
Jayden Gross	34	449	9	13.2
Brock Nagel	15	252	2	16.8
Dillon Doolittle	14	335	1	23.9
Al Gefroh	14	236	1	16.9
Cody Sehn	13	162	0	12.5
Lukas Holzer	10	132	1	13.2
Jordan Gross	2	23	0	11.5
Ryan Schneider	1	3	0	3.0
Totals	**103**	**1,592**	**14**	**15.5**

Scoring

Name	TD	XP	2XP	Total Pts
Cody Sehn	12	0	0	72
Jayden Gross	11	0	3	72
Tanner Purintun	8	0	2	52
Brock Nagel	6	5	1	43
Lukas Holzer	1	0	2	8
Dillon Doolittle	1	0	0	6
Mike Oien	1	0	0	6
Al Gefroh	1	0	0	6
Total	**41**	**5**	**9**	**269**

Canadian

Rushing

Name	Attempts	Total Yards	Average per Attempt/TD
Taylor Schafer	115	837	7.3/14
Isaac Lewis	59	526	8.9/7
Braden Hudson	121	483	4.0/8
Chris Marquez	51	352	6.9/3
Taylor Thompson	16	53	3.3/0
Ben Arbuckle	10	36	3.6/1
Jesse Sandoval	5	6	1.2/0
Matt Thompson	1	4	4.0/1
Chance Walker	1	2	2.0/0
Totals	**406**	**2502**	**6.2/33**

Passing

Name	Att	Comp	Yds	TDs	Int.	%
Braden Hudson	289	178	2394	30	11	66
Ben Arbuckle	15	13	191	1	1	87
Isaac Lewis	2	2	24	0	0	100
Taylor Schafer	1	1	67	1	0	100
Jesse Sandoval	1	1	8	0	0	100
Totals	**308**	**195**	**2684**	**32**	**12**	**63**

Receiving

Name	#	Total Yds.	TDs	Avg. Per Catch
Isaac Lewis	64	849	12	13.3
Boston Hudson	33	503	11	15.2
Taylor Schafer	21	283	3	13.5
Tyler Lynch	12	177	0	9.8
Brock Hegecoke	12	77	0	6.6
Chris Marquez	11	140	2	12.7
Taylor Thompson	6	71	0	8.0
Braden Galla	4	69	0	17.5
Chance Walker	2	61	0	30.5
Caden Cleveland	1	37	O	37.0
Totals	**195**	**2684**	**32**	**13.8**

Scoring

Name	Pts	Ave.	XP	TD	2pt.Con.	Safety
Isaac Lewis	120	10.0		20		
Taylor Schafer	116	9.7		19		1
Boston Hudson	56	4.7		9	2	
Braden Hudson	50	4.2		8	2	
Chris Marquez	30	2.5		5		
Salvador Escamilla	29	2.4	29			
Marcos Trevino	24	2.2	6	3		
Ben Arbuckle	6	1.0		1		
Jessie Sandoval	6	1.2		1		
Matt Thomasy	6	.7		1		
Chance Walker	2	.7			2	
Totals	**463**	**38.6**	**35**	**66**	**6**	**1**

Sacks

Name	Total	Avg. Per Game
Salvador Escamilla	6.0	.5
Taylor Schafer	5.0	.4
Andrew Ezzell	3.0	.3
Chris Marquez	3.0	.3
Deven Carson	2.0	.2
Paxton Galloway	1.0	.3
David Morales	1.0	.1
Matt Thomasy	1.0	.1
Camron Pearson	1.0	.1
Cole Banister	1.0	.5
Total	**24**	**2.0**

Defensive Stats

Name	Tackles	Assists	Total	Avg. per Game
Andrew Ezzell	23	100	123	10.3
Chris Marquez	21	58	79	6.6
Braden Hudson	38	39	77	6.4
Colton Cates	9	68	77	11.0
Deven Carson	16	53	69	6.9
Isaac Lewis	22	40	62	5.2
Taylor Schafer	12	42	54	4.5
Salvador Escamilla	10	44	54	4.5
Matt Thomasy	13	40	53	5.9
Caden Cleveland	14	35	49	4.1
Ty Morrow	6	27	37	3.7
David Morales	12	24	36	4.5
Marcos Trevino	15	19	34	3.1
Camron Pearson	2	30	32	4.0
Tyler Lynch	3	17	20	1.8
Taylor Thompson	6	13	19	2.4
Morgan Shrader	5	12	17	2.8
Boston Hudson	6	9	15	1.3
Jessie Sandoval	3	10	13	3.3
Julio Sandoval	2	8	12	2.4
Chance Walker	6	4	10	3.3
Brock Hedgecoke	3	5	10	1.7
Johnny Swires	1	8	9	1.1
Paxton Galloway	1	4	5	1.3
Jose Vigil	1	3	5	1.3
Cole Banister	1	3	4	2.0
Bo Dickinson	0	1	1	1.0
Ben Martinez	0	1	1	1.0
Ben Arbuckle	0	1	1	.2
Totals	**251**	**718**	**878**	**81.5**